Carlos Valcarcel

Eclipse 3.0

KICK START

SAMS

800 East 96th Street, Indianapolis, Indiana 46240

Eclipse 3.0 Kick Start

International Standard Book Number: 0-672-32610-8

Library of Congress Catalog Card Number: 2003116628

Printed in the United States of America

First Printing: August 2004

07   06   05   04   4   3   2   1

Trademarks

Warning and Disclaimer

Bulk Sales

Sams Publishing offers excellent discounts on this book when ordered in quantity for bulk purchases or special sales. For more information, please contact

U.S. Corporate and Government Sales

1-800-382-3419

corpsales@pearsontechgroup.com

For sales outside of the U.S., please contact

International Sales

international@pearsoned.com

Associate Publisher
Michael Stephens

Acquisitions Editor
Todd Green

Development Editor
Sean Dixon

Managing Editor
Charlotte Clapp

Project Editor
Dan Knott

Copy Editor
Bart Reed

Indexer
John Sleeva

Proofreader
Leslie Joseph

Technical Editors
Christian Kenyeres
Rob Byrom

Publishing Coordinator
Cindy Teeters

Designer
Gary Adair

Page Layout
Kelly Maish

Contents at a Glance

Table of Contents

About the Author

Carlos Valcarcel has been a developer for more than 15 years, and has used Java from its earliest availability. He is currently the director of technology at Trivera Technologies LLC and was a VP at Merrill Lynch. He has consulted for clients, including Jefferson National Laboratory, JPMorgan, Chase, John Hancock, and Lincoln Reinsurance, on the use of object-oriented technology, Java, design patterns, refactoring, and test-driven development. He has also led formal training for Sun and IBM. He is involved in the Eclipse community, is frequently tapped for quick answers about IBM and Eclipse technology, and helped to write the Web Services tutorial for IBM's "developerWorks" website.

Dedication

To my wife, Becky: I am reminded of a quote from the movie
Four Friends: *"I love you like the Pilgrim loves the Holy Land,*
like the wayfarer loves his wayward ways, like the immigrant
that I am loves America, and the blind man the memory of
his sighted days."

To my daughter, Lindley: The joy and love I feel for you grows
every day. Thank you for being patient when I declined to play
Lord of the Rings chess, video games, or watch movies because of
the book.

Acknowledgments

Without Eclipse there would be no book to write, so the first thanks must go out to IBM and the developers responsible for the 40-million-dollar source code gift that started it all.

Next is the army of open-source developers who have thought enough about Eclipse to spend countless hours developing plug-ins for the rest of us to use in our daily toil. I would like to extend thanks to the folks at Omondo, Sysdeo, the Jakarta Project (Struts and Cactus), Eclipse-Games at Source Forge, JFaceDBC, and JBoss. I used many plug-ins while I toiled over the pages of this book. If I left anyone out, please let me know and I will add your name to a future edition of the book.

Of course, this book would not be half as good as it is if not for the army of professionals at Sams Publishing. I would like to thank Christian A. Kenyeres, Robert Byrom, Bart Reed, and Dan Knott for their tireless work at making the chapters coherent and the content understandable.

Also, Todd Green and Sean Dixon of Sams Publishing deserve a huge measure of thanks for believing in me so much that they let me miss deadline after deadline and did not beat me mercilessly for it. Thank you both for this opportunity.

In addition, the following colleagues were able to take time out of their busy schedules to review chapters: Kevin Bedell, David Gallardo, Jon Norieka, and James Turner. Thank you, gentlemen! Let's do dinner!

Any outstanding errors are all mine and I beg the reader's indulgence in pointing out any problems so that I can correct them on the *Eclipse Kick Start* website. Eclipse was in a constant state of flux for most of the writing of this book, so any inconsistencies I can fix would be appreciated.

For a few months in 2003, I was fortunate enough to work with one of the development teams at Jefferson National Laboratory. Their encouragement kept me going when the book was first started, and it was their incessant inquiries about my page count that kept the content flowing. A huge thanks to Kari Heffner, Mike Staron, Dana Cochran, Geoffrey Barth, Bob Lawrence, as well as Dave Buckle, Margaret Ridley, Dave Sheppard, and Cindy Hall. Thanks also to Roy Whitney, CIO of Jefferson Lab. You were all part of my surrogate family and always made me feel that the commute from Long Island to Virginia was well worth it.

My colleagues at Trivera Technology, specifically Cindy Zmijewski, Joe Madden, and Lacy Bulterman, have all been supportive of my efforts and never made me feel guilty for missing conference calls or pre-sales meetings. Kim Morello, the CEO of Trivera, was always patient with my comments and complaints and also gave me the time I needed to complete this work (hi, Amanda, Chase, and Anthony). Kim, you are on the short-list of managers I have loved working for and with.

The Web services chapter would not have been possible if not for the hard work of Ken Kranz. He came in at the last minute and wrote an excellent chapter when he didn't even have the time to do his own work. Ken, since meeting you at a Java class at Fusion Systems Group so many years ago, your friendship has been a blessing.

Many thanks go out to my family. My wife Becky and my daughter Lindley have always been there for me and have supported me through the difficult task of writing this book as well as keeping me fed and feeling loved. As I've said before, if there is a bright center to the universe, you two are it. You fill the hole in my hugs better than anybody!

I also want to thank my parents, Luis and Regina Valcarcel, my brother, Luis, and my sister, Silvia Velez, for listening to me when I needed them to listen and telling me to be quiet when I was talking too much. And before anyone mentions it, I will now be quiet and let the book do its job.

Carlos Valcarcel
Bohemia, NY
carlos@triveratech.com
carlos@eclipsekickstart.com
carlos@eintech.com

We Want to Hear from You!

As the reader of this book, *you* are our most important critic and commentator. We value your opinion and want to know what we're doing right, what we could do better, what areas you'd like to see us publish in, and any other words of wisdom you're willing to pass our way.

As an associate publisher for Sams Publishing, I welcome your comments. You can email or write me directly to let me know what you did or didn't like about this book—as well as what we can do to make our books better.

Please note that I cannot help you with technical problems related to the topic of this book. We do have a User Services group, however, where I will forward specific technical questions related to the book.

When you write, please be sure to include this book's title and author as well as your name, email address, and phone number. I will carefully review your comments and share them with the author and editors who worked on the book.

Email: feedback@samspublishing.com

Mail: Michael Stephens
            Associate Publisher
            Sams Publishing
            800 East 96th Street
            Indianapolis, IN 46240 USA

For more information about this book or another Sams Publishing title, visit our website at www.samspublishing.com. Type the ISBN (excluding hyphens) or the title of a book in the Search field to find the page you're looking for.

Introduction

"The only thing better than writing a book is finishing writing a book."

—The author

"There ain't no rules here. We're trying to accomplish something."

—Thomas Edison

At the time I started writing this book, only two Eclipse books were available. Both books are (still) fantastic, mention many of the foundation features of Eclipse, and discuss how you can develop Java within this all-encompassing environment. However, the number of plug-ins available to the Eclipse community was growing, and continues to grow, at an impressive rate.

My goal from the beginning was to present Java developers with a slightly different view of Eclipse than just another IDE with cool features. The number of plug-ins available at the time of this writing (and I wrote this introduction last) was almost 500. Considering that the WebSphere Application Developer (WSAD) environment, IBM's Eclipse-based IDE, contains over 500 plug-ins, it would seem that the open-source IDE arena is catching up fast to the commercial arena. With that many open-source plug-ins, I felt that a useful Eclipse book would not only discuss the IDE at a feature level, including how to extend it using the Plug-in Development Environment (PDE), but would include a strong subset of free/almost-free plug-ins to allow developers the opportunity to develop industrial-strength applications at minimal cost, without having to worry about creating their own plug-ins.

Who Should Read This Book

This book is not for Java novices. You must understand Java syntax, object-oriented technologies, UML, design patterns, test-driven development, and framework concepts. An understanding of Tomcat, JBoss, and Java frameworks will also be a big help, but an in-depth knowledge is not necessary. The examples in this book will walk you through almost everything you need. However, Web servers and the concepts associated with enterprise technologies will not get a lot of attention. If you need to get information about various open-source projects and Java technologies, Appendix E, "Recommended Resources," will get you started on your quest for knowledge.

How This Book Is Organized

In addition to where you can get Eclipse and how to install it, you will be given enough information to use it productively and to extend it to make it an even better tool. This book is divided up into three sections:

▶ **The Eclipse Development Environment**—This section will cover most of the features that make Eclipse an environment worth using. Even though there are plug-ins to support languages such as C and COBOL, I will only discuss the Java support and the various ways you can develop Java applications using Eclipse. Support for the JUnit testing framework will be discussed, but additional testing frameworks, specifically Cactus, are discussed later in the book. If you only use Eclipse as a Java development environment, you will not be disappointed.

▶ **Developing Applications Using Plug-Ins**—This is the part of the book I expect most developers to use the most often. Java exists in a world where enterprise applications must be written in a minimum of time and with a minimum of fuss. The plug-ins examined are not all that are available, but they give a nice sampling of the kinds of extensions available to the Java development environment supported by Eclipse. You will get a chance to examine testing frameworks such as Cactus, as well as plug-ins covering UML, Struts, J2EE development, and GUI building.

▶ **Extending Eclipse**—The Eclipse plug-in architecture is last because it is the most interesting part of the tool, although it will be used the least by most developers. Although not difficult to use, the plug-in architecture is not trivial. I hope the plug-in examples inspire more developers to write additional views and editors for the myriad file types and technologies that continue to appear unabated by the lack of problems to solve.

Downloading and Installing Eclipse

Before you install Eclipse, make sure you have a Java Runtime Environment (JRE) or a full Java Development Environment (JDK) installed on your machine. Also, the Java environment should be 1.4.1 or better. To download Eclipse, you start your journey at http://www.eclipse.org. Here are the steps to follow:

1. On the Eclipse home page, look to the navigation menu on the left and click Downloads.

2. The Downloads page will take you to the list of locations that carry the Eclipse installation files. You can select the North America Main Eclipse Download Site or any of the volunteer mirror sites. When you click one of the site links, you will be taken to the Eclipse Project Downloads page.

3. The various available Eclipse downloads are listed here. At the time of this writing, the final release of Eclipse 3.0 is available. You should click the link that reads Latest Release and has a 3.0 build name.

4. The Build page for Eclipse 3.0 lists the various Eclipse releases for all the supported platforms as well the source code for Eclipse. Click either the HTTP or FTP link that appears in the third column on the same line as the platform on which you expect to run Eclipse. The status column for your platform must have a green check mark next to it. A red X next to a platform name means the build is not ready.

5. After you click the HTTP or FTP link, your browser should ask you for a location to save the file. If you do not intend to save the zip file after you install Eclipse, just save the file to your Desktop or some other location where you can remove it when you are finished. When the download completes, you are ready to install Eclipse on your machine.

6. The Eclipse zip file contains all the Eclipse files needed to run the IDE. If you already have Java installed, all you need to do is extract the contents of the Eclipse zip file into a selected directory. For example, extract the Eclipse zip file into `c:\tools`.

After you complete these steps, you are ready to go. On the Windows platform, navigate to the `eclipse` directory and run `eclipse.exe`. The splash screen will appear for a few moments and then the Workspace Launcher will open asking for the directory Eclipse should use as its default location for your project files. Click OK. If the Eclipse workbench opens up on the Welcome page, your installation was a success.

All the examples were run and tested on the Windows platform. The information is mostly platform independent, but there may be some instances where features are implemented differently. If you're using Unix or a Mac the information in the book should apply but be sure to check the Eclipse Release page for your OS and hardware platform for specifics on the differences. For Mac users there is a great article on Eclipse for the Mac at http:// developer.apple.com/tools/eclipse.html. For Linux, I recommend a Linux support forum such as http://www.linuxforum.com that covers each of the three Linux variants supported by Eclipse.

If you decide to download the code examples, you will find that all the code has a code marker next to string literals (`"//$NON-NLS-1$"`). This is used by the Eclipse incremental compiler to flag strings that *do not* need to be externalized. One of the many features of Eclipse is the ability of the Java nature to create a separate properties file for use in internationalization. I have removed these flags from the book text, but I've left them in the code in case you, like me, decide to let the compiler be as picky as it can.

Conventions Used in This Book

This book uses several conventions to help you prioritize and reference the information it contains.

Various typefaces are used to make code and input easily distinguishable from regular text:

- ▶ Program code appears in a special `monospace` font.

- ▶ Placeholders—words or characters used temporarily to represent the real words or characters you type in code—are typeset in *`italic monospace`*.

- ▶ Material that you are instructed to type appears in **`bold monospace`**.

In addition, the following special elements provide information beyond the basic instructions:

Headline Sidebars

Sidebars contain special tips, warnings, and extra facts that are related to the text where they are found. They often emphasize important topics, so you might find them very helpful.

SHOP TALK

Shop Talk

In most of the chapters, I use Shop Talks to share my personal experiences as they relate to the chapter subject. These elements often contain opinions or preferences; the rest of the book is confined strictly to the facts. My particular opinions or preferences might not always apply to your situation, so keep that in mind when you read a Shop Talk.

Source Code for This Book

The associated source code files described in this book are available on the Sams website at `http://www.samspublishing.com`. Enter this book's ISBN (without the hyphens) in the Search box and click Search. When the book's title is displayed, click the title to go to a page where you can download the code.

PART I

The Eclipse Java Development Environment

Using the Eclipse Workbench

1

"As a tool a loaded gun makes a lousy hammer."

—Anonymous

The Workbench

If you have not yet installed Eclipse, return to the Introduction for information on where and how to get it. The download and installation are so easy as to almost need no explanation. Start Eclipse by going to the directory where you installed it (for example, `c:\tools\eclipse`) and run the executable `eclipse.exe`. From Windows Explorer, navigate to the Eclipse installation directory and double-click the Eclipse executable.

When Eclipse starts up for the first time, it undergoes some internal housekeeping while the splash screen is displayed. When the GUI opens for the first time, it opens a Workspace Launcher dialog to ask you to decide where to make the default workspace. For the purposes of this book, you can simply click OK (meaning use the default Eclipse workspace), but you will need to decide where you want Eclipse to put your files when you are doing real development. The decision you make with the Workspace Launcher dialog is not irreversible. You can always change your mind the next time you start Eclipse, and you are always given the opportunity to decide where the files for a particular project should be saved every time you create a new project. In any case, either select a new directory to use as the location to store your projects or accept the default location; then click OK to close the Workspace Launcher and complete the startup of Eclipse.

When Eclipse 3.0 opens, the Welcome page is displayed. This page has a handful of links to help pages where you can find out about various areas of Eclipse. Feel free to use these links to navigate and discover both high-level and low-level information about Eclipse. Close this page by going to the tab for this page, located below the main menu, and clicking the X. Eclipse remembers the state of the IDE when you shut it down, so the next time you start Eclipse you will not see the Welcome page. If you ever want to see it again, go to the main menu and select Help, Welcome.

The window you are presented with is the Eclipse workbench. The Eclipse workbench is where everything happens. You can do everything from a single workbench, or you can open multiple workbenches at the same time. Eclipse is the base where any kind of work can take place based on the current plug-in in use.

The workbench is made up of a main menu bar located at the top of the Eclipse window, a toolbar located directly below the main menu bar that is plug-in configurable based on which plug-in has focus, a shortcut tab that contains one button for each open perspective and is located to the top right of the Eclipse window, and a displayed perspective. At any given time, you may have more than one perspective in use, but only one is displayed per workbench. To open more than one workbench, select Window, New Window from the main menu.

The workbench and the APIs available to implement plug-ins encourage the use of certain concepts within Eclipse. Because this book is about using Eclipse for Java development, everything we discuss will be slanted toward that end, but all the concepts are applicable for any use of the Eclipse core. The first group of concepts is the notion of perspectives, editors, views, and natures.

Perspectives, Editors, Views, and Natures

The main Eclipse window represents one workbench. The workbench is made up of a number of pieces that make understanding your current project much easier:

- **Perspectives**—A *perspective* represents a collection of editors and views within a particular workbench. What the editors and views are displaying will vary based on the kind of perspective in use. For example, a Debug perspective can display views of your thread stacks, variables, current file with associated breakpoints, and console output (see Figure 1.1).

- **Editors**—An *editor* allows you to read and/or write a particular file type. It can be used to edit a file, manipulate a bitmap, or draw a diagram (see Figure 1.2). An editor generally takes up the most real estate in a perspective, but the size of all views and editors can be changed at will.

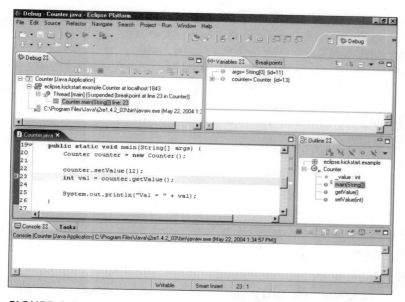

FIGURE 1.1   The Java Debug perspective displaying a file, suspended thread, and available variables.

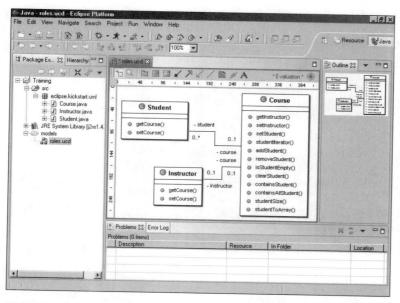

FIGURE 1.2   The Java perspective displaying a UML diagram in the UML Class Diagram Editor and the project structure in the Package Explorer view.

- **Views**—A *view* is a metadata presentation of information on the workbench. A view can have its own menus and can be displayed along with other views. For example, Figure 1.2 shows the Package Explorer view, on the far left, and the Problems view, at the bottom, which are two common views in the Java perspective. Another useful view is the Properties view, which displays information about selected resources.

- **Natures**—A *nature* is used by a plug-in to mark a project as being of a certain type. Plug-ins specific to Java would have little use for projects specific to COBOL.

Perspectives

When Eclipse starts for the first time, it defaults to displaying the Resource perspective (see Figure 1.3). The Resource perspective is made up of the following items:

- **The Navigator view**—Displays the file system from the starting point of a project.

- **The Outline view**—Displays information about a particular resource if it has an available Outline view to use.

- **The Tasks view**—Lists outstanding tasks. This particular view can be added to manually or programmatically.

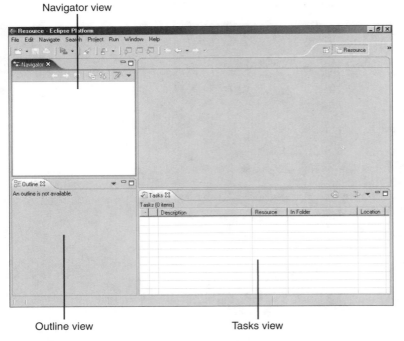

FIGURE 1.3   The Eclipse Resource perspective.

The shortcut tab on the top right of the workbench window displays a button per open perspective as well as the Open Perspective button. If you close all your current perspectives, the Open Perspective button still remains. It mirrors the functionality of the Window, Open Perspective command in the main menu in that it displays a subset of available perspectives, but you can always choose Other to see the full list.

You can have as many open perspectives as memory will allow, but you can only display one at a time. In order to view more than one perspective at the same time, you need to open an additional workbench window (Window, New Window) and then select the perspective you want to display in each (Window, Open Perspective or the Open Perspective button).

Editors

Editors in Eclipse take up the same area in a perspective, but you can have as many different editor types as file types. When you first start Eclipse, the Resource perspective displays the Welcome page in an editor that would be more accurately termed a *viewer*. When you open a Java file, the default Java editor opens in the editor area. If, for example, you have the Omondo UML plug-in installed and double-click a UCD file, the Omondo UML Class Diagram Editor will open.

Which editor opens for a particular file is controlled in two places. The first is in either the Navigator or Package Explorer view. Right-click the desired file and select Open With to view which editors are available for that file. The system will always have Default Editor as a selection, even if the default editor would not work with that particular file type.

The second place where file associations are controlled is within the Preferences dialog (see Figure 1.4). Open the Preferences dialog by clicking Window, Preferences from the main menu and go to Workbench, File Associations. When you install a new plug-in that contains one or more new editors, you can reassign file types by adding the new editor to the Associated Editors list. Select the file type to be modified and click Add to open the Editor Selection dialog. A newly installed plug-in will have its editor added automatically to the Internal Editors list. You can also select an external editor from the list of valid editors for a particular file type. Once you have added the editors for a file type, you can then assign one of them as the default. In any case, they will all appear as potential editors when you right-click the file to be opened (double-clicking opens the file using the assigned default editor).

Views

An Eclipse view displays metadata information about a resource in an alternative form. Generally speaking, a view is useful for navigation as well as displaying additional information about a resource (project, folder, or file). An example of a project navigator is the Resource perspective's Navigation view. It is a picture of the file system using a project as its starting point. An example of a file navigator would be the Outline view associated with a Java file (found in the Java perspective). It lists the class information in a tree view. When you select any of the nodes or leaves (for example, a method), the Java editor jumps to that point in the code.

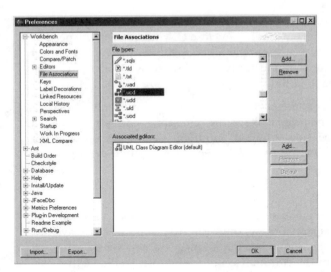

FIGURE 1.4   The file associations within the Preferences dialog displaying the UML editor associated with UCD files.

Views can be dragged and dropped in various locations and can be resized based on their location. Views can also have toolbars located on their title bar. When we discuss the various views in some of the alternative perspectives, they will be referred to in their default positions.

The shortcut bar on the bottom left side of the workbench can contain a button that, when clicked, displays a view until you click outside the view; this is known as a *Fast View*. As an example, from the Resource perspective, left-click the title bar of the Outline view and drag it over to the shortcut bar, the bottom left area displaying two separator bars. While you are dragging the view, the cursor changes to a stack of folders and then to an arrow pointing left. When you release the view, a new button appears. Click the new Outline view button, and the Outline view will open from the left side of the workbench. The Outline view is now the full height of the perspective (see Figure 1.5). Right-clicking the button in the shortcut bar opens a pop-up menu. Unchecking the menu item Fast View will put the view back from where you dragged it. However, instead of unchecking Fast View from the pop-up menu, click anywhere else on the Workbench to force the view to close.

Another interesting view is the Tasks view. Any plug-in that cares to use it can list tasks in this view. The Java development plug-in uses the Tasks view to display lines in a file that have been flagged using a task tag. Clicking an individual task will cause an already-open editor to go to the desired location. If the editor is not open, then double-clicking the task will cause the editor to open and go to the expected line. However, any problems that need to be attended to by a developer and discovered by internal project builders will be displayed in the Problems view.

The views supplied by the workbench are Bookmarks, Navigator, Outline, Problems, Progress, Properties, Search, and Tasks. Plug-ins can, and do, supply their own views specific to the tasks with which they are meant to help. The Java and Java Browsing perspectives add an additional 10 views.

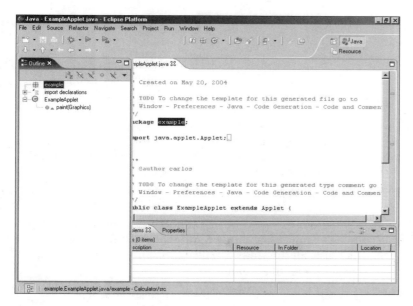

FIGURE 1.5   The Outline view in Fast View mode, covering part of an open editor.

Natures

Natures in Eclipse are artifacts of plug-in development. A plug-in defining a new project type will also associate a new or existing nature to go with the project. Having a nature affords other plug-ins the luxury of extending the capabilities of an existing project by supporting the project's nature. Natures can be grouped and given dependencies. You will find a much more in-depth discussion about natures and how to assign one to a project in Chapter 14, "Writing a Trivial (and Not So Trivial) Plug-In," when you walk through the creation of a new project type.

The Java Development Tooling (JDT)

The JDT offers the following four perspectives:

- Java
- Java Browsing
- Java Type Hierarchy
- Debug

Because they all have their strengths, let's examine each one in turn. They all share many of the same views, so we will discuss certain views only once, and you can safely assume that the view is valid at least in the perspective where it is discussed. Many views are valid in multiple perspectives of the same nature. However, some views, such as views belonging to the Debug perspective, will only be used in their respective perspective.

Java Perspective

The Java perspective is the most common perspective used in Java development and contains basic views of the resources. The Outline view from the Resource perspective is used and three are added.

Views

I would love to be able to say that some of the available views are not useful, but that would not be true. At worst, you will not use some as often as others, but they all contribute to the goal of developing Java code in a controlled fashion. Let's walk through most of the views, bearing in mind that some views are not directly related to Java development but are still quite useful.

FIGURE 1.6 The Show View dialog displaying the view categories for an Eclipse installation.

In order to display a view that is not already open, select Window, Show View, Other to display the Show View dialog, which lists all the views installed in Eclipse and the categories they fall under (see Figure 1.6).

Open the Tasks view within the Java perspective. From the main menu, select Window, Show View, Other to open the Show View dialog. Open the Basic category and double-click Tasks. The Tasks view displays comments in your Java code that use a task tag that you define in the Eclipse preferences. The default tags are TODO, FIXME, and XXX. Every time you add a comment in your code and use any of the default tags (or another task tag you defined in the Preferences dialog), the information will appear in the Tasks view (see Figure 1.7).

The Problems view displays problems encountered during a development session. While you're developing code, the Problems view may contain compiler errors, whereas various other plug-ins will list things such as badly formed XML or error messages related to missing resources. Clicking a problem encountered in a file will cause the editor to go to the line where the problem was encountered.

The Call Hierarchy view allows you to drag and drop a method from the Outline view into the view and see what classes/methods are calling the selected method or which classes/methods are called by the selected method. This is a convenient way to visually discover call trees (see Figure 1.8).

	Description	Resource	In Folder	Location
	TODO Check that 5 is the correct value.	Counter.java	CounterTest/src/eclipse/kicks...	line 43
	TODO To change the template for this gen...	Calculator.java	Calculator/src/calculator	line 4
	TODO To change the template for this gen...	Counter.java	CounterTest/src/eclipse/kicks...	line 4
	TODO To change the template for this gen...	CounterTest.j...	CounterTest/src/eclipse/kicks...	line 4

Tasks (17 items)

FIGURE 1.7   The Tasks view displaying tasks that use the TODO tag.

Call Hierarchy   Problems   Properties
Calls from method 'main(String[])' - in Workspace
main(String[]) - eclipse.kickstart.example.Counter
  Counter() - eclipse.kickstart.example.Counter
  setValue(int) - eclipse.kickstart.example.Counter
  getValue() - eclipse.kickstart.example.Counter
  println(String) - java.io.PrintStream

Line	Call
25	System.out.println("Val = " + val)

FIGURE 1.8   The Call Hierarchy displaying the call tree from Counter.

The Declaration view displays a read-only copy of the code of the selected node from the Outline view. If nothing is selected, nothing appears, but as soon as a class, method, or field is selected, the Declaration view displays just that block of code without the Javadocs. This is quite similar to the Show Source of Selected Element Only button in the toolbar. However, the Show Source button displays a block of code within the Java editor with the Javadocs (if any) and is writable.

The Hierarchy view is activated by right-clicking a node in the Outline view or by right-clicking in the editor, Call Hierarchy view, or Package Explorer after selecting a Java class and then selecting Open Type Hierarchy in the pop-up menu (see Figure 1.9). The Hierarchy view appears in the same area as the Package Explorer (the left side of the workbench). If the Hierarchy view obscures your view of the Package Explorer, click the Package Explorer tab located at the top of the view. This view has an upper half and a lower half. The upper half displays the selected class in one of three modes: the type hierarchy (class inheritance), the supertype hierarchy (class and interface inheritance), or the subtype hierarchy (the selected class and its subclasses). The lower half displays only the methods declared in the selected class or all the methods available due to inheritance. In addition, methods and fields can be hidden or made visible in the view.

Call Hierarchy   Problems   Properties
Calls from method 'main(String[])' - in Workspace
main(String[]) - eclipse.kickstart.example.Counter
  Counter() - eclipse.kickstart.example.Counter
  setValue(int) - eclipse.kickstart.example.Counter
  getValue() - eclipse.kickstart.example.Counter
  println(String) - java.io.PrintStream

Line	Call
25	System.out.println("Val = " + val)

FIGURE 1.9   The Hierarchy view displaying a class, its inheritance hierarchy, and the methods declared in the class.

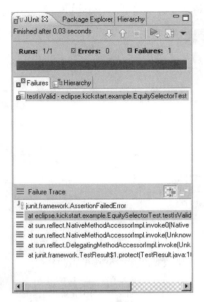

FIGURE 1.10 The JUnit view displaying an error in `testIsValid()`

The Javadoc view displays the Javadoc comments of the classes, methods, or fields if any exist. This might be one of the few views to see minimal use.

For those of you using JUnit as your framework for test-driven development, the JUnit view is an Eclipse-enabled version of the JUnit GUI. It displays the status of the running test with either a red or green bar. It also lists the tests that have run, indicates which methods passed and which failed, and displays the error messages generated by the selected methods (see Figure 1.10). This view is only useful if you are writing JUnit tests. If you are not using JUnit, you should make a point of reading Chapter 6, "High-grade Testing Using JUnit," which discusses JUnit and its integration within Eclipse.

The Package Explorer is my personal Eclipse favorite as a project view. The Package Explorer shows you the resources you are creating from an object-oriented point of view. A project contains packages, not directories with subdirectories that constitute a Java package, which is how the Navigator view displays its files. The Java plug-in takes care of translating the packages into the proper directory structure. Of course, the classes are still displayed with the `.java` suffix, but anything within a package is a class definition anyway (see Figure 1.11).

The Java Editor

For basic Java development, the only available editor is the default Java editor that ships with the JDT. Eclipse supplies a basic editor for use in editing text files, but it's only real feature is the ability to save the file after you have entered some text. The Java editor is a true developer's editor.

At first glance, the Java editor behaves like most Java editors currently available. It supports colored syntax (with configurable colors), programmer-configurable formatting, cut and paste, search and replace, macros (in Eclipse they are called *templates*), bracket matching, line numbers, space-for-tab substitution, and displayable print margins. In addition, the editor has support for refactoring, content assist, automatic indenting for pasted code, auto-bracket and parenthesis closing, auto-brace closing, automatic Javadoc comment

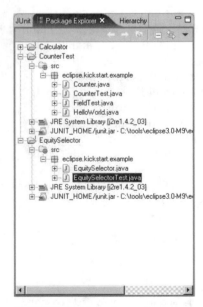

FIGURE 1.11 The Package Explorer view displaying a selected project, its associated packages, and associated JAR files.

creation, and association with existing Javadocs. All these features are configurable through the Preferences dialog and are discussed in more depth in a few pages.

The editor and the incremental compiler are inexorably linked as well. Every time you save a Java file, the incremental compiler takes care of compiling just the part of your code that has changed and any files that are dependent on it. You can change the build setting in Preferences, Workbench, Perform Build Automatically on Resource Modification. Remember, if you unset this flag, you must build the project on your own. If you forget, your code will appear to be missing functionality you may have already implemented.

Code Completion Within the Eclipse Java Editor

The Java editor supplied with the JDT allows you to write code regardless of what additional code may or may not exist. If you write code assuming that the methods you need already exist, you can have the editor take care of creating the missing pieces by allowing the Quick Fix feature to create nonexistent classes and their methods as you go along. For test-driven development, this feature makes the writing of tests almost trivial—because as you write the tests calling an API that doesn't exist yet, you can write the code as if the missing code were available and then the editor will create the missing pieces, whether they are classes, methods, or fields.

Java Browsing Perspective

The Java Browsing perspective is meant to mimic the general look and feel of the Java project view within VisualAge for Java. This perspective is ideal if you need to see the various drill-down levels of your project while you edit your code. The default Java Browsing perspective contains four views and an editor area. The four views are Projects, Packages, Types, and Members. Every time you select something in one of the previous views, it impacts the information in the succeeding views. For example, when you select a project in the Projects view, the Packages view will list the available packages for the selected project. When you select a package, the Types view will display all the available classes and interfaces contained within the package. When a class or interface is selected in the Types view, the schema of the class or interface will appear in the Members view (see Figure 1.12). It is not until you double-click one of the types in the Type view or anything in the Members view that the editor will open the selected file.

Notice in Figure 1.12 that an X within a red dot can be seen next to one of the classes displayed in the Types view. The Java Browsing perspective does not use the Problems view as one of its standard views. Therefore, select Window, Open View, Other to open the view dialog and then select Basic, Problems. The Problems view appears below the editor (see Figure 1.13).

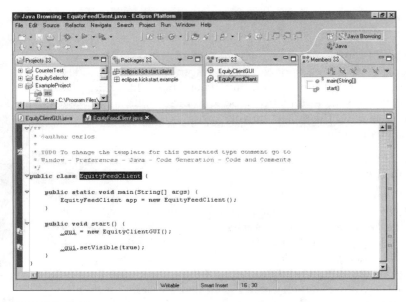

FIGURE 1.12   The Java Browsing perspective displaying the Projects, Packages, Types, and Members views together with the Java editor.

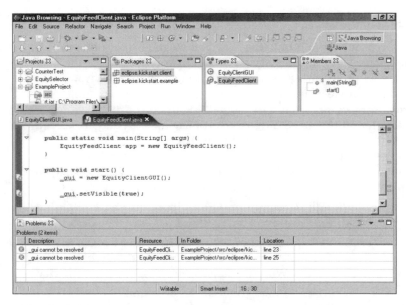

FIGURE 1.13   The Java Browsing perspective with the Problems view listing existing problems that must be handled.

Similarities Between VisualAge and Eclipse

Developers who have grown up using VisualAge for Java (VAJ) wonder if the migration to Eclipse, or IBM's commercial IDE, WebSphere Application Developer (WSAD), will be worth the effort. Moving to Eclipse/WSAD is IBM's migration strategy for users of its VisualAge for Java IDE. The two IDEs are different in quite fundamental ways. VAJ uses a repository to store everything under its control. It has a visual editor that supports visual programming using the JavaBeans component model. Eclipse uses the underlying file systems as its repository and does not have a GUI builder, much less a visual programming environment. However, VAJ developers will find the Eclipse model easy to adjust to, and much of VAJ's core functionality is available in Eclipse. WSAD adds even more VAJ functionality with its plug-ins, including a GUI builder.

Java Type Hierarchy Perspective

The Java Type Hierarchy perspective is made up of the Hierarchy view and editor space. When the Type Hierarchy first appears, the Hierarchy view is empty. If a Java file is open, you have to right-click the editor and select Open Type Hierarchy from the pop-up menu (or press F4). The Hierarchy view was discussed previously.

If you decide that you want to open another file from the Hierarchy perspective, you have one of two choices: You can return to a previous view, open the desired file, and return to the Hierarchy perspective, or you can open the Package Explorer view in the Hierarchy perspective and select a file to be opened.

Debug Perspective

The Debug perspective will be your new best friend when your JUnit tests refuse to behave. The Debug perspective consists of eight default views and can be opened by selecting Window, Open Perspective, Other to display the Select Perspective dialog so that you can choose Debug, or by running an application with Run, Debug As. Alternatively, if the Debug perspective had been opened before, you can click the Debug button in the shortcut tab on the top right of the workbench.

Views

Of the eight views, the Outline and Console views have already been discussed, so they will not be discussed in the context of the Debug perspective. Suffice it to say that any output from the program being debugged will appear in the Console view.

The Debug view, located at the top left of the Debug perspective, is probably the most important view of the Debug perspective because it displays the stack trace of the running program. The sample code running in Figure 1.14 has stopped at one of its methods, and the Debug view is displaying the current state of the application's stack. When a breakpoint is encountered, the Debug view will always display the current location where the code has been suspended and cause the Java editor to appear with the line containing the breakpoint selected.

The Variables view is one of four stacked views found to the right of the Debug view. This view displays the object where the breakpoint was set and any local variables created up to the breakpoint. If there are any fields declared in the object being debugged, a plus sign will appear next to the `this` variable. Any other object references will also have plus signs if the objects have any displayable fields. Otherwise, local primitive variables are displayed with their values, and objects have their `toString()` methods called to display these objects as strings.

The next stacked view to the right of the Debug view is the Breakpoints view. All the breakpoints available will be displayed here. If their boxes are checked, the breakpoints are enabled. If a box is not checked, the corresponding breakpoint is disabled. To reenable a breakpoint, check the box next to it. Right-clicking a breakpoint brings up a pop-up menu that allows you to enable/disable the breakpoint, delete the breakpoint, go to the file where the breakpoint is defined, suspend the VM, look at the properties for the breakpoint and do something such as set a condition under which the breakpoint will operate, and so on.

The Expressions view allows you to enter arbitrary expressions for evaluation during debugging. The left window displays the Watch expressions and the values to which they resolve, and the window to the right displays just the value the selected expression resolves to. For example, the sample class `Counter` has a local variable called `value` that is set to five. Right-clicking in the Expressions view allows you to add a Watch expression to evaluate the `value` variable while the program is being debugged. The Watch expression `"value == 0"` will resolve to `false` as long as `value` is not changed. However, adding a Watch expression of `"Math.random()"` works as well and displays a random value as its result (see Figure 1.14).

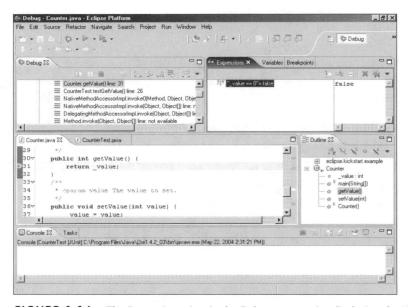

FIGURE 1.14   The Expressions view in the Debug perspective displaying the Watch expression `"value == 0"`, which resolves to `false`.

The Display view is used to display the value of a field or variable at a given point in time. Selecting a field, right-clicking it, and selecting Display from the pop-up menu will display the field name, the field type, and the current field value in the Display window. If you were to change the value in the field from the Variable view, the Display view would not automatically update itself with the new value. You would have to reselect the field and select Display from the pop-up menu. The Display view is useful in collecting field values over the course of a debug session to see how these values change over time.

The Java Editor, in addition to its normal capabilities, also displays any breakpoints within a file by showing either a blue or white dot on a line where a breakpoint is set. If the dot is blue, the breakpoint is enabled. If the dot is white, the breakpoint is disabled.

For more on the capabilities of the Debug perspective, go to the Debug Perspective section of Chapter 3, "Debugging."

JDT Preferences

To reconfigure the Java Development Tooling plug-in, you must open the Preferences dialog (Window, Preferences) and work your way down the workbench and Java preference nodes. The preferences are very personal, and the preference pages detailed in the following list are my own candidates for reconfiguration whenever I install a new version of the IDE. All the items in the Preferences dialog are useful in one context or other. Learn them all, but check out the ones listed here:

- **Workbench, Editors, Text Editor**—These preferences can be used by all the text editors. My Text Editor preferences are set to a Print Margin Column of 80, and Show Overview Ruler, Show Line Numbers, Highlight Current Line, Show Print Margin are all set.

- **Workbench, Appearance**—Eclipse defaults to displaying editor tabs on the top of the editor and view tabs at the top of the views. You can change the position of the tabs to the top or bottom of the editors and views from this page. Also, the perspective, which is displayed in a tab to the right, can be displayed at the top right or in a shortcut bar to the left. The changes take effect as soon as you click Apply.

- **Java, Build Path, Classpath Variables**—This page has no impact on the classpaths used by projects but rather allows you to set up variables available to all Eclipse projects when a third-party JAR file is needed by a project. When you right-click a project and select Properties from the pop-up menu, the Java Build Path page's Libraries tab displays a row of seven buttons to the right of the list of library files. Clicking Add Variable displays the New Variable Classpath Entry dialog. The entries in this dialog all come from the Preferences dialog's Java, Build Path, Classpath Variables page.

- **Java, Build Path**—A new project uses the `project` directory as its default. The standard location for plain Java files (that is, non-servlet, non-JSP, non-EJB, and so on) is the `src` directory, with class files being written to the `classes` directory. The Build Path page lets you change the default and, in addition, select the directories where source and class files go.

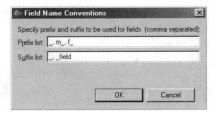

FIGURE 1.15   The Field Name Conventions dialog is where you enter a list of comma-separated prefixes and suffixes.

■ **Java, Code Style**—The preferences found here and in the Code Formatter, Code Templates, and Organize Imports subnodes are going to be the ones that have the greatest impact on your code if you use the wizards to generate stub code based on Quick Fix hints. The Code Style page is where you set any prefixes and suffixes used in your code so that the Generate Getters and Setters pop-up menu item will generate method names that ignore those parts of the field name. For example, if you've used leading underscores to identify instance fields, you would use the Code Style page to add an underscore in the Fields Prefix List cell (see Figure 1.15). Select the row of Variable Type Fields and click Edit. The Field Name Conventions dialog will open, allowing you to enter a comma-separated list of prefixes and suffixes that should be ignored when the wizards are using the field names to generate code. Enter into the Prefix List field _, **m**_, **f**_ and into the Suffix List field enter _, **_field**. Click OK and you will see your new field tags listed in the table. Click OK again and open up a Java file (if you don't have one, then create a project and create a new class or import one). Add the following instance fields to the Java class:

```java
private int aa_val;
private int _val1;
private int m_val2;
private int f_val3;
private int val4_;
private int val5_field;
private int val6;
```

Notice that each field has either a prefix or a suffix that would make the method name break the standard Java naming conventions. Right-click in the editor window and select from the pop-up menu Source, Generate Getters and Setters. The Generate Getters and Setters dialog opens, showing you the various instance fields for which you can generate accessors. All the preceding fields are listed with their associated method names. The only one that is not changed is aa_val, the one field whose prefix was not added to the Field Name Conventions dialog (see Figure 1.16).

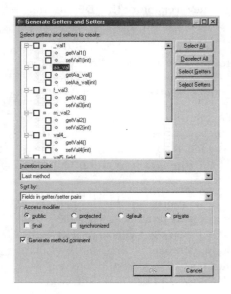

FIGURE 1.16   The Generate Getters and Setters dialog displaying auto-generated methods based on field name conventions entered in the Preferences dialog Code Style page.

- **Java, Code Style, Code Formatter**—The code-formatting options of the Java editor can all be found here. The Code Formatter page displays a window that shows how Java code would appear with the current format settings. You can create a new formatting profile or create a copy of an existing profile and modify it to suit your team's standards. You can create a new profile by clicking New, or you can change a modifiable profile by clicking Show. If you click Show, the Show Profile dialog will open with eight tabs that dictate what the editor will do about new lines, the length of lines, how comments are formatted, and so on. The combinations are many and varied.

Changing the Default Comments Used in Code Generation

The code-generation capabilities of the JDT will have you creating classes and interfaces faster than you ever have before. One of the most neglected facets of code writing, in general, is the use of comments. Eclipse's code-generation engine lets you decide where to place text stubs in various locations in your file based on whether you want to control the generation of comments or code. In the Preferences dialog on the Java, Code Style, Code Templates page, you can affect the comments for most, if not all, of the standard constructs found in Java code. In addition, the Java, Editor, Templates page lets you add new macros or change existing macros appearing in the content assist window that will output comments, method stubs, or any arbitrary text. In addition, the JDT supports internal variables that fill in information such as username, type name, and standard constructs.

- **Java, Compiler**—The Compiler page is where you get to show off how controlling you really are. The various compiler flags are set here, and the defaults are all quite reasonable. However, I set anything less than an Error up one level so that Warnings become Errors and Ignore becomes Warnings. After a few compiler runs, I reset certain flags back to their original settings or to Ignore. For example, on the Style tab, I always set Undocumented Empty Block to Error. Remember, your compiles should always be clean, and if a style issue keeps your code from compiling, you should fix the style error before going on. If you have style issues set to Ignore, they will accumulate over time. The next important tab is Unused Code. The field Local Variable Is Never Read should be a Warning, as should Parameter Is Never Read.

- **Java, Debug**—The Debug page and its associated subnodes, is where you check/uncheck items such as whether you want the debugger to stop when an uncaught exception is thrown. However, one of the most useful pages is the Debug, Detail Formatters page. On this page you can write a code fragment that will execute when an object of a specific type is selected in the debugger Variables view. Normally, when the debugger is running and a breakpoint has been reached, an object's `toString()` method is called to display information about the object. The `toString()` method has always played an important part in debugging, and the Eclipse debugger is no exception. However, you will not always have access to an object's source, and not all objects have a `toString()` method worth using. The Debug, Detail Formatters page allows you to write code that will format information about a selected object and display it in the debugger's Variables view. In effect, you are writing a custom toString() method for arbitrary data types. For example, add to the Detail Formatters page a formatter for java.util.Date with the following code snippet:

```
new java.text.SimpleDateFormat("MM/dd/yyyy").format(this)
```

Running the debugger and stopping it on a line that includes a Date object would output a date string formatted as follows:

```
10/23/2003
```

The normal toString() method for a Date object formats the date like this:

```
Thu Oct 23 20:32:20 CDT 2003
```

- **Java, Editor**—The Editor page is where you set line numbers, print margins, syntax colors, spaces for tabs, and so on. In the Appearance tab, set Show Line Numbers and Show Print Margin. In the Typing tab, set Insert Spaces for Tab. If you don't like the editor giving you matching quotes, braces, and parentheses, then turn them off as well. In Java, Editor, Code Assist, you might want to set Fill Argument Names on Method Completion.

  The Java, Editor, Templates page contains all the macros that appear along with the class, method, and field names when you do a content assist (Ctrl+spacebar). You can edit existing templates or add your own. The templates can be exported, imported, enabled, or disabled.

  To use them, just type a few letters of the template name in the Java editor, press Ctrl+spacebar, and the editor will do the rest (you can find more on content assist in Chapter 2, "Writing and Running a Java Application).

- **Java, Tasks Tags**—In prior versions of Eclipse, the Tasks view was the view where system problems and developer-added tasks were displayed. As of version 3.0, the system problems are displayed in the Problems view, while developer tasks appear in the Tasks view. In addition to adding tasks by right-clicking in the Tasks view, you can flag tasks in your code by using one of the tasks tags listed on this Preferences page. For example, you can add a new tag named DEFCON5 to the Task Tags list. If you add a comment using DEFCON5 as the first word, the comment will appear in the Tasks view (see Figure 1.17).

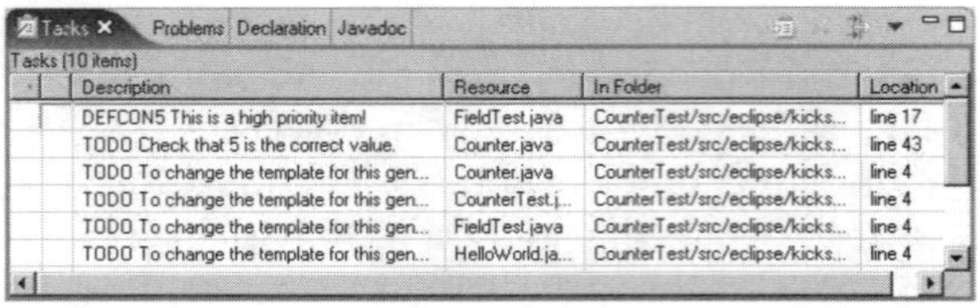

Description	Resource	In Folder	Location
DEFCON5 This is a high priority item!	FieldTest.java	CounterTest/src/eclipse/kicks...	line 17
TODO Check that 5 is the correct value.	Counter.java	CounterTest/src/eclipse/kicks...	line 43
TODO To change the template for this gen...	Counter.java	CounterTest/src/eclipse/kicks...	line 4
TODO To change the template for this gen...	CounterTest.j...	CounterTest/src/eclipse/kicks...	line 4
TODO To change the template for this gen...	FieldTest.java	CounterTest/src/eclipse/kicks...	line 4
TODO To change the template for this gen...	HelloWorld.ja...	CounterTest/src/eclipse/kicks...	line 4

FIGURE 1.17   The Tasks view with the DEFCON5 tag displayed.

Customizing a Perspective

Because perspectives define an arbitrary grouping of views and/or editors to assist you in the completion of a particular task it is a good idea to understand how to use perspectives to your advantage. Even though WebSphere Application Developer, the IBM IDE that uses Eclipse as its core, has over 80 views due to the over 500 plug-ins supplied by IBM, Eclipse starts out with a "measly" 37. As mentioned before, most of the views are useable between perspectives, so you get to decide what your ideal perspective would look like. With that in mind, let's take a look at what it would take to customize an existing perspective.

SHOP TALK

To IDE or Not to IDE

A rather interesting issue I find being ignored on a regular basis is the idea that a tool should be bypassed in favor of direct manipulation of code by a developer. Now, I have no problem with developers changing their own code, but one of the implied advantages of a tool is that the tool should take care of a myriad of details that developers should be cognizant of, but should not worry about implementing. Either buy into the tool or not, but don't blame the tool for doing its job and then screwing up because you bypassed it to accomplish something in a "quicker" fashion.

In your use of an IDE, the one thing of which you can be sure is a lack of some specific functionality you have been waiting for all your life. Whether it is a missing key binding or a wizard that should take care of one or more steps, there will always be something missing that would make your job more predictable or consistent. The JDT is a great development environment, but it is not the be-all-end-all. It can't be. The fact that IBM ships WebSphere Application Developer (WSAD) with over 500 plug-ins in addition to the Eclipse core should dispel that belief.

However, one of VisualAge for Java's shortcomings (VisualAge is Eclipse's direct predecessor) was its inability to keep up with the constant stream of changes to Java. When a new JDK would hit the streets, the other IDE vendors would have direct support for the new JDK within a few months, whereas VAJ was consistently a year or more behind. This was due to the Universal Virtual Machine that was the brains behind VAJ. It could not be updated fast enough and guarantee compatibility with the latest JVM.

Eclipse makes up for this by allowing you to arbitrarily change the runtime environment. There are some limitations to that flexibility, but overall it makes Eclipse resilient to change. Plug-ins may not always work properly based on the runtime you use, but that would be true in the case of any upgrade of an IDE.

The Eclipse environment is quite rich and shows no signs of slowing down. How could it? It's too busy keeping up with development best practices and with the ever-changing world of Java.

Every perspective can be customized. When you choose to customize a perspective, the changes are only applicable to the perspective you were viewing at the time of customization. Let's start with the Java perspective. Start Eclipse and open the Java perspective by going to the main menu and selecting Window, Show Perspective, Java. You have three areas where you can customize a perspective: the main menu, the toolbar directly below the main menu, and the views and editors area.

The main menu has three submenus where you can change default listings: the File, New submenu, the Window, Open Perspective submenu, and the Window, Show View submenu. Select Window, Customize Perspective to open the Customize Perspective dialog and get a look at the available choices (see Figure 1.18).

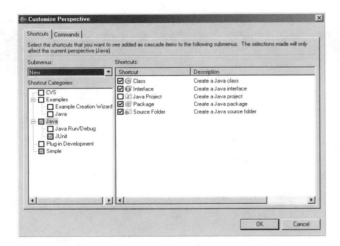

FIGURE 1.18 The Customize Perspective dialog.

The Customize Perspective dialog has a Shortcuts tab and a Commands tab. The Shortcuts tab affects the default selections displayed in menus that create resources, whereas the Commands tab adds or removes functionality on the main menu or the main toolbar.

In the Shortcuts tab, the New entry under Submenus displays two selected shortcut categories and five selected shortcuts. Because the default selections cover what you would need for a Java perspective, you can change Submenus to Open Perspective. In the Shortcuts table, check CVS Repository and Team Synchronizing. Change Submenus to Show View and check the CVS, Debug, and Team shortcut categories. Select the Basic category and check the Tasks shortcut. Click OK and check each of the main menus for the changes. Click Window, Open Perspective and the list should include CVS Repository and Team Synchronizing.

The toolbar is modified by selecting the Commands tab of the Customize Perspective dialog. Add the toolbar button that makes the Java editor show a selected source element, such as a method, by checking Editor Presentation in the Available Command Groups list. Click OK. A new button now appears in the toolbar. The icon looks like a page with a rectangle floating in the middle. Open a Java file and click Show Source of Selected Element Only. From the Outline view, select a method or field, and the editor will display just that section of code, including any associated comments. Because the button is a toggle, just click it again to get the full text view back.

Let's change the views displayed and the size of the editor; then the perspective can be saved. First, close the Package Explorer and Hierarchy views by clicking the X in the top-right corner of these views. Closing those two views will give the editor more area so you can view more of your code. Leave the Outline and Problems views. Add the Tasks view by selecting Window, Show View, Tasks. The Tasks view will list any code that uses the task tags defined in the Preferences dialog. The new perspective should look something like Figure 1.19 (the Problems view can be made visible by clicking the Problems tab to the left of the Tasks tab).

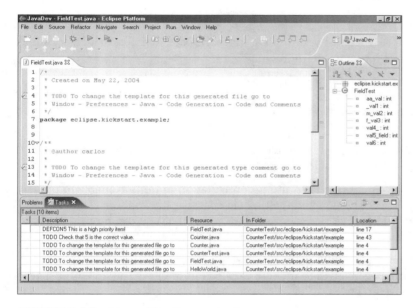

FIGURE 1.19 The new JavaDev perspective.

If you close Eclipse and open it again, you will find that the IDE has chosen to remember what your last perspective looked like. However, you should still save this new perspective under a new name so that you can display it whenever you need this combination of views. Select Window, Save Perspective As, and the Save Perspective As dialog will open. Enter the name **JavaDev**, or whatever name you prefer, and click OK.

Close the current perspective by right-clicking the button in the shortcut tab to the top right of the perspective and selecting Close. Click the Open a Perspective button, the only button in the shortcut tab, and select Other. When the Select Perspective dialog opens, you will see that the JavaDev perspective is now listed as a valid perspective.

The question that usually follows after saving a custom perspective is, "How do I delete a perspective? The one I just created is quite horrid (or at least something not to be desired)." To delete a perspective, open the Preferences dialog and select Workbench, Perspectives. Select the perspective you want to remove from the Available Perspectives list and click the Delete button to the right of the list.

In Brief

This chapter discussed the basics of Eclipse in an abbreviated form. The concepts of perspectives, views, and natures are fundamental to an understanding of Eclipse. No matter how many other features may be installed, they are all implemented within the Eclipse view of a development environment.

Here's a list of the concepts you should now be familiar with:

- The workbench is the GUI view of your underlying workspace. The workbench affords a consistent look and feel for your environment.

- An Eclipse perspective is a combination of zero or more views and zero or more editors. The various plug-ins may have their own combination of views and editors, depending on the task or role you are expected to play.

- Java Development Tooling (JDT) is the Eclipse plug-in you use to develop Java projects. It is a full-featured development environment that includes a commercial-grade editor that supports syntax coloring, refactoring, and code completion.

- The JDT Preferences pages contain the various configuration options available to the Java development plug-in. These include setting classpaths, editor options, compiler flags, debug settings, and many others. It is in these pages that you can modify the way code is generated, indicate which Javadoc's executable will be used, and more.

- Once you become comfortable with Eclipse's development model, the next step is to customize one or more perspectives to include a collection of views and an editor space that suits how you develop code.

Writing and Running a Java Application

"Give someone a fish and they will eat for a day. Teach them to fish and they will take your fishing pole."

—Anonymous

Implementing a Java Application

In many ways Java development in Eclipse using the Java Development Tooling is a dream come true: an open-source (read "free") IDE with over $40 million worth of code behind it, a well-thought-out core, and a Java development environment that rivals commercial products. Add the support of the Eclipse community, many of whom have contributed over 400 plug-ins, and you have the beginning of a beautiful friendship.

In this chapter you are going to accomplish the following:

- Create a Java project.

- Create and implement a few Java classes using the Eclipse Java editor.

- Create and implement a JUnit test to help you implement the aforementioned Java classes.

- Use a scrapbook page to test an algorithm prior to using it in a Java class.

- Use the search capability to track down fields and methods across multiple files and multiple projects and narrow the search to a subset of projects.

- Configure a launcher to run the Java application with command-line options.

Creating a Project

Before you create your first project, you should open the Preferences dialog to the Java, New Projects page. This page gives you the choice of either writing your source and classes directly into the project's folder or selecting alternate file locations. Eclipse uses src as the source directory but uses bin as the output directory. If you prefer alternate locations, select the Folders radio button and enter the subdirectory names where the source and output should go. The standard convention for Java is to name the source directory src and the output directory classes. For the examples in this book, the output folder is assumed to be called classes. When you have changed the names in your preference, click OK. All new projects will use the src and classes directories as their default source and output directories.

Start Eclipse and open the Java perspective either by selecting Window, Open Perspective, Java or by clicking the Open Perspective button in the tab to the right of the Eclipse window and selecting Java from the list of perspective choices. When you create a new Java project, Eclipse will ask if you want to switch to the Java perspective if you are not already there.

Resources in Eclipse are projects, folders, and files. To create a project, you can select a shortcut in the main menu (File, Project or File, Other), the toolbar (the first button from the left has a short list of resources that can be created, including Other), by right-clicking in the Package Explorer and selecting from the pop-up menu New, File or New, Other, or by pressing Ctrl+N from the keyboard. In every case, the New dialog will open expecting you to click Next or Cancel.

Because it is a good idea to learn keyboard shortcuts, press Ctrl+N to open the New dialog, select Java Project and then click Next. When the Java Project page appears, enter as the project name Calculator. The project name is arbitrary and does not have to match the directory where the code will be located. All Java projects go into a workspace somewhere on your filesystem, and Eclipse has a default workspace path that is located in the installation path of the IDE. I strongly recommend not using the default workspace path as the location for your projects. If you uninstall Eclipse, your projects will disappear along with the IDE. Locating your projects in a separate location will keep them safer and make it easier to create backups.

To use a different directory than the one displayed on the Java Project page of the New dialog, uncheck Use Default and either enter a new page in the Directory field or click the Browse button to open the Browse For Folder dialog (see Figure 2.1). Unless you have a small path to enter, you should click Browse and navigate to a safe location you can use as your personal workspace. Click OK to close the Browse For Folder dialog and then click Next on the Java Project page.

The next page, the Java Settings page, is where you can confirm that the source and the output folders for your code match your development conventions. In the Source tab, your preference settings for the source and output directories will be used. The Source Folders on Build Path will list Calculator/src, and the Default Output Folder will be Calculator/classes. The Projects tab will display any projects in your workspace, and any that are selected (that is, that have their check boxes selected) are included in the build of the current project. If this is your first Java project in Eclipse, this list will be empty.

The next tab, Libraries, is where you set your Java classpath. You never have to worry about manually setting your classpath during development ever again! You have five different ways of adding libraries/packages to your environment:

- With an Eclipse alias that is available for all projects to use

- By selecting a JAR file within an Eclipse project

- By selecting a JAR file external to Eclipse

- By selecting a new or additional JRE or plug-in library

- By adding a folder that contains class files

Click Finish to close the New dialog. If you ever need to see this page again, you can right-click the project and select the Properties pop-up menu item. The Package Explorer will display the new project, and all the other views are empty. The editor area should also be blank. If this is the first time you have started Eclipse, the Welcome page might be displayed. Close it by clicking the X on the Welcome page tab.

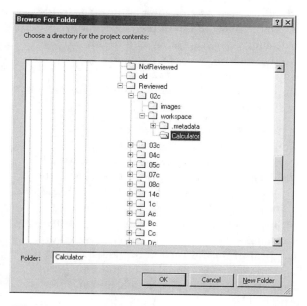

FIGURE 2.1   The Browse For Folder dialog with the `Calculator` directory created and selected.

Open the project. You'll see that only two resources are located within it: the `src` directory and the JRE System Library. The `classes` directory will not be seen in the Package Explorer,

FIGURE 2.2 The Navigator view displaying the actual filesystem resources related to the Calculator project.

FIGURE 2.3 The Extended Interfaces Selection dialog displaying the Serializable interface.

but it can be seen in the Navigator view, which displays a filesystem-oriented view. You can open the Navigator view by selecting Window, Show View, Navigator (see Figure 2.2). It overlays the Package Explorer, so click the Package Explorer tab, located at the bottom of the leftmost views, to bring the Package Explorer view to the top. If you prefer to keep an OO perspective of your project, the Project Explorer is going to be your view of choice.

Creating an Interface

It is time to create an interface for the calculator object you are going to implement. If the project is not selected in the Package Explorer, select it to have one less field to fill in the wizard. Once again, press Ctrl+N to open the New dialog. If only two items are listed, check Show All Wizards to display the full list of available choices. Select Java, Interface and then click Next. The Java Interface page needs only one field filled in—the name of the interface—but it is poor form to define a new data type without locating it inside of a package. Move the cursor to the Package field and enter calculator as the package name. Notice that the top of the page complains that the type name is empty. You can safely ignore this message because you will be entering the type name next. Enter Calculator as the interface name in the Name field. The Modifiers setting should be left as public, and the Extended Interfaces list should be left blank.

If there were additional interfaces Calculator needed to extend, you would click Add to display the Extended Interfaces Selection dialog (see Figure 2.3), and you would begin typing the name of the additional interfaces (not the package name). For the purposes of this example, let's add the Serializable interface located in java.io. Click Add to open the Extended Interfaces Selection dialog and type the first few letters of Serializable. Notice that two interfaces called Serializable appear in the 1.4 version of the JDK. Select the java.io package and click OK. The Java Interface page now displays a package name, an interface name, and an interface that will be inherited by Calculator. Click Finish.

The JDT configures its look based on this new resource. It will open the src folder, revealing the calculator package, which reveals the Calculator.java file you just created. The Java editor also opened automatically, revealing the code generated by the wizard based on your input (see Figure 2.4). The various generated pieces are consistent between interfaces and classes: a file comment, a package statement, any imports (if you declared any inherited types), and a type comment for the interface (or class). When we discuss the Java editor, you will configure it to display line numbers, a print margin, and new templates to replace the default comment blocks used when you generate code-creating interfaces, classes, methods, and fields.

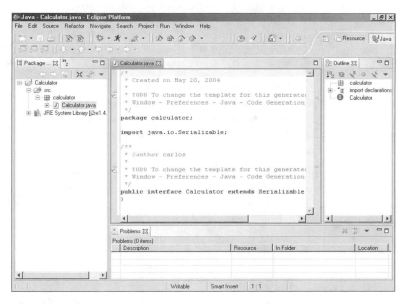

FIGURE 2.4   The Java editor displaying the Calculator interface.

Creating a Class

Creating a class is marginally different from creating an interface. Select Calculator.java or calculator in the Package Explorer and press Ctrl+N. When the New dialog appears, select Java, Class and then click Next. The input fields Source Folder, Package, and Superclass are already filled. Enter in the Name field SimpleCalculator and click the Add button. When the Implemented Interfaces Selection dialog appears, type in the Choose Interfaces field Calculator and click OK. The Calculator interface appears in the Interfaces list. Click Finish. Once again, the Java editor opens, only this time it displays the SimpleCalculator class. There are no methods or fields declared. In keeping with test-driven development, you will now define a test to show that the Calculator works as expected.

Creating a JUnit Test

You will spend more time on JUnit and testing in Chapter 6, "High-grade Testing Using JUnit," but this preview is meant to show how you can develop tests and code seamlessly within Eclipse. For now, let's look at developing a test for this example. Test-driven development dictates that the test is always written first. Well, in Eclipse, if the class you are trying to test does not exist, the JUnit Wizard complains about its nonexistence. Because you have already created the SimpleCalculator class, you can now safely create a test to prove that it behaves in the manner you expect.

Select SimpleCalculator.java from the Package Explorer. Press Ctrl+N and, after the New dialog appears, open the Java node to reveal JUnit. Select Java, JUnit, TestCase. When you click Next, the New Test Case dialog appears, asking if you would like the wizard to add junit.jar to the build path. Because you cannot write any JUnit test without junit.jar, click Yes.

The New JUnit Test Case page displays almost everything filled in for you (if it does not have all the input fields filled in, you should cancel out, select SimpleCalculator from the Package Explorer, and try again). The standard convention for JUnit is to name the test class after the class to be tested and append "Test". The only thing you need to do is check setUp() and tearDown(). Click Finish. The editor opens on the test class.

At this point you need to edit the file, and it will be easier after you configure the editor to display line numbers. Select from the main menu Window, Preferences. Open the Java node and select Editor (see Figure 2.5). Check Show Line Numbers from the Appearance tab and click OK. All the Java editors will now display line numbers.

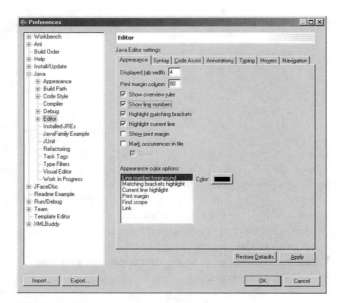

FIGURE 2.5   The Preferences dialog displaying the Appearance tab, where the line numbers configuration is found.

Let's set up our test. Replace the line

```
super.setUp();
```

with this:

```
calculator = new SimpleCalculator();
```

Replace the line

```
super.tearDown();
```

with this:

```
_calculator = null;
```

Both of these new lines have light bulbs and X's in the margin to the left and thin red bars in the margin to the right. If you have already saved the file, you will also see that the two errors appear in the Problems view directly below the editor. You could correct these problems yourself, but the editor can do the job with less work.

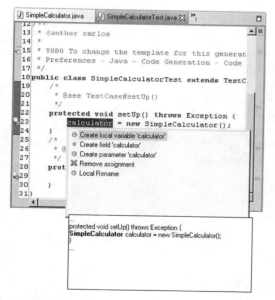

FIGURE 2.6 The Content Assist window with choices to fix a perceived syntax error.

Using the Java Editor

Move the mouse cursor over the first light bulb located in the left margin. If you wait a second or two, a tooltip will appear, notifying you that the problem it encountered was "_calculator cannot be resolved." Well, you knew that. Click once on the light bulb, and a Content Assist window opens, listing possible solutions to the error (see Figure 2.6). The choices cover the most obvious solutions: define a local variable, define an incoming parameter, define an instance field, and simply remove the assignment. For this test you need _calculator as an instance field, so select Create field '_calculator'. The code generator places the new instance field above the methods and assigns it a scope of private.

The code generator also selects calculator and the generated instance field and highlights them with a rectangle. The reason for this elaborate selection is to allow you to change the name of the variable in the code while staying in sync with the field declaration. To test how this works, while the field is still selected and underlined, begin typing _calculator. The instance declaration will update to match the new field name. When you are done, press Esc. Now that the field declared in tearDown() has a match with the declaration within teardown(), both compile errors have been corrected.

Save `SimpleCalculatorTest` by pressing Ctrl+S or by selecting File, Save in the main menu. Save your file as often as you can while you complete this example.

The next thing you need to do is test one of the `SimpleCalculator` methods. Not having any defined methods in `SimpleCalculator` should not stop you from writing your test code. Add a blank line after the instance field and enter the following code:

```
public void testAdd() {
```

Pressing Enter after the curly brace will cause two lines to appear: a blank line with the cursor waiting for input and a line with a closing brace. Before you write any test code, change the class type declaration of the instance field from `SimpleCalculator` to `Calculator`. The reason for this change is meant to keep the `Calculator` interface and the `SimpleCalculator` class API in sync when the editor generates additional stubs. This will soon become self-evident. Add the following code to `testAdd()`:

```
public void testAdd() {
    int expected = 0;
    int actual = _calculator.add(0, 0);
}
```

The `add()` method will take two numbers and return the result of the addition. The next syntax error is the nonexistence of `add()`. Click once on the yellow light bulb to the left of line 23 to see what suggestions the editor has to correct the problem (see Figure 2.7). The only choice you have is to create an `add()` method in the `Calculator` interface. Press Enter or double-click the entry in the Content Assist window. The code generator will cause the `Calculator.java` editor window to come to the front and display the generated method declaration. Every component of the method declaration is selected and outlined. Move the cursor and press Esc to remove the underline. Save `Calculator.java`. Click once on the editor tab for `SimpleCalculatorTest` to see that the error is now gone. If the error is still listed, save all of the files to have Eclipse recompile any dependent files.

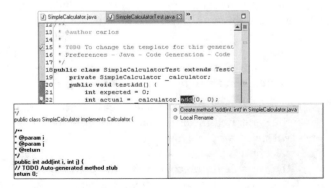

FIGURE 2.7   The Content Assist window with choices to handle the missing method syntax error.

To complete this simple test, add one more line after the call to add() to check that the expected result matches with the actual result:

```
assertEquals(expected, actual);
```

When you type this line, you should only have to type "assert" before pressing Ctrl+spacebar to allow the editor to find assertEquals(). Once the editor has found the method, press Enter and type "exp", press Ctrl+spacebar, and press Enter on expected. Type ", ac", press Ctrl+spacebar, and press Enter on actual. Pressing Ctrl+spacebar may take some work, but it is well worth the effort. You will code faster and with more accuracy.

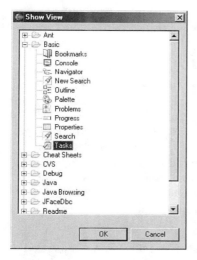

FIGURE 2.8 The Show View dialog with the Tasks view item selected.

Another error has now surfaced: The SimpleCalculator class needs to implement add(). The Problems view lists an error within SimpleCalculator having to do with implementing the missing method. Double-click the Problems view entry to bring the editor for SimpleCalculator to the front. A light bulb is to the left of the class declaration, and if you click it once, the Content Assist window lists three possible solutions. Press Enter or double-click the entry "Add unimplemented methods" to have the code generator take care of creating a syntactically valid version of add(). A gray X will appear in the left margin until you save the file.

Once you have saved the file, a new icon appears in the left margin at line 21: the TODO icon. Whenever the TODO token appears in a comment, the editor adds it to the Tasks view, which you can open by selecting Window, Show View, Other, and opening the category named Basic (see Figure 2.8). The Tasks view will display the items flagged with TODO across all projects and files (see Figure 2.9).

	Description	Resource	In Folder	Location
	TODO Auto-generated method stub	SimpleCalcul...	Calculator/src/calculator	line 21
	TODO To change the template for this ge...	Calculator.java	Calculator/src/calculator	line 4
	TODO To change the template for this ge...	SimpleCalcul...	Calculator/src/calculator	line 4
	TODO To change the template for this ge...	SimpleCalcul...	Calculator/src/calculator	line 4
	TODO To change the template for this ge...	Calculator.java	Calculator/src/calculator	line 14
	TODO To change the template for this ge...	SimpleCalcul...	Calculator/src/calculator	line 12
	TODO To change the template for this ge...	SimpleCalcul...	Calculator/src/calculator	line 15

FIGURE 2.9 The Tasks view displaying the TODO items from the Calculator project files.

Keeping Track of Your Daily Tasks

A common coding convention is to use a token such as TODO or FIXME to alert developers to the fact that a change needs to be made to the code they are working on. The only items that appear in the Tasks view are comment lines flagged with TODO, FIXME, XXX, or items added manually by right-clicking in the Tasks view and selecting Add Task from the pop-up menu. Going to the Preferences dialog and selecting Java, Task Tags will show you a table where you can add your own custom tags that will appear in the Tasks view whenever they are used in any kind of Java comment. The default task tag is TODO, and it has a priority of Normal. You can change TODO's priority to Low, Normal, or High or add your own tags and assign a priority to them. Low-priority tasks have a downward pointing arrow associated with them, a normal priority has no icon, and a high-priority item has an exclamation point.

At this point you have no compile errors, an interface that defines what calculators should do, a subclass that implements that behavior, and a test class. Let's run the test class and see if the calculator object adds our simple case of "0 + 0." To run the JUnit test, you must either have the SimpleCalculatorTest editor as the current editor or select the SimpleCalculatorTest class in the Package Explorer. From the main menu select Run, Run As, JUnit Test. JUnit Plug-in Test is available as a selection, but do not choose it to run your test because you are not testing a plug-in. If the JUnit test does not appear as the top view to the left of the editor, click its tab, which is located toward the bottom of the Package Explorer view (see Figure 2.10).

The fact that the test passed is a good sign, but a few more tests need to be run. Add the following code to testAdd() after the current working test:

FIGURE 2.10   The JUnit GUI displaying the green bar, which means the test passed.

```
expected = 1;
actual = _calculator.add(0, 1);
assertEquals(expected, actual);
```

Run the test again by selecting Run, Run As, JUnit Test or by pressing Ctrl+F11, which executes whatever you ran last. This time the test fails because the stub is only set to return 0. Asking the calculator to add "0 + 1" had to fail. Correct SimpleCalculator's add() method by changing the current implementation to something a little more general:

```
public int add(int i, int j) {
    return i + j;
}
```

This new implementation is not perfect because it does not take overflow or underflow into account, but it is better. Run the test again. The bar is now green.

Now let's look at how you can customize the editor, create a scrapbook page to allow for the running of arbitrary code outside of a Java class/object, and how to search for files, types, and fields.

Customizing the Java Editor

As mentioned in Chapter 1, you customize the Java editor through the Preferences dialog. Open the Preferences dialog (Window, Preferences) and go to Java, Editor. In the Appearance tab, check Show Print Margin. This will draw a thin line at the margin column set in the Print Margin Column field in this tab. The Print Margin Column default is 80. Next, click the Code Assist tab and check Fill Argument Names on Method Completion. This editor setting will best-guess which variables you might want to use as incoming arguments when you use code-completion to find a method. In the Typing tab, check Insert Spaces for Tab.

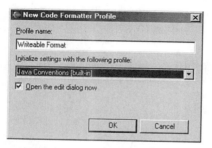

FIGURE 2.11   The New Code Formatter Profile dialog set to the new writeable profile using the Java formatting conventions as its base.

Now select the Java, Code Style, Code Formatter node in the Preferences tree view to the left. The Code Formatter page displays a named profile list and a Preview window with sample code formatted using the selected profile. The default formatting profile is named Default and is one of two built-in read-only profiles. To change the current formatting settings, you need to create a copy of an existing profile and modify the desired settings. Click New to open the New Code Formatter Profile dialog. Enter "Writeable Format" for Profile Name and "Java Conventions" for Initialize settings with the following profile (see Figure 2.11). Click OK. The Edit Profile dialog opens to show eight different tabs, where you can change the format settings for your Java code:

1. Under the Indentation tab, uncheck Use Tab Character.

2. Under the White Space tab, in the Insert Space window, select Expressions, Type Casts, and in the window below, uncheck After Closing Parenthesis. The Preview window to the right shows the change on a single line of code.

You can change numerous settings to suit your needs. In addition, you can save your settings to share with your team or load the formatting agreed on by your team. Click OK to close the Edit Profile dialog.

Finally, there are two areas where you can impact the code generation of the Java editor. The first is Java, Code Templates. This page is where you can change what code is used when new code is generated. For example, when you created the previous three files, the editor gave you the default file comment, default type comment, and default method comments. The Code Templates page is where you can change what code is output as part of a generated file (see Figure 2.12). For example, the comment block that appears above the class definition is defined under Comments, Types. The comment block used when a new file is generated (for example, when creating a new class or interface) is found under Code, New Java Files. This file template defines the file's comment block as well as defines that a package statement follows the file comment and that a type comment and type follow the package statement. These additional template hints are defined using template variables. You can get a peek at the template variables by selecting one of the nodes and clicking Edit. The Edit Template dialog has a button labeled Insert Variable. Click Insert Variable for the list of available template variables. When you are done looking at the list, click Cancel to return to the Preferences dialog. Feel free to change any of the comments or code-generation templates that you feel you need to customize. For this book, the default templates are used.

The second area where you can affect code generation is under Java, Editor, Templates (see Figure 2.13). The templates listed are customizable, and you can add, edit, or delete any of them. You can add your own shortcuts, and you can export one or more of the templates for later import into another instance of Eclipse. You can include these templates in your code by pressing Ctrl+spacebar. Click OK to save all your changes and return to the workbench.

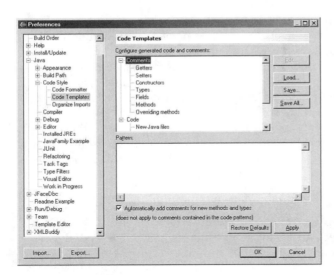

FIGURE 2.12   One of the code-generation pages found in the Preferences dialog.

Now you have a slightly different setup for code generation as well as code formatting. Feel free to return to the three files you have been working with and reformat them by pressing Shift+Ctrl+F on each. As you update the three files in this chapter, you will get a chance to try out some of the editor-customization features.

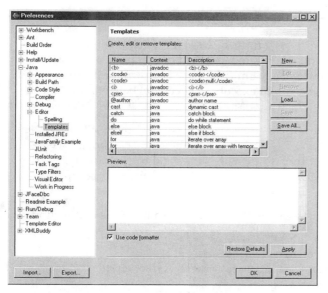

FIGURE 2.13   A partial list of customizable templates.

SHOP TALK

On the Shoulders of Giants, or Why Guns Can Be Dangerous

If you enjoy having your hand held, then tools such as Eclipse are going to tickle you pink. Although it is true that some developers prefer to use non-colored-syntax editors and command-line compilers, there are many more who prefer to spend their time in other development-related activities. The JDT, with its wizards and incremental compiler, should make you more productive as you use the tool to execute the steps you performed by hand in the past. The refactoring support alone is worth its weight in Au. (Go ahead and look it up in the Periodic Table. I can wait.)

A good tool is all about low complexity and high usability. The more we learn about the problems we encounter in our day-to-day work, the easier it is to create general solutions so we don't have to keep solving the same problem in ways that don't vary by much. Design patterns are nice, but sometimes you just want the concrete solution to your problem without having to customize a previous solution. Our tools reflect that. Eclipse is popular, not because it has a cool name or has a lot of buzz associated with it, but because it codifies best practices, thereby helping you become more productive. The tools we use reflect aggregate knowledge. We stand on the shoulders of those who came before us, and sometimes on the shoulders of those we work with every day (metaphorically speaking, or course).

But a cautionary note: The same way that owning a gun doesn't make you a marksman, using an IDE, even a great one, will not make you a good developer. Remember, you just have to take a written test to get behind the wheel of a car. A learner's permit may expire, but the holder of the permit can cause a great deal of damage before it does. Experience still counts for a great deal in this field. As our tools become more abstract and hide more and more complexity, knowledge about tools and how to extend them will define the next level of shoulders on which we will stand.

Creating a Scrapbook Page

Whereas the Java editor allows you to write fully formed class types, the scrapbook page allows you to write code snippets that you can run independent of any particular class. A scrapbook can be used as a scratch pad where experimental code is grown, or it can be saved with a collection of code snippets that you would execute to check the behavior of the code being called.

Create a scrapbook page by selecting the current project and pressing Ctrl+N. When the New dialog appears, select Java, Scrapbook Page. Click Next. When the New Scrapbook Page appears, select project Calculator and enter into the File Name field the name scrap. When you click Finish, the JDT creates a file with the .jpage extension (in this case, scrap.jpage), and the editor opens on this new file.

Enter the following code into the scrap.jpage file (be sure to use some of the editor short-cuts you have learned so far):

```
java.util.Date d = java.util.Calendar.getInstance().getTime();
java.text.DateFormat format = new java.text.SimpleDateFormat("yyyy/MM/dd");
System.out.print("Date: " + format.format(d));
```

All the preceding code is doing is creating a Date object and a SimpleDateFormat object and calling System.out.println() to display the date in the format yyyy/MM/dd. Make sure the scrap.jpage editor has focus and then press Ctrl+A. This will select all the code on the page for execution. Right-click in the editor window and select Execute from the pop-up menu. The current date in a string format will be displayed in the Console view (if the Console view does not come forward, click the Console tab to bring it forward). No method was declared to contain the code, and no class was declared to contain the method. The scrapbook is an ideal place to experiment with algorithms until you are sure they work the way you expect. Even though scrapbook pages can be saved and reused, you should not use a scrapbook file as a substitute for a JUnit test.

Searching for Files, Types, Fields, and Plug-Ins

What happens when you need to find where various symbols or strings are being called either in one project, all projects, or a subset of projects? The JDT has search capabilities to search files, the Help area, Java files based on various types, and plug-in code. Each of these areas has its own set of search criteria and can search either the full workspace or a subset. Bear in mind that the search functionality does not search the general file system; the only resources searched are those under the control of Eclipse, which translates to projects, folders, and files. For the purposes of the following examples, and because we only have one project to begin with, all the search examples will use the Calculator project for its output.

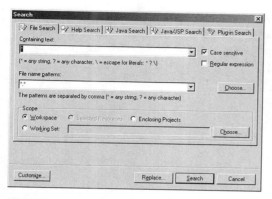

FIGURE 2.14 The Search dialog with the File Search tab selected.

If the Calculator project is selected, unselect it by holding down the Ctrl key and clicking the project once. Press Ctrl+H to open the Search dialog. The Search dialog is made up of five tabs: File Search, Help Search, Java Search, Java/JSP Search, and Plug-in Search (see Figure 2.14). The first tab from the left is File Search. The first time you open the Search dialog, it is liable to default to the Java Search tab. To follow along, click the File Search tab.

File Search allows you to enter a string of arbitrary text with the choice of making the search case sensitive and/or interpreting the search string as a regular expression. Output from the search will appear in the Search view, which will open when results are found. The regular expression characters are listed directly below the input field, labeled Containing Text: An asterisk (*) matches any string, a question mark (?) is used to match individual characters, and the backslash (\) is used to escape the asterisk and the question mark if they are part of the search string. If you enter an asterisk, leave File Name Patterns set to *.*, and leave Scope set to Workspace. Clicking Search will return everything from your current workspace, which in this case only contains one project (see Figure 2.15). If you had a number of projects in your workspace, they would all be checked, and every line from all the projects would be returned.

FIGURE 2.15 The Search view displaying the result of a search string of "*" on all the files in all the projects on the workbench.

Notice in Figure 2.15 that the editor, displaying SimpleCalculator, has multiple arrows pointing at each individual line. In the Search view, double-click Calculator.java. This will open the file in the editor and take you to the first matching line. In this case, all the lines match, so the file simply opens. Click within the New Search view, select a non-Java file such as scrap.jpage, and press Ctrl+H again, but this time enter the word *Calculator* into the Containing Text field. Leave Case Sensitive and Workspace checked and click Search. This time, only four items appear: `Calculator.java`, `SimpleCalculator.java`, `SimpleCalculatorTest.java`, and `.project`. Double-click `SimpleCalculatorTest.java` in the Search view and it will open, displaying arrows pointing at the three lines where the case-sensitive word *Calculator* appears (see Figure 2.16).

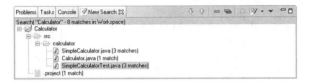

FIGURE 2.16   The Search view displaying the three files that match the search string "Calculator".

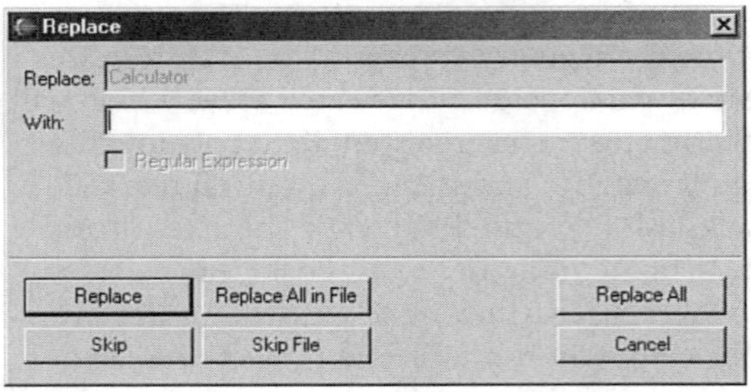

In addition to finding every location of an arbitrary string or regular expression, you can also do a search-and-replace of that string or regular expression by clicking the Replace button instead of Search. Every time the search engine finds a match, it displays a Replace dialog and gives you the following choices: skip the current selection, skip the entire current file, replace the current string, replace all matches within the current file, and replace every occurrence within every matching file (see Figure 2.17).

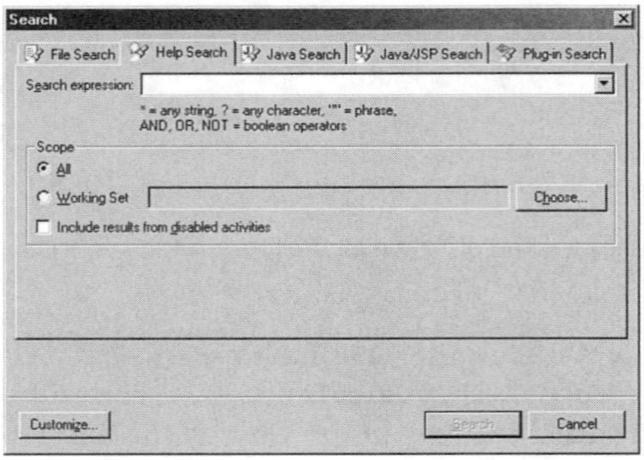

FIGURE 2.17   The Replace dialog waiting for a decision on what to do with the matching strings.

The Help Search tab allows you to search through the Eclipse Help files (see Figure 2.18). For example, if you were to enter the string *SWT* in the Search Expression input field and click Search, you should get approximately 87 documents found. Double-clicking any of the documents listed in the Search view will cause the Eclipse Help system to start and display the main Help window, with the selected document in the window to the right and all the matching words highlighted (see Figure 2.19).

FIGURE 2.18   The Help Search tab.

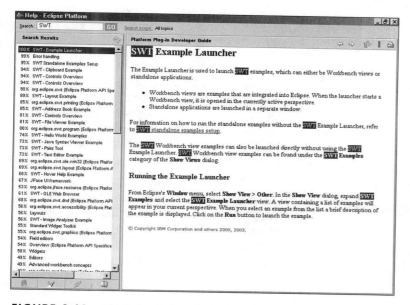

FIGURE 2.19 The Help window displaying the results of the Help search with the search word *SWT* highlighted.

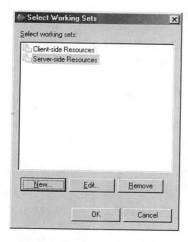

FIGURE 2.20 The Select Working Sets dialog displaying named search subsets.

The procedure to create a resource subset is valid for all the search tabs. To create a subset of the Workbench resources, thereby making the search more focused, you select the Working Set radio button and click Choose. The Select Working Sets dialog lists all existing named subsets and allows you to create a new named subset (see Figure 2.20). Each named subset can contain zero or more projects, zero or more folders, and zero or more files in any combination. Click New to open the New Working Set dialog (see Figure 2.21) and select a Working Set type. The Java type would be appropriate for Java and plug-in searches, whereas Help would be appropriate for Help searches. Also, any of the three types (Java, Help, and Resources) would be valid for file searches. Select Resources and click Next.

FIGURE 2.21   The New Working Set dialog listing the three working set types.

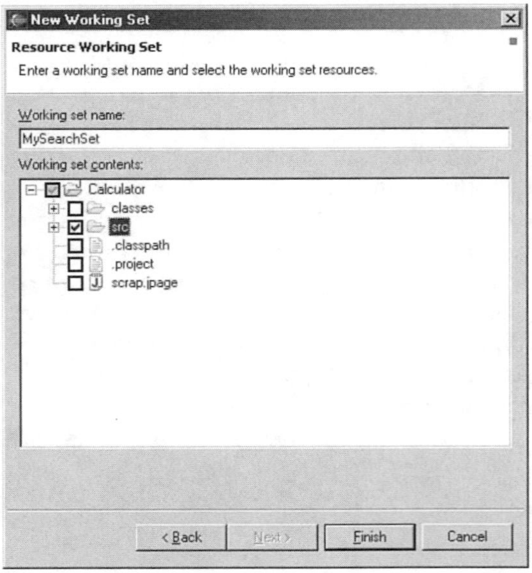

FIGURE 2.22   The Resource Working Set page with a set name and the chosen folder (src).

Resource Working Set is the last page of the New Working Set dialog. Give your new set a name, such as MySearchSet. Then, after opening the nodes, check the box next to the src folder (see Figure 2.22). Click Finish. Make sure MySearchSet is selected and then click OK. To test the use of the working set, perform another file search for the word *System* with Workspace selected in the Search dialog and then again with MySearchSet selected as the current working set.

The Java Search tab is much different from either File Search or Help Search. This tab allows you to search for strings that match targeted Java language constructs (see Figure 2.23). Of the three search tabs discussed so far, Java Search is the most complex. In both File Search and Help Search, you enter a string, and the system does a full-file search for the requested string. In Java Search, the string you enter is only checked against a particular language construct. For example, if `Calculator` is entered as the search string, the Search For area has the Constructor radio button selected, and the scope is Workspace (not MySearchSet), no item will be selected because there is no constructor defined for `Calculator`. Change the search string to `SimpleCalculator`, and two files will be found: `SimpleCalculator.java`, whose constructor is used in `main()`, and `SimpleCalculatorTest.java`, which uses the constructor in `setUp()`.

Open the Search dialog again and enter `setUp` as the search string. Check the Case sensitive check box, change the Search For setting from Type to Method, the Limit To setting to All Occurrences, and the Scope setting to Workspace. These settings will make sure the search engine performs a case-sensitive compare, only compares the search string to

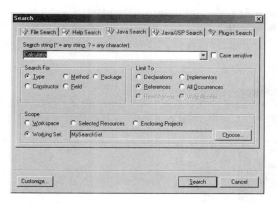

FIGURE 2.23 The Java Search page in the Search dialog.

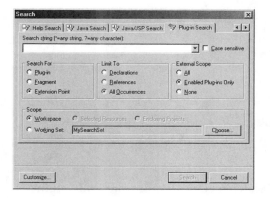

FIGURE 2.24 The Plug-in Search page.

methods, and lists both the declaration of setUp methods as well as where they are used. Click Search to see the results. Three files will be found: SimpleCalculatorTest.java and two files from junit.jar, TestSetup.java, and TestCase.java.

Use the Java Search tab when an arbitrary search for a string would not achieve the results for which you are looking. An alternative to using Java Search would be the refactoring mechanism in Eclipse, which takes care of searching the files that use a symbol prior to changing it. A more in-depth discussion of refactoring can be found in Chapter 4, "Refactoring."

Similar to the Java Search tab is the Plug-in Search tab. This search tab has been available since release 2.1.2. Without worrying too much about the details behind plug-ins, let's look at one example of searching for plug-in information (see Figure 2.24).

The Plug-in Search field defaults to accepting a string that is a regular expression. Plug-ins come in three flavors: plug-ins, fragments, and extension points. A *plug-in* is additional Eclipse functionality that you can add by pointing Eclipse to the directory where the plug-in has been installed. A *feature* is an addition to a plug-in, and an *extension point* is an entry point into the plug-in architecture where you can add your own plug-in. Plug-ins are discussed in more depth in Part 3, "Extending Eclipse." The Plug-in Search tab allows you to search for symbols within all three types as well as just the declarations or references (or both) of a plug-in. You can also include just the enabled plug-ins, all plug-ins recognized by Eclipse, or no plug-ins whatsoever.

As a sample search, let's try to find the extension point for preferences pages. Perhaps you want to add a new page to the Preferences dialog. The full name of the preferences extension point is org.eclipse.ui.preferencePages. In the Plug-in Search page, you can enter the following into the Search String input field:

- org.eclipse.ui.preferencePages

- *.preferencePages

- *.preference*

The three are equivalent, and all return the same number of matches (three `plugin.xml` files for Eclipse 3.0 M8). If you double-click one of the results located in the Search view, Eclipse will open the Plug-in Manifest editor and select the `org.eclipse.ui.preferencePages` item located in the file (see Figure 2.25).

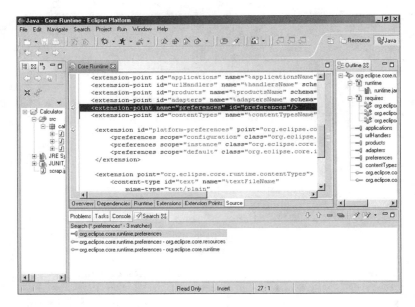

FIGURE 2.25   Search results displayed in the Search view, and the `plugin.xml` file open in the Plug-in Manifest editor.

So what is the point of having so many different search methods? A file search will return everything it finds based on an arbitrary string, whereas a Java search will only return matches within Java files based on usage. You can search by type, method, package, constructor, or field. For example, if you only want to know which classes are using a particular method, you would search based on references, and it would be safe to assume you will only get classes where a method is used and not where it coincidentally appears in a comment. The plug-in search makes it easier to search either the entire set of `plugin.xml` files or a subset based on whether it is enabled or just poised to be loaded.

In all these cases, you can disable case sensitivity as well as create custom subsets of data that you want to search.

Running a Java Application

The various examples in this chapter have been executed directly from the Run menu, which gave Eclipse the opportunity to make its own decisions about how to call the JVM. When you need more control over the execution of your Java code, you open the Launcher dialog.

The Launcher

Time to run the calculator as a standalone Java application. The first requirement for any Java application is that it contain `main()`. Your `SimpleCalculator` does not, but that is easily remedied. Move the keyboard cursor to the closing curly brace of `add()`, press Enter, type `main`, and press Ctrl+spacebar. When the Content Assist window opens, press Enter on the entry that states "main - main method." Save the file. Enter the following code into `main()` and save the file:

```java
public static void main(String[] args) {
    Calculator calculator = new SimpleCalculator();
    int result = calculator.add(5, 5);
    System.out.println("Result: " + result);
}
```

Formatting Your Code

If you are like me, the fact that the code is not properly formatted can be quite irritating. In Eclipse, this is solved by right-clicking in the editor and from the pop-up menu selecting Source, Format or pressing Ctrl+Shift+F. If you only need a section of code formatted, select the lines needing formatting and press Ctrl+Shift+F or select Source, Format from the pop-up menu. Better yet, under the Typing tab in the Preferences dialog select Java, Editor and make sure that Pasting for Correct Indentation is checked.

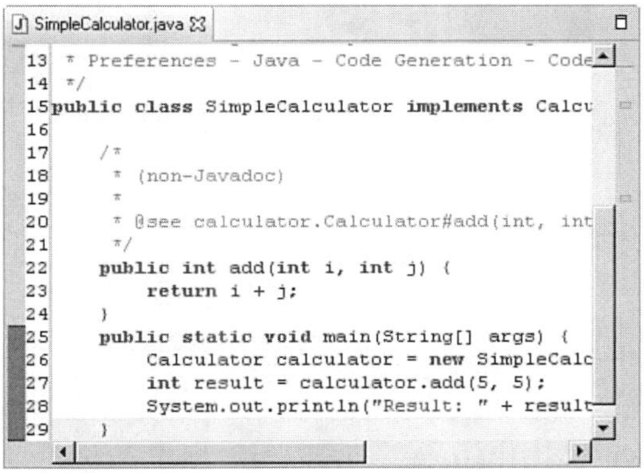

FIGURE 2.26 The Console view displaying the output of `SimpleCalculator`.

You are now ready to run this version of the calculator. Eclipse, in its never-ending quest to help you along, will run this application in a transparent fashion because it does not need any command-line arguments to run. With `SimpleCalculator` as the current editor, go to the main menu and select Run, Run As, Java Application. Because `main()` is printing to the output stream, the Console view opens and displays the calculator's output (see Figure 2.26).

The execution of `SimpleCalculator` is not based solely on its definition of `main()`. Eclipse uses launch configurations to allow you to run Java programs using varying execution information. Rather than selecting Run, Run As to execute the program, from the main menu select Run, Run to open the Run dialog, which displays all the available launch configurations (see Figure 2.27).

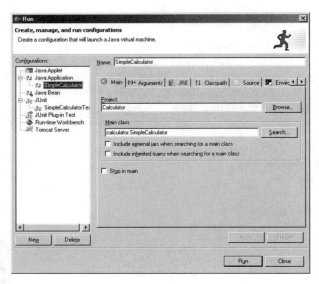

FIGURE 2.27   The Run dialog displaying the `SimpleCalculator` launch configuration.

If you opened the Run dialog, close it and change the code in `SimpleCalculator` to use the command line to discover the two values to add together:

```java
public class SimpleCalculator implements Calculator {

    private static final String USAGE =
        "java calculator.SimpleCalculator val1 val2";
    /*
     * (non-Javadoc)
     *
     * @see calculator.Calculator#add(int, int)
     */
    public int add(int i, int j) {
        return i + j;
    }
    public static void main(String[] args) {
        if (args == null || args.length < 2) {
            System.out.println(USAGE);
        } else {
            Calculator calculator = new SimpleCalculator();
            int val1 = Integer.parseInt(args[0]);
```

```
            int val2 = Integer.parseInt(args[1]);
            int result = calculator.add(val1, val2);

            System.out.println("Result: " + result);
        }
    }
}
```

Press Ctrl+F11 to run `SimpleCalculator` again. This time, the console output displays

```
java calculator.SimpleCalculator val1 val2
```

The original launch configuration was simply running `SimpleCalculator` against the JVM with no command-line arguments. The launch configuration is now incorrect. To correct it, select from the main menu Run, Run, select `SimpleCalculator` from the configurations listed to the left of the dialog, and click the Arguments tab. Enter the numbers 5 and 10 into the Program Arguments text area (see Figure 2.28).

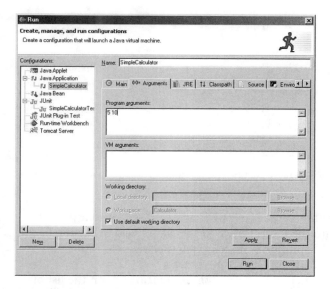

FIGURE 2.28   The Arguments tab displaying the command-line values to be used when SimpleCalculator is executed.

Click Run, and the Console view will display the new result:

```
Result: 15
```

Creating Custom Launchers

Let's walk through creating a new launch configuration for our application. Reopen the Run dialog again (Run, Run). Select Java Application from the tree view to the left. The tab to the right of the configurations allows you to control which perspective should appear when a configuration is run (see Figure 2.29). All configuration types can have their default perspectives set to activate in either debug or non-debug mode. Any available perspective can be chosen for use in the Launcher, including custom perspectives created by you. If no perspective is chosen, the chosen launch configuration will run under the current perspective.

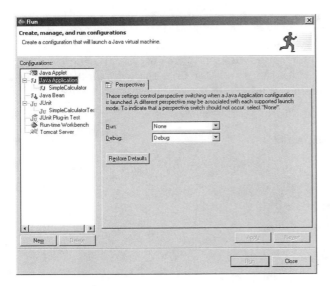

FIGURE 2.29   The Launcher's Perspectives tab with no default perspective for Run and the Debug perspective set when an application is run in debug.

Click New with Java Application selected. Because project Calculator is our current project, the wizard entered the project name into the Project field. In the Name field at the top of the Run dialog, change the name of the configuration from New_configuration to SimpleCalculator with Formatter. In the Main Class field, enter calculator.SimpleCalculator or click Search and select SimpleCalculator from the list of available classes in the Choose Main Type dialog (the wizard will fill in the full class name). Click the Arguments tab, only this time enter 100 1 as the program arguments. In the VM Arguments text field, enter -Dformat=000000. Click Apply and Close and change your main() code once again. This time it will use the incoming property to format the result of the calculation with leading zeroes for anything less than six digits:

```java
public static void main(String[] args) {
    if (args == null || args.length < 2) {
        System.out.println(USAGE);
    } else {
        Calculator calculator = new SimpleCalculator();
        int val1 = Integer.parseInt(args[0]);
        int val2 = Integer.parseInt(args[1]);
        int result = calculator.add(val1, val2);

        String format = System.getProperty("format");
        String strResult = null;
        if (format != null) {
            DecimalFormat formatter = new DecimalFormat(format);
            strResult = formatter.format(result);
        } else {
            strResult = Integer.toString(result);
        }
        System.out.println("Result: " + strResult);
    }
}
```

If you run or encounter any compile errors, press Ctrl+Shift+O to have the editor insert any missing imports. When you have updated the code and saved the file, select Run, Run As, Java Application. The Launch Configuration Selection dialog will appear asking you to choose a launch configuration; choose SimpleCalculator with Formatter. Now your result should print a six-digit number with leading zeroes because you entered into the launch configuration a property named format with a value of 000000. This property was used in the code to create a DecimalFormat object, which formatted the calculated result using the format string. Feel free to change the format string and see how the number format changes as you run the SimpleCalculator over and over again (if you are not familiar with java.text.DecimalFormat, you can read more about it in the Javadocs):

Result: 000101

Let's get a better look at some of the tabs available to you from the Launcher. Reopen the Launcher Run dialog by selecting Run, Run. Select the Simple Calculator with Formatter configuration. The Main tab is where you enter the project that contains the class with main(). You have the choice of stopping in the first line of main() by checking Stop in Main and running the configuration in debug mode (selecting Run, Debug As, Java Application). We will discuss debugging in Chapter 3, "Debugging." The application will start and stop at the first executable line within main(), even if a breakpoint is not set.

The remaining check box, Include External Jars When Searching for a Main Class, has the Launcher load all the class names it can find using the JAR files defined in the current project's classpath.

The Arguments tab allows you to enter arguments to be passed to main() in an identical fashion as they would be passed if the program were run from the command line. If you uncheck Use Default Working Directory, you have a choice to make: Make the working directory (meaning the directory in which the application thinks it is running) either the project directory or an arbitrary local directory. This is similar to opening a command prompt, changing directories, and running the program in a directory other than the directory where the code is located. Either choice changes the relative path of any file lookups being done by the application.

The two remaining tabs to be discussed, JRE and Classpath, are not used that often, but they afford you the opportunity to change which Java runtime environment you want used and to change the classpath environment used by the application, respectively.

Launching an Applet

Launching an applet is not much different from launching an application. You can define an applet within Eclipse by creating a class and changing its superclass from java.lang.Object to java.applet.Applet (there is no wizard support for the creation of an applet class). Assign the applet to package example. The typical sample applet overrides paint() and uses the incoming Graphics object to draw the string "Hello, world!" Use Ctrl+spacebar to fill in any missing imports:

```
public class ExampleApplet extends Applet {

    /* (non-Javadoc)
     * @see java.awt.Component#paint(java.awt.Graphics)
     */
    public void paint(Graphics graphics) {
        graphics.drawString("Hello, world!", 50, 50);
    }

}
```

To force the JDT to create a default launcher for the applet, from the main menu click Run, Run As, Java Applet. After a few seconds, the Appletviewer will open displaying "Hello, world!"

Exit the Appletviewer by clicking Applet, Quit.

Click Run, Run and select Java Applet from the Launcher dialog list to the left. Click New and change the Name setting to ExampleApplet with Parameters. The project should be set to Calculator (or whatever name you have been giving the current examples) and the Applet class should be set to example.ExampleApplet. If any of this information is different, change your information to match what you see here.

One of the only ways to pass variable information to an applet is through the use of parameters. Normally, the parameters would be passed to the applet through the HTML page where the applet is defined. You can mimic that behavior by filling in parameters in the Parameters tab. Click the Parameters tab and click Add. The Add Parameter Variable dialog will open asking for a name/value pair. For this example, enter "book" and "Eclipse" for Name and Value. Before you can check whether the parameters were accepted, you need to change the code in ExampleApplet. Click Apply and then click Close. Change paint() as shown:

```
public void paint(Graphics graphics) {
    String book = getParameter("book");
    graphics.drawString("Hello, " + book + "!", 50, 50);
}
```

Select Run, Run As, Java Applet. When the Select an Applet Configuration dialog opens, select ExampleApplet with Parameters and click OK. The Appletviewer should open and display the string "Hello, Eclipse!"

A JUnit test will not require a custom launch configuration, but you do have the option to customize it. Here are some examples:

- **Test tab**—You could execute a collection of JUnit tests from one configuration instead of manually selecting the tests from the Package Explorer (select Run All Tests in the Selected Project, Package, or Source Folder). In addition, to cut down on the overhead of startup, you could have the JUnit GUI always running when you are debugging (check Keep JUnit Running After a Test Run When Debugging).

- **Arguments tab, VM Arguments**—You could have your JUnit test load up a property file containing information specific to a particular test or any other arbitrary information your tests, or the code you are testing, need to run.

Launching a plug-in is a little bit different from running an application, applet, or JUnit test. Whereas the aforementioned program types run within the current instance of the IDE, a plug-in needs to run in its own instance of Eclipse. The reason for this is simple: The life cycle of a plug-in is controlled by the IDE in much the same way that a servlet has its life cycle controlled by the servlet engine. However, you do not want to run your still-in-development plug-in within the actual IDE because the plug-in may cause an IDE error that causes the IDE to stop functioning. In order to avoid this circumstance, Eclipse starts another instance of the IDE, called the Runtime Workbench, that loads your plug-in as if it were complete so that you can run it independent of the development environment.

Launching a JUnit plug-in test is only marginally more difficult than launching/running a plug-in from within Eclipse. When you launch a JUnit test specific to a plug-in, you not only get the Runtime Workbench, but integration with JUnit as well.

In Brief

We covered a significant number of features found in the Java Development Tooling environ-ment. Any self-respecting IDE has to be able to support at least the features discussed in this chapter.

- Project-based development allows you to organize your resources in a controlled fashion, where your view of the information is both object oriented and task oriented.

- The New dialog is the centerpiece of resource creation. Through it you create Java projects, interfaces, classes, and JUnit tests. Depending on the resource to be created, having a resource selected before opening the wizard can take care of prefilling neces-sary information.

- The Preferences dialog is where you can customize the Java editor to do things such as display line numbers, write templates, and customize the formatting of code.

- A scrapbook page is a convenient place to work on code in isolation without the explicit overhead of creating a Java class.

- Eclipse search capabilities range from a standard string search across files to a Java search, which understands how to search for a string by type, method, package, constructor, and field. The creation of a working set also gives you the opportunity to create a custom set of searchable resources.

- The Launcher is used to create custom configurations to allow you to set up different environments in which your code can run. These configurations work in debug and non-debug mode. You can create launch configurations for applications, applets, plug-ins, and JUnit tests.

Debugging

3

"*Debugging is twice as hard as writing the code in the first place. Therefore, if you write the code as cleverly as possible, you are, by definition, not smart enough to debug it.*"

—Brian W. Kernighan

Debugging in the Java Development Tooling Environment

No matter how hard you try to make your code bullet-proof, at some point you will find yourself confronted with a bug that needs to be examined under the micro-scope. The Eclipse debug environment gives you the tools you need to examine and exterminate bugs as they surface.

Of course, out of the box, Eclipse only gives you enough debugging capabilities as plain-old Java objects can handle. If you want to debug servlets, you can always use a remote agent (which will be discussed at this end of this chapter), but you are much better off getting a plug-in such as Sysdeo or MyEclipse that gives you native app server support. Also, when you look at the remote agent, it will be in the context of a standalone program, not in terms of connecting to an app server.

On the subject of debugging, much can be said, but the less the better. The methodology of Test-Driven Development is mentioned in various places in this book without going into it in any real depth (you can always read Chapter 6, "High-grade Testing Using JUnit"), but take the opening quote to heart: If you find yourself spending a great deal of time in front of your debugger, perhaps you need to write more, or better, tests. Of course, when you reach the point where all else fails, there is always the all-purpose `println()`.

Debugging in Eclipse happens within the Debug perspective. You can open the Debug perspective in all the usual ways:

- From the main menu, select Window, Open Perspective, Debug.

- From the main menu, select Window, Open Perspective, Other and then select Debug from the Select Perspective dialog.

- From the main menu, select Run, Debug As, and then select the program type to run after opening the Debug perspective.

- From the main menu, select Run, Debug to open the Launcher dialog. Once you have created or modified a run configuration, click Debug to run your program after opening the Debug perspective.

- From the toolbar, click the bug icon and Eclipse will start the last program you were debugging after opening the Debug perspective.

- From the toolbar, click the arrow to the right of the bug icon and select the program to be run after opening the Debug perspective.

As usual, the most important thing to recognize is which of the many ways available to accomplish a task is the most comfortable for you.

Let's look at the Debug perspective and then look at debugging standalone Java code, plug-ins, and server-side Java code as well as remote debugging.

The Debug Perspective

The default Debug perspective is made up of the following views:

- **Debug**—This view is where you track and control the execution of your code (see Figure 3.1). You can have more than one program running at a time, and you can open or close the list of associated threads by double-clicking the selected program. Standard debugging functionality is also available through the buttons on the Debug view toolbar—you can pause, resume, kill, and disconnect processes as well as clear the view of any terminated processes. On any given line of code, you can also go into any given method or constructor (Step Into), execute the current line (Step Over), or leave the current execution point and return to the caller (Step Return). In addition, the Step With Filters/Step Debug feature allows you to step into a method, but skip any code that meets the filter criteria (for example, anything defined within a particular package could be skipped).

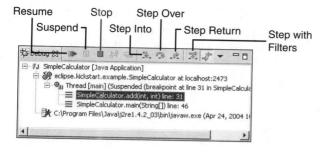

Resume   Stop   Step Over
Suspend   Step Into   Step Return   Step with Filters

FIGURE 3.1   The Debug view displaying the running threads, the stack leading to the program's current location, and the current suspended thread.

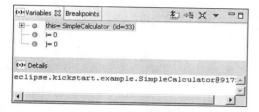

FIGURE 3.2   The Variables view displaying the running threads, the stack leading to the program's current location, and the current suspended thread.

- **Variables**—The Variables view displays the object and local variables available at the current position in the execution stack (see Figure 3.2). The top half of the view lists the variables, whereas the lower half displays the value of the selected variable. The menu bar for this view has five selections:

  - Display the type names next to the variable names

  - Display the logical structure

- Select from one of the logical structures

- Collapse an expanded node

- A menu that allows you to change the orientation of the variable list to the Details window, turn Word Wrap on and off, display or hide constants, static variables, full package names, null array entries, and select how to display primitive data values (hex, ASCII, or unsigned)

- **Breakpoints**—The Breakpoints view allows you to enable, disable, or remove listed breakpoints (one at a time or all at once). If you double-click a breakpoint, the file in which it is located will open to the location of the breakpoint. You can also set values such as the breakpoint hit count and display the breakpoint's properties by right-clicking the selected breakpoint.

- **Expressions**—The Expressions view is similar to the Variables view except that you can arbitrarily add a variable or an expression for the debugger to display. The menu items available are the same as for the Variables view. This view is most valuable in displaying a variable that is changed by different levels of code.

- **Display**—The Display view can be thought of as an extension of the Scrapbook page, only the results are displayed in the same view and are resolved within the context of the current stack frame. You can either cut and paste code from the current editor and execute, display, or inspect it (where inspecting the code opens the Expressions view) or you can type in code and then select and execute it.

The Variables, Breakpoints, and Expressions views are stacked in the top-right corner of the Debug perspective by default, but the Expressions view does not appear unless you select Window, Show View from the main menu. The Display view also does not appear unless you select it but rather opens in the lower part of the perspective. You are free to move or resize these views in any way you like. Three of the remaining views you have already seen and used (Outline, Console, and Tasks), leaving only the Progress view:

- **Progress**—This view displays JVM activity while the process is running. Every line of code causes some activity in Eclipse as well as within itself.

The Debug perspective also contains an area reserved for editors. When you select an entry in the stack frame, the editor will jump to the location specified at the breakpoint in the correct level of the stack, if the code is available.

Using Debug Views Outside of the Debug Perspective

Eclipse makes no distinction between a view and the perspective in which it is displayed. Views are views are views: You can open other views in the Debug perspective (for example, the Package Explorer view), and you can open debug views (for example, the Variables view) in other perspectives. However, where other views could be helpful to have in Debug, the reverse is generally not true: Debug views are not of much value outside of the Debug perspective. Displaying the Debug view's current stack trace in the Java perspective or Registers in the Resource view does not help you to accomplish the task of debugging in an easier way.

SHOP TALK

Debugging as a Complement to Testing

To debug, or not to debug; that is the question. Bug-hunting can be a very satisfying part of the development process because it allows you to focus on a very specific problem-solving exercise, but it can also sometimes cause you to fail to see the forest for the trees. At this stage in the evolution of various development processes, it is easy to forget that without a good test suite in place, you will spend more and more of your time tracking down bugs than writing code. Try to think of debugging as a development tool to keep your tests working and not as a tool to keep your code working. Once you bypass the testing step, no amount of debugging is going to save you. Always have a test written to prove that a feature works as advertised, and use the debugger to help you figure out why a straightforward-looking piece of code is failing.

Without doing anything fancy, let's walk through debugging `SimpleCalculator` using as many of the debugger features as possible. Using the debugger in most other situations is similar, with the exception of necessary setup. For example, debugging server-side code assumes the server can either run within Eclipse or is available for a remote connection.

Debugging Standalone Java Code

Start Eclipse if it is not already running. Create a new project, a Java class, and a JUnit test to go with it. If you created the Calculator project from Chapter 2, "Writing and Running a Java Application," then simply refer to that project for the next few pages. If you have not created the Calculator project, perform the following steps:

1. Press Ctrl+N and from the New dialog select Java Project and click Next. In the Project Name field enter "Calculator".

2. Leave the Location section set to its default workspace location.

3. In the Project Layout section, select Create Separate Source and Output Folders and click Configure Defaults. When the Preferences dialog opens, click the Folders button. Leave the Source Folder Name set to `src`, but change the Output Folder Name to `classes`. Click OK.

4. Click Finish.

Now you need to create two classes: the class to be run and the class that tests it. In order to create them, perform the following steps:

1. Press Ctrl+N to open the New dialog. If only two selections appear, put a check next to Show All Wizards toward the lower-left corner of the dialog. When the remaining resource wizards appear, select Java, Class and click Next.

2. On the Java Class page, enter a Package of `eclipse.kickstart.example` and Class Name of `SimpleCalculator`. Click Finish.

3. Select `SimpleCalculator` in the Package Explorer view.

4. Press Ctrl+N again to open the New dialog. Select Java, JUnit, JUnit Test Case and click Next.

5. On the JUnit Test Case page, all the test case information should be filled in. If it is not, click Cancel, select `SimpleCalculator`, and return to step 4. If the JUnit Test Case page is filled in, check `setUp()` and `tearDown()` and click Finish.

If you did not implement the `SimpleCalculator` class from Chapter 2, open the `SimpleCalculator` class and add the following code:

```
package eclipse.kickstart.example;

import java.text.DecimalFormat;
```

```
public class SimpleCalculator implements Calculator {

    private static final String USAGE =
➥"java eclipse.kickstart.example.SimpleCalculator val1 val2";

    public int add(int i, int j) {
        return I + j;
    }

}
```

If you did not implement SimpleCalculatorTest in Chapter 2, open the
SimpleCalculatorTest class and add the following methods (if you already implemented this
class then just add the code in bold):

```
package eclipse.kickstart.example;

import junit.framework.TestCase;

public class SimpleCalculatorTest extends TestCase {

    private Calculator _calculator;

    public void testAdd() {
        int expected = 0;
        int actual = _calculator.add(0, 0);
        assertEquals(expected, actual);

        expected = 1;
        actual = _calculator.add(0, 1);
        assertEquals(expected, actual);

        try {
            actual = _calculator.add(Integer.MAX_VALUE, 1);
            fail("add() passed on an overflow value.");
        } catch (RuntimeException e) {
            // If we come here then an exception was
            // thrown and the test passed.
        }
    }

    protected void setUp() throws Exception {
        _calculator = new SimpleCalculator();
    }
```

```
protected void tearDown() throws Exception {
    _calculator = null;
}
```

}

The code in the try/catch block is checking if SimpleCalculator's add() method can handle an integer value overflow. The expected behavior is for the method to throw an exception if the value is too large to contain in an int, and the caller then needs to do something about it. If the test passes, you should get a green bar in the JUnit GUI. (It will fail, of course. Make the code changes, select SimpleCalculatorTest, and then select Run, Run As, JUnit Test. Red bar!)

Let's set a simple breakpoint in SimpleCalculator's add() method at the line that reads return i + j. Double-click in the editor margin to the far left, just past the line numbers. A blue dot appears. Press F11 or select from the main menu Run, Debug As, JUnit Test. The debugger stops the code in add() and displays the various stack frames in the Debug view. Select the stack frame for SimpleCalculator.testAdd() (see Figure 3.3). The selected code is for the first of the three tests run in testAdd(). Because you want the debugger to stop on the third test, you have two choices on how to proceed: You can either set the breakpoint in the testAdd() method of SimpleCalculatorTest or you can modify the breakpoint to become activated based on a condition. For the purposes of this example, you are going to do the latter.

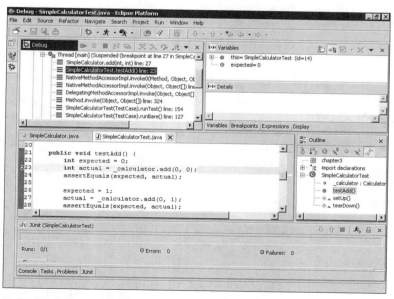

FIGURE 3.3 The Debug perspective with the stack frame for SimpleCalculatorTest selected.

FIGURE 3.4 The Breakpoints view display-ing the single available breakpoint.

Go to the Breakpoints view in the upper-right corner (see Figure 3.4). If it is not visible, click the Breakpoints tab. Double-click the breakpoint in the Breakpoints view to bring the editor forward with the breakpoint line selected. Because you are debugging the code and you are at the particular line, you will also see an arrow pointing toward the line in question. Right-click where the blue dot is to open a pop-up menu and then select the Breakpoint Properties menu item. This menu item will open a Properties dialog (see Figure 3.5) for this breakpoint, allowing you to do the following:

- Disable the breakpoint.

- Set the breakpoint to be called only after it has been accessed a certain number of times.

- Set the breakpoint to halt execution when a condition has been met.

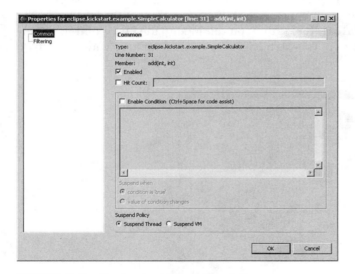

FIGURE 3.5 The Breakpoint Properties dialog.

Let's try all three. Uncheck Enabled and click OK. To resume execution, go to the Debug view and click the right-pointing triangle or just press F8. The breakpoint, now disabled, was ignored, and the test completed with the red bar.

Reenable the breakpoint by right-clicking the breakpoint and, when the Properties dialog opens, checking Enabled. Now check Hit Count and enter 3 into its input field. Click OK. Press F11 to restart the debug session.

Now, when the breakpoint is hit in the add() method, it will only stop the third time the breakpoint is accessed. To prove it, select the stack frame just below the breakpoint frame (the one for SimpleCalculatorTest.testAdd()). Instead of stopping at the first call to add() in testAdd(), it has stopped at the third call. This is useful when you have a bug that only surfaces when a piece of code executes a certain number of times. Press F8 to resume and complete the test run (still a red bar!).

What about those situations where you need to stop only after a particular condition is met? For example, when the value of a variable enters a certain range, you would like the breakpoint to activate. Once again, right-click the breakpoint and open the Breakpoint Properties dialog. Uncheck Hit Count and check Enable Condition. In the text area, enter i == Integer.MAX_VALUE. Code Assist is active in this text area, so feel free to use it in completing Integer and MAX_VALUE. Click OK and press F11 to restart the debugging session. Click the Variables tab to bring the Variables view forward. The variable i is set to 2147483647, which, not coincidentally, equals Integer.MAX_VALUE. Just to double-check, click the stack frame for SimpleCalculatorTest.testAdd() again. The breakpoint stopped at the third test once again. Press F8 to complete the test run.

In case you are tired of seeing the red bar, add the following code to SimpleCalculator's add() method:

```
public int add(int i, int j) {
    int result = 0;

    long op1 = i;
    long op2 = j;
    long longResult = op1 + op2;
    if (longResult > Integer.MAX_VALUE) {
        throw new RuntimeException(
                "The addition of the values would result in an overflow.");
    } else {
        result = (int) longResult;
    }
    return result;
}
```

Let's look at the Expressions view before we move away from the SimpleCalculator example. Set a breakpoint at the first line of the add() code and another at the if statement. Press F11 to restart the debug session. When the breakpoint stops at the top of add(), select the variable longResult, right-click to open the pop-up menu, and select Watch. Because longResult is a local variable, the debugger complains that it cannot evaluate the expression. Press F8 to resume execution to the next breakpoint. Now that longResult is declared, the Expressions view shows the variable set to 0 (which is correct because the first JUnit test checked that 0 + 0 equals 0). Press F8 again, and the Expressions view once again complains that longResult has encountered evaluation errors. Press F8 again, and now longResult equals 1.

Continue pressing F8 until the program completes. If you want to clear the Debug view of all the terminated processes you created, click the fifth icon from the left in the menu bar of the Debug view (the one that looks like a stack of rectangles). To remove the breakpoints, click the Breakpoints tab, right-click in the Breakpoints view, and select Remove All from the pop-up menu.

Close all the editors.

Debugging Server-Side Java

Server-side debugging of Java code is not supported in Eclipse, but it can be added through additional plug-ins. The section titled "Debugging Servlets, JSPs, and EJBs" of Chapter 9, "J2EE and the MyEclipse Plug-In," covers J2EE development using the MyEclipse plug-in, including the installation of the plug-in, how to set up the configuration of a server, implementing a servlet and JSP, and debugging server-side components within Eclipse.

Once the plug-in J2EE support is installed and the server configuration is entered, debugging proceeds as before. Set breakpoints, examine variables, edit files, and observe the various views in the same way you would for a standalone.

Remote Debugging

The debugging of an external process from within Eclipse is supported through remote debugging. The process can be running on the same machine as the debugger or a separate machine on the network. Unfortunately, the VMs of various vendors do not all turn on their debug-listening capabilities in the same way. The following example uses the standard Java VM and its documented command-line options.

The first step is to ensure that the compiler has debugging turned on. Open the Eclipse Preferences dialog and go to the Java compiler page (Window, Preferences, Java, Compiler). Click the Compliance and Classfiles tab and look at the settings for Classfile Generation. For this example, make sure all the boxes are checked, although in general, Preserve unused local variables can be unchecked (see Figure 3.6). Clicking OK will force a rebuild of the current projects.

In the Calculator project, create a new class named `CalculatorInput`. This class will read a string of digits from the command line, add them up, and print the result of the addition. All the generated comments have been removed:

```
public class CalculatorInput {

    private BufferedReader _in;
    private SimpleCalculator _calculator;
    public CalculatorInput() {
```

```java
        InputStreamReader reader = new InputStreamReader(System.in);
        _in = new BufferedReader(reader);

        _calculator = new SimpleCalculator();
    }
    public static void main(String[] args) {
        CalculatorInput app = new CalculatorInput();
        try {
            app.start();
        } catch (IOException e) {
            System.out.println("Exception found: " + e.getMessage());
        }
    }

    public void start() throws IOException {
        String calcStr = null;

        System.out.println(
                "Enter a space-separated list of numbers to add (q to exit):");
        calcStr = _in.readLine();
        int [] value = null;
        int result;
        while(calcStr.equals("q") == false) {
            result = 0;
            value = parseValues(calcStr);
            for (int i = 0; i < value.length; i++) {
                result = _calculator.add(value[i], result);
            }

            System.out.println("Result: " + result);
            calcStr = _in.readLine();
        }
    }

    private int[] parseValues(String calcStr) {
        int [] result = null;

        Vector v = new  Vector();
        StringTokenizer tokenizer = new StringTokenizer(calcStr);
        while (tokenizer.hasMoreTokens()) {
            String strVal = (String) tokenizer.nextToken();
            v.add(strVal);
        }

        result = new int[v.size()];
```

```
        for (int i = 0; i < result.length; i++) {
            result[i] = Integer.parseInt((String) v.get(i));
        }
        return result;
    }
}
```

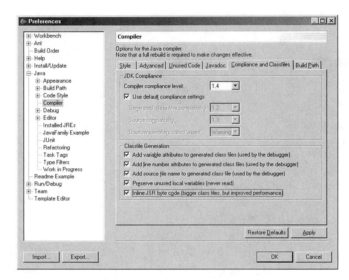

FIGURE 3.6   The Preferences dialog with all classfile generation options checked.

Do not worry about the missing package imports. When you have typed the preceding code into Eclipse, you can press Ctrl+Shift+O and all the missing imports will be added to the file. Save CalculatorInput.

Export the Calculator project by right-clicking the project name and selecting Export from the pop-up menu. When the Export dialog opens, select JAR file as the export destination. Click Next. In the list to the right of the project, uncheck .classpath, .project, and calculator.jpage. Exporting them will not cause any damage, but they are not needed. In the Select Export Destination field, enter c:\calc.jar or any safe location where you can find the file later, but still name the JAR file calc.jar. Click Next. The JAR Packaging Options page can be left alone, so click Next. In the JAR Manifest Specification page, click the Browse button, located toward the bottom of the page, and select CalculatorInput from the Select Main Class dialog. Click OK. The new class, eclipse.kickstart.example. CalculatorInput, is now assumed to be the class to be run when you run the JAR file from the command line. Click Finish to complete the export process.

Open a command-line window and change directory to wherever it is you saved calc.jar. If you are running on Windows, the easiest location to run this from is the C drive, which is why you entered c:\calc.jar as the target export directory. Make sure you can run Java from the command line. If not, update your path variable to include Java's bin directory so that you can run CalculatorInput from the command line.

Enter the following on the command line:

```
C:\> java -Xdebug -Xrunjdwp:transport=dt_socket,address=8000,suspend=n,server=y
➥ -jar calc.jar
```

All this must be on one line. Press Enter, and the program prompts you to enter a string of space-separated numbers, or you can enter the letter *q* to exit. If the program does not prompt you, check that you have entered everything as listed here.

The JVM -X Options

If you are using the standard Javasoft-supplied JVM, here is a caveat on the preceding command-line listing: The -X command-line option for the JVM defines options that may go away someday. The two options have been around for a few years, but there are no guarantees they will stay that way. Always refer to your vendor documentation to discover what options are available to turn on remote debugging.

The command-line options are as follows:

- -Xdebug—Notifies the VM that an external process may connect to it.

- -Xrunjdwp:—Contains the list of comma-separated configurations needed by the VM to allow an external process to connect to it:

    - transport=dt_socket—The VM can expect the external process to connect via a socket.

    - address=8000—The external process will connect using this port.

    - suspend=n—The VM should not suspend the program while it waits for the external program to attach.

    - server=y—The VM should behave like a server.

Enter the string 0 1 and press Enter. The program will display Result: 1. Let's attach the Eclipse debugger to this process.

To attach the Eclipse debugger to an external Java program, it has to be told which machine the external program is running on and what port it can use to communicate with it. This information is entered through the Launcher dialog. Select from the main menu Run, Debug to open the Launcher dialog specific to debugging. Select Remote Java Application as the configuration type and click New. This configuration information will be used by the debugger to connect to the external program. Enter the following configuration information:

- Name: Remote Calculator

- Project: Calculator

- Connection Type: Standard (Socket Attach)

- Connection Properties: Host: localhost

- Connection Properties: Port: 8000

Click Debug to start up the debugger and have it attach to `CalculatorInput`. The Debug perspective will open and the Debug view will display the Calculator as running in a Java HotSpot Client VM. Right-click the third line of the stack frame (`Thread [main](Running)`) and select Suspend from the pop-up menu. The external VM will suspend the named thread "main" and the debugger displays what the current stack looks like (see Figure 3.7). The second-to-last line of the stack is the call from `CalculatorInput.start()`. Select this line and the `CalculatorInput` file will open in the editor at the proper location.

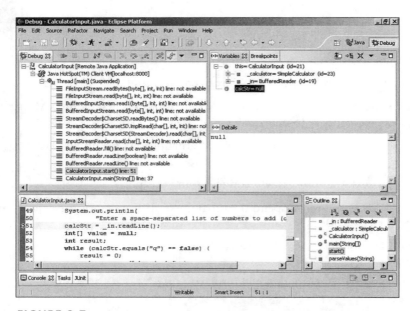

FIGURE 3.7   The debugger with the Debug view showing the stack trace for the remote `CalculatorInput` program. The editor is open to the line at which the process is suspended.

The Variables view displays the `this` and `calcStr` references as set in the external process. Set a breakpoint at the first line inside the `while` loop and press F8 to resume the thread. Bring the command-line window forward, enter the string "2 2" and press Enter. The debugger will suspend execution of `CalculatorInput` and display the line within the code where the breakpoint was hit. The Variables view displays three variables: `this`, `calcStr`, and `value`, which was created after the call to `in.readLine()`.

From within the Variables view, double-click `calcStr` and change its value from "2 2" to "5 5". When the Set Variable Value dialog opens, do not enter quotes around the values. Click OK and then press F8 to resume execution. The result of the addition of "2 2" is now 10. From the command line window, type **q** to end the `CalculatorInput` session.

Once the debugger has connected to the external process, you can use many of the standard features of the debugger, but remember that you cannot do things like hot-swap code. If you change the code in the debugger while you are debugging, the debugger will flag the code as out of sync with the running code and will not allow you to use the file for the debugging session.

In Brief

The Eclipse debugger can examine Java code locally or remotely. In Chapter 13, "The Eclipse Plug-in Architecture," you will find information about debugging plug-ins. Here are the salient points about out-of-the-box Eclipse debugging:

- The Debug perspective presents the basic grouping of views to help you debug your code. You can use a number of additional views by selecting Window, Show View, Other and looking in the Debug category.

- The debugging of standalone Java code is quite straightforward and complements JUnit testing. Standard features such as Step Into, Step Over, and Resume are all supported. Use Step Filter tells the debugger what code it can safely skip when it is stepping into code during a debug session.

- Remote debugging is activated by running the process to be debugged using command-line options that make the JVM listen on a socket for external commands. Once the Eclipse debugger is connected to the external process, it becomes just another debug target with most of the available features of the debugger.

Refactoring

4

Overview

When an author writes a book, it is a safe bet that the first unedited version will have some mistakes. No matter how closely an author checks over his work, an editing phase is still required. When a developer implements code meant to represent a business process or an algorithm, it is not until the work is done that the developer realizes how little was known at the time and how much still needs to be done. With any luck and a few tests, a developer can look over the code and decide what to change to make the code more maintainable or more object-oriented or less obscure. If the developers of the code do not take the time to improve their code, over time, as more and more code is written, the system represented by the code will become harder to change, harder to contain, and harder to extend. The code needs to be edited.

Refactoring is the conscious editing of code to minimize the duplication of logic and maximize the ability of the code to remain flexible in the face of change. The external behavior of the code does not change, but the code to implement that behavior changes in a way that could easily introduce bugs. Without tests to show that the code's behavior has not changed, it is a bad idea to introduce refactoring into your development methodology. The one thing you must be able to prove after a refactoring session is that the behavior has not changed.

In other words, test-driven development and refactoring are made for each other.

For those of you who have not heard of refactoring, pick up *Refactoring* by Martin Fowler, which is *the* book on a task that developers perform all the time, but do not necessarily view in the light of a formal methodology, to help them keep their code flexible and robust. *Refactoring* lists 72 different types of refactorings that can be applied to code, and it lists them under seven different categories, such as Simplifying Conditional Expressions and Dealing with Generalization. Eclipse supplies much in the way of support for the refactoring of Java code. As of the writing of this book, Eclipse supports 18 different kinds of refactorings.

There is nothing about refactoring that demands a tool like Eclipse. All the refactorings performed by Eclipse could be done by hand, either within Eclipse or outside Eclipse. Once you understand what the various refactorings are, you can easily begin modifying files by hand to achieve your goal. However, if you refactor by hand, with or without tests, you run the risk of missing some dependency and damaging the build process for one or more projects.

Let's look at the following four refactorings supported by Eclipse as well as the whys and wherefores of their use:

- Renaming resources

- Extracting an interface from a class

- Moving methods to a superclass

- Extracting a method from existing code

SHOP TALK

Refactoring and Test-Driven Development

Looking at various examples of refactoring supported by the JDT might lead you to think that you should refactor your code on a regular basis, and you would be right in many cases. There are certain places where you will find yourself using JDT-based refactoring all the time, and others where refactoring will not happen that often. The renaming of projects, packages, classes, methods, and fields happens often enough that you will become familiar with the Rename refactoring right away. However, once you've made any refactoring changes, you need to be confident that they were positive. The only way to be sure is with tests.

Whenever you decide to make a change to your code, whether it is to add functionality or to refactor it, you should always have tests in place to prove that the system behaves in expected ways. *Test-Driven Development (TDD)* is a development methodology that encourages you to grow your system through the extensive use of automated tests. For every piece of functionality you add, you should have a test that proves the functionality works. After a certain number of iterations, you refactor your code using the existing tests to check that you have not introduced any bugs into your system. Refactoring and TDD go hand-in-hand. TDD supports refactoring without making you write additional tests. Remember, refactoring does not add functionality to your code; instead, refactoring should improve your design and code over time. Your existing tests are enough to prove your refactoring did not break your code.

Renaming Resources

The renaming of resources within Eclipse can appear to be a trivial task, but allowing the Java Development Tooling plug-in to keep track of changing symbols will keep the myriad of dependencies synchronized with each other. In addition, the renaming of projects, folders, files, and classes, all of which are self-contained entities, can only be performed through refactoring. Entities within a file can be changed by hand, but you run the risk of missing a change that Eclipse can take care of. For example, you can change the name of a public class/interface within a file, but the compiler flags the new name as an error because the file must also be named after the public class (nonpublic classes can be contained in a file with an arbitrary name). Refactoring is a safe way to rename these resources.

The high-risk point in renaming is resources such as projects or packages, but within the class definition itself, it's methods and variables, including static, instance, and local items. Dependencies are not always obvious, and the renaming of a method or variable can have nonobvious side effects if a method or variable with a similar name is changed by accident. If you have a project that depends on a particular class you have implemented and you decide, for example, that the class has a misnamed method, you have two choices:

- **Rename the method by hand**—You do a search and begin changing the name of the method one file at a time. If you have other classes that have a name similar to the method you are renaming, you need to be careful not to change the wrong method, the wrong file, or both. This is not recommended, but if the change is isolated to the originating file, then this is an acceptable decision.

- **Choose Refactor, Rename**—You let Eclipse worry about finding and changing the original and all matching declarations. This may seem like overkill for a change within a single file, but it guarantees a successful and consistent rename.

Because projects, folders, and files can only be renamed within Eclipse using Refactor, Rename, the JDT deals with updating dependencies for those names in various ways based on the resource:

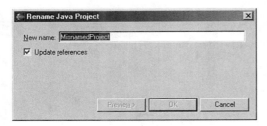

FIGURE 4.1 The Rename Java Project dialog with the Update References box checked.

- Projects are Eclipse-defined constructs. As such, Eclipse takes care of updating the references from dependent projects to the project about to be renamed if you configure the dialog to do so, as shown in Figure 4.1.

- Java packages and source files, as standalone resources, get a Rename dialog that not only changes the name of the resource, but also gives you the choice of updating references to the package/class, updating references in comments or strings to the renamed resource, and updating non-Java files if the fully qualified name is found.

■ Within a Java file, you can modify class names and method names by editing the file. As mentioned before, this is an acceptable means as long as the scope of the change is local. When you select a method name and right-click the selected name, for example, Eclipse opens a Rename dialog that will update the method and, if you decide, any references to the method. After you have dependencies to your class and its methods, using Refactor, Rename is the best way to do a method rename. Changing a method variable opens the same dialog and only affects the code within the method.

■ Instance fields within a Java class are renamed the same way as methods, but you have the choice of updating references to the field, updating comments, and updating the getter and setter methods to the field if any are available (see Figure 4.2).

■ Generic resources (folders and non-Java files) are renamed with no consideration for possible dependencies. The Rename dialog only gives you the ability to enter the new name.

FIGURE 4.2   The Rename Field dialog with the default setting checked for the update of the _calculator field.

Let's start with an example of renaming the various elements of two classes. Create a project, call it Refactoring, and create two classes: RenameExample and RenameDependent (see Listings 4.1 and 4.2). The class RenameExample defines a method used both within its own code and by RenameDependent. (Note that the autogenerated comments were removed to make the code more compact.)

LISTING 4.1   RenameExample.java

```java
package example;

public class RenameExample {
    public void renameThisMethod() {
        System.out.println("This message is from renameThisMethod().");
    }

    private void privateMethod1(){
        renameThisMethod();
    }

    private void privateMethod2(){
        renameThisMethod();
    }
}
```

LISTING 4.2 RenameDependent.java

```java
package example;

public class RenameDependent {
    public void dependentMethod() {
        RenameExample renameX = new RenameExample();

        renameX.renameThisMethod();
    }
}
```

In RenameExample, select and right-click the method name renameThisMethod() and select Refactor, Rename from the pop-up menu (or select Refactor, Rename from the main menu or press Alt+Shift+R). The Rename Method dialog will open with the name of the selected method and a check box giving you the choice of changing the current declaration and any code within

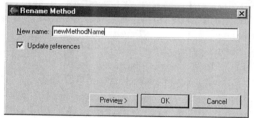

the project that refers to it or changing the name of the method without changing references to it. For this example, make sure the Update references box is checked (see Figure 4.3). Change the method name to newMethodName and click Preview. If you are already used to renaming code elements, it would now be safe for you to click OK. However, let's first look at the code preview of our method name change (see Figure 4.4).

FIGURE 4.3 The Rename Method dialog.

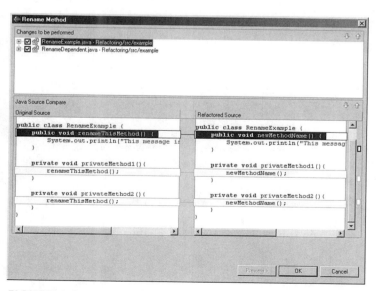

FIGURE 4.4 The Preview dialog. The top window lists the files to be changed, and the lower two windows display the changes to be made.

The top view lists the files that would be affected by the change (in this case, two files). All the checked items will have code changed in them unless you uncheck one or more of the files.

The next two windows are the standard JDT Java Source Compare windows. The window to the left shows the original code, and the window to the right shows the new code. If you scroll the window on the right, you can see that the string "This message is from renameThisMethod()." has not been changed. The string is neither a reference nor a declaration, so it is left untouched. Click OK to complete the renaming. Both files have `renameThisMethod` changed to `newMethodName`.

Changing the Signature of an Existing Method

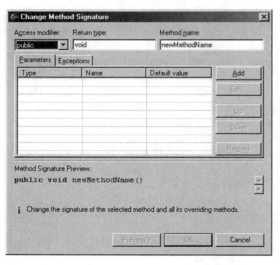

The Change Method Signature refactor lets you change the visibility, return type, parameter list, or exceptions thrown by a method. From the Outline view, or the editor, select the method to be modified—for example `newMethodName()`—and right-click (or go to the main menu) and select Refactor, Change Method Signature. The Change Method Signature dialog appears, giving you the opportunity to modify the selected method and see what the new signature will look like (see Figure 4.5). Notice that you can change the name of the method as well as its signature.

FIGURE 4.5 The Change Method Signature dialog displaying the current signature in the Method Signature Preview area just below the Parameters table.

Change the return type to String. Click Add and enter `String` as the Type setting, `name` as the Name setting, and `""` (empty double quotes) as the Default Value setting. Any place where the method is called, the default value will be used as the incoming value. This serves a double purpose: The compiles will succeed, and your code will continue to work until you go back and enter any additional logic needed to use the new method signature. Notice the new signature in the Method Signature Preview area. Click Preview to take a look at the changes that will take place.

While the JDT is making the changes, it notices that `newMethodName()` does not return a String, even though it is part of its signature. It will allow you to change the signature so that it does not return anything (`void`), or you can click Continue and change the code in the editor later. Click Continue.

Again, the Preview mode lists the files to be affected (these can be ignored when you uncheck their boxes) and the original and new contents of the files. To view any particular file, select it in the top view, and the lower view will display the original and changed versions (see Figure 4.6). Click OK to finalize the changes.

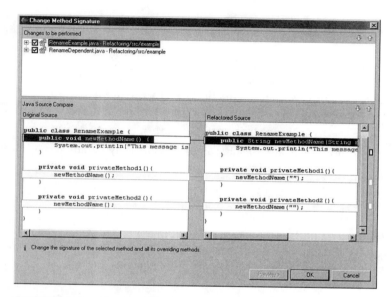

FIGURE 4.6   The Preview mode displaying the original file and the file with its new content.

Add `return null;` at the end of `newMethodName()` to remove the compile errors listed in the Problems view. Notice that all the calls to `newMethodName()` use the default value of an empty string as the incoming argument:

```
newMethodName("");
```

Extracting an Interface from a Class

The Extracting Interface refactor takes an existing class, creates an interface with a user-defined name, and copies an arbitrary set of method declarations into the interface. Let's take a `Circle` class and create a hierarchy for the next few refactorings.

In the same project (Refactoring), create a new class named `Circle` in a package named `shape`. Give the `Circle` class three instance fields—a radius, an x position, and a y position—as follows:

```
package shape;

public class Circle {
    private int _radius;
    private int _x;
    private int _y;
}
```

Right-click the editor window and select Source, Generate Getters and Setters. When the Generate Getters and Setters dialog appears, click Select All to select both `get` and `set` methods for all three fields. Also, just for this exercise, uncheck the Generate Method Comment box at the bottom of the dialog. This will give you code that's uncluttered with comment blocks.

Next, add a `draw` method that takes in a `java.awt.Graphics` object as its only parameter:

```
public void draw(Graphics g) {
    g.drawOval(getX(), getY(), getRadius(), getRadius());
}
```

If you get a complaint from the compiler about the `Graphics` class being resolved, just press Ctrl+Shift+O to automatically have the import for the `Graphics` class added to the `Circle` definition. At this point, you should have the `Circle` class with three `get` methods, three `set` methods, and one command method (`draw()`).

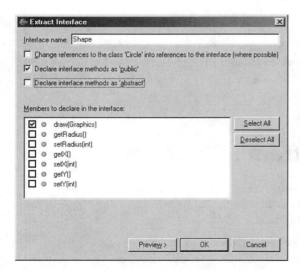

Let's extract the interface from this class. Right-click anywhere in the editor and go to Refactor, Extract Interface. When the Extract Interface dialog opens, enter `Shape` as the Interface Name setting and check `draw(Graphics)` from the list of available methods (see Figure 4.7). The getter and setter methods for `Circle` are specific to `Circle`, but `draw()` is common to all shapes. When you check the box next to `draw()`, the second and third check boxes near the top of the dialog become enabled. Uncheck Declare Interface Methods as Abstract because all methods declared in an interface are abstract by definition. When this box is unchecked, the code generator will not add the `abstract` keyword to the method declarations. Click OK.

FIGURE 4.7   The Extract Interface dialog configured to create an interface named `Shape`, with a `draw()` method that will not have an explicit `abstract` keyword in the method definition.

The `Circle` class now has the following definition:

```
public class Circle implements Shape {
```

The `shape` package now has the interface `Shape` as a new definition. The only declaration in `Shape` is `draw()`, and it also has `import java.awt.Graphics` included.

Moving Methods to the Superclass

Methods in an inheritance hierarchy can be moved up or down the tree one level at a time. To show off this functionality, you will do the following:

1. Create a new class called `ShapeImpl` that will inherit from `Shape`. `Circle` and any other shapes will inherit from it.

2. Create a class called `Square` that inherits from `ShapeImpl`.

3. Pull the X and Y accessor methods into `ShapeImpl`.

To begin, create a new class called `ShapeImpl` in the Refactoring project. Make sure that the package is `shape`, `abstract` is checked in the Modifiers section, `shape.Shape` is included in the interfaces implemented by `ShapeImpl`, and Inherited Abstract Methods is unchecked. If all this is correct, click Finish. `ShapeImpl.java` will be opened, and it will be an empty abstract class definition.

Go to the `Circle` class and change the class definition to `extends ShapeImpl` instead of `implements Shape`.

Create a new class, called `Square`, that extends `ShapeImpl`. Make sure the package is `shape` and that Inherited Abstract Methods is checked so the code generator will create an empty method for `draw()`. Click Finish if the preceding is correct. Within the editor, add the `int` instance fields `_x`, `_y`, `_side`. Once again, right-click in the editor, select Source, Generate Getters and Setters, and then generate the accessor methods for all the instance fields. Finally, remove the `TODO` comment and insert a call to `Graphics.drawRect()` in `draw()`:

```
public void draw(Graphics g) {
    g.drawRect(getX(), getY(), getSide(), getSide());
}
```

The hierarchy you have just created is made up of a parent type named `Shape`, an intermediate abstract class called `ShapeImpl`, and the two subclasses called `Circle` and `Square`. `ShapeImpl` is empty, but it's abstract because it does not define the method defined in `Shape`. `Circle` and `Square` both have positional information.

In the editor window of `Square`, right-click and select Refactor, Pull Up. (If the Refactor menu item does not display a variety of choice, the cursor is not in the class itself. Make sure you click within the class definition first and then right-click.) The Refactoring dialog opens and displays the name of the parent class where one or more methods and/or fields are going to be moved. Check `_x`, `_y`, `getX()`, `setX()`, `getY()`, and `setY()` (see Figure 4.8). Click Next.

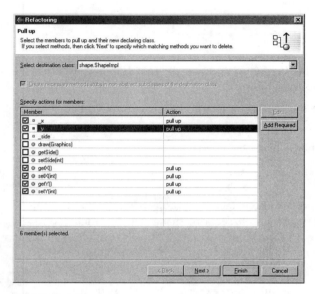

FIGURE 4.8   The Pull Up Refactoring dialog with a combination of fields and methods to be moved to the `ShapeImpl` parent class.

The next page of the dialog displays the subclasses of your hierarchy, including the `Circle` class. At this point, you can select which methods you would want removed from the various subclasses. Check the `Circle` class to include all the matching methods that should be removed because they contain the exact same logic as the methods from `Square`. Click Next.

The Preview page displays the files in alphabetical order, so the original source for `Circle` is displayed on the left and the new code on the right. The only code that will remain in `Circle` is `draw()`, `getRadius()`, and `setRadius()` (see Figure 4.9). Click Finish.

Here's what the hierarchy looks like after the preceding changes:

- The `Shape` interface did not change.

- `ShapeImpl` now has the positional information needed by all shapes.

- `Circle`, inheriting from `ShapeImpl`, contains an implementation of `draw()` and the radius property.

- `Square`, also inheriting from `ShapeImpl`, contains its own implementation of `draw()` and the `side` property.

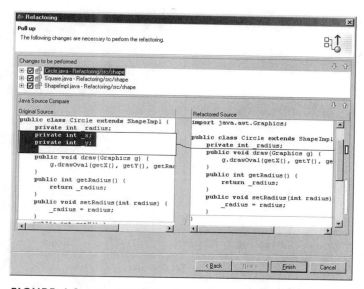

FIGURE 4.9 The Pull Up Preview page displaying the original and soon-to-be modified code for `Circle`.

You can see how using the Pull Up Refactoring dialog can save you time by taking care of the tedious details of pasting methods into a parent class and deleting them from any subclasses where the method is no longer needed.

Extracting a Method from Existing Code

This next refactoring technique involves extracting lines of code to create a new method with the intent of making your logic clearer. Because comments can get out of sync as soon as code is changed, it can be easier to name your methods in a verbose fashion to describe the goal of the algorithm than expecting comments to keep up. Let's look at a method with a substantial amount of logic and how it can be subdivided to better explain its intent.

Using the Refactoring project, create two new classes in the package `extract`. Name one class `OrderFactory` and the other `Order`. These classes are shown in Listing 4.3 and Listing 4.4, respectively. The `OrderFactory` code is incomplete, but it's sufficient to walk through the Method Extraction refactoring.

In `OrderFactory`, the `findLessThan()` method will return an array based on the number of orders found that have individual totals less than the value passed in as the method's argument. The method performs three tasks:

- Retrieves the rows from the database

- Creates and collects the `Order` objects using the returned rows

- Cleans up after itself by closing the connection to its data source

Listing 4.3 has all the gory details. Let's break the method up according to this functionality.

LISTING 4.3 OrderFactory.java

```
1. package extract;
2.
3. import java.sql.Connection;
4. import java.sql.ResultSet;
5. import java.sql.SQLException;
6. import java.sql.Statement;
7. import java.util.Vector;
8.
9. import javax.sql.DataSource;
10.
11. public class OrderFactory {
12.     // This would be retrieved from a JNDI source
13.     private DataSource _dataSource;
14.
15.     public Order[] findLessThan(int maxTotal) throws SQLException {
16.         Order[] result = null;
17.
18.         Connection con = null;
19.         Statement stmt = null;
20.         String query = "select id, customer_id, total from order";
21.         try {
22.             con = _dataSource.getConnection();
23.             stmt = con.createStatement();
24.             ResultSet rs = stmt.executeQuery(query);
25.             Vector v = new Vector();
26.             while (rs.next()) {
27.                 int total = rs.getInt("total");
28.
29.                 if (total <= maxTotal) {
30.                     int orderId = rs.getInt("id");
31.                     int customerId = rs.getInt("customer_id");
32.                     v.add(new Order(orderId, customerId, total));
33.                 }
34.             }
35.
36.             result = new Order[v.size()];
37.             v.copyInto(result);
38.
39.         } finally {
40.             if (stmt != null) {
41.                 stmt.close();
```

LISTING 4.3 Continued

```
42.                }
43.                if (con != null) {
44.                    con.close();
45.                }
46.            }
47.
48.            return result;
49.        }
50. }
```

LISTING 4.4 Order.java

```
package extract;

public class Order {

    public Order(int orderId, int customerId, int total) {
    }

}
```

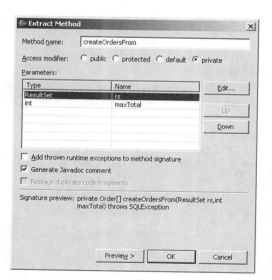

FIGURE 4.10 The Extract Method dialog displaying the method name, incoming parameters, and a preview of the method signature to be used.

You are not going to change Order in any way. OrderFactory has a few snippets of code that are prime candidates for making findLessThan() more legible.

In OrderFactory, select lines 25–37, right-click the highlighted lines of code, and select Refactor, Extract Method to open the Extract Method dialog (see Figure 4.10). Enter createOrdersFrom as the name of the new method and leave private as the access modifier. Notice the ordering of the parameters: ResultSet is the second argument, when logically it should be the first, and the maxTotal variable should be second. In the list of parameters, select the ResultSet row and click the Up button to the right of the parameter list. This makes ResultSet the first parameter. Click OK.

Let's look at the generated code:

```
/**
 * @param rs
 * @param maxTotal
 * @return
 * @throws SQLException
 */
private Order[] createOrdersFrom(ResultSet rs, int maxTotal) throws SQLException {
    Order[] result;
    Vector v = new Vector();
    while (rs.next()) {
        int total = rs.getInt("total");

        if (total <= maxTotal) {
            int orderId = rs.getInt("id");
            int customerId = rs.getInt("customer_id");
            v.add(new Order(orderId, customerId, total));
        }
    }

    result = new Order[v.size()];
    v.copyInto(result);
    return result;
}
```

Because Generate Javadoc Comment was checked in the Extract Method dialog, a Javadoc header was generated for this new method. There are two @params with names that match the names of the variables we declared in the original code (rs and maxTotal). The @return method is empty because it is still up to you to document the return value, and the @throws method declares the method as throwing a SQLException. Why a SQLException? The signature for findLessThan() is already declared as throwing a SQLException, and the selected code did not include a try/catch block. Connection, Statement, and ResultSet all have the potential of throwing a SQLException, but the refactoring engine will not surround the code with a try/catch block because it cannot determine what your intentions are; hence, it added the exception to the method signature. The variable you were using to return the array of Order objects was called result, so the refactoring engine uses the same name for its return variable.

Meanwhile, back at the original location of the code, you now have a single line of code that states its purpose and can be reused in OrderFactory.

Another method that could be extracted is the closing of the Statement and Connection objects used in findLessThan(). Select all the code within the finally block (lines 40–45 from the original line count, or lines 28–32 of the new count), right-click the highlighted lines of code, and select Refactor, Extract Method to open the Extract Method dialog again. Enter closeDataSource as the name of the new method and leave private as the access modifier. Notice the ordering of the parameters this time: Connection is first and Statement is second, which is an acceptable order. Click OK. The new method is inserted above createOrdersFrom() and below findLessThan().

The new version of findLessThan() is short and to the point: Execute some SQL, create an array of Order objects based on the returned ResultSet, and close the data source. Here's the code:

```java
public Order[] findLessThan(int maxTotal) throws SQLException {
    Order[] result = null;

    Connection con = null;
    Statement stmt = null;
    String query = "select id, customer_id, total from order";
    try {
        con = _dataSource.getConnection();
        stmt = con.createStatement();
        ResultSet rs = stmt.executeQuery(query);
        result = createOrdersFrom(rs, maxTotal);

    } finally {
        closeDataSource(con, stmt);
    }

    return result;
}
```

In Brief

The refactoring support within Eclipse makes refactoring your code convenient and predictable. The engine understands the context of the change you are trying to make and assists you making the change consistent across files. Here are some other points to keep in mind:

- Eclipse provides extensive dependency checking to help you avoid naming conflicts when you rename resources.

- You can extract an interface from an existing class and make it available for use by subclasses. You have full control as to the extracted interface's name and available API.

- You can remove duplicate methods by using the Pull Up refactoring technique. With Pull Up, you can remove duplicate methods from multiple classes and move them to their shared superclass in a reliable way.

- The Extract method refactoring only affects the file where the code to be extracted is located. You select the lines of code to be extracted, and using the Extract Method dialog you give the method a name and correct parameter information.

Writing GUIs in Eclipse

5

Installing the Visual Editor

The Visual Editor Project is divided into three zip files located under the Eclipse Tools group at http://www.eclipse.org/vep/. At the time of this writing, the Visual Editor would only work with particular versions of its support files. Here are the three files for version 1.0 M1 of the Visual Editor:

- emf-runtime-I200403250631.zip—This is the latest runtime version of the Eclipse Modeling Framework classes.

- GEF-runtime-I20040330.zip—This is the latest runtime version of the Graphical Editing Framework.

- VE-runtime-M1RC1.zip—This zip file contains the classes that constitute the Visual Editor plug-in.

- VE-examples-M1RC1.zip—Optionally, you can also download this file. It contains examples of what can be done using the Visual Editor.

Extract all the zip files into the Eclipse install directory. For example, if you installed Eclipse into c:\eclipse, extract the EMF and GEF zip files into c:\eclipse. Extract the VE-runtime zip file (and the VE-example file if you downloaded it as well) into the directory where you installed Eclipse (for example, c:\tools). All the zip files contain files that will be distributed between the features and the plugins directories. Do not extract the files into the plugins directory because Eclipse will not be able to load them.

Unless these files are extracted properly, the Visual Editor will not work at all. As a quick test, start Eclipse, press Ctrl+N, and look under the Java node in the Wizards list of the New dialog. Under the Java node, you should see the Visual class and nodes for AWT and Swing. If the only subnode listed is JUnit, the install failed.

If the install failed, only a couple things could have gone wrong. The first is that you extracted the files to the wrong location, and the second is that the Eclipse Update Manager has become confused by creating a duplicate plug-in directory target (which I have only seen in Eclipse 2.1.x).

In the first case, make sure you extracted the zip files to the base Eclipse home directory (not the `plugins` directory). If you inadvertently extracted the files into the `plugins` directory, delete the duplicate `features` and `plugins` directories under the main `plugins` directory first.

In the second case, go to the Update Manager and access the Install Configuration view (the view in the upper-left corner), open the Eclipse Platform node, and disable all but one of the duplicate plug-in directory targets. Restart Eclipse and check the New dialog for the addition of AWT and Swing under the Java node. If the Java node does not have AWT and Swing listed, return to the Update Manager, disable the currently enabled directory, and enable one of the others. Restart Eclipse and check the New dialog again. The AWT and Swing choices will appear eventually.

The Visual Editor

The Visual Editor Project (VEP) is a relative newcomer to Eclipse, having only been added as an official project on November 18, 2003. The Visual Editor (VE) is a contribution from IBM's WebSphere Application Developer and, as of the 1.0M1 release, supports the building of AWT, Swing, and SWT GUIs. The addition of a GUI builder is an important contribution to Eclipse because the first version of a GUI can be built within VE and then necessary customization can be accomplished by hand.

This chapter assumes you understand AWT and/or Swing concepts.

Overview

When you open the Visual Editor, it automatically displays the JavaBeans view, Properties view, and the Visual Editor (see Figure 5.1). The JavaBeans view displays the containment hierarchy of the current class. From this view, you can rename components, delete components (except for the root component), and add event handling. When you select a component in this view, it is also selected in the Visual Editor and the Properties View.

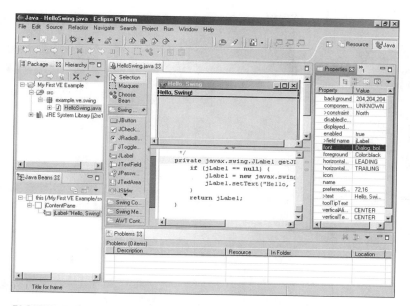

FIGURE 5.1 The Java perspective, in addition to the standard views, displaying the JavaBeans view, the Properties view, and the Visual Editor.

The Visual Editor is divided into three areas: the design window, the source window, and the JavaBeans palette (see Figure 5.2). At any time, you can hide the various windows by clicking the sash-based arrowhead that points toward the window you would like to close, thus releasing space to any of the remaining windows (the palette sash bar only has one arrow because you can either hide or reveal the palette). For example, closing the palette gives the design and source windows additional display room. The design window is a WYSIWYG editor where you can see changes made to the GUI in real time. You can drag and drop components from the palette or make changes to the source code, and the design window will reflect the changes immediately. The palette contains both AWT and Swing components with the usual caveats about mixing the two in the same container: The two toolkits can be used together, but they have a well-known list of issues that must be taken into account. Also, as of version 1.0 M1, the VE does not support SWT GUI components from the palette, but you can add SWT palette support with a minimum of effort. True SWT support will no doubt be added by the time this book is available.

The source editor is the standard Java source code editor. Changes you make to the Java code are reflected almost immediately in the visual window if they have an impact on the current visual representation.

JavaBean palette   Design window

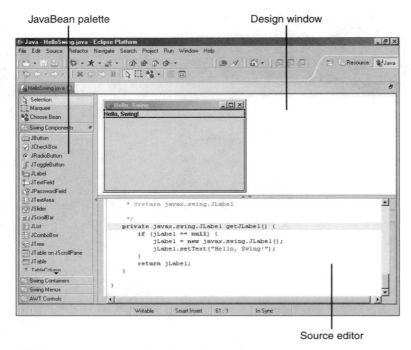

Source editor

FIGURE 5.2 The Visual Editor is divided into the design window and source window. The design window has an associated JavaBeans palette.

The Properties view is the same one discussed previously. With the addition of the Visual Editor, the Properties view also displays JavaBean property information. What you will notice is that certain properties start with a greater-than sign. Any property that starts with a greater-than sign will be set through the generation of code. For example, when you create a class that inherits from JFrame, the VE adds code to set the size and the content pane. Every time you change a property, you will see a greater-than sign appear at the start of the property name. The only way to remove the greater-than sign is to reset the default property value by right-clicking the property and selecting Restore Default Value.

Palettes

The JavaBeans palette to the left of the design window covers AWT, Swing, and any custom JavaBean components you implement, including invisible JavaBeans. The palette categorizes the various GUI components into four areas:

- **Swing Menus**—Includes menu bars, menus, pop-up menus, and various menu items, such as check box menu items and radio button menus.

- **Swing Containers**—Includes frames, panels, scrolling panes, tabbed panes, dialogs, toolbars, and applets.

- **Swing Components**—If the Swing component is not a menu or a container, then it is a standard component. Buttons, labels, text fields, sliders, progress bars, scrollbars, trees, and tables all fit into this list.

- **AWT Controls**—This is a subset of the AWT GUI components. Many items are included, but a number of other AWT components are not to be found. If you are designing an AWT client, you will find yourself using Choose Bean to include FileDialog, Menu, and Canvas components.

As you will see when you implement the examples, the behavior of the VE is what you would expect out of a GUI builder. If you are a fan of the VisualAge for Java GUI builder, you will miss the visual programming aspect, because this is purely a GUI builder, not a visual programming environment.

Using the Visual Editor

Let's build a few GUIs, adding complexity at each step.

Possible Visual Editor Lock-up Problem

If you encounter a syntax error that the VE cannot handle, the VE is liable to lock up. If Eclipse locks up, kill the process, correct the syntax error outside of Eclipse, and restart the IDE.

The smallest possible GUI would be a standalone window with a label displaying "Hello, world!" (or in this case, "Hello, Swing!"). The following are the steps involved:

1. Create a Java project.

2. Create a JFrame.

3. Add a JLabel to the JFrame.

4. Change the text of the label.

5. Run the JFrame using the JavaBean launcher or as a Java application.

Create a new Java project and name it "My First VE Example." To do this, press Ctrl+N, select Java Project, and click Next. Enter "My First VE Example" as the project name and in the project Layout section select Create Separate Source and Output folders. Click next and, if the project output directories are src and classes click Finish. If you updated your Java Preferences (Window, Preferences, Java, New Projects), there should be a src directory under the project node. If there is no src directory because you did not update the Java project preferences, just take that into account everywhere I mention the src directory; your packages will be listed under the project node instead. If you prefer, delete the project, change Preferences, Java, New Projects to use src and classes, and re-create the project.

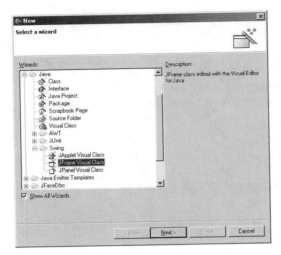

FIGURE 5.3   The New dialog with Swing and JFrame Visual Class selected.

With the src folder selected under your project (or with the project itself selected if you don't have an src directory), press Ctrl+N to open the New dialog. Open the Java node to the left and select Swing. In the list to the right, select JFrame Visual Class (see Figure 5.3) and click Next.

In the Java Class page of the New dialog, enter example.ve.swing as the package name and HelloSwing as the class name. This dialog page has a couple of notable features. The first is the collection of radio buttons located below the question, Which visual class would you like to extend? These buttons (frame, panel, applet, and other) define the kind of container from which this class will inherit. Selecting "other" enables the Superclass field, allowing you to choose an arbitrary parent class type. The other notable feature is the check box next to the radio buttons, which toggles between Swing as the underlying GUI toolkit (if checked) and AWT.

Make sure that the check box next to public static void main() is unchecked. Click Finish.

When the Visual Editor opens for the first time, it will also open the JavaBeans view and the Properties view. The JavaBeans view displays the object containment hierarchy for the current class displayed in the VE. If the hierarchy is not opened, click once on the plus sign next to the object named this. The first Swing component to be listed in the hierarchy is jContentPane. The jContentPane component is the root container for all GUI components, whether they are components or containers. Every JFrame starts life with a root container that it uses to hold all GUI components. This content pane can be changed at any time through a call to setContentPane(), and the first thing the code does is reset the content pane.

Select the topmost node in the JavaBeans view. The design window and the Properties view change to accommodate the selection. The design window has an outline around the entire frame with resizing dots in the center of each side. The Properties view displays the properties for the JFrame (such as background and foreground color, size, window title, and font). In the Properties view, click and change defaultCloseOperation to EXIT. Because this is a behavior change, you do not see any direct change in the HelloSwing GUI. However, when you run this GUI and then close it using the X button in the top-right corner (or using Alt+F4) the JVM will exit, giving you a clean application shutdown.

Click the title property and set it to "Hello Swing". Press Enter, or change the cursor's focus, and you will see the window title change immediately in the design window.

Let's add the label that will hold our string to the frame. In the palette, click once on JLabel. Move the cursor over the frame. The cursor displays a plus sign in the lower-right corner of the pointer and highlights the available layout position where the component may be placed. The content pane outlines the container's boundaries and names the position where the component is hovering (see Figure 5.4). In this case, click in the North position to drop the label in the topmost position of the panel. The JavaBeans view displays the JLabel component and its association with the jContentPane object. In addition, the VE also named the JLabel object jLabel. If you were to add other JLabel objects, they would be named jLabel1, jLabel2, and so on.

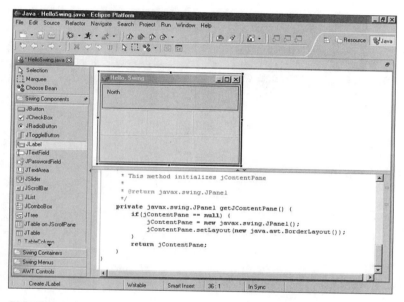

FIGURE 5.4 The design window with the JFrame content pane divided up into the various positions defined by the BorderLayout manager.

To change the label's text, you need to select the label and change its text property. You have two ways to select it: Either go to the JavaBeans view and select the jLabel node or go directly to the design window and click the component. In either case, the Properties view will display the available component properties. Click the text property, enter "Hello, Swing!", and press Enter. The label now appears with the entered string (see Figure 5.5).

You have just accomplished enough to run HelloSwing as a complete component. There are two ways you can now run it to see how well it works. You can add main(), which would allow you to run it as a Java application, or you can use the JavaBean launcher.

The JavaBean launcher is a new configuration type that is specific to the Visual Editor. This configuration type recognizes the component as a GUI component and will either place it in a dialog or, if the component is already a window, simply tell the component to make itself visible. From the main menu, select Run, Run. In the Configurations list, select Java Bean and click New. The Launcher may automatically select the VE project. If it does not, set the fields to the following:

- Name: HelloSwing

- Project: My First VE Example

- Java Bean: example.ve.swing.HelloSwing

- Swing Look and Feel: <none>

- Locale: Check "Use Default"

- Pack: Uncheck "Pack"

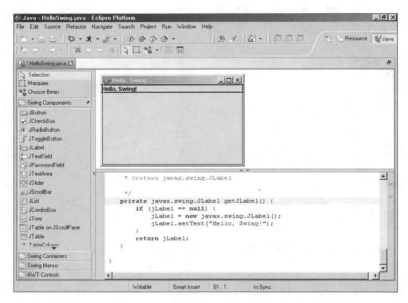

FIGURE 5.5   The Visual Editor displaying a frame with a label with the text "Hello, Swing!"

By leaving Pack unchecked, you are allowing the HelloSwing JFrame to use the default size property (defined in the Property view) to determine its default window size. Click Run. HelloSwing opens looking just like it did in the design window (see Figure 5.6). Click the X in the top-right corner to kill the frame. Select Run, Run again, select Java Bean, HelloSwing, and check then Pack. Now the HelloSwing JFrame is being instructed to only use as much space as needed to display any GUI components under its control. In effect you are causing a call to the JFrame's pack() method. Click Run again. The HelloSwing frame now opens with the minimum amount of space needed to display the label (see Figure 5.7). When you are done admiring your handiwork, click the X in the top-right corner to close the window.

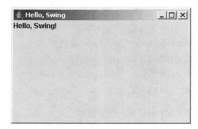

FIGURE 5.6 HelloSwing, unpacked, displaying its greeting to the world.

FIGURE 5.7 The packed version of HelloSwing.

If you were to delete the Java Bean configuration for HelloSwing and selected Run, Run As, Java Bean, the Java Bean launcher would create a default configuration that takes into account the fact that the component is a frame. HelloSwing would be started with its default as the size to which it was set in the VE, and it would appear as shown in Figure 5.6.

Turning HelloSwing into a Java application is as trivial as adding main() to the class and running it as a Java application from the Run menu:

```java
public static void main(String[] args) {
    HelloSwing gui = new HelloSwing();

    gui.pack();
    gui.setVisible(true);
}
```

SHOP TALK

Hand-coding GUIs Versus GUI Builders, or John Henry Versus the Machine

A religious argument that refuses to go away is the use of GUI builders instead of just writing the GUI by hand. I have to admit to living on both sides of the argument at various times in my development career, and I can say that this discussion has moved into the Pointless Issues category. Like so many other tools, a GUI builder is there to help you achieve a particular goal. If the idea of using a tool to make your life easier seems contrary to your nature, then what are you doing holding this book? Like all good tools, GUI builders have their limitations, but so does hand-coding. GUI builders are not the be-all-end-all, and they certainly do not purport to be full-blown development environments. I will probably mention this a few dozen times throughout the book, but what the heck: Use a tool where it is most appropriate and nowhere else. Code by hand when you must; use a tool when you can. The only advantage to using a GUI builder is to let it give you the ability to create a screen quickly. If you don't know the GUI toolkit and what the GUI components are capable of, then a GUI builder is no better than a scratch pad. Then again, even a scratch pad can be pretty useful.

Building a Database Viewer

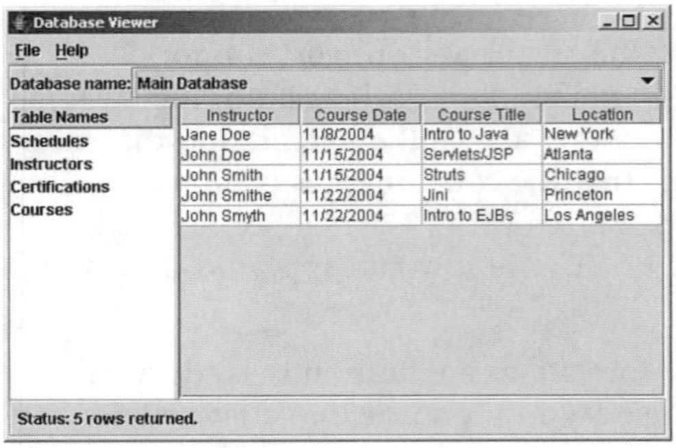

FIGURE 5.8   The complete
DatabaseViewerGUI.

The following is a working, but nonfunctional, GUI. It uses a menu to exit the program or display an about dialog, a combo box to display a list of databases, a list box to display tables for the database, and a JTable to display table data from the database (see Figure 5.8). Of course, none of the database-related pieces actually exists.

Create a Java project called "My Second VE Example". As before, there is nothing special about the project. It is not until you create a visual class that VE is brought to bear.

To keep things simple, open the new project in the Package Explorer and select src. Press Ctrl+N and select Java, Swing, JFrame Visual Class. Click Next and enter example.ve.swing as the package name and DatabaseViewerGUI as the class name. Click Finish. The JavaBeans view displays the DatabaseViewerGUI as the root node of this component, giving it the name this, and also displays as its only subnode jContentPane. All JFrames need a default container to store GUI components, and programmatically you add GUI components to the JFrame by adding to its content pane.

During this example, the Save All Modified Resources dialog may appear, asking you to save one or more files before completing a command. This is normal, and you should click OK to complete the save operation.

The Properties view will probably be empty at this stage. Select the root node from the JavaBeans view or click the title of the JFrame to alert the Properties view to display the selected component's properties. Within the Properties view, change the JFrame's title property to "Database Viewer" by clicking the property name or the empty cell to the right of the title property and entering the string when the cursor appears in the empty cell. The new title should appear as soon as you press Enter or change focus from the input cell. Next, click the defaultCloseOperation property and select EXIT from the drop-down list. If you were to launch this component as a JavaBean, you would see an empty window with the title set to "Database Viewer," and clicking the X would close the window and terminate the program.

In the palette to the left of the design window, click Swing Menus. Select JMenuBar and click the title bar of the JFrame. A very thin line will appear where the menu has been positioned. From the JavaBeans view, right-click the jMenuBar component and select Rename Field. When the Rename dialog opens, change the menu bar name from jMenuBar to mainMenuBar and click OK. The JavaBeans view will display the menu bar with its new name (see Figure 5.9).

FIGURE 5.9 The `DatabaseViewerGUI` composed of a JFrame and JMenuBar.

From the palette, go to the Swing Menus again, select JMenu, and either click the menu bar (which can be a challenge due to the menu bar being thin) or in the JavaBeans view click `mainMenuBar`. In the JavaBeans view, right-click the new menu, named `jMenu`, select Rename Field, and change its name to `fileMenu`. In the Properties view, change the `text` property to File and change `mnemonic` to F by selecting the `mnemonic` property, clicking the "..." button in the value field, and selecting F from the displayed list in the Java Property Editor. When you click OK to close the Java Property Editor dialog, the menu appears on the JFrame with the label File and the *F* in File underlined. Add another JMenu and perform the same steps. In the JavaBeans view, change the menu's name to `helpMenu`, and in the Properties view change the `text` property to Help and `mnemonic` to H (see Figure 5.10). Of course, the menu is not of much value without a selectable menu item, so let's do that next.

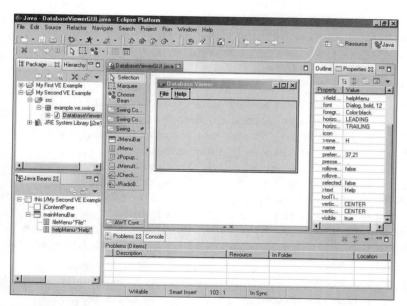

FIGURE 5.10 The JMenuBar with File and Help.

From Swing Menus, click JMenuItem and add it to `fileMenu` by clicking the word *File* or, within the JavaBeans view, by clicking the `fileMenu` object. Change the name of the

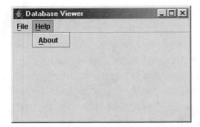

FIGURE 5.11   The `DatabaseViewerGUI` displaying one of the working menus.

`jMenuItem` to `exitMenuItem`. With `exitMenuItem` selected in the JavaBeans view, or by clicking it in the design window, go to the Properties view and change the `text` property to Exit and `mnemonic` to X. Do the same for the Help menu: Add a JMenuItem to `helpMenu`, change its name to `aboutMenuItem`, change the `text` property to About, and change `mnemonic` to A. Run the GUI as a JavaBean to check your handiwork so far (see Figure 5.11). Close the window by clicking the X icon.

The next few steps are going to add header and footer containers to the JFrame and a JScrollPane to the center (the JFrame's content pane is using a BorderLayout manager).

First the header. Click Swing Containers in the palette. Click JPanel and click somewhere in the empty area to the right of the JFrame. Do not place the JPanel in the JFrame. Because it is created with a small default size, resize `jPanel` so that you can at least click inside it. Change the `jPanel` field name to `headerPanel` from within the JavaBeans view. Go to the Properties view and change the `layout` property to BorderLayout by clicking in the cell next to the property name and selecting BorderLayout from the drop-down list. Rather than leave the panel with a plain appearance, click the `border` property. A button with "..." will appear to the far right side of the cell. Click the button to open the Java Property Editor dialog, which, in this case, allows you to choose a border type for this container. From the drop-down button, select Etched and Lowered Etched. Click OK. Now the `headerPanel` will be nicely bordered.

Let's put some GUI components in the `headerPanel`. Start by clicking Swing Components in the palette. Select JLabel and add it to the WEST area of `headerPanel`. Change the text of `jLabel` from within the Properties view to read "Database name:". Next, select JComboBox and place it in the CENTER area of `headerPanel`. Change the `jComboBox` field name to `databaseNameComboBox` (JavaBeans view). The panel might look rather odd if you did not resize it to be a long, thin rectangle, but your next move will take care of that. Select `headerPanel` in the JavaBeans view. From within the design window, drag and drop the `headerPanel` into the NORTH area of the `jContentPane` or drag and drop it within the JavaBeans view from the bottom of the tree view up into `jContentPane` (see Figure 5.12). If the `headerPanel` does not get positioned in the NORTH area of the `jContentPane`, select the `headerPanel` in the JavaBeans view, and in the Properties view change `constraint` to NORTH.

Let's assemble the footer panel. From the Swing Containers palette, click JPanel. Again, click to the right of the JFrame in the empty area. Resize the panel so you can drop components into it later. From the JavaBeans view, change the field name of `jPanel` to `statusPanel`. In the Properties view, click the plus sign next to `layout` and change the FlowLayout's alignment property to LEFT. This will force any components to be left-justified. Add a JLabel to the `statusPanel`, change the field name of the label to `statusLabel`, and change the label's text to "Status: 5 rows returned." With that done, add the `statusPanel` to the SOUTH area of the `jContentPane` by selecting it in the JavaBeans view and then dragging it in the design window and dropping it in the proper position within the JFrame (see Figure 5.13).

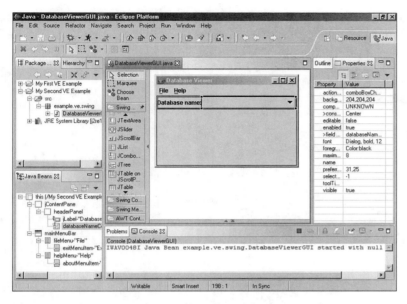

FIGURE 5.12 The `DatabaseViewerGUI` with the header panel installed.

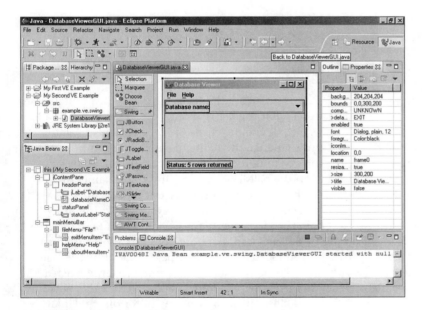

FIGURE 5.13 The `DatabaseViewerGUI` with the status panel to the south.

The center of the JFrame is going to hold a JList and a JTable. In órder to do that, and to give the GUI the option of controlling the amount of visible space between these items, you are going to drop a JSplitPane in the center of the jContentPane. From the Swing Containers palette, select JSplitPane and click in the center of the jContentPane in the design window. Go to the Properties view and set the divider size to 5 and the divider location to 125 (see Figure 5.14).

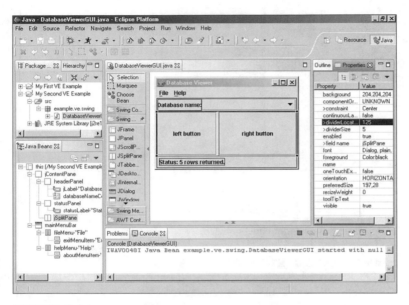

FIGURE 5.14 The DatabaseViewerGUI with the JSplitPane added to the center.

Now that you have two areas available for use, let's create the JList to hold the list of database tables. The JList should have a title explaining what the list is about, so you are going to add a JLabel to the top of the JList. Once again, click JPanel from the Swing Containers palette and drop the panel to the right of the JFrame. Change the name of the JPanel component to tableNamePanel and change its layout property to BorderLayout. Place a JLabel in the NORTH area of tableNamePanel and a JList in the CENTER (rename it to tableNameList). Select the JLabel in the JavaBeans view and change its text property to "Table Names". Because JLabel looks flat, you need to change its border to a raised beveled look. If you look at the Properties view, there appears to be no border property for JLabel, but in fact, there is; border is considered an advanced property of JLabel and therefore does not appear unless you click the Show Advanced Properties button located in the title bar of the Properties view (second button from the left). Click Advanced Properties, and the border property is listed fifth from the top. As before, click border to make the "..." button appear. Click this button and select Bevel and Raised Bevel. Click OK to close the Java Property Editor dialog. Finally, drag and drop tableNamePanel into the left side of the JSplitPane (select it in the JavaBeans view and move it within the design window), as shown in Figure 5.15.

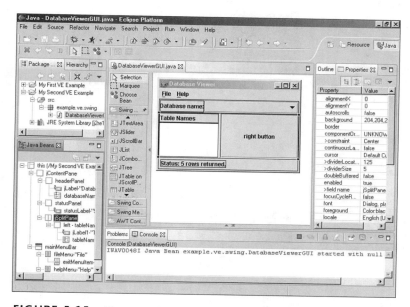

FIGURE 5.15 The `DatabaseViewerGUI` with the `tableNamePanel` in the left side of the JSplitPane.

The only piece left is the JTable. Click "JTable on JScrollPane" from the Swing Components palette. Click in the right panel of the JSplitPane. The JTable has default values in the design window. From the JavaBeans view, rename the JTable to `resultSetTable` (see Figure 5.16).

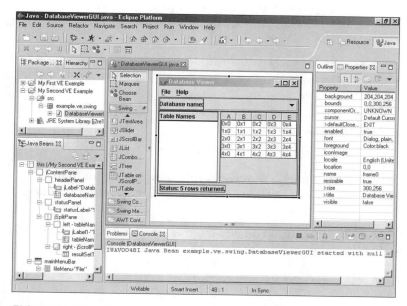

FIGURE 5.16 The `DatabaseViewerGUI` complete with its JTable.

Click the title bar of the JFrame and resize the JFrame to give the components viewing space. Run the `DatabaseViewGUI` by selecting Run, Run As, Java Bean (see Figure 5.17).

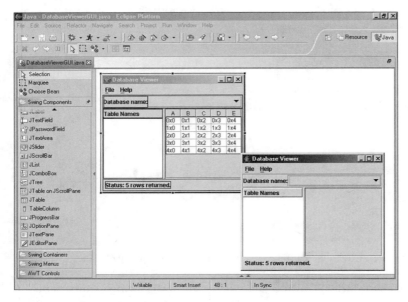

FIGURE 5.17   The running `DatabaseViewerGUI`.

The `DatabaseViewerGUI` is devoid of data because the default models do not contain anything. Also, the menus do not have behavior. Let's create some models for the visible components and some event handlers for the menus.

Let's prepare the `DatabaseViewerGUI` for the inclusion of three external model objects. Add to the end of the instance fields three model declarations—one for the JComboBox, one for the JList, and one for the JTable:

```
private ComboBoxModel _comboBoxModel = new DefaultComboBoxModel();
private ListModel _listModel = new DefaultListModel();
private TableModel _tableModel = new DefaultTableModel();
```

The default Swing model objects are used to give the code consistency. Right-click in the editor and select Source, Generate Getter and Setter. In the Generate Getter and Setter dialog, look for the three model variables and only select their get methods. Click OK.

Finally, add one line of code to each of the three GUI components' get methods, as shown in Listings 5.1 through 5.3, so that the `databaseNameCombobox`, `tableNameList`, and `resultSetTable` components set their models to the objects referenced by the instance fields. The line of code is in bold and is the line after the constructor call.

LISTING 5.1   The getDatabaseNameComboBox() Method

```java
private javax.swing.JComboBox getDatabaseNameComboBox() {
    if (databaseNameComboBox == null) {
        databaseNameComboBox = new javax.swing.JComboBox();
        databaseNameComboBox.setModel(getComboBoxModel());
    }
    return databaseNameComboBox;
}
```

LISTING 5.2   The getTableNameList() Method

```java
private javax.swing.JList getTableNameList() {
    if (tableNameList == null) {
        tableNameList = new javax.swing.JList();
        tableNameList.setSelectionMode(
            javax.swing.ListSelectionModel.SINGLE_SELECTION);
        tableNameList.setModel(getListModel());
    }
    return tableNameList;
}
```

LISTING 5.3   The getResultSetTable() Method

```java
private javax.swing.JTable getResultSetTable() {
    if (resultSetTable == null) {
        resultSetTable = new javax.swing.JTable();
        resultSetTable.setModel(getTableModel());
    }
    return resultSetTable;
}
```

If you run the DatabaseViewerGUI, the look is still the same as before. Now it is time to add model objects that will hold fake data for the components to display.

Create three new classes—DatabaseNameComboModel, DatabaseTableModel, and TableNameListModel—as shown in Listings 5.4 through 5.6. Each class represents a model for the JComboBox, JList, and JTable and will supply each GUI component with default display data. You will wrap this GUI up with a facade class that will create the GUI and give it the needed model objects.

LISTING 5.4   DatabaseNameComboModel.java

```java
package example.ve.swing;

import javax.swing.DefaultComboBoxModel;

public class DatabaseNameComboModel extends DefaultComboBoxModel {
    public DatabaseNameComboModel() {
        addElement("Main Database");
        addElement("Backup Database");
    }
}
```

LISTING 5.5   TableNameListModel.java

```java
package example.ve.swing;

import java.util.Vector;

import javax.swing.AbstractListModel;

public class TableNameListModel extends AbstractListModel {

    private Vector _tableName = new Vector();

    public TableNameListModel() {
        _tableName.add("Schedules");
        _tableName.add("Instructors");
        _tableName.add("Certifications");
        _tableName.add("Courses");
    }

    public int getSize() {
        return _tableName.size();
    }

    public Object getElementAt(int index) {
        int length = _tableName.size();
        if (index < 0 || index >= length) {
            throw new IllegalArgumentException("Bad index requested: " + index);
        }
```

LISTING 5.5   Continued

```
            return _tableName.get(index);
        }


    }
```

LISTING 5.6   DatabaseTableModel.java

```java
package example.ve.swing;

import javax.swing.table.DefaultTableModel;

public class DatabaseTableModel extends DefaultTableModel {
    public DatabaseTableModel() {

        String [] name = { "Jane Doe", "John Doe", "John Smith", "John Smithe",
                "John Smyth" };
        addColumn("Instructor", name);

        String [] courseDate = { "11/8/2004", "11/15/2004", "11/15/2004", "11/22/2004",
                "11/22/2004" };
        addColumn("Course Date", courseDate);

        String [] courseName = { "Intro to Java", "Servlets/JSP", "Struts", "Jini",
                "Intro to EJBs" };
        addColumn("Course Title", courseName);

        String [] location = { "New York", "Atlanta", "Chicago", "Princeton",
                "Los Angeles" };
        addColumn("Location", location);
    }
}
```

The three models will give the three components something to display, but how will the GUI get them? If we add a new constructor to DatabaseViewerGUI, how can we be sure the GUI will be properly constructed? As it turns out, the VE code generator uses a single method, initialize(), as the entry point into the construction of the GUI. You have two choices for how to implement the additional constructor: You can call the default constructor through the use of super(), or you can call initialize() directly. Because you need to set the models prior to the GUI components becoming visible, in this case you will do the latter:

```java
public DatabaseViewerGUI(DatabaseViewerModel model) {
    _comboBoxModel = model.getDatabaseNameComboBoxModel();
    _listModel = model.getTableNameListModel();
    _tableModel = model.getDatabaseTableModel();
    initialize();
}
```

Because DatabaseViewGUI is just a courser-grained GUI component, it makes sense to create a model object that it can use as the model for all its internal components. Create a new class in this package called DatabaseViewerModel, as shown in Listing 5.7. When you added the new DatabaseViewerGUI constructor, the JDT was already asking if it could generate the new class for you. Therefore, create the class either by pressing Ctrl+N and filling in the New dialog or by clicking the light bulb in DatabaseViewerGUI and letting Eclipse create the class. In either case, the DatabaseViewerModel holds all the finer-grained models needed internally by DatabaseViewerGUI.

LISTING 5.7   DatabaseViewerModel.java

```java
package example.ve.swing;

import javax.swing.ComboBoxModel;
import javax.swing.ListModel;
import javax.swing.table.TableModel;

public class DatabaseViewerModel {

    private ComboBoxModel _databaseNameComboBoxModel;
    private ListModel _tableNameListModel;
    private TableModel _databaseTableModel;

    public DatabaseViewerModel() {
        _databaseNameComboBoxModel = new DatabaseNameComboModel();
        _tableNameListModel = new TableNameListModel();
        _databaseTableModel = new DatabaseTableModel();
    }

    public ComboBoxModel getDatabaseNameComboBoxModel() {
        return _databaseNameComboBoxModel;
    }
```

LISTING 5.7 Continued

```java
    public TableModel getDatabaseTableModel() {
        return _databaseTableModel;
    }

    public ListModel getTableNameListModel() {
        return _tableNameListModel;
    }

}
```

Creating the DatabaseViewerModel presents its own challenge: how to pass in a DatabaseViewerModel object to the GUI? Time to create one more class: DatabaseViewer. This class will be the application class that takes care of assembling the various pieces of your client application (see Listing 5.8). Now, instead of running DatabaseViewerGUI as a JavaBean, you can run DatabaseViewer as a Java application.

LISTING 5.8 DatabaseViewer.java

```java
package example.ve.swing;

public class DatabaseViewer {

    private DatabaseViewerGUI _gui;
    public DatabaseViewer() {
        DatabaseViewerModel model = new DatabaseViewerModel();
        _gui = new DatabaseViewerGUI(model);

    }
    public static void main(String[] args) {
        DatabaseViewer app = new DatabaseViewer();
        app.start();

    }

    public void start() {
        _gui.setVisible(true);
    }
}
```

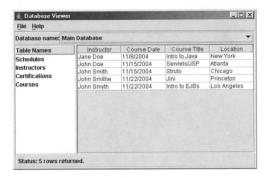

FIGURE 5.18   The DatabaseViewerGUI called from DatabaseViewer with the DatabaseViewerModel carrying the various models to be used by different GUI components.

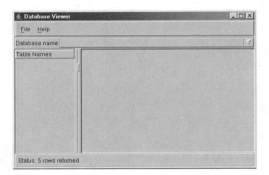

FIGURE 5.19   The DatabaseViewerGUI using the Motif look and feel.

Once you have all these classes implemented and saved with no syntax errors, you can select the DatabaseViewer editor and then select Run, Run As, Java Application to execute your functional, but nonworking, database viewer (see Figure 5.18).

Swing is also well-known for its ability to shift its look and feel based on either the platform on which it is running or a programmatic choice made by the developer and/or user. To see the DatabaseViewerGUI component using the Motif look and feel, open the launcher again (Run, Run), select Java Bean, DatabaseViewerGUI, and select CDE/Motif under Swing Look and Feel. Click Run, and your component uses Motif as its look and feel (see Figure 5.19). Of course, none of the data from the models is displayed.

Visual Editor Preferences

The Visual Editor is configurable from the main Preferences dialog under the Java node. The three configuration areas cover the VE's appearance, how code is generated, and the naming conventions used for initialization and access to components:

■ **Appearance**—The default appearance of the Visual Editor and its views can be modified. The source window can be given its own tab (not a new editor tab, but a new page tab that appears at the bottom of the VE window), and the palette can default to hidden when the VE first opens. The Properties and JavaBeans views can be made optional, and you can force the use of a particular look and feel (none, Metal, Motif, or Windows).

■ **Code Generation**—In the days of VisualAge, code markers delimited where you were allowed to add your own code and what code would be regenerated by VisualAge. The Visual Editor in Eclipse parses Java code looking for code that affects the Visual Editor and updates the WYSIWYG window. In the Generation Style section, if you check Generate a Comment for New Expressions, the VE code-generation engine would add the comment // Generated after every line of code created by the Visual Editor. Checking the Generate try{}catch{} block option will surround the GUI-generated code with a try/catch block. The Source Synchronization Delay section defines how long the VE update threads wait to update either the Visual Editor with the source or vice versa.

- **Pattern Styles**—This tab defines some of the code rules used by the VE to determine if a JavaBean is a valid component for display on the canvas and if it is capable of being modified by the VE code generator. If the JavaBean is a subclass of `java.awt.Component` or if the field name starts with `ivj` (a holdover from VisualAge for Java), then it is a valid candidate to appear on the canvas. The VE also checks all the fields of the bean to determine which fields should be included in the bean's visual representation. Another rule is that the JavaBean be instantiated within a `get` method or in one of the methods listed in the Pref tab.

In Brief

The Visual Editor is a welcome addition to the Java Development Tooling environment. With its support for AWT and Swing, it makes the construction of GUIs simpler than coding by hand and gives you a head start on implementing client-side presentation components. SWT support is forthcoming.

- You can build a simple GUI using the Swing components JFrame and JLabel.

- You can build a more complex GUI using various Swing containers and GUI components such as JComboBox, JList, and JTable.

- You can use the Visual Editor Configuration page in the Preferences dialog to control the Visual Editor's appearance, code-generation options, and code pattern rules.

High-Grade Testing Using JUnit

6

"Test, code, refactor, design. Repeat."

—Anonymous

Overview

Test-driven development. Testing frameworks. JUnit, Cactus, StrutsTestCase, HttpUnit, HtmlUnit, JWebUnit, SwingUnit. These days there is almost as much to be learned about testing APIs as the libraries with which you are writing your code. JUnit, the most popular of the current testing frameworks, was created by Erich Gamma and Kent Beck. You may remember Erich Gamma as one of the authors of the groundbreaking book *Design Patterns*. Kent Beck, in addition to various contributions in software analysis and design, is responsible in part for a small earthquake called *Extreme Programming* (sometimes called *Agile Programming* so as not to upset the faint of heart).

Documentation, source code, and binaries for JUnit can be found at http://www.junit.org, which will point you to SourceForge (http://sourceforge.net/projects/junit/) where the latest version can be found. However, you are one of the select few who have downloaded a tool that already has the latest version of the most popular testing framework on the face of the planet. The real issue is why you should use it.

Eclipse makes the creation and use of tests almost trivial (almost because you still have to decide what to test and how to test it). Having JUnit built in is not unique to Eclipse as a Java IDE, but as an additional piece to an already feature-rich IDE, it makes the decision to go with Eclipse all the more easy.

I am not going to spend time trying to convince you that writing tests is good for you, your programs, and your paycheck. What I will say is that without tests to prove your code works, you don't know for sure that it does work. Do tests prove that your code works in every instance? Of course not. Your users will be certain to remind you of that. What tests will do for you is guarantee that the situations you've planned for work, the situations that don't work fail gracefully, and bugs that have been squashed stay that way. Let's take a look at how you can do all this using Eclipse.

The JUnit Framework

The JUnit framework is made of a number of classes that take care of the nitty-gritty details of running your tests, as well as running a GUI to visually display which of your tests have passed and which have failed. From your perspective, you need to learn one class: `TestCase`. Once you become comfortable with `TestCase` then you may, on occasion, use `TestSuite`.

The process of using JUnit can be summed up as follows:

1. Write a test class that subclasses `TestCase`. It should not be able to compile because you have not yet written the class to be tested. Your first test has just failed.

2. Write the class that needs to be tested. Your first test now passes.

3. Add to the test class a test of functionality you have not yet written in the other class. As your second test, this also fails.

4. Write the smallest amount of functionality in the other class. Your second test now passes.

5. Test another bit of nonexistent functionality. This test fails.

6. Add the missing functionality. The test now passes.

By now you should see a pattern emerging. Write the test, which fails, and then write the functionality for which the test is checking, which causes the test to pass. You start with the simplest functionality and work your way up. As the functionality gets more complex, you know that prior functionality continues to work. If prior functionality stops working, you know it right away and you can fix it before the complexity grows out of hand.

Writing JUnit tests in Eclipse is only marginally different. In order to take advantage of the JUnit Wizard, the class to be tested must exist. In Eclipse's case, the previous list would look like this:

1. Create an empty class to be tested.

2. Create a subclass of `TestCase` to test the other class.

3. Write a test of simple functionality of the other class. The test fails.

4. Write the simplest piece of functionality for the other class. The test should now pass.

5. Write another test and watch it fail.

6. Add the functionality that will cause the test to pass.

Perform steps 5 and 6 until it is time to go home, until you hit a milestone date, or until you have to deliver your code. If you used use cases to drive your schedule and test-driven development to prove that the use cases pass the good scenarios and know how to behave in the bad scenarios, you win.

TestCase

When you write a test case, you subclass `junit.framework.TestCase`. In the same way that a servlet subclasses `HttpServlet` so that the servlet engine knows how to manage its life cycle, you are responsible for subclassing `TestCase` so the JUnit framework can walk your test object through its life cycle. The TestCase API includes assert methods that you will use to confirm the validity of results returned by the object under testing.

Let's discuss what happens when a test case runs within Eclipse. The JUnit framework starts up, loads the test class selected on the workbench (your test class does not need `main()`), creates as many copies of your test case as there are methods that start with the word `test` (for example, `testFindCustomer()`), and begins to run the test objects one at a time. Before the test method is run, an initialization method called `setUp()` is called to give you the opportunity to create whatever objects you need to make your test work. When your test method completes, either with a success or failure, a cleanup method called `tearDown()` is called so your code can safely dispose of used resources.

The Granularity of Tests

A question that always comes up in discussions about tests and testing frameworks is, how many tests (meaning assertions) should you put in a test method? The quick answer would be to put one assertion per test method because it gives JUnit the opportunity to run all your tests rather than just the ones that passed prior to the one that failed. However, the number of tests can get rather high, in which case you would have an immense number of test methods, which would be hard to maintain (the second argument against tests). The longer answer is, group associated tests together as long as they make sense. Start with one test method per method being tested. As you find that the methods are getting too long, break them up into functional test areas. In other words, use refactoring as a way of controlling the inevitable onslaught of success.

TestSuite

A suite of tests can be run by creating a subclass of `junit.framework.TestSuite`. Within this class, you would list the various subclasses of `TestCase` that you would like JUnit to run by overriding `suite()`. When you create a test suite using Eclipse, the code generator uses code markers so that it can regenerate the suite as often as you like. After you complete the example, you will get a chance to create, and re-create, a test suite.

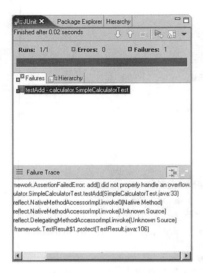

FIGURE 6.1   JUnit's TestRunner displaying the red bar, signaling it is not time to go home yet.

TestRunner: The JUnit GUI

So how does JUnit run within Eclipse? Do you simply select a test and run it like a Java application? When JUnit, or one of its variants, runs within Eclipse, it opens TestRunner, the GUI used by JUnit to display the results of completed tests (see Figure 6.1). The most visible part of TestRunner is the colored bar that runs below the title bar. You will learn to question a red bar when you expected a test to pass and a green bar when you expected a test to fail. Below the colored bar are three status values: how many tests of the available number of tests have run, how many errors (non-JUnit exceptions) occurred, and how many failures (assertion failures) occurred. Below these counters are two tabs: The Failures tab lists the methods that failed, and the Hierarchy tab lists all the methods with either a red X (error), a grey X (failure), or a green check (success).

Below the method list is the output of the currently selected method. If the method succeeds, there should be no output. If the result bar is red, expect to find output.

The title bar of TestRunner has five convenience buttons:

- **Next or Previous Failed Test**—Either of these buttons will take you directly to the method that encountered a failure or error.

- **Stop JUnit Test Run**—In case the test class has encountered an infinite loop or has simply decided to hang, you can kill JUnit from here.

- **Rerun Last Test**—The same as pressing Ctrl+F11, except it only runs the last JUnit test, not the last class that was run.

- **Scroll Lock**—Used to keep the selected test and its output in sync.

Creating a Test Case

In order for you to get a good feel for how to use JUnit, let's create a class that simply prints out a greeting. The greeting is changeable, as is the name of the person being greeted.

Create a Class

Start Eclipse and create a Java project called Greeter. Due to the way the JUnit Wizard works, you need to create the class to be tested first. Create a new class called Greeter in package example (you can create the package at the same time you are creating the class). The class should be quite empty after the code generator is done creating it.

FIGURE 6.2   The New dialog with the JUnit test case selected.

Create a Test Case

Let's look at creating a JUnit test. With the Greeter class selected in the Package Explorer, press Ctrl+N (or you can right-click the Greeter class and select New, Other). When the New dialog appears, select Java, JUnit, JUnit Test Case (see Figure 6.2). Click Next. Because this is the first time you are creating a JUnit test, the JUnit Wizard will ask if you would like it to add the JUnit JAR file to your class path. Click Yes to go to the JUnit Test Case page.

If you selected the Greeter class before you pressed Ctrl+N, the JUnit Test Case page should be almost completely filled in. If the page does not appear to be populated, click Cancel and start again.

This page lists all the information needed to generate the class:

- The name of the source folder to which the class should be written.

- The package into which the test class will go. You could put the test class into a different package, but conventionally the test classes live in the same package as the class they are testing. This gives the test class access to package/protected methods that may need to be tested.

- The name of the class to be tested.

- The name of the test class. The wizard uses the convention of appending the word *Test* to the end of any test classes. Other IDEs use the word *Test* as a prefix for the JUnit classes they generate. If you come up with another convention, just be consistent.

- The super class of the test class. This will almost always be junit.framework.TestCase, unless you come up with another class that you would prefer to extend. Be aware, though: if the class does not ultimately extend TestCase, it will not work within the JUnit framework.

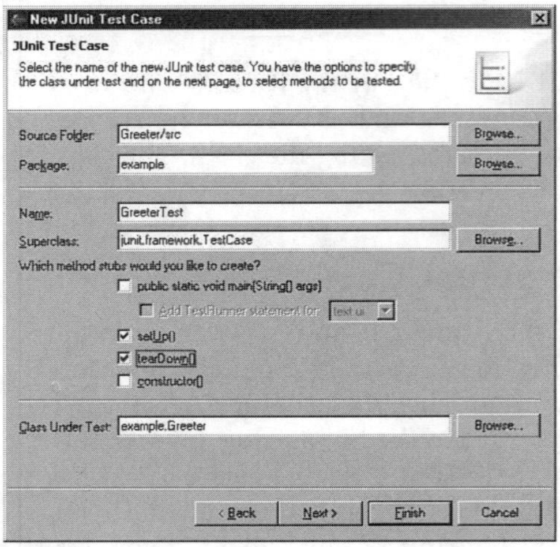

FIGURE 6.3   The JUnit Test Case page with the two main life cycle methods selected.

The only missing information needed is which of the lifecycle methods you want the class to include. Check setUp() and tearDown() and then click Finish (see Figure 6.3).

When the GreeterTest class opens in the Java editor, go to setUp() and remove the call to super.setUp(). In its place create a Greeter object and store it in an instance field called _greeter:

```
protected void setUp() throws Exception {
   _greeter = new Greeter();
}
```

A light bulb and red X appear in the left margin on the line where _greeter is declared. Click once on the light bulb and, when the content assist window opens, double-click Create Field _greeter. Save the file once the instance field is created.

The code in setUp() affords you the opportunity to single-source the creation of objects used through the test class. Because all your tests will need a Greeter object, setUp() is an ideal place to create it.

Next, empty out the tearDown() method and set _greeter to null:

```
protected void tearDown() throws Exception {
   _greeter = null;
}
```

Now, no matter what happens, you will always have a good object to work with before the test starts, and the object will always be released to garbage collection when the test completes. This may not seem like a big deal for a single test, but you can safely assume that you will have dozens, hundreds, maybe even thousands of tests running as your code development progresses.

One of the things we want the Greeter class to do is to return a greeting for display. A string returned as a result for display should not be null. (Yes, I know there are plenty of reasons why you might want a null returned from a method, but not in this case.) Our first test is now defined: a call to the method that returns the greeting should not return null. Above setUp(), define the method testGreeting() as follows:

```
public void testGreeting() {
}
```

Within `testGreeting()`, make a call to the `Greeter` method `getGreeting()`:

```
public void testGreeting() {
    String actual = _greeter.getGreeting();
}
```

Yes, it is true that there is no method in the `Greeter` class called `getGreeting()`. Remember step 3 of the development of JUnit tests? Your first test just failed. In order to make it succeed, you need to add the method to the `Greeter` class. Eclipse makes this a trivial task. Just single-click the light bulb and double-click the suggested fix in the content assist window:

```
Create method 'getGreeting()' in Greeter.java
```

The `Greeter` class comes forward, showing you the new method that has just been added. Save the `Greeter.java`.

Return to the GreeterTest editor window and save the file. The light bulb is gone, and our test-by-implication test is now successful. Because your first real test is to make sure you don't get a null from the call to `getGreeting()`, you need to take the result of the call and compare it against an expected result. By extending `TestCase`, you have an extensive selection of methods to check the result of a call and either do nothing if the result was as expected or complain if the result was invalid.

`TestCase` extends the `Assert` class, which has the following assertion methods:

- `assertEquals()`
- `assertTrue()`
- `assertFalse()`
- `assertNotNull()`
- `assertNull()`
- `assertNotSame()`
- `assertSame()`
- `fail()`

All the `assertXXX()` methods will throw an `AssertionFailedError` if the value they are passed is false. The `fail()` method throws an `AssertionFailedError` as soon as it is called. Each one gives you the choice of using its default error message or one you supply. For the test in `testGreeting()`, you could make a call to `assertEquals()` and compare the result to null, but the `assertNotNull()` method will work much better:

```
public void testGreeting() {
    String actual = _greeter.getGreeting();
    assertNotNull("getGreeting() returned null.", actual);
}
```

Running the Test

Save your files and make sure that GreeterTest is the active editor. From the main menu, select Run, Run As, JUnit Test. You already know that the getGreeting() method is going to return a null, so running TestRunner should give you a red bar (see Figure 6.4). If a green bar appears, make sure you are calling the proper assert method and that you are passing in the result of the call to getGreeting().

Let's fix getGreeting() so it does not return a null:

```
public String getGreeting() {
    return "";
}
```

Simply returning an empty string should cause the test to be successful, and pressing Ctrl+F11, which runs the last thing you executed, causes TestRunner to return a green bar. Success!

SHOP TALK

White Box Testing Versus Black Box Testing

A *black box test* is a test run on code without you knowing its internal makeup. A *white box test* is a test where you know exactly what is going on in the code. JUnit tests are usually white box tests, but you could also write black box tests against third-party vendor libraries.

When I first started writing tests, I found it a little disconcerting to know that I was writing tests to prove that code would behave in the fashion I had written it. Checking whether a method returns (or doesn't return) an expected result seemed trivial, especially when I knew what the code was doing. Why should I check, for example, that a method does not return a null when I know it will never return a null? There was no code anywhere (in the code I had written) that could possibly return a null.

I found out the reason as soon as I used someone else's code in my algorithm.

If the set of acceptable values is known, a test needs to be written to check that the result does not fall outside of this set or, if the value does fall outside the acceptable set, that the bad value is returned under known conditions.

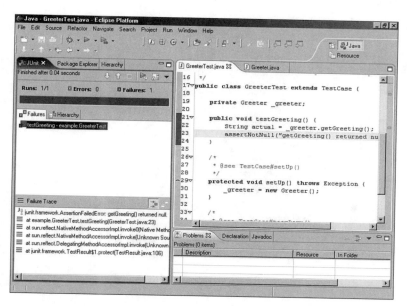

FIGURE 6.4 The TestRunner GUI with the expected red bar and the message passed in as the first argument to `assertNotNull()`.

If this were a chapter on writing tests in an incremental fashion, here are the next tests you would try to write:

1. Test for a default greeting.

2. Test the ability to change the current greeting with a null (throw an exception), a blank string (throw an exception), and a nonblank string.

3. Test whether the greeting can be reset to the default.

4. Test for a default greeting that can be personalized.

5. Test the ability to change the personalizable greeting with a null (throw an exception), a blank string (throw an exception), and a nonblank string.

6. Test whether the personalizable greeting can be reset to the default.

The number of things that can be implemented in the Greeter class is not insignificant, but you can check them reliably by adding slightly more complex tests in each iteration. But I digress.

When you discover a test that fails and the code has reached a complexity level where simply eye-balling it does not suggest where the problem may be, you need to debug the code through your test. Debugging a JUnit test is the same as debugging any other Java code: set a breakpoint in the test code or in the class being tested and from the main menu select Run, Debug As, JUnit Test. The Debug perspective opens and displays TestRunner at the bottom of the screen after the first full run, with the debug views and editor above it (see Figure 6.5).

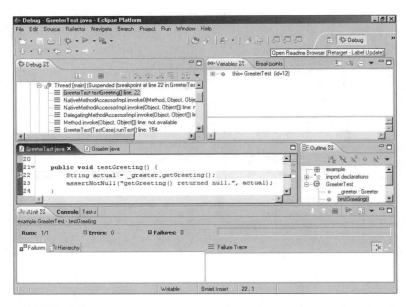

FIGURE 6.5   The Debug perspective with the JUnit TestRunner displaying the methods to be run.

Everything discussed so far would give you the impression that you can only run tests at the object level. In fact, you can select one method for execution to the exclusion of all the other test methods. Select the method to be executed from the Package Explorer or the Outline view, or double-click the method name in the Java editor. From the main menu, select Run, Run As, JUnit Test. Only the selected method will be run within JUnit. Unfortunately, you can only select one method at a time; this is not an arbitrary selection.

Creating and Running a Test Suite

As mentioned before, a JUnit test suite contains one or more tests that should be run as a unit. TestSuite is a composite object that contains Test objects (including other test suites) that are prepared to run all or one of their tests. When the JUnit framework starts, it uses reflection to make a call to the suite() method of the object created from the incoming class type. Because JUnit uses reflection, the only thing the class has to define to work within the framework is suite(). The incoming class does not have to be a type of Test. The suite() method must return an object of type Test so that the framework can begin running tests. The suite() method returns a Test object that contains whatever test objects you decide. Internally, JUnit performs the same operation, only it creates enough objects of your test type to run each individual method.

To make this explanation clearer, let's look at a class that defines `suite()` and returns a TestSuite object composed of a combination of single-method tests and multiple-method tests:

```
package example;

import junit.framework.Test;
import junit.framework.TestSuite;

public class AllTests {

    public static Test suite() {
        TestSuite suite = new TestSuite("Test for example");

        // Only run the named methods.
        suite.addTest(new TimeSeriesServiceTest("testGetTimeSeries"));
        suite.addTest(new OTCQuoteServiceTest("testGetOTCQuote"));
        suite.addTest(new QuoteServiceTest("testGetQuote"));

        // Run all of the tests contained within each class.
        //$JUnit-BEGIN$
        suite.addTestSuite(OTCQuoteServiceTest.class);
        suite.addTestSuite(QuoteServiceTest.class);
        suite.addTestSuite(TimeSeriesServiceTest.class);
        //$JUnit-END$
        return suite;
    }
}
```

The `AllTests` class has the following features:

- It does not extend any JUnit class.

- It declares a `suite()` method that will return an object of type `Test`.

- Within `suite()`, a TestSuite object is created.

- The TestSuite object has three method-specific tests added to it through calls to `addTest()`. Because method names are being passed into the test class constructors, only those tests will be run.

- The TestSuite object has three test classes added to its internal list through calls to `addTestSuite()`, and all the tests within each test class will be executed.

If the three test classes mentioned in the `AllTests` class have two test methods each, the call sequence might look something like this:

```
In testGetTimeSeries().
In testGetOTCQuote().
In testGetQuote().
In testGetOTCQuote().
In testGetOTCQuoteName().
In testGetQuote().
In testGetQuoteSymbol().
In testGetTimeSeries().
In testGetTimeSeriesFloat().
```

FIGURE 6.6 The JUnit Test Suite page with all the available tests checked.

The three single tests were run first. Next the test classes were called, in turn, and all their tests were run before moving on to the next test object. All these methods have a `System.out.println()` line, but normally the tests are silent if they succeed.

To generate a class that creates a `TestSuite` object, you open the New dialog and select Java, JUnit, TestSuite and then click Next. The JUnit Test Suite page will display the source folder in which the code will be generated, the package to which the class will belong, and the name of the class, which defaults to `AllTests` (see Figure 6.6). In the list below the test suite name are the various JUnit tests the builder recognizes. You can select zero or more JUnit tests for inclusion in `TestSuite`.

Also for the purposes of the example, I have deleted the comments from the code that was generated by the JUnit Wizard. Let's look at what was created:

```java
package example;

import junit.framework.Test;
import junit.framework.TestSuite;

public class AllTests {

    public static Test suite() {
        TestSuite suite = new TestSuite("Test for example");
        //$JUnit-BEGIN$
```

```
            suite.addTestSuite(OTCQuoteServiceTest.class);
            suite.addTestSuite(QuoteServiceTest.class);
            suite.addTestSuite(TimeSeriesServiceTest.class);
            //$JUnit-END$
            return suite;
        }
    }
```

The first line in `AllTests.suite()` is the instantiation of a `TestSuite` object. `TestSuite`, as a composite object, is the container of the various tests you want to run. The next line is a code marker used by the JUnit builder in case you decide to regenerate the suite. Anything outside of the code markers will be saved, whereas anything within the markers will disappear when you regenerate the code. The next line of code adds a class definition to the `TestSuite` object using `addTestSuite()`. This has the effect of creating a new `TestSuite` object and adding all the methods that start with *test* to the new `TestSuite` object, which is then added to your topmost suite. At the end of all this, `suite()` returns the `TestSuite` object.

What happens as you add and remove individual tests in the course of development? Regenerate the test suite class. You can do this in one of two ways:

- Press Ctrl+N (which opens the New dialog), select Java, JUnit, Test Suite, and then click Next. The JUnit Test Suite page will display a warning that `suite()` already exists and that it will be replaced unless you give the test suite class a new name (see Figure 6.7).

- Right-click the test suite class in the Package Explorer and select Recreate Test Suite from the pop-up menu. The Recreate Test Suite dialog will list the available JUnit tests for you to choose from. Select the tests you want to have appear in the code and click OK (see Figure 6.8).

FIGURE 6.7   The JUnit Test Suite page displaying the warning about `suite()` being replaced.

Running the test suite is no different from running a regular JUnit test (you select Run, Run As, JUnit Test). If you try to run the test suite as a regular Java class, it will not work (unless you add `main()` and a call to TestRunner).

I have been very careful not to say that the JUnit Wizard creates a `TestSuite` class. The wizard does not. The wizard generates a class that contains the `suite()` method, which will instantiate a `TestSuite` object and return it to any callers.

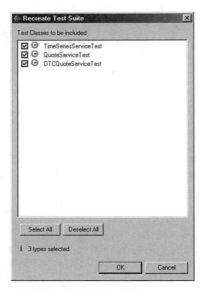

FIGURE 6.8   The Recreate Test Suite dialog listing the available JUnit tests that can be added to suite().

In addition, the JUnit Wizard only creates test suites made up of complete tests. If you want to have the suite() method call certain test methods, you have the task of adding by hand the calls to addTest() in suite().

Custom JUnit Launch Configurations

By selecting to run the JUnit test (which is either a subclass of TestCase or a test suite) using Run, Run As, JUnit Test, you allow the Launcher to create a default launch configuration and execute the TestRunner GUI using this default configuration. If you were to open the Run dialog (by selecting Run, Run), you would see in the Configurations list to the left the JUnit category with GreeterTest as a configuration entry (you did not get the opportunity to create all the classes for the test suite example, so there is no launch configuration for it). Running a JUnit test with the default launch configuration will do the job for most runs; however, creating a custom launcher lets you decide whether you want to run one test or many (see Figure 6.9).

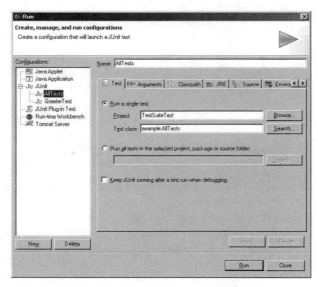

FIGURE 6.9   The Run dialog of the Eclipse Launcher.

The Launcher Run dialog has the base functionality discussed in previous chapters (configurable name, configurable environment variables, and sharable launch configurations as well as the ability to create new configurations, pass arguments both to the VM and the running class, select a JRE, and have a custom source path). The Test tab allows you to do the following:

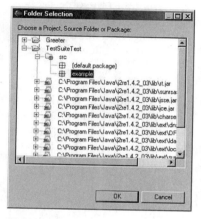

FIGURE 6.10   The Folder Selection dialog of the Eclipse Launcher Test tab.

- **Run a single test**—You can use the Browse button to select a new project, or you can use the Search button to display the list of available tests. You can only select one.

- **Run all the tests from either a project, a package, or a folder**—Selecting the radio button for this choice enables the Select button, which, when clicked, displays a dialog listing the available projects, packages, and folders (see Figure 6.10).

Finally, the check box labeled Keep JUnit Running After a Test Run When Debugging is useful only if you are using a JDK that supports the hot-swapping of code. When you are debugging a JUnit test and you modify and recompile the code, the hot swap will only work if you have checked the Keep JUnit Running... box.

To create a new JUnit configuration, remember to select either the JUnit category in the Configurations list or one of the JUnit configurations and then click New.

Extensions to JUnit

Not to be outdone in the open-source marketplace for testing frameworks, a number of additional packages have emerged that allow testing of Java technologies that are not easily tested due to their inclusion in application frameworks. For example, servlets, JSPs, and EJBs only run within a container framework that the average JUnit test cannot easily test against.

Developers abhor a vacuum. Almost before anyone realized how cool JUnit really was, extensions were already being written to allow for the testing of client-side and server-side Java components in their native environment. Here are some examples:

- **Cactus**—A server-side testing framework for the testing of servlets, EJBs, and other server-side Java technologies.

- **HttpUnit/HtmlUnit/jWebUnit**—Various frameworks for testing Web applications. The best thing about testing at this level is that the tests are really user-level tests. Pick a use case and write your HttpUnit, HtmlUnit, or jWebUnit test as proof that the use-case scenario works based on how the user acts and reacts to the system and that the system behaves predictably when the use-case failure scenarios occur.

- **JMXUnit**—A testing framework for JMX Beans.

- **StrutsTestCase**—A testing framework for Struts.

- **VirtualMock**—An AOP-based framework that uses the concept of *mock objects*, which allow for the testing of objects without concern as to the objects the objects being tested call. A mock object is an object that returns predictable values to the object under test. For example, database functionality is always difficult to test due to the necessary setup involved in making the tests repeatable. If the objects to be tested call mock database objects, you can test these objects based on what they believe they are receiving rather than what they would actually receive.

Please do not take inclusion in this list as an endorsement as to the usefulness of the these frameworks. Their usefulness will vary depending on your needs and where the developers of the frameworks are with their projects. However, performing a quick search on SourceForge results in the following available testing frameworks and utilities: JFCUnit, StrutsTestCase, jWebUnit, JUnitEE, Pounder, Artima Suite Runner, Cricket Cage, JUnitEJB, JXUnit, GroboUtils, JUnitDoclet, NoUnit, AgileDox JUnit-addons, Quilt, JUB, Hansel, and JFunc. This is not a complete list, and I expect it to grow.

Cactus has emerged as one of the more popular server-side testing pieces for Java. It tests server-side components from the safety of a client-side position.

Using a Non-Plug-in-Based JUnit Extension

As of the writing of this chapter, a Cactus plug-in for Eclipse has not seen the light of day (well, it did and then it was pulled back into the closet kicking and screaming). However, all is not lost. You can still write Cactus tests with the existing JUnit Wizard. A nontrivial example will explain how to set up everything needed to make that happen.

Let's begin by installing Tomcat and Cactus. When those two items are ready to go, you will write a sample servlet and its test and then display the results of the test.

In order to run a servlet, you need a servlet engine. If you don't already have Tomcat, you can download it from `http://jakarta.apache.org/site/binindex.cgi` and install it in your favorite location (for example, `c:\tools\jakarta-tomcat-5.0.25`). From the same Web page, you can also download Cactus (scroll up to look for it and install Cactus into your favorite location—for example, `c:\tools\jakarta-cactus-13-1.6.1`). Your versions will probably be newer.

At this stage, you have completed the most difficult part of this example: downloading and installing the latest versions of Tomcat, and Cactus. Cactus needs no configuration, and you will configure Eclipse to run Tomcat from the Eclipse Launcher.

In a more complete J2EE environment, such as MyEclipse from Genuitec, there would be editors, wizards, and builders specific to servlets and JSPs. However, due to the addition of Tomcat support in Eclipse 3.0, you can develop basic J2EE applications by setting up the proper directory structure in your project and creating a valid `web.xml` file.

Create a servlet and deploy it to Tomcat using the following steps:

1. Create a new project by pressing Ctrl+N. When the New dialog opens, select Java Project and then click Next. Enter the project name **CactusTest** and click Next. In the Java Settings page on the Source tab, set the Default Output Folder to CactusTest/WEB-INF/classes. Click the Libraries tab, click Add External JARs, and navigate to <Tomcat Install Directory>/common/lib. Select servlet-api.jar and click Open. Click Finish to close the New dialog. The use of the WEB-INF directory gives you the Web application structure you will need when you deploy to Tomcat, and servlet-api.jar gives you the J2EE symbols needed to compile servlets.

2. Create a servlet class by pressing Ctrl+N. From within the New dialog, select Java, Class and then click Next. Enter example for Package, HelloWorldServlet for Name, and javax.servlet.http.HttpServlet for Superclass. Click Finish.

3. HelloWorldServlet will open in the Java editor. Right-click in the editor and click Source, Override/Implement Methods. When the Override/Implement Methods dialog opens, check doGet() and click OK. Delete the TODO line and super.doGet(arg0, arg1). Add code to get the PrintWriter from the HttpServletResponse object and write a message. If you don't add code to produce some output, the servlet will fail to run:

```
protected void doGet(HttpServletRequest arg0, HttpServletResponse arg1)
    throws ServletException, IOException {
    PrintWriter out = arg1.getWriter();

    out.print("This is a message from the HelloWorldServlet!");
}
```

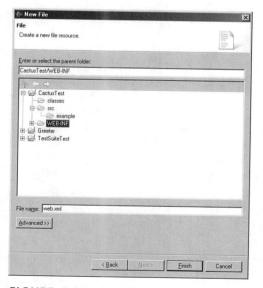

Fix any compile errors by pressing Ctrl+Shift+O to add any missing imports. Save the file.

4. Create a web.xml file by pressing Ctrl+N. From the New dialog, select Simple, File and then click Next. Make sure the parent folder is CactusTest/WEB-INF and enter web.xml as the filename (see Figure 6.11). Click Finish.

5. In the web.xml file, create a Web application entry that maps your HelloWorldServlet to the servlet name helloworld. This allows you to access the servlet using the name helloworld. Save the file:

FIGURE 6.11 The New dialog preparing to create an empty web.xml file.

```
<!DOCTYPE web-app PUBLIC
  '-//Sun Microsystems, Inc.//DTD Web Application 2.3//EN'
  'http://java.sun.com/j2ee/dtds/web-app_2_3.dtd'>
<web-app>
  <servlet>
    <servlet-name>helloworld</servlet-name>
    <servlet-class>example.HelloWorldServlet</servlet-class>
  </servlet>

  <servlet-mapping>
    <servlet-name>helloworld</servlet-name>
    <url-pattern>/helloworld</url-pattern>
  </servlet-mapping>
</web-app>
```

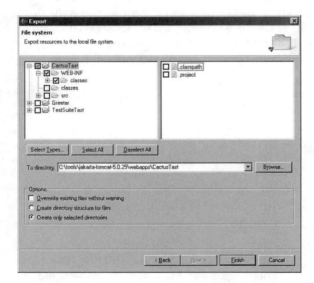

FIGURE 6.12   The Export dialog, set up to copy the project files into the Tomcat webapps directory.

6. Deploy the CactusTest project to Tomcat. The simplest way to do that is to export CactusTest into the Tomcat webapps directory. In the Package Explorer, right-click the CactusTest project and select Export from the pop-up menu. When the Export dialog opens, select File System and click Next. On the File System page, select the CactusTest project in the window to the left and uncheck the .classpath and .project files in the window to the right. Click the plus sign to the left of the CactusTest node to reveal the WEB-INF, classes, and src directories. Check only the WEB-INF directory. This will export everything under WEB-INF, including classes and web.xml. The To Directory field needs to reference the Tomcat webapps directory. Click Browse and navigate to your Tomcat installation directory. When you find it, select it and click New Folder. Enter the folder name CactusTest, press Enter, and click OK to see the export directory target (see Figure 6.12). If the To directory does not display a path that includes CactusTest, click Browse, navigate to it, and click OK. Click Finish to deploy your project to Tomcat.

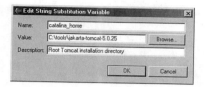

FIGURE 6.13 The catalina_home variable set with the Tomcat home directory.

7. In order to start Tomcat from within Eclipse, you need to create a Tomcat launch configuration. Eclipse already defines a string-substitution variable called catalina_home, but it is not assigned a default value. From the main menu, select Window, Preferences and Run/Debug, String Substitution. The Variable column lists catalina_home with an empty Value. Select the catalina_home row and click Edit. When the Edit String Substitution Variable dialog opens, click Browse, navigate to the Tomcat installation directory, and click OK to return to the Edit String Substitution Variable dialog (see Figure 6.13). Click OK to close the Edit String Substitution Variable dialog and then click OK to close the Preferences dialog.

8. From the main menu, select Run, Run. When the Run dialog opens, select Tomcat Server from the Configurations list and then click New. For Name, enter CactusTest, and for Web Application Root, enter /CactusTest (see Figure 6.14). Click Run. When the Run dialog closes, the Console view will come forward and begin to output Tomcat logging statements. You are ready to check your servlet when the Console has a statement similar to this:

```
INFO: Server startup in 9494 ms
```

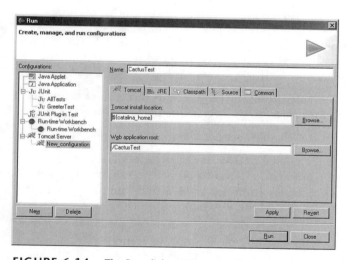

FIGURE 6.14 The Run dialog with a new Tomcat Server configuration for the CactusTest Web application.

9. Open a browser and set the URL to http://localhost:8080/CactusTest/helloworld. You should see your message in the browser (see Figure 6.15).

FIGURE 6.15   The `HelloWorldServlet` output displayed in a browser.

At this point, you now have a working servlet that in practice may or may not have a JSP to which it is redirecting. Now let's take a look at what it would take to run a test on it.

The intention of this part of the chapter is not to explain the hows and whys of Cactus, but to show you how you can implement Cactus tests even without direct Cactus support within Eclipse. However, in order to appreciate what needs to be done, you will need a certain amount of Cactus background.

Cactus, as a server-side testing framework, has both a client-side and a server-side component. The server-side piece runs on the same server as the servlet, and the client-side component receives messages from the server-side piece via sockets. In order for that to work, you will need to update the Web app `web.xml` file and carry along certain JAR files that must be deployed on the server with the servlet and the servlet test code.

Here's the short list of things that need to be done to write Cactus tests in Eclipse:

1. Copy a collection of JAR files needed by Cactus into `WEB-INF/lib`. This is for the Cactus test that runs on the Web server. These will be deployed along with the servlet to be tested.

2. Add a collection of JAR files to the classpath of the project. This way, you can run the Cactus test as a client so that it can connect to the server-side Cactus test.

3. Update `web.xml` to include the Cactus filter and servlet mappings.

4. Write a Cactus test either by extending `ServletTestCase` or by instantiating a `ServletTestCase` object within a JUnit test. If Tomcat is properly set up within Eclipse, you can run the Cactus test as a standalone JUnit test and it will communicate with the server-side code returning the results of the tests.

Cactus can be used to test servlets, JSPs, EJBs, and any server-side Java components. For this example, because you are going to write a servlet test, you will not look at some of the other test classes you could have extended. The CactusTest project will contain both the servlet to be tested and the test code.

Let's fill in the preceding steps. Before you create the test class, you need to import the following JAR files into the `WEB-INF/lib` directory for use by the Cactus server-side piece (all the JAR files are from the Cactus install directory):

- `aspectjrt-1.1.1.jar`

- `cactus-1.6.1.jar`

- `commons-logging-1.0.3.jar`

- `commons-httpclient-2.0.jar`

- `junit-3.8.1.jar`

Add these to your `CactusTest project` by right-clicking `WEB-INF` and selecting Import from the pop-up menu. Because you want to copy the JAR files into the project, when the Import dialog opens, from the Select page choose File System as the import type and click Next.

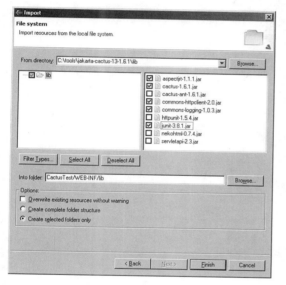

From the File System page of the Import dialog, click the top Browse button to navigate to the `lib` directory of the Cactus installation (for example, `C:\tools\jakarta-cactus-13-1.6.1\lib`) and select the `lib` node from the tree view in the window to the left. When you select the `lib` node, the available JAR files in that directory will be listed in the window to the right. Select the five JAR files listed previously (even if the version numbers are different—they should be higher [see Figure 6.16]). Change the Into Folder from

`CactusTest/WEB-INF`

to

`CactusTest/WEB-INF/lib`

FIGURE 6.16 The Import dialog listing the JAR files found in the Cactus installation `lib` directory.

and click Finish. Your WEB-INF directory now has a `lib` directory, and it contains the Cactus JARs. These JAR files will be used by your test when it runs on the server.

The next step is to add a collection of JAR files needed by Cactus onto the project classpath. Open the project's Properties dialog by right-clicking the CactusTest project name in the Package Explorer and selecting Properties from the pop-up menu. Select Java Build Path from the list to the left and the Libraries tab from the Java Build Path page to the right. Click Add External JARs and navigate to your Cactus installation `lib` directory (again, for example, `C:\tools\jakarta-cactus-13-1.6.1\lib`). Holding down the Ctrl key, select the following JAR files:

- `aspectjrt-1.1.1.jar`

- `cactus-1.6.1.jar`

- `commons-httpclient-2.0.jar`

- `commons-logging-1.0.3.jar`

- `junit-3.8.1.jar`

Click Open to select these five JAR files. They will be added to the Libraries tab's build path (see Figure 6.17). Click OK.

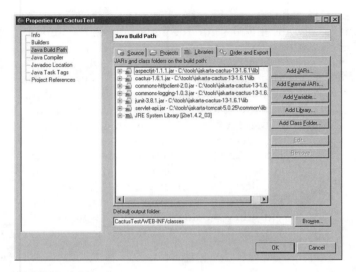

FIGURE 6.17   The five JAR files needed from the Cactus installation by the client-side Cactus test.

The third step is to add the Cactus-specific filter and servlet information into the Web application web.xml file:

```
<!DOCTYPE web-app PUBLIC
  '-//Sun Microsystems, Inc.//DTD Web Application 2.3//EN'
  'http://java.sun.com/j2ee/dtds/web-app_2_3.dtd'>
<web-app>
    <filter>
        <filter-name>FilterRedirector</filter-name>
        <filter-class>org.apache.cactus.server.FilterTestRedirector</filter-class>
    </filter>

    <filter-mapping>
        <filter-name>FilterRedirector</filter-name>
        <url-pattern>/FilterRedirector</url-pattern>
    </filter-mapping>
```

```
<servlet>
  <servlet-name>helloworld</servlet-name>
  <servlet-class>example.HelloWorldServlet</servlet-class>
</servlet>

<servlet>
    <servlet-name>ServletRedirector</servlet-name>
    <servlet-class>org.apache.cactus.server.ServletTestRedirector</servlet-class>
</servlet>

<servlet-mapping>
    <servlet-name>ServletRedirector</servlet-name>
    <url-pattern>/helloworld/ServletRedirector</url-pattern>
</servlet-mapping>
<servlet-mapping>
  <servlet-name>helloworld</servlet-name>
  <url-pattern>/helloworld</url-pattern>
</servlet-mapping>
</web-app>
```

This web.xml file is the complete file you will use. It contains both the HelloWorldServlet servlet mapping as well as the filter and servlet information needed to call Cactus (the shaded code). The only item of note is the way the Cactus ServletRedirector servlet is defined: Because our HelloWorldServlet is mapped to the name helloworld, the ServletRedirector must be defined relative to the servlet to be tested, so /helloworld is placed before ServletRedirector in the <url-pattern> tag of the servlet mapping.

FIGURE 6.18 The Superclass Selection dialog displaying the Cactus ServletTestClass.

After all that setup, it is time to create a Cactus test. Select HelloWorldServlet in the Package Explorer view. Create a class that extends ServletTestCase by pressing Ctrl+N to open the New dialog and selecting Java, JUnit, JUnit Test Case. Click Next. In the JUnit Test Case page, all the standard information should be filled in for you. The one change you need to make is to change the superclass to ServletTestCase. Click Browse, enter ServletTest in the topmost text field of the Superclass Selection dialog, and select ServletTestCase (see Figure 6.18). Click OK to close the Superclass Selection dialog. Click Finish on the New JUnit Test Case page to close the dialog and accept the class information. The HelloWorldServletTest opens in the Java editor and is quite empty.

A standard JUnit class has a setUp() method, a tearDown() method, and one or more test methods that start with the word *test*. Cactus can use the setUp() and tearDown() methods, but it also adds the capability to add custom setup and teardown methods per test. The custom setup and teardown methods are called begin<name of method being tested>() and end<name of method being tested>(). The test method for the servlet is going to test the doGet() method, so you could create three methods: beginDoGet(), endDoGet(), and testDoGet(). For this example, you will only create the last two. To check whether the call to doGet() streamed information to the caller, you are going to check the servlet output in endDoGet().

For the purposes of this exercise, you are only going to look at calling doGet(), but Cactus allows you to call any method defined in the servlet. Two objects created by Cactus to predictably test servlets are WebRequest and WebResponse. WebRequest represents an HTTP request message to the servlet, and WebResponse represents the HTTP response from the servlet. When endDoGet() is called, its single argument is going to be a WebResponse object. You will use it to find out what the servlet printed out, as shown here:

```java
package example;
import java.io.IOException;

import javax.servlet.ServletException;

import org.apache.cactus.ServletTestCase;
import org.apache.cactus.WebResponse;


public class HelloWorldServletTest extends ServletTestCase {

    public void testDoGet() {
        HelloWorldServlet servlet = new HelloWorldServlet();

        try {
            servlet.doGet(request, response);
        } catch (ServletException e) {
            e.printStackTrace();
        } catch (IOException e) {
            e.printStackTrace();
        }
    }

    public void endDoGet(WebResponse response) {
        String actual = response.getText();
```

```
        String expected = "This is a message from the HelloWorldServlet!";
        assertNotNull(actual);
        assertEquals(expected, actual);
    }
}
```

The `testDoGet()` and `endDoGet()` methods are quite small. To test a servlet, Cactus asks that you instantiate your servlet in the test method as well as check its response in the end method. The code in `testDoGet()` does the following:

- Instantiates the servlet.

- Calls `doGet()` and passes in predefined request and response objects. The `try/catch` code is there as protection in case the method call throws an exception.

As you'll recall, the `doGet()` method of `HelloWorldServlet` gets the `PrintWriter` object and then prints a greeting. The `testDoGet()` method makes the call to `doGet()`, and the test method `endDoGet()` gets the text from the response object and compares what it finds to what it was expecting.

Your Web application needs to be deployed to Tomcat. Right-click the CactusTest project and select Export from the pop-up menu. Select File System from the Select page and click Next. Select and open the CactusTest node and uncheck `classes` and `src` in the list to the left and uncheck `.classpath` and `.project` in the list to the right. Make sure To Directory is set to the Tomcat `webapps/CactusTest` directory. Click Finish. When the Question dialog opens asking if you want to overwrite existing files, click Yes To All.

There is only one thing left to do before you run the test: You need to create a launch configuration to give the Cactus framework the URL to use in calling the servlet. Select `HelloWorldServletTest` in the Package Explorer and select Run, Run from the main menu. In the Run dialog, select any of the JUnit tests or the JUnit node and click New. A new configuration page appears with as much information as the system could glean from the file you selected before opening the dialog. The only thing left for you to configure is the URL for Cactus to use in testing the servlet. Even though you could pass Cactus the URL to use by setting up a `cactus.properties` file, you will instead put the URL in an environment variable that the JVM will place in the runtime environment. Click the Arguments tab and enter the following in the VM Arguments area (see Figure 6.19):

```
-Dcactus.contextURL=http://localhost:8080/CactusTest/helloworld
```

Click Apply and then click Close to shut down the Run dialog. You're done! Time to run the test.

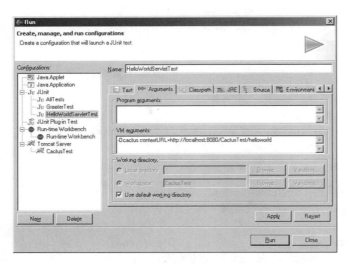

FIGURE 6.19   The Run dialog with the environment variable entry for `cactus.contextURL`.

If you have not stopped Tomcat since you last started it, go to the Console view and click the red square button located on its toolbar (it is the first button on the left). The Console view title will display a message similar to the following:

```
Console (<terminated> CactusTest [TomcatServer] ...
```

FIGURE 6.20   The JUnit TestRunner displaying the green bar of success for the Cactus servlet test.

Restart Tomcat from within Eclipse by opening the Launch Configuration dialog (select Run, Run and then select Tomcat Server, CactusTest). Click Run. The Console view should have fresh output from the Tomcat server. When the Console states that the server has started, you are ready to run the Cactus test using JUnit.

Check that the servlet is available by opening a browser and going to `http://localhost:8080/CactusTest/helloworld`. You should see the same page as before with your welcome message displayed.

Select `HelloWorldServletTest` in the Package Explorer. From the main menu select Run, Run As, JUnit Test. The Launcher will use the launch configuration you just created and will start the JUnit TestRunner with `HelloWorldServletTest` as its only test class. If all goes well, the TestRunner GUI will open and display the green bar of success (see Figure 6.20). Click the Hierarchy tab to see that `testDoGet()` was run and that it succeeded.

If you already had the TestRunner GUI open, it may not come to the front if the test passes, so click the JUnit tab to see it.

The test that just ran went through the following steps, assuming Tomcat is running and the servlet is available (this is a very abbreviated version of the actual process):

- The client code, `HelloWorldServletTest`, ran and performed standard JUnit initialization.

- The Cactus framework looked for the `beginDoGet()` method. Because you did not write `beginDoGet()`, this did not do anything.

- Cactus opened a connection to the `ServletRedirector` running within Tomcat. The `ServletRedirector` was deployed with the `HelloWorldServlet` and will take care of running the server-side component of the test.

- `ServletRedirector` reinstantiated `HelloWorldServletTest` on the server side within Tomcat and called `testDoGet()`, which created an instance of the `HelloWorldServlet`. Because `HelloWorldServletTest` was running within the servlet engine, it safely created `HelloWorldServlet` and was able to call any and all methods available in the `HelloWorldServlet` API.

- When `testDoGet()` completed, `ServletRedirector` returned to the client side, which promptly called `endDoGet()`. The `endDoGet()` method received the `WebResponse` object, which contained the text output by `HelloWorldServlet`.

All this is independent of Eclipse. The most interesting thing about the Cactus test is that you are able to run the server side and client side within one environment.

So what did it really take to complete these steps? You copied a number of JAR files into WEB-INF/lib so that the server-side code would work. You also updated the web.xml file to support the Cactus ServletRedirector, and you put a number of JAR files in the project's classpath so the client-side component would work. You wrote a test that extended a Cactus base class, you deployed the code to Tomcat, and then you ran your test code as a JUnit test.

This example may have seemed like it needed a lot of setup. In the normal course of your day-to-day development, you will probably use a more comprehensive plug-in to make the development of your J2EE application simpler. Plug-ins such as Lomboz and MyEclipse not only control the configuration, starting, and stopping of application servers, but they also create support files like web.xml.

Perhaps by the time this book comes out the Cactus Eclipse plug-in will be released again, and the preceding steps will be reduced a bit. Go to http://jakarta.apache.org/cactus/integration/eclipse/index.html to check on the plug-in's progress. Better yet, join in and help to get it ready.

Ant Support for JUnit

Ant already has a task tag called `junit` that will take care of running your tests in a batch mode. In addition, Ant also has a task called `junitreport` that will take care of generating a report with useful information about the test run.

Many JUnit (or JUnit-like) extensions are available for you to choose from. The amount of support varies, depending on the current popularity of the tool and whether or not it behaves well with existing frameworks. Take a stroll through JUnit.org and SourceForge.net to look for help in your testing efforts.

To quote Mae West, "Too much of a good thing can be wonderful!"

SHOP TALK

Test/Integrate Daily

Something we will not discuss at any length is the fact that even though we develop our software using tools such as Eclipse, we will rarely deploy the files created by the IDE. Build tools, such as Ant, should be used to extract, build, and deploy the final production systems. In many cases, what is missing is the additional step of checking the integrity of the system about to be deployed.

In order to prove the integrity of a system, it is necessary to run all the tests written by the various developers in one giant testing marathon. Of course, if the first time you run all the tests needed by the system is before deployment, you were in trouble long before you got out of bed. The concept of continuous integration has been gaining favor as something that should be done to any nominally nontrivial system as a way of checking the system every day. No, you did not read that wrong. Every day. Multiple times a day.

And if you have inherited a system already in production with no supporting tests, remember that you can add tests as bugs are reported. Rather than spend all your time dreaming up tests to check the code, just write tests that prove a reported bug exists and that it has been fixed. If you write a test every time a bug is reported, not only will the number of bugs be reduced, they will not reappear.

Anyway, many books and articles are available to you to begin looking up information about continuous integration and the tools that support it, such as CruiseControl. Appendix E, "Recommended Resources," lists just a few Web sites to begin your journey to more predictable software.

In Brief

The Eclipse support for JUnit is quite extensive and convenient. The JUnit TestRunner is a full-fledged SWT GUI and is well-integrated with the Java Development Tooling plug-in. As an accepted standard, JUnit goes a long way in encouraging the use of tests in day-to-day development and continuous integration. JUnit's small API makes it easy to learn and easy to use.

In this chapter you looked at the following JUnit capabilities:

- Implementing a JUnit test involves writing a Java class and selecting it before opening the New dialog to select the JUnit Test Case. The results of JUnit tests are viewed through the TestRunner GUI.

- The creation and execution of JUnit tests are supported from within Eclipse.

- The JDT debugger let's you set breakpoints and debug JUnit tests.

- JUnit test suites can be created using the JUnit Wizard. You can re-create the test suite through the wizard as well as modify the test suite by hand.

- There are many JUnit extension frameworks. Non-plug-in JUnit extensions, such as Cactus, can be included in your projects in two ways: by inheriting from a base class such as `ServletTestCase` or by instantiating objects of type `ServletTestCase` in your JUnit test.

- Tomcat and Cactus can be downloaded from the Jakarta site for use by Eclipse in the development of Web applications.

- Cactus programs to test servlets can be implemented and run from within Eclipse using the built-in support for Tomcat and the JUnit launcher support.

Painless Code Sharing Using Team Support

7

It's the source control, stupid.

—Anonymous

Eclipse Support for CVS

No matter what your views may be about the use of an IDE versus a text editor, the one thing developers can agree on is the use of source control. Once your source code has found its way onto the filesystem, it is imperative that you save it in some kind of repository when you feel it has reached a level of functionality you can snapshot. Test-driven development techniques allow you to feel confident about the state of your code at any given milestone, whereas the use of source control gives you the knowledge that, if you had to, you can always roll back to an earlier version. Don't let test-driven development make you cocky; always use source control.

The advantage of source control is that you can work on your copy of the source for as long as you like, and when you decide to check the code into the repository, CVS will let you know that either your code is acceptable or someone else changed the code since you checked it out and now you need to resynchronize your code with the repository. Let's look at Eclipse support for CVS and how it will assist you in importing code for you to work on as well as exporting source code when you are finished.

Eclipse support for source control is at the same level of support as Java development. The CVS perspective contains views of the available CVS repositories, including a repositories view, an editor view, and resource history. Unfortunately, Eclipse does not support local CVS repositories. The only way Eclipse can perform its source control tasks is through the use of a CVS server available on some port on some machine.

CVS Perspective

The CVS perspective is displayed by either going to the main menu and selecting Window, Open Perspective or by clicking the Open Perspective button in the shortcut bar at the top right of the workbench. In either case, the CVS perspective appears as shown in Figure 7.1. The first time you use the CVS perspective, it will not display any repositories. Eclipse waits for you to enter a server and repository name so it can connect to the remote server and display whatever CVS information the server is willing to supply. You can add or remove repositories at any time, but be careful: Eclipse does not confirm the removal of a repository from the CVS Repositories view unless you have imported code into a project. This does not affect the actual repository in any way; it only removes it from the view.

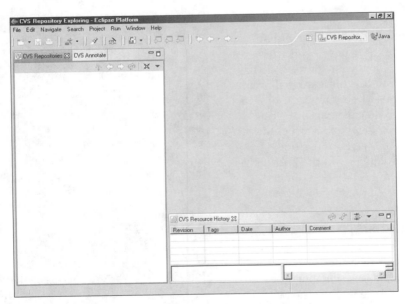

FIGURE 7.1   The CVS perspective with no displayable CVS repositories.

Creating a New Repository Entry

Let's look at the various views and how they support each other by connecting to a public CVS repository on the Web.

To illustrate creating a new repository entry, let's go to SourceForge and use Eclipse to browse the CVS repository of a SourceForge project. You will start by going to `http://sourceforge.net` and selecting one of the projects under the Most Active list in the left navigation bar. At the time of this writing, JBoss was the fourth most active project on the site. After selecting the JBoss.org project (`http://sourceforge.net/projects/jboss/`), you should see the "Project: JBoss.org: Summary" page appear. Select the CVS link from the headers list directly below the Summary bar. The CVS link leads you to the "Project: JBoss.org: CVS" page, which briefly discusses CVS, anonymous CVS access, and developer CVS access. The information you are looking for is located in the Anonymous CVS Access section. When I accessed the CVS page for JBoss.org, the Anonymous CVS Access section displayed the following CVS information:

```
cvs -d:pserver:anonymous@cvs.sourceforge.net:/cvsroot/jboss login
```

This line tells us three things:

- The CVS server name is `cvs.sourceforge.net`.

- The CVS root path to the project is `/cvsroot/jboss`.

- The CVS user login name is `anonymous`.

Something else the JBoss.org CVS page tells us is that user anonymous has no password. Using this information, the next few steps will connect you to the SourceForge CVS server and allow Eclipse to display the CVS repository for the JBoss.org project.

CVS, Firewalls, and Connectivity

If the CVS server you need to access is not located on your local machine, you need to be set up to connect either across the Internet or on your local network. Connecting to SourceForge is a trivial exercise that gives you a rich selection of code from which to choose. Remember, however, that this will not work if you are situated behind a firewall or are not connected to the Internet.

First, right-click in the CVS Repositories view and select New, Repository Location to display the Add CVS Repository dialog (see Figure 7.2). Once you enter all the required information, this dialog will take care of finding the machine on the network and displaying its repository in the CVS Repositories view located on the left side of the workbench.

In the Add CVS Repository dialog, enter **cvs.sourceforge.net** into the Host field, **/cvsroot/jboss** into the Repository Path field, and **anonymous** as the user. The Connection Type field should be set to pserver; if it is not, change it to pserver. The CVS servers at SourceForge use the standard CVS password server to authenticate any users coming into the repositories, so you must set the connection type to pserver. Use Default Port should be the selected radio button, and Validate Connection on Finish should be checked. Figure 7.2

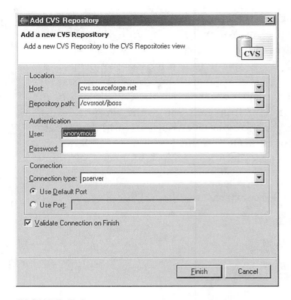

FIGURE 7.2   The Add CVS Repository dialog with all the information necessary to connect to the SourceForge CVS server.

shows all the information discussed here. Click Finish. A Progress Information dialog should briefly appear. When it closes, the CVS Repositories view should display the JBoss.org CVS source tree (see Figure 7.3).

A Brief Tour of the Various Views

Let's look at the various parts of the CVS perspective using the JBoss CVS repository.

The default CVS perspective is made up of three views:

- The view to the left is the CVS Repositories view.

- Directly to the right of the CVS Repositories view is an editor area.

- The area below the editor is the CVS Resource History.

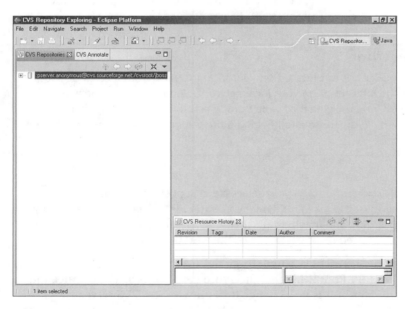

FIGURE 7.3   The CVS Repositories view with the JBoss.org CVS repository being displayed.

The CVS Repositories view is where CVS repositories are displayed in a tree view (see Figure 7.4). The CVS Repositories view can display zero-to-many CVS repositories. Double-clicking the repository name, or clicking once on the plus sign, will open the view, revealing the HEAD, Branches, and Version nodes.

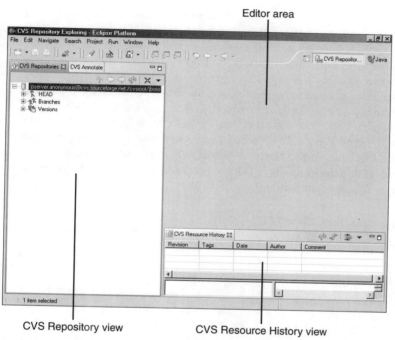

FIGURE 7.4   The CVS perspective with its two views and one editor area.

The HEAD node is the main branch of the CVS tree for that repository. It represents the main branch or trunk of the repository tree. Double-clicking HEAD, or clicking once on the plus sign next to the HEAD branch, will display everything in the main branch of the repository, which includes directories and files. Double-click HEAD to close the node.

Double-clicking the Branch node, or clicking once on the plus sign next to the Branch node, will reveal that there are no branches currently available. What does this mean? Well, you would create a branch in a CVS repository when you need a safe place to make changes that will end up in the HEAD branch. If you were to decide to make changes to the JBoss.org source (assuming you had developer privileges), you would create a branch where the files you wanted to work on would be associated. After the file changes were complete, you would check to see if the files had changed since you took them out. If they had changed, you would have to reconcile the new changes with your current changes. If no changes were made, you could safely check your files into HEAD.

Opening the Version node displays version tags associated with various directories and files for a particular version. For example, selecting the version tag jbossmq and right-clicking it will display the pop-up menu. Choosing Configure Branches and Versions causes a dialog to appear that allows you to select branches and/or versions of a directory associated with a particular branch or version (see Figure 7.5).

Let's walk through an interesting JBoss directory and add it to the Branch node. Once that directory has created a new branch, you will add the directory's contents as a project within Eclipse. Open the Version node in the CVS Repositories view, scroll down, and right-click jbossmq. Select Configure Branches and Versions from the pop-up menu. When the dialog appears, open the src folder by clicking the plus sign next to it and then open the main folder by clicking the plus sign next to main. Open the org directory, followed by jboss and then mq. Select the Connection.java file. The list box to the right now displays the various branches and versions associated with that file. Click the Deselect All button and check the Branch_2_4 and Branch_3_0 boxes. Click Add Checked Tags, and a plus sign will appear next to the Branches node in the tree view in the center of the dialog. If you open that Branch node, you will see that Branch_2_4 and Branch_3_0 have been added to it. The dialog and all the preceding information is displayed in Figure 7.5. Click OK.

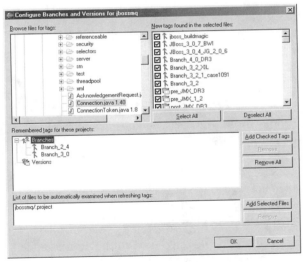

FIGURE 7.5   The Configure Branches and Versions dialog for jbossmq displaying the two selected branches.

The Branch node in the CVS Repositories view now has a plus sign next to it. Open the Branch node and you will see two branches associated with it: Branch_2_4 and Branch_3_0. Open either branch and you will see that jbossmq has been added as a branch associated with the JBoss.org repository. These branches have no connection with the public CVS repository with which we started. However, if you right-click the jbossmq folder, you'll see the pop-up menu item Check Out As Project (the second item in the list). If you select Check Out As

Project, the CVS plug-in will extract all the code in the folder and create an Eclipse project named jbossmq made up of the code from the particular branch of JBoss.org you selected, which in this case is not the latest branch.

The Editor view is used to display a read-only view of a selected file. Because the file is not associated with an Eclipse project, you are not allowed to change the file in any way. Select Branches, Branch_2_4, jbossmq Branch_2_4, src, main, org, jboss, mq and then double-click Connection.java. The file will appear in the editor view fully syntax-colored and with a moveable cursor. Cutting and pasting from the editor into another destination is supported.

The final view is the CVS Resource History. This view displays the CVS revisions, tags, time-stamps, author, and comments associated with a file. Right-clicking the Connection.java file used earlier will display the selection Show in Resource History in the pop-up menu. Select that item, and the current known CVS information for Connection.java will appear. Of course, all the CVS information is displayed, not just the information up to the version you selected.

The two text areas below the CVS Resource History table will display detail data for a chosen row. Select one of the rows of CVS data from the CVS Resource History. The left window will display version tags, if any are available, and the right window will display the full comment.

Accessing CVS

An interesting point to note is that the CVS perspective does not care if you are looking at a repository of Java code or a repository of COBOL code. Source control is source control. CVS is CVS. The JBoss.org repository consists of Java code, but the information we will be viewing pertains to anything under the control of the repository.

Checking In

Now that you have seen how easy it is to connect to an external CVS server, create working branches from versions within the CVS repository, and create projects from CVS folders, let's create a new project and make it available to the rest of our team. For the sake of argument, assume that we have a project called Greeter with one package and one class, called GreetingFactory, in the package. You will export GreetingFactory so others can use the class.

If you do not have a CVS server to which you can safely connect and you are running on a Windows machine, you can download and install CVSNT from http://www.cvsnt.org/. You'll find plenty of instructions and help at the CVSNT site to get you going. However, I ran into problems the first time I configured CVSNT, so be sure to read Appendix B, "Setting Up and Running a Local CVS Server," which goes into some of the setup issues involved in getting CVSNT up and running so that Eclipse can connect to it. Be aware that some of the functionality may not work correctly due to incompatibilities between Eclipse and CVSNT.

Because you are creating this project for the first time, we will create a new repository location and then commit the project files into it.

Select the CVS perspective using either the Perspective button or by selecting Window, Open Perspective, CVS Repository Exploring from the main menu. Once the perspective is visible, right-click in the CVS Repositories view and select New, Repository Location. When the Add CVS Repository dialog appears, enter the name of the machine where you installed CVSNT, the absolute path to the repository, and the username and password to allow you to log in to the repository. Click Finish to complete the connection to your CVS server. If you have a repository path problem, make sure you unchecked the Repository Prefix box in the CVS for NT admin program.

Before you can check in the Greeter project, you need to create it. Go to the Java perspective, create a project named Greeter and create a new class, GreetingFactory, in the package example. The code for this class should look something like this:

```
package example;

public class GreetingFactory {

    public String greetingsTo(String name) {
        return "Hello, " + name + "!";
    }
}
```

After saving the class, right-click the project name in the Package Explorer view. From the pop-up menu, select Team, Share Project. The Share Project dialog will appear, asking you to choose a repository type for the shared code to reside in. Select CVS and click Next. The next panel in the dialog, the Share Project with CVS Repository panel, needs to know if the code will be shared in an already existing CVS repository or if you are going to add a new repository location. Part of the process of configuring CVSNT is the registration of CVS repositories. If you did not create any repositories, go to Appendix B and read the section titled "Registering a Repository."

Once you have a repository registered, you can do one of two things: You can register the repository location in the CVS perspective ahead of time and then, within the Share Project dialog, select Use Existing Repository Location, or, again from the Share Project dialog, you can select Create a New Repository Location.

If you select Create a New Repository Location, the panel you used to enter the repository information (host, repository path, username, and password) is displayed. In addition, once you've entered the repository information, the dialog's Enter Module Name panel will request a module name under which the project will reside. It will try to best guess your intention by using the existing project name as the module name, but you are also allowed to enter your own module name. For this example, you should use the project name. At this point, clicking Next or Finish accomplishes the same goal: connecting to a repository and starting the first step in checking in the new project.

However, if you chose Use Existing Repository Location instead, clicking Next will take you directly to the Enter Module Name panel, and you can either use the existing project name or enter a new name after selecting Use Specified Module Name. Again, for this example, use the existing project name for clarity.

Clicking Next or Finish will now set up an initial connection between your project and the CVS repository. If you have not clicked Finish, do so now. In addition, the CVS plug-in will compare your incoming code to code that may already be in the repository. In this case, there is nothing to compare, so right-click the project folder in the Synchronize view and select Commit from the pop-up menu. The Add to CVS Version Control dialog appears asking if you want to add the files to CVS because the resources do not appear to be under its control. Click Yes and enter a comment, such as "My first CVS commit." And click OK Select the CVS perspective and open the repository location you selected as the destination for your code. Open the HEAD node and you will see a folder with your project name (unless you chose to name your project something else, in which case the folder will have that name). Open the project folder, also known as the *module* folder, and you will see the same directory structure as your project. The only piece that appears to be missing is the JRE System Library component of your project. In fact, in your actual project, the Package Explorer view combines the JAR files listed in your classpath with your source code to give you a consolidated view of your work. The JAR files are not actually located in your project directory.

The process works the same if you want to check in an arbitrary number of individual files, with only one caveat: Before you check in your file, you should synchronize your changes with the current contents of the branch you are committing to.

For example, someone else can update the very basic `GreetingFactory` you committed with additional code while you have been working on it as well. This would imply the following development steps when using CVS:

1. Check out, or create, a project.

2. Make changes.

3. Synchronize with the CVS repository.

4. Update any code that is in conflict.

5. Commit the files once any conflicts have been resolved.

Return to the Java perspective. Change the `GreetingFactory` code by adding a comment:

```
/**
 * This is a comment.
 */
```

The code should now look like this:

```
package example;

/**
 * This is a comment.
 */
public class GreetingFactory {

    public String greetingsTo(String name) {
        return "Hello, " + name + "!";
    }
}
```

SHOP TALK

Practicing Safe Source Control

A search on various search engines for "source control best practices" does not yield much in the way of direction for the use of source control in environments where *continuous integration* is the watchword. In practice, if developers on a team can be convinced that source control is useful—and there are many who pay lip service to it but in fact don't use it or use it badly—then how often it is used becomes the driving force in your process. If your team wants to test/integrate your system every day, then enough code has to churn into the source control system to trigger the checkout of the system so that it can be deployed and tested.

Consider the following when you extract code from source control to perform a bug fix or a feature addition/extension:

- Make sure you also take out the test associated with the class you are about to modify. Add whatever tests you need to confirm that your changes work.
- Although this might be too obvious, you should push only working code back into source control. The code might still break when your scripts perform a full system test, but it should have worked when it left your machine.
- If you are fixing a bug, push back all the files associated with the change, including the tests.
- Consider branching HEAD to make your changes rather than making the changes to HEAD. Although this is a little extra trouble, it allows others the opportunity to work the main source trunk if needed.
- If you are adding/completing functionality, push back all the files/tests for the working functionality. Consider granularity at a use-case level until you find a finer or coarser granularity that you and your team are comfortable with.

Save the file and notice the greater-than signs (>) that appear next to all the names in the project hierarchy in the Package Explorer. The greater-than sign tells you that you have checked out the changed file and, by implication, you are going to check it in at some later point in time.

Before you check in the code, you have to synchronize your version of the file with whatever happens to be out in the branch. You are still using the HEAD branch, so right-click the file in the Package Explorer and go to Team, Synchronize with Repository. The Synchronize CVS Workspace dialog opens, displaying the available resources that can be synchronized. Select the Greeter project and click Finish. A confirmation dialog opens, asking for permission to switch to the Team Synchronizing perspective. Click Yes to open the new perspective. When the Team Synchronizing perspective opens, another dialog opens, reporting the results of the synchronization. In this case, it found two outgoing changes, no incoming changes, and no conflicting changes. Click OK to close the reporting dialog. To the left of the perspective is the Synchronizize view. In this view, open Greeter, src/example, GreetingFactory.java. Double-click GreetingFactory.java to open the Compare editor (see Figure 7.6).

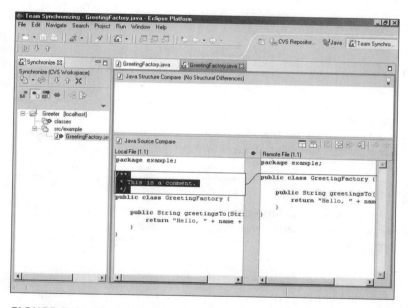

FIGURE 7.6   The Team Synchronizing perspective displaying the Synchronize view and the Compare editor.

The Compare editor is showing you three different views of the file about to go into CVS. The Java Structure Compare view, located at the top of the Compare editor, displays the class structure and the differences between the current structure and the structure of the class coming from the branch to be merged. Any selected elements will appear in Java Source Compare. Any elements flagged in red are conflicts that must be resolved. Because there are no structural changes, the window is empty.

The Java Source Compare view, the bottom half of the Compare editor, displays the work-bench file to the left and the branch file to the right. All changes go from right to left. In this example, this is not a problem, but if you had been trying to synchronize a branch, it might be a problem (more on branches later). However, because the change in the workbench code is going to overwrite whatever is in the HEAD branch, you can safely ignore the code differences.

The toolbar on the title bar of the Java Source Compare view can be used to copy conflicting code from right to left for an incoming change, from left to right on an outgoing change, or to display a direction-insensitive file compare. In this case, you don't need to do anything to update the file to contain the changes because they are in the file you are about to commit. The fourth button from the left copies all nonconflicting changes from right to left, and the sixth button copies the current change from the right file to the left file.

For this example, you want to take all the changes from your workbench code (the window on the left) and commit them to the repository. Right-click the GreetingFactory.java file in the Synchronize view and select Commit from the pop-up menu. When the Commit dialog appears, enter the comment "My second commit." Click OK. Return to the CVS perspective, right-click in the CVS Repositories view and select Refresh View, and then open your local repository location. Open HEAD, Greeter, src, example. The GreetingFactory.java file will be version 1.2. Close all open editors.

Checking Out

In order to proceed through the steps of checking out an existing project, you will now delete your project from the Java perspective and check out as a project the code you committed into the repository. You will then modify your file, check it back in as an individual file, and view the file in CVS to ensure that the check-in was successful.

Keyboard Shortcuts Considered Useful

Remember that Ctrl+F8 will take you to the next open perspective on your workbench. Pressing Ctrl+F8 will toggle you between your current perspective and your last perspective.

Return to the Java perspective. Select project Greeter and delete the project, either by pressing the Delete key or by right-clicking the project name and selecting Delete from the pop-up menu. When the Confirm Delete Project dialog appears, select Also Delete Contents Under [your project path here]? and click Yes. Your code is now gone from the local filesystem.

Return to the CVS perspective. Right-click the Greeter folder located under HEAD and select Check Out As Project from the pop-up menu. Because the project does not exist in the work-space, the checkout proceeds without any more prompting from the system. Had the project already existed and you chose Check Out As Project, the CVS plug-in would have prompted you for permission to delete the destination project so that the code checkout could proceed. If you go back to the Java perspective (press Ctrl+F8), you will find the Greeter project is back safe and sound.

Also notice that the project name has a greater-than sign (>) as its prefix. This means that the project was taken out of source control.

Now that you have successfully checked in and checked out your project, bear in mind that all the work you have accomplished so far has been to the HEAD branch of your repository. At some point you will need to make changes to your code that you can commit without affecting HEAD. This is where branching comes in.

Branching

In the Java perspective, right-click the Greeter project and select Team, Branch. Enter the branch name **Greeter_1_0**, leave the check box Start Working in the Branch checked, and press Enter or click the OK button. The string "Greeter_1_0" and the name of your CVS server appearing within square brackets should now follow your project name. Return to the CVS perspective. Anywhere within the CVS Repositories view, right-click and select Refresh View from the pop-up menu, or press F5. A plus sign will appear next to the Branches node. Open the Branches node and you will find a branch called Greeter_1_0. If you open branch Greeter_1_0, you will find a folder named after your project with the branch name displayed next to it.

The Use Of Branch Naming Conventions

Not to belabor the obvious, but branch naming conventions are important. At the very least, enter a branch name that will not conflict with any other branch name in your repository.

Branch Greeter_1_0 is where your code will go when you update it and commit it to the repository. Return to the Java perspective. Add the following code to GreetingFactory:

```
private String _greeting = "Hello, ";

/**
 * @param string
 */
public void setGreeting(String string) {
    _greeting = string;
}
```

You should insert the code above greetingsTo(). Save the code, right-click the filename in the Package Explorer, and select Team, Commit from the pop-up menu. When the Commit dialog appears, enter the comment "Added setGreeting()." Click OK.

Press Ctrl+F8 to return to the CVS perspective. Refresh the view by pressing F5. Open Branch, Greeter_1_0, Greeter Greeter_1_0, src, example. The version number for GreetingFactory.java is different (higher) from the version number of GreetingFactory.java under HEAD.

Merging a Branch

Your next task is to take the code change you made to GreetingFactory and move it into HEAD. In order to accomplish the move to HEAD, you are going to overwrite the code in the workbench and merge it with the code for your custom branch. This is a safe procedure because the updated code is, in fact, in branch Greeter_1_0.

Return to the Java perspective. Right-click the project name in the Project Explorer view and go to the Replace With, Another Branch or Version item. When the Select with Branch or Version dialog appears, select HEAD and click OK. The CVS plug-in has now overwritten the changes you made, but the changes are still in Greeter_1_0. Now that the workbench reflects the code from HEAD, you will update the workbench code with the changes from the branch.

Right-click GreetingFactory.java and select Team, Merge from the pop-up menu. Select as the starting point Root_Greeter_1_0 and click Next. In the next panel, open the Branches node, select Greeter_1_0, and click Finish. The Confirm Perspective Switch dialog opens, asking to switch to the Team Synchronizing perspective. Click Yes. In the Editor view of the Team Synchronizing perspective, the Compare editor will be open with information displayed in all three Compare editor windows (see Figure 7.7). The Java Structure Compare window, the one at the top of the Compare editor, allows you to compare the file in the branch with the source in the workbench, which matches the source in HEAD. To make it easier to compare the files, double-click the title bar of the Compare editor to fill the screen.

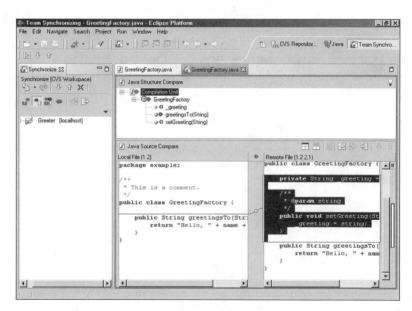

FIGURE 7.7   The Team Synchronizing perspective's Compare editor with the HEAD and branch versions of GreetingFactory.java.

The Java Structure Compare window shows you the differences in the structure of your class definition. In this case, the blue arrows with the embedded plus signs mean that the branch has changes that need to be incorporated into the workbench code. Once again, the Java Source Compare window is directly below the Structure Compare window. The left window is the workbench code, and the right window is the branch code, which contains the changes you made. In this case, the HEAD code is to the left and the branch code is to the right. However, bear in mind that the changeable code is *always* going to be in the left window. It is because of this that you overwrite the workbench code with the target branch that does not contain your changes, and you compare it to the branch that contains the actual changes. The color code used by the two windows is as follows:

- Incoming changes are blue.

- Outgoing changes are gray.

Simply update the workbench files with the changes committed to the branch. Click the sixth button, Copy Current Change from Right to Left, to update the workbench file with your changes. If more changes were available, you would continue adding changes to the workbench file until no more changes were available. Save the file and shrink the editor window back to normal by double-clicking the title tab.

The final step in updating the HEAD branch is the actual commit to the repository. This is no different from what you did earlier when you checked in the project. However, in this example you are only going to enter one file. Right-click GreetingFactory.java and select Commit. Enter a comment into the Commit dialog and click OK. Return to the CVS perspective and press F5 to refresh the CVS server view. Note that GreetingFactory has had its version number updated.

In Brief

The CVS perspective is a quick-and-easy way to connect to a CVS server. The sharing of files is a trivial task, and support for combining out-of-sync files is intuitive.

You were able to accomplish a number of CVS-related tasks:

- The creation of a new repository entry is handled by using the Add CVS Repository Wizard.

- The CVS Repositories view lists the various CVS servers with whose repositories you can interact. The editor area will use an appropriate editor to display a file, but the file is read-only. The CVS Resource History allows you to see the CVS audit trail of any given file.

- The check-in process involves synchronizing with the repository to ensure that no one else has changed the file since you took it out and, after you correct any changes, committing the file into the repository after you enter a descriptive comment about any changes made.

■ The check-out process involves finding a module of folder in the CVS repository and selecting Check Out As a Project.

■ Branches are created by selecting a project or a file and choosing Team, Branch from the Java perspective Package Explorer view.

■ File merges are accomplished by committing your current changes to the non-HEAD branch, checking out the HEAD branch, and selecting the branch and HEAD as the merge source and target, respectively. After reconciling all file differences, you can safely commit your files to HEAD.

PART II

Developing Applications Using Plug-Ins

Finding, Installing, and Using Plug-Ins

"Seek and ye shall find. Install and ye shall be more productive. Configure and ye shall forget how you got something to work."

—Anonymous

The Eclipse Plug-In Site(s)

If you used Eclipse "out of box" and added nothing else to it, you could develop an immense amount of code and accomplish quite a bit of work. However, it is because of Eclipse's plug-in architecture that so much buzz has been generated about its capabilities. Although the number of sites with links to Eclipse plug-ins is still rather small, a large number of plug-ins is available.

The granddaddy of all Eclipse sites is the Eclipse Plugins page:

```
http://www.eclipse-plugins.info/eclipse/index.jsp
```

As a general rule of thumb, when you are looking for an open-source project, the first place to go is SourceForge. However, for Eclipse plug-ins, the place to go is Eclipse Plugins. The plug-ins are listed in various orders. I generally scan the list using date order. This way, when I find a plug-in version submitted since the last time I checked, I stop looking. It is always interesting to see what kinds of plug-ins are the most popular and what new plug-ins are being worked on by the Eclipse community.

Second on the list is SourceForge. Many of the plug-ins listed in Eclipse Plugins are hosted by SourceForge. Type **Eclipse** in the search input field and dozens of Eclipse projects will be listed:

```
http://sf.net
```

What is interesting is that no matter which plug-in project I find in SourceForge, I can find it already listed in Eclipse Plugins. Therefore, I find it more efficient to start my search for plug-ins at the Eclipse Plugins site.

Another site vying for the position of main Eclipse plug-in portal would have to be Eclipse Plugin Central at

`http://www.eclipseplugincentral.com/`

Although nicer looking than `eclipse-plugins.info`, it does not yet list as many plug-ins.

Freshmeat.net, at

`http://freshmeat.net/search/?q=eclipse&section=projects&x=0&y=0`

and Resources for Java Server-side Developers, at

`http://www.java201.com/resources/browse/5-2003.html`

are also good sources for Eclipse plug-ins.

However, the odds are in your favor that the plug-in you are looking for can be found at the Eclipse Plugins site, if at all.

Once you have found the plug-in of your dreams, or perhaps your manager's dreams, you have three ways in which to install a plug-in into Eclipse:

- Unzip the plug-in file into the Eclipse installation directory.

- Unzip the plug-in into an arbitrary directory and have Eclipse point at this external directory through the use of a `links` directory.

- Use the Find and Install feature to direct Eclipse to search for a plug-in at a URL, a local directory, or an archived site.

Installing a Plug-In in Two (Maybe Three) Steps

Installing a plug-in is straightforward in almost every instance. The MyEclipse plug-in is one of the only plug-ins that does not follow the standard plug-in installation model. MyEclipse takes care of installing the plug-in into an arbitrary directory and just makes sure that Eclipse can find it.

▶ For a walkthrough of the MyEclipse plug-in installation, **see** "Downloading and Installing MyEclipse," **p.182**.

You can install a plug-in in one of two locations: either in the Eclipse installation directory or in the directory of your choice. Installing a plug-in in the Eclipse `plugins` directory has the virtue of being easier to accomplish, but it makes reinstalling Eclipse harder if you decided to dispose of your current installation. Let's go over both scenarios. In either case, you will need a program that recognizes and can extract zip files. These instructions are specific to Windows, but should map to the various flavors of Unix. For example, copying to a directory is still copying to a directory.

The steps are straightforward:

1. Exit Eclipse if it is running.

2. Uncompress the plug-in file into the Eclipse installation directory.

Simple, yes? Let's add a little more detail and then move on to installing a plug-in in an arbitrary location. If you are using a compression program that has a GUI, such as WinZip or UltimateZip, you can use it to open the plug-in zip file. If you are running the compression program from the command line, run the program on the file and have it simply list the contents of the zip file. Take a good look at the path used by the plug-in in the zip file. The path will start in one of three ways:

- `eclipse`

- `features` and/or `plugins`

- With the plug-in directory specific to the plug-in (using the Java package-naming convention). It will also probably have a version number as its suffix. For example, a typical plug-in directory name could be `org.aspectj.ajde_1.1.4`.

All plug-ins delivered with Eclipse are stored in the `plugins` directory located below the `eclipse` directory. There is also another directory, called `features`, where some plug-ins place additional files for their use. The path you find in the zip file will dictate whether you uncompress the zip file in the directory where the Eclipse installation is found, directly below the `eclipse` directory, or below the `plugins` directory.

For example, if you installed Eclipse under `c:\tools` and the plug-in zip file contains a path that looks like a Java package name, you should extract the file directly into the `c:\tools\eclipse\plugins` directory.

If the zip file contains a path of either `features`, `plugins`, or both `features` and `plugins`, you should extract the file into `c:\tools\eclipse`. The plug-in has additional files that must go into both locations.

On rare occasion, you will find a plug-in that has a starting path of `eclipse`. If the zip file contents start their path with `eclipse`, you should extract the zip file into the directory where you installed Eclipse (in this case, `c:\tools`).

Once you have copied the files into the proper directory, restart Eclipse. At this point, the installation is complete.

Installing Your First Plug-In

On occasion, a plug-in can be fun even when you are not developing code, so for a first run let's install a plug-in that installs a few games playable within Eclipse. Exit Eclipse and, for the purposes of this example, download `eclipse-games_3.0.1.zip` from `http://eclipse-games.sourceforge.net`. Click the Latest Release link to download the games plug-in zip file. Opening the zip file will show that the file paths start with `eclipse`. If you installed Eclipse directly into a directory such as `C:\tools`, extract the `eclipse-games_3.0.1.zip` directly into that directory. If you extract the file into the `eclipse` directory, you will have a subdirectory named `eclipse` with an undetectable plug-in.

Restart Eclipse. The main menu of every perspective now has a menu titled Games. If you select Games from the main menu, it will list the four games you can play from within Eclipse (Minesweeper, Minesweeper II, Snake, and Sokoban). If that seems too easy, welcome to the world of Eclipse. At runtime Eclipse checks the `plugins` and `features` directories to determine which plug-ins are available, what perspectives they are valid under, and whether they should be displayed. Using the Product Configuration dialog, you can take a look at what Eclipse believes is its current collection of plug-ins. To do that, you must select Help, Software Updates, Manage Configuration to open the Product Configuration window (see Figure 8.1). When you open the node below the Eclipse Platform root, Eclipse-Games 3.0.1 is listed as the first plug-in node. Close the Product Configuration window.

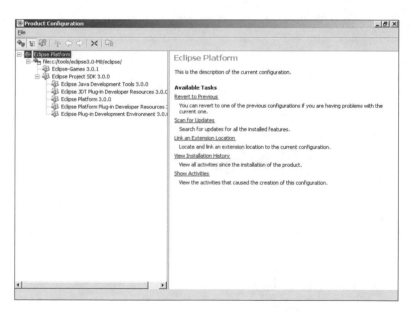

FIGURE 8.1   The Product Configuration window.

The appearance of a plug-in in the menu bar, including the games plug-in, can be controlled by customizing the perspective. Open the Customize Perspective dialog (Window, Customize Perspective) and select the Shortcuts tab, if it is not already selected. From the Shortcuts tab, you control which menu subitems appear in the New, Open Perspective and Show View menu items, the pop-up menu, and the shortcut buttons. Select Show View under Submenus and check Games from the Shortcut Categories (see Figure 8.2). Click OK to close the dialog. From the main menu, select Window, Show View. You will find that the four games now appear as shortcut menu items.

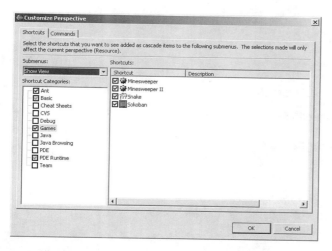

FIGURE 8.2 The Customize Perspective dialog with submenu Show View Games checked.

If you want to remove the Games menu from the menu bar, open the Customize Perspective dialog (Window, Customize Perspective) and select the Commands tab. The appearance of various menu items are controlled by checking these items in the Available Command Group list (see Figure 8.3). Because the Games Actions item is checked, it appears in the main menu. To remove Games from the main menu, uncheck Games Action. Remember, anything you select (or unselect) in this dialog only affects the current perspective.

If you left the Games Actions item checked and you are in the Resource perspective, the main menu will have a Games menu inserted after the Project menu but before the Run menu. Run MineSweeper by selecting Games, Minesweeper from the main menu. Then double-click its title bar to fill the window (see Figure 8.4). If you run into a problem with this plug-in, just select Window, Reset Perspective and try again.

Enjoy playing the game. It is one of my favorites (yes, I am easily amused). I taught my daughter, Lindley, how to play it while we were on a plane on our way to one of my consulting assignments when she was about five years old.

If you have been following along with the exercise, exit Minesweeper and exit Eclipse.

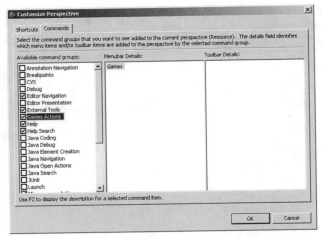

FIGURE 8.3   The Customize Perspective dialog with Available Command Group Games Actions checked.

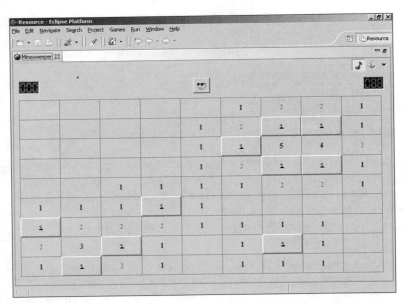

FIGURE 8.4   Beginner-level Minesweeper, from the Eclipse-Games plug-in, displayed in Eclipse.

Installing a Plug-In to an External Location

Let's download another plug-in, only this time let's extract it outside of the Eclipse installation. Go to the Sysdeo Web site and download the latest Tomcat plug-in:

```
http://www.sysdeo.com/eclipse/tomcatPlugin.html
```

The plug-in name will be something like `tomcatPluginV3beta.zip`, where *V3beta* will probably be different by the time this book makes it to print. To install the plug-in in an arbitrary location:

1. Create a directory structure into which you can copy the plug-ins (for example, `c:\eclipse-plugins\eclipse`).

2. Create a `plugins` and a `features` directory under `c:\eclipse-plugins\eclipse` (or whatever you named the new location).

3. Uncompress the zip file in the directory of your choice.

4. When you uncompress the zip file make sure that you overlay the directories properly; otherwise, the plug-in will not be found. The topmost directory under `eclipse-plugins` does not have to be called `eclipse`, but I have found plug-in zip files that start their path at `eclipse`, so having a directory with that name will make life easier for you in the long run. The Sysdeo plug-in starts its file paths at `com.sysdeo.eclipse.tomcat_2.2.1`, which means you need to extract the Sysdeo files under `c:\eclipse-plugins\eclipse\plugins` (if that is the name you gave your external plug-ins directory).

In order for Eclipse to recognize this external directory, or any number of external directories where you might have plug-ins installed, you have to modify the Eclipse installation. Create a directory called `links` under the Eclipse installation directory (for example, `c:\eclipse\links`). When Eclipse starts up, it searches for the `links` directory. If the IDE finds this directory, it attempts to read a file ending with `.link`. If you have created an external plug-in directory and have downloaded a plug-in and extracted it to this external directory, you can create the `links` directory under your Eclipse installation directory and create a `plugins.link` file inside the `links` directory. The `.link` file must contain a name/value pair that tells Eclipse where to find any additional plug-in directories:

```
path=C:\\eclipse-plugins
```

Notice that the `eclipse` directory is not included in the path. You can have as many `.link` files as you like, with each one pointing to a different plug-in directory.

When you restart Eclipse, it will recognize this external directory and add it to its Product Configuration. Start Eclipse and go to Help, Software Updates, Manage Configuration. The Product Configuration dialog opens, displaying all the known plug-in locations, both enabled and disabled. Your plug-in path will appear along with any other plug-in directories you might already have.

You have a few different ways to check that the Sysdeo plug-in was installed:

1. Look at the main menu. You should see Tomcat added as a menu item, and on the toolbar you will find a new group containing three Tomcat buttons.

2. Switch to the Java perspective. The menu and toolbar changes should still be visible.

3. Open the Customize perspective dialog (from the main menu select Window, Customize Perspective) and select the Commands tab. Scroll down to the bottom of the Available Command Groups list to find Tomcat (see Figure 8.5). From this location you can decide to either display the menu and toolbar additions or remove them. Click OK to close the dialog.

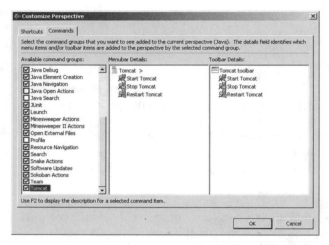

FIGURE 8.5   The Customize Perspective dialog's Command tab with the Select Tomcat command group.

4. Next, go to Window, Preferences and look for Tomcat as an additional node in the list to the left. This is where you configure the plug-in to recognize the desired Tomcat installation. Close the dialog.

5. The Sysdeo plug-in adds a Tomcat project type. Press Ctrl+N to open the New dialog. The Tomcat Project type is located within the Java folder. Close the New dialog.

Let's recap what you've done to install a plug-in in an external directory:

1. You created a directory that contains at least a directory called `plugins`. Eventually, you will install a plug-in that needs the `features` directory, but the extraction process will take care of creating that directory for you.

2. You exited Eclipse.

3. You downloaded a plug-in and extracted it into the aforementioned external `plugins` directory (or at the same level, depending on the file paths in the zip file containing the plug-in).

4. In the Eclipse installation directory, you created a directory called `links`, and inside that directory you created a file called `plugins.link` (this could have been called anything as long as the extension is `.link`). Inside the `plugins.link` file you assigned your plug-in path to the property name `path`.

5. You restarted Eclipse and went to Help, Software Updates, Manage Configuration. The new plug-in directory was listed together with any other plug-in directories.

This plug-in has just given you the ability to run Tomcat from within Eclipse. Congratulations! Unfortunately, it did not install Tomcat, so you will still have to download Tomcat and install it for the plug-in to work (`http://jakarta.apache.org/tomcat/index.html`). This is not a problem because the Tomcat download is a zip file that is extracted into the directory of your choice. As long as `JAVA_HOME` is defined in your environment, Tomcat will work by executing the `startup.bat` command. The configuration of the plug-in is done through the Preferences dialog.

SHOP TALK

Too Much of a Good Thing Is...

There are a number of good reasons why you would want to install a plug-in somewhere other than in the Eclipse `plugins` directory, but the one I find the most compelling is organization. By creating a separate location (or multiple locations, depending on how many plug-ins you use), you can easily add and remove plug-ins from your Eclipse install. Once you have added more than two nontrivial plug-ins (and there are very few that are trivial), you will find that reinstalling Eclipse can cause you to lose a great deal of time as you reextract your plug-in zip files. Many plug-ins have multiple plug-in directories, and some also expect you to add additional plug-ins before they will work at all.

Keeping your plug-ins organized is just another way of keeping your system stable. The first time you set up an external plug-in target, it will seem like a lot of work (create the external directory, create the `links` directory in your Eclipse installation, create a file that lists your external directory, and so on). However, it is a one-time hit. After that, the thought of adding another directory--say, for new editors, miscellaneous plug-ins, or games--won't seem so tedious.

One of the features of Eclipse is its extensibility. If you let your plug-ins get out of hand at the first sign of trouble, you will begin to limit the number of plug-ins you install for less-than-legitimate reasons (there might be better reasons not to load up so many plug-ins, but organization shouldn't be one of them).

Installing a Plug-In Using the Eclipse Update Manager

The third way to install a plug-in is to point Eclipse toward a location where update informa-tion exists. This location can be local to your machine, on the Web, or in an archive. Let's add each of these lookup sites, one at a time.

To add an external lookup site, select Help, Software Updates, Find and Install to open the Install/Update dialog. Select Search for New Features to Install and then click Next. The next visible page will be titled Update Sites To Visit. The first time you run this, the site list will be empty. Let's add an external update site by clicking Add Update Site.

When the New Update Site dialog opens, enter the following information:

- Name--Hibernate Synchronizer

- URL--http://www.binamics.com/hibernatesynch

This URL is to the Hibernate Synchronizer plug-in.

Click OK. The update site will appear using the name Hibernate Synchronizer and will have a node named Synchronizer (see Figure 8.6). Check the box next to either node and then click Next. The Search Results page displays the available plug-ins from the external site, and you should check the entry for Hibernate Synchronizer. The current version number is displayed, as is the public name of the author of the plug-in (see Figure 8.7). Click Next.

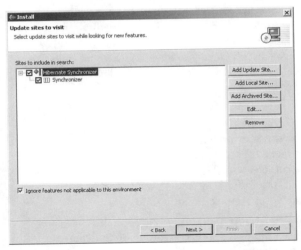

FIGURE 8.6   The Search Results page from searching through an Eclipse plug-in update site.

The next page is the Feature License. This page displays the standard Apache License and asks you to accept, or not, the license. For this exercise, select "I accept" and click Next.

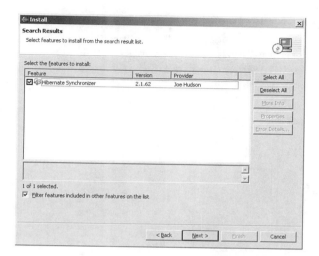

FIGURE 8.7 The Search Results page displaying the feature name, version number, and author name.

Now it's time to install the plug-in. The Install Location page lists the plug-ins to be installed and the available locations to which they can be installed. Because an additional point of this exercise is to install the plug-in in a location external to Eclipse, you need to add an additional install site. Click Add Site and, using the Browse For Folder dialog, navigate to c:\eclipse-plugins. Click New Folder and add a directory called update-manager so that now you have the directory path c:\eclipse-plugins\update-manager. Click OK. This new folder can be called anything, but to keep this example clean, you will install this plug-in into a different location than the plug-in you installed earlier. When you created the local install location for the update site using the Install/Update dialog, Eclipse took care of creating an internal file named .eclipseUM.

Installing Local and Update Site Plug-ins in the Same Location

Could you have installed this plug-in into the first external directory you created (c:\eclipse-plugins\eclipse)? The answer is a qualified yes. Qualified because the Install/Update mechanism is expecting to find a file named .eclipseUM in the directory where the plug-in is being installed to. The contents of the file are three name/value pairs:

```
id=org.eclipse.platform
name=Eclipse Platform
version=3.0.0
```

If you were to create .eclipseUM in the c:\eclipse-plugin\eclipse directory with these contents, the Install/Update dialog would have recognized it as a valid local update site and listed it in the Install Location page. When you do a local install from a zip file, the .eclipseUM file is not necessary, but to successfully install a plug-in from an update site, this file must exist.

The Install dialog now displays two installation directories: the standard Eclipse plugins directory and your new c:\eclipse-plugins\update-manager directory (see Figure 8.8). Select c:\eclipse-plugins\update-manager and click Finish. When the Jar Verification dialog appears, click Install. Eclipse will ask to be restarted when the installation is complete, so click Yes.

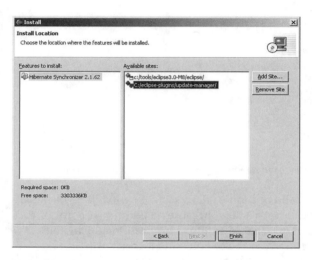

FIGURE 8.8   The Install Location page of the Update/Install dialog displaying the available installation directories.

Let's check for the installation of Hibernate Synchronizer. This plug-in does not contribute a new perspective, but it does contribute a new editor specific to .hbm files, templates, and wizards. The first thing you can check is the Eclipse About dialog (Help, About Eclipse Platform). Click Plug-in Details and you will find the entry HibernateSynchronizer Plug-in near the bottom of the list. The provider listed is Joe Hudson, and the table is sorted by provider (see Figure 8.9).

The next thing to check is the inclusion of the Hibernate Synchronizer editor. Open the Preferences dialog and go to Workbench, File Associations. Under file type, select *.hbm. The Synchronizer editor is the only listed editor for that file type (see Figure 8.10). Success once again!

Installing a plug-in that you have locally using the Install/Update feature is a little different, but not by much. The Install/Update capability expects whatever you are installing to have a features directory. If it does not, Eclipse will not recognize the plug-in as valid. Most plug-ins do not have a features directory, even though it is recommended that all plug-ins have one. If you have a plug-in that includes a features directory, the process is almost identical to the process of installing from an update site.

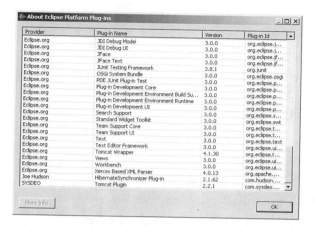

FIGURE 8.9 HibernateSynchronizer Plug-in listed on the second-to-last line of the Plug-in Details window.

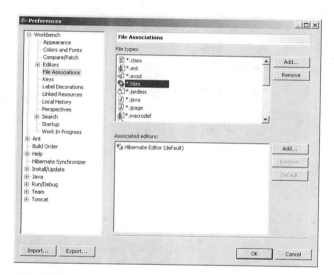

FIGURE 8.10 The Preferences dialog displaying the file association between .hbm files and the Hibernate editor.

For the purposes of this exercise, I have selected the JFaceDbc plug-in, which at the time of this writing was one of the few plug-ins that included a features directory. JFaceDbc is a database plug-in by Joe Hudson (joe@binamics.com). It installs a new perspective with seven additional views, a SQL editor, and a selection of plug-in extension points to extend the plug-in if you are so inclined. In order to keep all these files within reach of each other, create a downloads directory under c:\eclipse-plugins. Create another directory under downloads called jfacedbc.

Download JFaceDbc from

`http://sourceforge.net/projects/jfacedbc/`

At the time of this writing, the latest version of JFaceDbc was 2.2.1. Expand the zip file into `c:\eclipse-plugins\downloads\jfacedbc`.

Let's walk through the process of installing this local plug-in, with a `features` directory, using the Install/Update mechanism:

1. Do not exit Eclipse.

2. Select Help, Software Updates, Find and Install to open the Install dialog.

3. Once again, select Search for New Features to Install and then click Next.

4. On the Update Sites To Visit page, click Add Local Site, navigate to `c:\eclipse-plugins\downloads\jfacedbc`, and click OK.

5. The Install dialog will display the path in the Sites to Include in Search list. Uncheck Hibernate Synchronizer and check `c:\eclipse-plugins\downloads\jfacedbc`. Click Next.

6. In the Search Results page, check JFaceDbc and click Next.

7. On the Feature License page, accept the license and again click Next.

8. The Install Location page will display JFaceDbc 2.2.1 as the feature to install, and you must select `c:\eclipse-plugins\update-manager` as the installation location. Click Finish to start the install process.

9. The system will not display the Install dialog; it simply goes into the installation process. When it is finished, it will ask for permission to restart Eclipse. Click Yes.

If the install completed successfully, the JFaceDbc Welcome page should be opened when Eclipse restarts, and you should be able to find the JFaceDbc plug-in listed in the About dialog by clicking the Plug-in Details button. Another check would be to click the Open Perspective button in the shortcut bar, select Other, and then see whether JFaceDbc is an available perspective.

The installation of an archived site is as simple as finding a plug-in file that has both `features` and `plugins` directories and `site.xml`. In step 4 in the preceding list, instead of clicking Add Local site, you click Add Archived Site. Eclipse will display a standard File dialog to display either JAR or zip files.

With all this installation activity, you might think that Eclipse could end up with more plug-ins than you need. Aside from the fact that Eclipse only loads a plug-in when it is used, it is very straightforward to disable or delete a plug-in.

As of this writing, the simplest way to uninstall a plug-in is to delete the directories in which the plug-in was installed when you extracted the file. It used to be that you could just delete the directories where the plug-in files are located to uninstall it. Due to possible dependencies between plug-ins, there is always the possibility that the removal of a plug-in will have a negative effect on one or more plug-ins. For example, the Omondo UML plug-in is dependent on the Eclipse Modeling Framework (EMF) and the Graphical Editing Framework (GEF), so removing either plug-in will cause the Omondo plug-in to stop working.

Rather than uninstall a plug-in, you also have the ability to disable the directory where the plug-in is located. Let's disable the Hibernate Synchronizer plug-in. From the main menu, select Help, Software Updates, Manage Configuration. From this window you can either disable an entire directory of plug-ins or individual items. Select file:C:/eclipse-plugins/update-manager in the tree view to the left and click Disable or right-click and select Disable from the pop-up menu. A dialog will open asking for confirmation of the disabling of all the features under the C:/eclipse-plugins/update-manager directory. Click OK. When the Restart dialog appears, click Yes. To check whether the features under that directory have been disabled, open the About dialog and check the listing of plug-ins by clicking the Plug-in Details button. You can reenable a disabled plug-in by opening Manage Configuration, selecting the disabled plug-in, and clicking Enable.

Displaying and Configuring Plug-Ins

Some of the information in this section might seem repetitious to you, but I think it is important to take a look at how Eclipse displays and configures plug-ins you add yourself. Let's take a look at where you can add visibility to a plug-in to make accessing it as convenient as possible.

In this chapter, you have added three plug-ins. However, if you were to examine any of the menus or buttons where views or perspectives are displayed, you would not find any of the plug-ins listed. For example, opening the New dialog after selecting File, New, Other will display choices from two of the four plug-ins. Sometimes it is convenient to have a selection of views or perspectives listed as default items in the main menu or in pop-up menus. For the following examples, you will set up JFaceDbc as the target plug-in.

From the main menu, select Window, Customize Perspective. The Customize Perspective dialog is divided into two areas: Shortcuts and Commands. The Shortcuts tab is where you control what is displayed in the menus when you are trying to create new resources, open perspectives, and/or show views. From the drop-down list under Submenus, select New and check JFaceDbc from the list to the left (see Figure 8.11).

Change the Submenus drop-down to Open Perspective and check JFaceDbc from the list to the right. Select Show View from the drop-down. Then, after selecting (but not checking) JFaceDbc on the left, check Connections and Database Structure View from the list on the right (see Figure 8.12). Click OK.

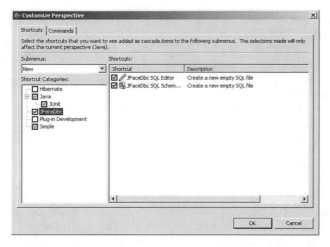

FIGURE 8.11   The Customize Perspective dialog with JFaceDbc checked.

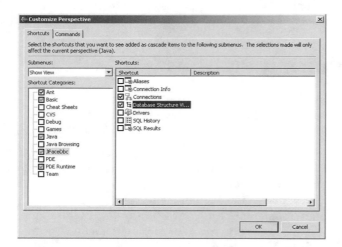

FIGURE 8.12   The Customize Perspective dialog with two of the seven views for JFaceDbc checked.

Check the changes you have just made, one at a time.

- Right-click in the Package Explorer and select New. The two JFaceDbc selections have been added to the list of default choices (see Figure 8.13).

- Click the Open Perspectives button in the shortcut bar to the left, and JFaceDbc is listed as an available perspective (see Figure 8.14). Selecting Other also displays JFaceDbc as an available perspective, but the point of the exercise is to add a new default to the pop-up menus.

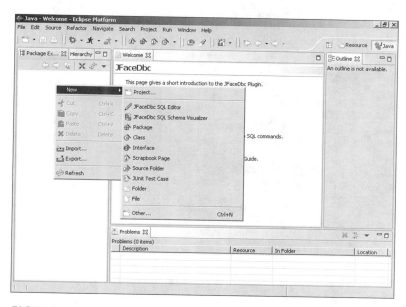

FIGURE 8.13   The JFaceDbc SQL Editor and Schema Visualizer added to the default new resources list.

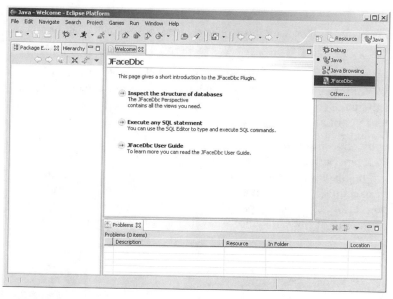

FIGURE 8.14   JFaceDbc added to the default available perspectives.

■ Finally, select Window, Show View from the main menu, and Connections and Database Structure View appear in the default view list (see Figure 8.15).

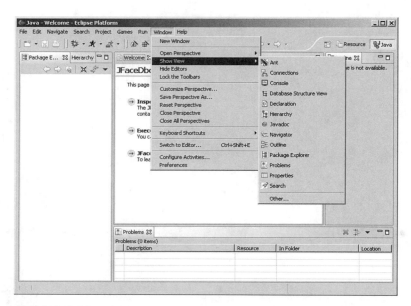

FIGURE 8.15   The JFaceDbc Connections and Database Structure View added to the default list of available views.

Configuring a plug-in is the same as configuring any other part of Eclipse: You open the Preferences dialog and search for an entry in the list to the left that matches the desired plug-in. In the case of JFaceDbc, there are two pages: one to set up defaults for the execution of SQL statements, and another to configure the JFaceDbc SQL editor.

Open the Preferences dialog by choosing Window, Preferences. Select JFaceDbc from the tree view on the left. The first Preferences page for JFaceDbc (see Figure 8.16) lets you set the maximum number of lines to be displayed when previewing SQL output, the maximum number of lines to get when executing SQL, whether to auto-commit lines of SQL, and whether to turn on auto-completion. The second page (JFaceDbc, SQL Editor) allows you to configure the SQL editor with many of the same choices available with the Java editor (see Figure 8.17).

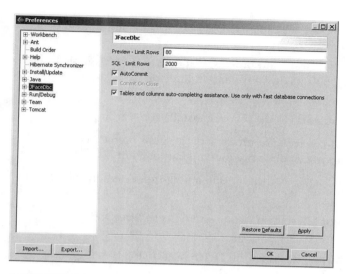

FIGURE 8.16   The JFaceDbc Preferences page.

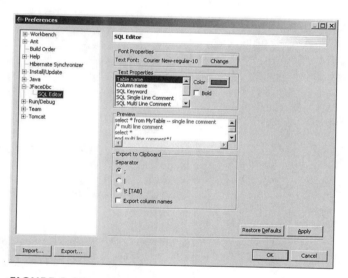

FIGURE 8.17   The JFaceDbc SQL Editor Preferences page.

In Brief

Finding and installing plug-ins is a straightforward process, made all the more simple by Eclipse's ability to find plug-ins located in its own installation directory or in arbitrary locations.

- You can install a plug-in by extracting it into Eclipse's installation directory.

- You can install a plug-in in an arbitrary location by adding a `links` directory with a `.link` properties file that lists in which directory plug-ins can be found.

- Using the Install/Update functionality, you can install a plug-in located on an external site as well as a local directory.

- The Customize Perspective dialog allows you to add shortcuts to JFaceDbc for the creation of new resources, a new perspective, and a collection of new views.

- You can configure the JFaceDbc plug-in using the Preferences dialog to set up basic defaults for the SQL editor and the execution of SQL statements.

J2EE and the MyEclipse Plug-In

9

*"Abstracting many of the complexities of an intractable system
can be very expensive. In this case, $30."*

—Anonymous

J2EE and Eclipse

Out of the box, Eclipse does an incredible job with Java
development. The editor is impressive, the incremental
compiler gives Java the feel of a scripting language, and
the various views give you numerous ways to view your
resources and be a better developer. Of course, Java technology is not about plain-vanilla Java, but about Java's
(rather large) niche on the server side. The Java 2
Enterprise Edition is not about standalone applications,
but about hosting a controlled distributed computing environment where components can run in a robust fashion
accessible to many different kinds of clients.

When it comes to J2EE and its high-abstraction framework,
Eclipse falls short. Various plug-in developers have stepped
into the vacuum and implemented tools to assist in the
development of certain facets of J2EE applications, but it
wasn't until the Lomboz plug-in (http://www.lomboz.com)
that an integrated plug-in was available to help in the
complex world of J2EE. Soon after, Genuitec began to
collect the plug-ins of various developers and repacked
them into a larger fully integrated plug-in called
MyEclipse. One install takes care of adding numerous plug-
ins to give you the tool support for J2EE technologies such
as servlets, JSPs, EJBs, and Struts. MyEclipse is not free (it
has a 30 day trial period), but for $30 you have a full year's

use of the product as well as support and all the updates you can handle. Genuitec has been funding the implementation of MyEclipse, and the plug-in is quite useful for J2EE development.

I'll assume you are familiar with servlets, JSPs, and EJBs; if you are not, this chapter is going to be a waste of time, as will most of the chapters in this section on plug-ins. A number of very good books and resources are available that discuss various J2EE technologies, but this is not one of them. Where covering a particular technology will help to explain what a tool is doing, an explanation will be given.

You will now download and install MyEclipse, implement servlets, JSPs, and EJBs.

Downloading and Installing MyEclipse

If you have the Sysdeo Tomcat plug-in installed, or any plug-in that controls Tomcat, make sure you uninstall it before going through any of these steps.

The MyEclipse plug-in can be found at `http://www.myeclipseide.com`. You will have to register to see the download list, but once you do, you can download the `EnterpriseWorkbenchInstaller_nnnnnn.exe` file onto your PC. Make sure that the file corresponds with the version of Eclipse you are running. During the milestone builds prior to the final release of 3.0, it was difficult for all the plug-in developers to keep up with the subtle changes being made to the plug-in extension points.

Let's walk through the installation procedure, starting with the basics:

1. Start Eclipse.

2. Close all open perspectives.

3. Exit Eclipse.

4. Double-click the MyEclipse file.

The MyEclipse installer walks you through the necessary steps to install the MyEclipse Workbench:

1. The first two pages of the dialog are informational. Read them and move along by clicking Next.

2. The Choose Eclipse Folder page is where you get to enter the location of Eclipse that will be using MyEclipse. The directory you enter (or navigate to using the Choose button) must end in `eclipse`. Click Next.

3. Choose Install Folder is the easiest page to get wrong. The installer wants to know where it should install the MyEclipse plug-in files; it is not recommended that you install them into the Eclipse directory. Wherever you install MyEclipse, make sure that

the path has MyEclipse as the last component; otherwise, the various pieces will be installed incorrectly. Click Next.

4. The Choose Shortcut Folder page can be left alone. Click Next.

5. You are one step short of installing the MyEclipse Workbench. Check that the path for the install folder ends in MyEclipse and that the Eclipse home path is correct. If the Eclipse home directory is wrong and you install MyEclipse into it, you will probably have to reinstall Eclipse and then install MyEclipse again. If everything is correct, click Install.

6. The installation page displays a progress bar that will automatically advance to the next page when the install is done.

7. When the install is complete, the Release Notes page will ask if you want to see the current release notes. It is to your advantage to read the release notes so you understand where MyEclipse stands with a particular release, but this is optional. Click Next.

8. The Install Complete page lets you know that the installer has done its job. Click Done.

You can confirm that the installation was successful by starting Eclipse and checking that MyEclipse has been added to the main menu and then opening the Preferences dialog (Window, Preferences). The MyEclipse node has additional subnodes for the configuration of app servers, editors, project structures, and XDoclet. Also, you can enter your subscription code on the MyEclipse, Subscription page.

If you are curious as to what MyEclipse did to install itself, go to your Eclipse installation directory. You will find a links directory that wasn't there before (unless you have been implementing the examples in previous chapters). The links directory will contain the file com.genuitec.eclipse.MyEclipse.link. The only information in the file is a name/value pair that directs Eclipse to add a new directory to its plug-ins search path:

```
path=C:\\tools\\eclipse3.0-M8\\MyEclipse
```

The information in your file will vary based on where you installed Eclipse. The preceding path is specific to my machine.

If you have not already downloaded Tomcat, do so now. You can download it from http://jakarta.apache.org/site/binindex.cgi (scroll down until you see latest Tomcat build) and install it anywhere on your hard drive that is convenient. In order to install Tomcat, you only need to unzip the installation file onto your file system. For use in this chapter, installing it to a directory named C:\tools is convenient.

In addition, MyEclipse expects a directory named temp to exist under your Tomcat installation. Open a Windows Explorer and create temp in your Tomcat home directory (for example, C:\tools\jakarta-tomcat-5.0.25\temp).

Before using Tomcat, you must configure it for MyEclipse's use. From the main menu, select Window, Preferences, and from the Preferences dialog, select MyEclipse. Open the MyEclipse, Application Servers node and select Tomcat 5 (see Figure 9.1). Click the Enable button so that the server will appear in the toolbar with Start and Stop menu items; then click the Browse button next to the Tomcat Home Directory field. Navigate to the Tomcat home directory and click Open. The wizard will take care of filling in the remaining fields using the home directory as its starting point.

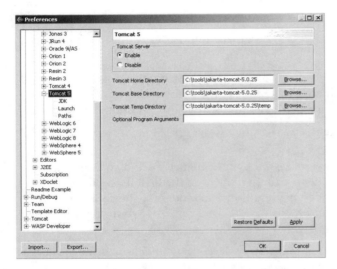

FIGURE 9.1   The Application Server Tomcat 5 page with the Enable button selected and the various required directories filled in.

Select Tomcat 5, JDK from the list to the left in the Preferences dialog. Click Add next to the Tomcat JDK drop-down button to open the Tomcat > Add JVM dialog (see Figure 9.2). Enter a descriptive name in the JRE Name field, such as J2SDK1.4.2_03, and click the Browse button next to the JRE Home Directory field. Navigate to the home directory of your Java SDK and click OK. The remaining fields of the dialog are filled with information based on the path you entered. Click OK. Your new JDK configuration should be the selected item in the Tomcat JDK name field.

Still in the Preferences dialog, select MyEclipse, Application Servers, Tomcat 5, Launch. The Launch page sets the startup mode of the server: Debug or Run. Click Run mode, for faster startup during your development, and then click OK. You are finished with the MyEclipse Tomcat configuration.

Now that the MyEclipse Workbench is installed and recognized by Eclipse, and you have Tomcat installed and configured, let's implement a few J2EE applications.

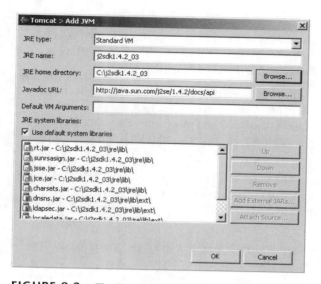

FIGURE 9.2 The Tomcat > Add JVM dialog allows you to configure a JDK target for Tomcat.

Using MyEclipse to Implement Web Applications

MyEclipse has wizards for the creation of the following:

- Enterprise Application Projects
- EJB Module Projects and EJBs
- Web Module Projects, HTML, servlets, and JSPs
- XML files
- Applets
- Struts Modules

You will get a chance to use all these (except for applets) in one capacity or another in the examples in this chapter.

Creating Enterprise Application Projects

The first question that must be asked is, to which server are you deploying? You are going to create a servlet/JSP/Struts-based application, so it is acceptable to start with a server such as Tomcat because it is included in so many application servers as its servlet engine. Make sure you configured MyEclipse to recognize the location of your Tomcat installation. If at any time during the Tomcat server startup a problem is encountered, first check the Preferences dialog configuration of Tomcat under MyEclipse. The most common errors are to have an incorrect Tomcat home directory and not to have the JDK set properly.

The J2EE specification states that a J2EE application belongs in an Enterprise Application Archive (EAR) file, which is made up of individual Web modules. An EAR file is really an aggregation point for the various parts of one or more Web applications. For completeness sake, you will start by creating an Enterprise Application Project and a Web Module Project.

Let's build the beginning of a Web-based call center application. The Web application includes an opening page to allow support staff to look up the information about a customer based on the customer's phone number. You will create an enterprise archive file that will point to the Web application and eventually to an EJB that will act as a customer search service.

To create an Enterprise Application Project, press Ctrl+N to open the New dialog. MyEclipse adds a J2EE project category with three project types and four categories. You will get a chance to create items from every level of the J2EE category as we proceed, but for now select J2EE and Enterprise Application Project. Click Next.

In the New Enterprise Application Project page, enter the project name CallCenterEAR. This page is where you create the basis for your EAR file and also have the opportunity to create a Web or EJB project at the same time, so the Web or EJB project will be automatically associated with the Enterprise Application Project. In this case, uncheck the Define EJB Project Modules item and leave Define Web Project Modules checked as you will be creating a Web application first. Click Next.

The Define Web Project Modules page is where you set up the initial configuration for your Web application. Check the option Create Web Project Module to enable the fields listed on the page. Make sure the information listed on your page matches the following:

- **Project Name**—CallCenterWeb

- **Location**—Use Default Location is checked. (Feel free to change this to your preferred project workspace location.)

- **Source Folder**—src

- **Web Root Folder**—WebRoot

- **Context Root URL**—/CallCenter

You changed the project name from CallCenterEARWeb to CallCenterWeb and the context root URL from CallCenterEARWeb to CallCenter to make it easier to type as a URL when you finally deploy your Web application. You can name your context root anything you like within the standard Web server naming constraints. Click Next to view the Summary page, which lists the EAR and Web projects to be created. Click Finish. The Confirm Perspective Switch dialog may open, asking for permission to change from your current perspective to the MyEclipse perspective. Click Yes.

Just to confirm what you have just done, open the CallCenterEAR project in the Package Explorer and then open the META-INF directory. Double-click the application.xml file to open it in the XML editor supplied with MyEclipse. The XML file lists the CallCenterWeb.war file as a component of the Enterprise Application and changes its context name to /CallCenter, as shown here:

```
<?xml version="1.0" encoding="UTF-8"?>
<!DOCTYPE application PUBLIC "-//Sun Microsystems, Inc.//DTD J2EE Application 1.3//EN"
➡ "http://java.sun.com/dtd/application_1_3.dtd">
<application>
    <display-name>CallCenter</display-name>
    <module id="myeclipse.1076791914090">
        <web>
            <web-uri>CallCenterWeb.war</web-uri>
            <context-root>/CallCenter</context-root>
        </web>
    </module>
</application>
```

If you had not changed the context root name, the default context URL would have been the name of the Web project (for example, because the name of the project is CallCenterWeb, the .war file that would have been created would be named CallCenterWeb.war and the context URL would have been /CallCenterWeb). Close the editor window by clicking the X in the tab or by pressing Ctrl+F4.

Creating Web Module Projects

The Web application is going to do three things:

- Display an input HTML page.
- Execute a servlet to perform a search.
- Display the dynamic output from the servlet in a JSP.

Because the creation of the Enterprise Project created a Web project as well, you will use the existing CallCenterWeb project to create the HTML, servlet, and JSP. In the Package Explorer, select CallCenterWeb, WebRoot. WebRoot is the location where the HTML and JSP files will be stored.

To create the HTML page, press Ctrl+N to open the New dialog. Select J2EE, Web, HTML and then click Next. In the HTML Wizard page, change the filename to search.html, leave the other fields unchanged, and click Finish. The search.html file opens in the MyEclipse HTML Editor, which has two tabs displayed at the bottom of the editor: Source and Preview. The Source tab is selected first and displays the HTML for a stubbed-out search.html page. Notice the string "This is my HTML page." located between the <body> tags. Click Preview to see the HTML displayed as a browser page.

Return to the Source view of the HTML editor. Remove all the code between <head></head> and <body></body> and save the file:

```
<!DOCTYPE HTML PUBLIC "-//W3C//DTD HTML 4.01 Transitional//EN">
<html>
    <head>
    </head>

    <body>
    </body>
</html>
```

Insert a blank line in between the <head> tags and press Ctrl+spacebar. All the possible tags available to you are displayed in the Content Assist window (see Figure 9.3). Type <ti, and the only selection that will be left is <TITLE>. Press Enter, and the editor will fill in the opening tag. Move the cursor to the end of the current line and press Ctrl+spacebar again. The second entry is </TITLE>. Move the cursor to the closing tag for <TITLE> and press Enter to have the editor display it. Save the file.

Configuring the MyEclipse JSP Editor

Let's briefly examine some of the configuration options for the HTML editor. In the Preferences dialog (Window, Preferences) under MyEclipse, Editors, you can find the node for the JSP/HTML Editor. Under the General tab, when you check Use Separate Settings, you control the following basic editor functions:

- The location of the print margin

- The display the overview ruler

- The display of line numbers

- Highlight of the current line

- The display of a print margin

- The customization of the colors used for line highlighting, the line number foreground, and the print margin

FIGURE 9.3 The Content Assist window listing the available tags for the HTML page.

You can switch these items back to their default values by unchecking Use Separate Settings. The one piece of JSP functionality in this tab is the ability to turn off JSP compilation when you save the file.

The Colors and Format tabs present the functionality you would expect. The Colors tab has the same functionality as the Syntax tab in the Java editor: You can select a background color for the entire editor and individual colors for various syntactical tokens (HTML tag names, JSP directives, and so on). The Format tab lists various formatting options, including a preview window to see the effect the changes will have on a sample file (see Figure 9.4). I generally set my tab size to 4, insert spaces for tabs, use lowercase HTML tags, force a line break before and after all tags, remove superfluous line feeds, and update all the tags to reflect a consistent case (all lowercase, in my case).

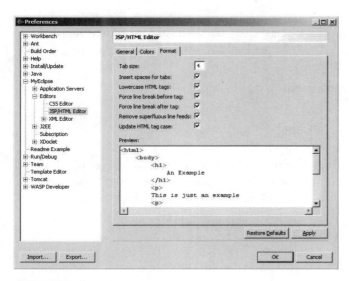

FIGURE 9.4 The Format tab for the JSP/HTML editor.

If you made any formatting changes to the JSP/HTML editor, make sure you press Ctrl+Shift+F to have the editor reformat the file. For example, any tabs will be changed to spaces if you selected that as a formatting option.

Setting Up the Input HTML Page

Add a title (Call Center Customer Search Page), a header (Enter a customer phone number), and a form to search.html. The title should be in the <head> section, and the header and the form should be in the <body> section. The form will take in a phone number to be sent to the (as yet unwritten) servlet. Note that after each of the following steps, I pressed Ctrl+Shift+F to reformat the code; therefore, your code may look different:

1. Add the title within the <head> tags:

```
<head>
    <title>
        Call Center Customer Search Page
    </title>
</head>
```

2. Add the header within <h2> tags within <body>:

```
<body>
    <h2>Enter a customer phone number.</h2>
</body>
```

3. Within the <body> tags, add the <form> tags. Use Ctrl+spacebar for Content Assist to present the available valid tags:

```
<body>
    <h2>Enter a customer phone number.</h2>
    <form>
    </form>
</body>
```

4. Within the opening <form> tag, add a space and press Ctrl+spacebar to see the list of available attributes for form tags. Add name="searchForm", method="POST", and target="search" (make sure there is no leading slash in front of "search"):

```
<form name="searchForm" method="post" action="search" >
</form>
```

5. Insert a line in between the <form> tags. Add a label for the phone number field and add an input field of type input:

```
<form name="searchForm" method="post" action="search" >
    Phone number:
    <input type="input" name="phoneNumber" />
</form>
```

6. Add a line break tag, `<br>`, after the `<input>` line. Add a button to the form using the `<input>` tag. Give the button a name and a value of `"submit"`. Use Ctrl+spacebar whenever possible:

```
<form name="searchForm" method="post" action="search" >
    Phone number:
    <input type="input" name="phoneNumber" />
    <br>
    <input type="submit" value="Submit" />
</form>
```

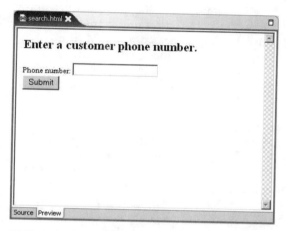

FIGURE 9.5   The preview of the HTML page.

FIGURE 9.6   The Project Deployments dialog.

7. Click the Preview tab at the bottom of the editor to take a look at your HTML page (see Figure 9.5).

Deploying the Web Application

To deploy the HTML (or servlets, JSPs, or EJBs), you need to create a MyEclipse project deployment entry. In the Package Explorer, right-click the CallCenterWeb project and select MyEclipse, Add and Remove Project Deployments from the pop-up menu. This feature is also available from the toolbar. The Project Deployments dialog opens, displaying an empty page, so you must select CallCenterWeb from the drop-down (see Figure 9.6). Click Add to enter a new deployment. The New Deployment dialog will open. Select Tomcat 5 from the drop-down and click Finish.

An entry for CallCenterWeb is now available for use to deploy your Web application to Tomcat. When the entry is first entered, MyEclipse deploys it to the target so Tomcat is ready to be started. Click OK to close the Project Deployments dialog.

Make sure you do not have any other processes listening on port 8080 because this is the default port for Tomcat. The easiest way to discover whether you have any other processes already listening to port 8080 is to simply run Tomcat from a command prompt window and see if a message appears in an output window that reads similar to this:

```
java.net.BindException: Address already in use: JVM_Bind:8080
```

Another choice is to download a freeware program called ActivePorts that lists all the processes listening on sockets on your machine. You can download ActivePorts from

```
http://www.snapfiles.com/get/activeports.html
```

After installing and running ActivePorts, you can sort the list by ports and check to see if anyone is using 8080. If you do have another process listening on 8080, you can either stop the process (recommended for this chapter) or change the port Tomcat uses by modifying server.xml. The server.xml file can be found under the Tomcat conf directory. Perform a search for the string 8080, and when you find the <Connector> element, change the value 8080 to a free port number (for example, 8090). If you decide to change the port assignment of your Tomcat installation, make sure you use the new value everywhere this chapter refers to port 8080.

FIGURE 9.7   The Run Server button on the toolbar displaying Tomcat 5, Start.

On the toolbar is a group with only two buttons. One of the two is a running guy with a large smiling face behind him. Click the little downward-pointing triangle next to the running guy to open up the Tomcat menu that has items for starting and stopping the previously configured Tomcat server (see Figure 9.7). Click on Tomcat 5, Start. The Console view will open and display Tomcat's output. The server will have completed its startup when the output has a message that looks something like the following:

```
INFO: Server startup in 11106 ms
```

Double-clicking the title bar of the Console will maximize the size of the view so that you can see your output better. Remember to double-click it again to restore its last size.

Open a browser window and enter the target address http://localhost:8080/CallCenter/search.html (see Figure 9.8).

Implementing a Controller Servlet

Next, let's create a servlet. By rights, the only thing you should have to do is create a Java project and create a class that extends javax.servlet.http.HttpServlet. Unfortunately, the directory structure expected of a Web application is different from a standard project, so you need to either create a project and take care of building the directory required by a Web application, including creating a web.xml file, or let Eclipse, with the help of the MyEclipse Workbench, take care of the task for you.

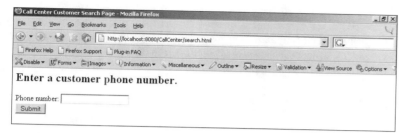

FIGURE 9.8 The HTML output of `search.html`.

The CallCenterWeb project, as a Web module, is already structured for Web application use. All that remains is to create a servlet, make sure it is recognized by Tomcat, create a JSP that will display the customer information, and modify the servlet to send back an object with customer data.

Create a servlet using MyEclipse by doing the following:

1. Press Ctrl+N to open the New dialog. Select J2EE, Web, Servlet and then click Next.

2. Enter `SearchServlet` and `kickstart.j2ee.servlet` into the Name and Package fields, respectively. Notice that Superclass is already set to `javax.servlet.http.HttpServlet`. In the Options area, the only fields that need to be checked are Create Inherited Methods and Create doPost. The form is defined as using method POST, so `doPost()` is the method that will be called. Click Next.

3. The XML Wizard page is where you enter the information for the `web.xml` file. Leave the Generate/Map web.xml option checked. To make the URL used by the HTML page more legible, change the Servlet/JSP Mapping URL from `/servlet/SearchServlet` to `/search`, which is how it is called in `search.html`. You can change the Display Name and Description fields if you like, but they are purely informational. Click Finish.

Two new files will open: `web.xml` and `SearchServlet.java`. Let's take a brief look at them and then run what you have so far. The `web.xml` file contains the Web application–specific configuration (see Listing 9.1), whereas `SearchServlet` is the entry point into the CallCenter search capability.

LISTING 9.1 `web.xml`

```
<?xml version="1.0" encoding="UTF-8"?>
<!DOCTYPE web-app PUBLIC "-//Sun Microsystems, Inc.//DTD Web Application 2.3//EN"
➡ "http://java.sun.com/dtd/web-app_2_3.dtd">
<web-app>
  <servlet>
    <servlet-name>SearchServlet</servlet-name>
    <display-name>This is the display name of my J2EE component</display-name>
```

LISTING 9.1   Continued

```
    <description>This is the description of my J2EE component</description>
    <servlet-class>kickstart.j2ee.servlet.SearchServlet</servlet-class>
  </servlet>
  <servlet-mapping>
    <servlet-name>SearchServlet</servlet-name>
    <url-pattern>/search</url-pattern>
  </servlet-mapping>
</web-app>
```

Click the editor tab for web.xml. The first thing you should notice is that the editor does not display line numbers. You configured the Java editor and the HTML editor to display line numbers, but this is the MyEclipse XML editor. If you want to see line numbers and substitute spaces for tabs, open the Preferences dialog, navigate down to MyEclipse, Editors, XML Editor, Style, and then check Show Line Numbers and Insert Spaces for Tabs. Unfortunately, the Ctrl+Shift+F keyboard shortcut does not work.

Now that you have line numbers, let's examine web.xml. Go to <display-name> and change the text to "Call Center Customer System". You can leave <description> alone. The rest of the information is as we entered it, including <servlet-mapping><url-pattern>, which you changed to /search.

An interesting element in web.xml is the use of <welcome-file-list>. The web.xml file is used to configure everything about a particular Web application, including error pages and the like. Manually add <welcome-file-list> after </servlet-mapping>, and within <welcome-file-list> add <welcome-file>. Within the <welcome-file> element, add search.html. This change means that a user of the site just has to type in http:// localhost:8080/CallCenter to get the search page.

Without making any other changes, you are going to redeploy the Web application and restart Tomcat. The changes you made to web.xml are purely cosmetic. You would have been able to deploy even without the changes. MyEclipse generates a good web.xml and servlet file right out of the wizard.

To rerun and check the application, follow these steps:

1. Redeploy the Web application. Right-click the CallCenterWeb project and select MyEclipse, Add and Remove Project Deployments or, on the toolbar, select the button directly to the left of the running guy with the smiling face behind him. When the Project Deployments dialog opens, make sure that Project is set to CallCenterWeb, select the only entry in the deployment list, and then click Redeploy. A progress dialog will briefly appear and disappear. Click OK.

2. Look in the Console view. The following message may appear:

   ```
   INFO: Reloading this Context has started
   ```

This message means that the deployment was successful and recognized by Tomcat. If you see any other messages, stop Tomcat and redeploy. If you get an error message after the redeploy, wait a few seconds and redeploy again. When you get an error-free redeployment, restart Tomcat. This step is necessary because you need Tomcat to reload the `web.xml` file, which is only read once unless Tomcat reloads the Web application. If you have to restart Tomcat, then monitor its output in the Console until you see the "INFO: Server startup" message.

3. Open a browser and enter `http://localhost:8080/CallCenter`. The `search.html` page should be displayed again. Click the Submit button, and the output from the servlet should appear (see Figure 9.9).

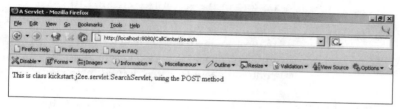

FIGURE 9.9 The `SearchServlet` streamed this HTML output when it was called by `search.html`.

If the HTML page does not fire the servlet, check that the form is using the `action` attribute with `"search"`.

Adding a JSP as the Data View
In this next step, the servlet is going to forward the request to a JSP. You will create the JSP first, add forwarding code to the servlet, and check the flow under Tomcat before we update the servlet to return an object for the JSP to display.

Create the JSP using the following steps:

1. Select the CallCenterWeb project in Package Explorer. Selecting it will allow the wizard to prefill many of the fields you would otherwise have to fill in.

2. Press Ctrl+N and select J2EE, Web, JSP from the New dialog. Click Next.

3. The JSP Wizard page is where you decide what kind of JSP to create. You have four templates to choose from. You are going to use the default JSP template, but if this were a Struts app, you could select one of the two Struts JSP templates or the default HTML template you have already used. Leave the template set to its default and change the filename from `MyJsp.jsp` to `results.jsp`. Click Finish.

If all has gone well, you have `results.jsp` opened along side the other three files. However, Eclipse does bring its own JSP editor, which is not much better than the plain-text editor it uses when your `results.jsp` file was created. Close the `results.jsp` file, open the

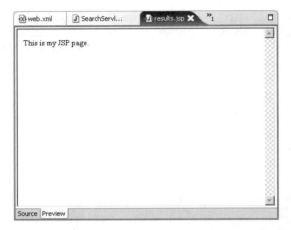

FIGURE 9.10   The preview of the JSP page to which the SearchServlet will forward the request.

Preferences dialog, and go to Window, File Associations to change the default JSP editor assignment. From the File Types list, select *.jsp. In the Associated Editors window, select MyEclipse JSP Editor. Click Default to make the MyEclipse editor the default for JSP files (the word *default* should be appended to the selected editor). Double-click the results.jsp file from the Package Explorer view to open the file. Look at the expected output of results.jsp by clicking the Preview tab at the bottom of the editor (see Figure 9.10).

You are now going to forward the incoming request to results.jsp. Click the editor tab for SearchServlet.java. Delete all the code in doPost(). The compiler will complain about the extraneous import of java.io.PrintWriter, so remove it by pressing Ctrl+Shift+O. Save the file. Add a call to forward() from the RequestDispatcher sending the incoming request and response:

```
public void doPost(
    HttpServletRequest request,
    HttpServletResponse response)
    throws ServletException, IOException {
    getServletContext().getRequestDispatcher("/results.jsp")
    ➥.forward(request, response);
}
```

The Web application is ready to go again. The search page will send the form information to the servlet, which will forward the request to the results page. Stop Tomcat, redeploy CallCenterWeb from the Add and Remove Web Deployments dialog, and then restart Tomcat. Open (or refresh) your browser to http://localhost:8080/CallCenter and click Submit. A few seconds will pass while the request is handled because the first time any JSP is called, it goes through its standard processes to generate, compile, load, initialize, and start the code, but eventually you will see in your browser the output you saw in the JSP editor preview.

Let's modify the servlet and JSP to display some data. In a standard Web application, an HTML form would send a collection of information to a servlet, which would take care of finding data based on the incoming request, and then the servlet would send this new information to a JSP for display. Let's fake the lookup of a customer by phone number by returning a collection of strings for display. Click the SearchServlet editor, add code to store some strings in a Hashtable, and put the Hashtable object in the request object:

```java
public void doPost(HttpServletRequest request,
                   HttpServletResponse response)
                     throws ServletException, IOException {
    Hashtable info = new Hashtable(2);
    info.put("name", "Thomas Anderson");
    info.put("street", "42 Wabash Street, Apt. 101");
    info.put("city", "Chicago");
    info.put("state", "Illinois");
    info.put("zipcode", "60615");


    request.setAttribute("results", info);


    getServletContext().getRequestDispatcher("/results.jsp")
.forward(request, response);
    }
```

Update the JSP with `<jsp:useBean>` and get the information out of the `results` object you just finished putting into the request scope. Add a table to keep the appearance of the information neat:

```html
<body>
    <h2>Enter a customer phone number.</h2>
    <form name="searchForm" method="post" action="search" >
        Phone number:
        <input type="input" name="phoneNumber" />
        <br>
        <input type="submit" value="Submit" />
    </form>

    <h2>Customer Results</h2>
    <jsp:useBean id="results" class="java.util.Hashtable" scope="request" />
    <table border="1">
        <tr>
            <td>
              Name
            </td>
            <td>
              <%= results.get("name") %>
            </td>
        </tr>
        <tr>
            <td>
              Street
```

```
            </td>
            <td>
              <%= results.get("street") %>
            </td>
        </tr>
        <tr>
            <td>
              City
            </td>
            <td>
              <%= results.get("city") %>
            </td>
        </tr>
        <tr>
            <td>
              State
            </td>
            <td>
              <%= results.get("state") %>
            </td>
        </tr>
        <tr>
            <td>
              Zipcode
            </td>
            <td>
              <%= results.get("zipcode") %>
            </td>
        </tr>
      </table>
</body>
```

Stop Tomcat again and redeploy. Start Tomcat, open your browser to http://
localhost:8080/CallCenter, and click Submit. An HTML table with the hard-coded
data is displayed (see Figure 9.11).

To make the previous example more "real life," you would have to take a more conventional
approach. A staple of Web development is the use of an HTML form for sending data to a
servlet, which takes care of finding data for display by a JSP. In order to make that flow somewhat object oriented, you would take the form data from the request object and put it into
an object whose only reason for existing is to hold the data and perhaps to copy the data
into another object type or perform data validation.

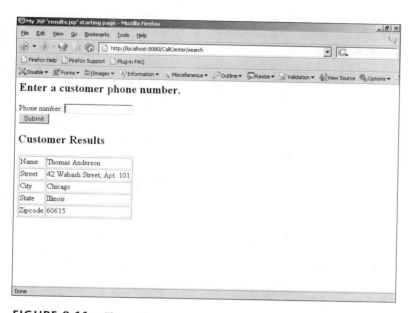

FIGURE 9.11 The results of the empty telephone number search from the welcome page.

Using the previous example, you would leave search.html alone, update SearchServlet to use two additional class types, and implement the two class types, CustomerSearchForm and CustomerSearchService (see Figure 9.12). Listing 9.2 has the servlet creating a form object, performing data validation, and then sending the data (a phone number, in this case) into the search service to retrieve information to be displayed by the JSP (the comments have been removed for brevity).

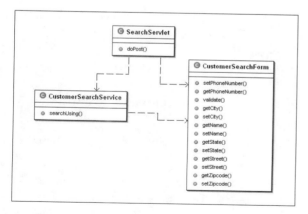

FIGURE 9.12 The SearchServlet and its associations with the CustomerSearchForm and the CustomerSearchService.

LISTING 9.2 SearchServlet.java

```java
public class SearchServlet extends HttpServlet {

    private CustomerSearchService _searchService = new CustomerSearchService();

    public void doPost(HttpServletRequest request, HttpServletResponse response)
        throws ServletException, IOException {

        CustomerSearchForm form = new CustomerSearchForm();
        String phoneNumber = request.getParameter("phoneNumber");
        form.setPhoneNumber(phoneNumber);
        boolean isValid = form.validate();
        if (isValid) {
            Hashtable info = _searchService.searchUsing(phoneNumber);

            request.setAttribute("results", info);
        } else {
            request.setAttribute("errormsg", "Please enter a phone number.");
        }

        getServletContext().getRequestDispatcher("/results.jsp").forward(
            request,
            response);
    }

}
```

The initial HTML page, as a gateway page, really does nothing more than collect data for use by the servlet. The servlet, as a controller object, needs to take many things into account:

- What should happen if the form data is bad?

- What should happen if the form data is good?

- How can the servlet return error messages to the JSP page that is meant to display any retrieved data?

- How will the servlet keep track of error pages based on a particular action taken based on incoming data?

- If the servlet handles requests from multiple pages, how will it keep track of what page is asking for what data?

- If the servlet handles requests from multiple pages, how will it keep track of initialization for each request type?

This is not an exhaustive list. The preceding is not only typical of expected behavior, but the answers are always being reimplemented. When enough similar code is written, some developer somewhere decides to codify it, and in today's environment the codification takes place in the creation of a framework. The J2EE presentation framework many developers have chosen is Struts. The chapter on Struts will look at this same example, but using Struts to reimplement it.

Implementing and Deploying an EJB Using EJB Module Projects

Before moving onto the debugging of Web components, you will have the opportunity to create an EJB within Eclipse, deploy it to an application server that supports an EJB container, have the servlet find the EJB using JNDI, and pass data from the EJB to `results.jsp`.

This example will show you how to do the following:

- Create an EJB project.

- Implement an entity bean.

- Generate the various support files needed by an application server, such as RMI stubs and `ejb-jar.xml`.

- Generate the various support files, such as the home and remote interfaces needed by a client.

- Deploy the EJB to JBoss, a J2EE-compatible application server.

- Update the CustomerSearchService to use the entity bean to retrieve customer information.

In addition, you will download and install the JBoss app server and configure it for use with an entity EJB. Because of the number of variations on the way EJB can be used, this example is going to focus on a single EJB that maps to a single table and returns the same data as before: a name, street, city, state, and ZIP Code based on a customer's current phone number.

The various files created for the app server and the client should go into different JAR files, but during development you will make sure they are visible by updating the appropriate build paths.

EJB Development Using XDoclet

The implementation of all the aforementioned pieces has never been a trivial undertaking, and rather than tackle it anew MyEclipse chose to use XDoclet as its code-generation engine. XDoclet is a code-generation engine that started as a means of creating EJB support files and grew to include many different Java technologies.

XDoclet works through the use of Javadoc tags you add to your code. The tags allow the XDoclet code-generation engine to understand your code and create files appropriate to your current task. The implication is that you have only one file to modify, and XDoclet creates the associated support files. For example, EJBs prior to 3.0 needed seven or more files to be properly deployed. XDoclet let's you worry about the one EJB file that contains the business logic, and the additional files are created when you run an Ant build file. In addition to EJBs, XDoclet also has support for Hibernate (an Object Relational Mapping tool), Java Data Objects, Java Management Extensions, and Portlets, to name a few.

Anyone doing serious EJB development should learn the various <ejbdoclet> tags and their uses in EJB development to take full advantage of XDoclet's code-generation capabilities. Also, because XDoclet can only be used in conjunction with Ant, you should add the various XDoclet code-generation tags to your main build.xml file so XDoclet can create the exact support files needed by your system.

Download and Installing JBoss

In keeping with the free, or almost free, theme of this book, you will run the next example using the JBoss J2EE application server. To download JBoss, open your browser to http://www.jboss.org and surf to the download page. Download the 3.2.3 release, which is the version used to test the example in this chapter. Extract the zip file to a convenient location (for example, into the same directory where you extracted Tomcat, C:\tools). JBoss needs only one other thing to work: a reference to the Java SDK. If you already have JAVA_HOME declared as an environment variable, your JBoss installation is ready to go. If you do not have JAVA_HOME declared, either declare it as an environment variable or edit the JBOSS_HOME/bin/run.bat file to include JAVA_HOME in the batch file.

More Information about JBoss

The JBoss organization sells documentation about its application server, but it also has a free Getting Started manual you can download from http://www.jboss.org/docs/index#free-32x. It includes a quick look at JBoss and how to run some of the standard J2EE examples, such as the ones found in the J2EE Tutorial.

Before using JBoss, you must configure MyEclipse with the location of JBoss and a valid Java SDK, just like you did with Tomcat. From the main menu select Window, Preferences, and when the Preferences dialog opens, select MyEclipse, JBoss 3 (see Figure 9.13). Click Enable in the JBoss Server section to have MyEclipse add JBoss to the MyEclipse app server toolbar button so you can start and stop the app server from within Eclipse. Click Browse and navigate to the JBoss home directory (for example, `c:\tools\jboss-3.2.3`).

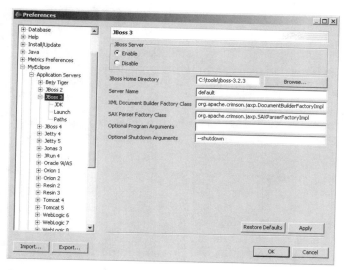

FIGURE 9.13   The MyEclipse configuration page for JBoss.

Select MyEclipse, Application Servers, JBoss 3, JDK from the tree view in the Preferences dialog to the left. This page sets the JDK to be used when JBoss is run from within Eclipse. Because you created a full JDK entry when you configured Tomcat, you can use the same JDK entry for JBoss. From the JBoss JDK Name drop-down button, select J2SDK1.4.2_03.

Update the launch configuration by going to MyEclipse, Application Servers, JBoss 3, Launch. Make sure the launch configuration for JBoss is set to Run Mode and then click OK to close the Preferences dialog.

FIGURE 9.14   The MyEclipse app server toolbar button displaying both JBoss and Tomcat as available servers.

To ensure that all these changes have been accepted, go to the Eclipse toolbar and click the triangle button next to the running guy with the smiling face behind him. JBoss 3 is now on the list of available servers that can be started and stopped from the toolbar (see Figure 9.14). Select JBoss 3, Start and then examine the JBoss output in the Console view. There should be no exceptions or error message displayed, and the server will complete when it states something like the following:

```
19:33:52,919 INFO  [Server] JBoss (MX MicroKernel)
➥ [3.2.3 (build: CVSTag=JBoss_3_2_3 date=200311301445)] Started in 28s:591ms
```

Configuring the Hypersonic Database

Now that you are sure JBoss is operational, you need to configure its default data source, the Hypersonic database, for use with this example. The Hypersonic database is an open-source Java database that can be found at `http://hsqldb.sourceforge.net`. It already ships with JBoss, so you do not need to download any additional software. However, if you want to read up on the capabilities of Hypersonic, you can go to the Hypersonic website and research its many features.

Because the Hypersonic database is already part of the JBoss installation, you can use it for the following example. However, JBoss has external access to Hypersonic turned off by default, so you will have to modify the Hypersonic configuration file, `hsqldb-ds.xml`, in order to create a table and populate it with a minimal dataset.

Stop JBoss by selecting JBoss 3, Stop from the MyEclipse server button on the toolbar (the running guy with the smiling face behind him). You will need to restart it once you update the JBoss Hypersonic configuration file:

```
10:32:53,775 INFO  [Server] Shutdown complete
Shutdown complete
Halting VM
```

Once JBoss has stopped, navigate to `<JBoss installation directory>/server/default/deploy` and open `hsqldb-ds.xml` by going to the main menu and selecting File, Open External File.

The `hsqldb-ds.xml` file contains, in addition to other information, datasource configuration, such as the following:

- The JNDI name to use to access the data source. Hypersonic's JNDI name is DefaultDS.

- A connection URL.

- The JDBC driver name.

- A JMX MBean entry to administer the Hypersonic database.

The first thing to do is to uncomment the first `<connection-url>` entry:

```
<!-- for tcp connection, allowing other processes to use the hsqldb
database. This requires the org.jboss.jdbc.HypersonicDatabase mbean.
-->
<connection-url>jdbc:hsqldb:hsql://localhost:1701</connection-url>
```

Next, you need to comment out the other connection URLs:

```
<!-- for totally in-memory db, not saved when jboss stops.
The org.jboss.jdbc.HypersonicDatabase mbean is unnecessary
<connection-url>jdbc:hsqldb:.</connection-url>
-->
```

```
<!-- for in-process db with file store, saved when jboss stops. The
org.jboss.jdbc.HypersonicDatabase is unnecessary
<connection-url>jdbc:hsqldb:${jboss.server.data.dir}/hypersonic/localDB
</connection-url>
-->
```

Finally, uncomment the <mbean> tag at the bottom of the file:

```
<!-- This mbean should be used only when using tcp connections. Uncomment
when the tcp based connection-url is used.
-->
<mbean code="org.jboss.jdbc.HypersonicDatabase"
  name="jboss:service=Hypersonic">
  <attribute name="Port">1701</attribute>
  <attribute name="Silent">true</attribute>
  <attribute name="Database">default</attribute>
  <attribute name="Trace">false</attribute>
  <attribute name="No_system_exit">true</attribute>
</mbean>
```

Restart JBoss using the MyEclipse app server toolbar button. To make sure that the changes were accepted first, check the Console view and verify no errors or strange messages appear. Open a browser and go to http://localhost:8080/jmx-console. You should see the JBoss JMX page with the Hypersonic database listed as a service under the jboss section.

Creating a table with columns and populating it with a few entries is done through a JBoss-supplied Hypersonic GUI. In your browser, click jboss, service=Hypersonic. The JMX MBean View page will open, displaying manageable attributes and operations associated with Hypersonic on JBoss. Scroll to the bottom of the page to find the list of available operations and then click Invoke on startDatabaseManager. This will open the HSQL Database Manager, a Swing GUI to administer the Hypersonic database (see Figure 9.15). You will create a table with three columns and data using this GUI. You could also load a SQL file and execute it within the Manager to accomplish this task.

In the HSQL Database Manager's main menu, click Command, CREATE TABLE. This will display a template of the CREATE command for your use while you write the SQL to create a table. In the top-right window, enter the SQL to create the Customer table with a phone number column (which will also be used as a primary key), a name column, and a city column:

```
CREATE TABLE CUSTOMER
(
ID INTEGER PRIMARY KEY,
PHONE_NUMBER VARCHAR(15) NOT NULL,
NAME VARCHAR(30) NOT NULL,
STREET VARCHAR(30) NOT NULL,
```

```
CITY VARCHAR(20) NOT NULL,
STATE VARCHAR(30) NOT NULL,
ZIPCODE VARCHAR(10) NOT NULL
)
```

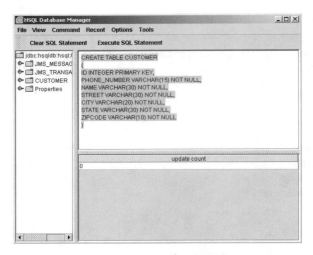

FIGURE 9.15   The HSQL Database Manager after creating the Customer table.

Click Execute SQL Statement, and Hypersonic responds with an update count of 0 (refer to Figure 9.15). Inserting data into the table is no more difficult than the previous step. From the main menu, click Command, Insert and then enter in the top-right window the SQL needed to enter a single row of data. Use single-quotes around the string values:

```
INSERT INTO CUSTOMER
(ID, PHONE_NUMBER, NAME, STREET, CITY, STATE, ZIPCODE)
values
(1, '1-222-333-4444', 'Ronald Weasley', '4 Privit Drive',
➥ 'Burrow', 'Outside Surrey', '11111')
```

Click Execute SQL Statement again to insert the single row. Change the data if you like and execute the statement again. To check the data you have just inserted, select Command, Select and enter a simple select of the customer table to view its data (see Figure 9.16):

```
SELECT * FROM customer
```

Exit the HSQL Database Manager by selecting File, Exit.

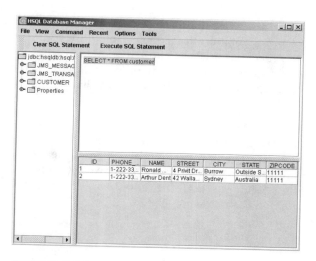

FIGURE 9.16   Output from the SQL `select * from customer`.

Configuring JBoss and its default embedded Hypersonic database gives you one less thing to do: install and set up an external database to interact with your EJB. The setup of an external data source is explained in the JBoss documentation that can be found at the JBoss site. Shut down JBoss using the MyEclipse app server button located on the Eclipse toolbar.

Implementing and Deploying an Entity Bean Using XDoclet

With the external tool setup complete, and your app server and database, you can now return to Eclipse and create an entity EJB. Here is a brief reminder of what you are going to do:

1. Create an EJB module.

2. Create an entity EJB.

3. Generate the support files needed by the EJB and JBoss.

4. Deploy the EJB to JBoss.

5. Update the CustomerSearchService to access the entity bean.

Create an EJB project by pressing Ctrl+N to open the New dialog. Select J2EE, EJB Module Project and then click Next. In the New J2EE EJB Project page, enter the project name CallCenterEJB in the EJB Project Details section and then click Finish. The CallCenterEJB project now appears in the Package Explorer view. The CallCenterEAR project will not appear in the next few screenshots because it does not have an impact on the following example. Do not remove it from your workspace, however, because you will need CallCenterEAR later.

With the creation of an EJB Module, you can add the XDoclet support it needs. Adding XDoclet to the EJB Module sets up the XDoclet configuration the module should use during code generation. In addition to setting up the generic EJB XDoclet configuration, you will also add the JBoss support for the generation of JBoss-specific deployment information. Right-click the CallCenterEJB project and select Properties. When the Properties dialog opens, select MyEclipse-XDoclet from the list to the left.

Right-click in the top window of the MyEclipse-XDoclet page and from the pop-up menu select Add Standard. A dialog opens, listing the selection of available XDoclet tags. Select Standard EJB and click OK. The MyEclipse-XDoclet page now lists Standard EJB as a checked item. Standard EJB maps to the `<ejbdoclet>` Ant task. Select Standard EJB to display the list of supported subtasks `<ejbdoclet>` supports (see Figure 9.17). All the subtasks are checked by default, but you only need to check the subtasks in the following list:

- `ejbdoclet`
- `deploymentdescriptor`
- `entitycmp`
- `fileset`
- `homeinterface`
- `localhomeinterface`
- `localinterface`
- `packageSubstitution`
- `remoteinterface`
- `utilobject`

The checked subtasks configure XDoclet to run the Ant tasks that will create the various support Java files and deployment descriptors defined by the EJB 2.0 specification. Each checked item represents an Ant subtask that will be executed when you decide to run XDoclet from within the project.

The next XDoclet piece that must be added is the subtask that will generate the files needed by JBoss. Right-click `ejbdoclet` in the lower-left window and select Add from the pop-up menu. The dialog that opens lists, among others, the supported application servers. Select `jboss` and click OK.

The `<jboss>` tag needs two properties to be set: `Version` and `destDir`. In the Properties list to the right of the XDoclet tasks, check `Version` and double-click on the cell that contains `Version`. Double-clicking will open up the Attribute Value dialog, where you must enter `3.2`, which is the version of JBoss you are using for this example, in the Value field. Click OK.

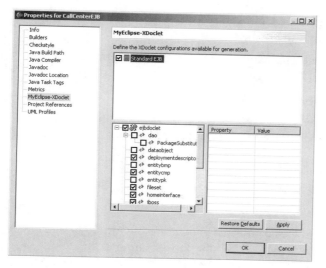

FIGURE 9.17 The list of supported `<ejbdoclet>` subtasks in the lower-left window.

The second `<jboss>` property you must set is the `destDir` property. This directory is the target where the JBoss deployment files must be generated. Check the `destDir` property, double-click the field to open the Attribute Value dialog, and enter `src/META-INF` in the Value field. Click OK. With all that information in place, you can now close the Properties dialog by clicking OK.

The XDoclet configuration you just completed constitutes the extent to which you have to configure XDoclet within Eclipse, at least until you try something a lot more complicated. This configuration will generate both remote and local interfaces, the EJB implementation class used by the EJB container, `ejb-jar.xml`, `jboss.xml`, and `jbosscmp-jdbc.xml`. MyEclipse will accomplish this through the use of an Ant build script called `xdoclet-build.xml`. You can find `xdoclet-build.xml` under the CallCenterEJB project. It has a collection of pathelements and two targets. It is this build script that will take care of generating the EJBs support files in MyEclipse.

Create an EJB by selecting the CallCenterEJB project (just click it once) and pressing Ctrl+N. When the New dialog opens, select J2EE, EJB on the left and EJB (session, entity and message) on the right. Then click Next.

The EJB Wizard page needs the following information to create your EJB:

- Source Folder must be set to the project name and the `src` subdirectory. In this case, it should read `CallCenterEJB/src`.

- The Package field must be a name that ends with `ejb` as the package of the EJB. XDoclet expects the EJB package to end with `ejb`, so enter a package name of `eclipse.kickstart.ejb`.

- The Name field contains the name of the EJB. Again, XDoclet defaults to looking for a class name that ends with `Bean`. Enter the name `CustomerBean`.

- Set the Modifiers entry to `public` and `abstract`. When you add the methods that map to the columns in the database, you declare those methods as `abstract`.

- Superclass should be `java.lang.Object`.

- The Interfaces field defaults to `javax.ejb.SessionBean`. Change Template to Use to `Entity EJB`, and it will update the interface to `javax.ejb.EntityBean`.

- In the Options section, leave Check Required Methods and Create Optional Example Methods checked.

Once you have entered all this information, click Finish.

`CustomerBean.java` opens when MyEclipse has completed generating the Ant build file. If you updated your compiler configuration to complain about unused imports, the `CustomerBean` class will complain about the unused import of `java.rmi.RemoteException`. Delete that line and save the file.

The next few steps involve manual operations. You need to add Java to define the primary key, the phone number field, and the two supporting fields, name and city. In addition, you must add the XDoclet tags that define which table this EJB maps to and which of the fields are persistent fields. MyEclipse does not support the visual editing of the EJB, so you will have to add this information by hand.

Scroll down to the Javadoc above the `CustomerBean` class declaration (see Listing 9.3). There are two general comments and the XDoclet tags in the Javadoc block. The XDoclet tags facilitate the centralization of the EJB information within one file. The XDoclet engine parses the `CustomerBean` file and uses the various tags to create the support files. In the Javadoc block, add the XDoclet tag `primkey-field` to define the primary key used with `CustomerBean` and add `@ejb.persistence` to associate the `CustomerBean` with the `CUSTOMER` table (the lines in bold). The `ejb@finder` tag allows you to define a search method based on the phone number.

LISTING 9.3   `CustomerBean.java`

```
/**
 * XDoclet-based CMP entity bean. This class must be declared
 * <code>public abstract</code> because the concrete class will
 * be implemented by the CMP provider's tooling.<br>
 *
 * To generate code:
 * <br>
```

LISTING 9.3 Continued

```
 * <ul>
 * <li> Add Standard EJB module to XDoclet project properties
 * <li> Customize XDoclet configuration
 * <li> Run XDoclet
 * </ul>
 * <br>
 * Please see the included XDoclet Overview
 * and the XDoclet Reference in the help system for details
 *
 * @ejb.bean name = "CustomerBean"
 *             type = "CMP"
 *             cmp-version = "2.x"
 *             display-name = "CustomerBean"
 *             description = "CustomerBean EJB"
 *             view-type = "both"
 *             jndi-name = "ejb/CustomerBeanHome"
 *             local-jndi-name = "ejb/CustomerBeanLocalHome"
 *             primkey-field = "ID"
 *
 * @ejb:util
 *      generate="physical"
 *
 * @ejb.persistence table-name = "customer"
 *
@ejb.finder signature = "eclipse.kickstart.ejb.CustomerBean
                          findByPhoneNumber(java.lang.String phoneNumber)"
query = "SELECT OBJECT(c) FROM CustomerBean as c
         where c.phoneNumber = ?1"
 */
```

Now add the five fields that map to the CUSTOMER columns, flag the various methods as visible in the EJB remote/local interfaces, and flag the id field as the primary key (see Listing 9.4). Just for visibility, place the code as the first entries in the class. Notice that setID is not tagged in any way. Tagging the get method is sufficient to map the column to the EJB, but not tagging the set method means that the primary key cannot be changed outside of the EJB container. Also, the id field has an explicit mapping to the ID column, whereas the other fields do not have explicit mappings to their columns. The reason is that the name of the field, determined using the JavaBeans naming conventions, is used as the default column name by XDoclet and, by extension, the EJB container.

LISTING 9.4   CustomerBean.java

```java
/**
 * @ejb.interface-method
 * @ejb.persistence column-name = "ID"
 */
public abstract String getID();
public abstract void setID(int id);

/**
 * @ejb.interface-method
 * @ejb.persistence column-name = "PHONE_NUMBER"
 */
public abstract String getPhoneNumber();
/**
 * @ejb.interface-method
 * @ejb.persistence column-name = "PHONE_NUMBER"
 */
public abstract void setPhoneNumber(String phoneNumber);

/**
 * @ejb.interface-method
 * @ejb.persistence
 */
public abstract String getName();
/**
 * @ejb.interface-method
 * @ejb.persistence
 */
public abstract void setName(String name);

/**
 * @ejb.interface-method
 * @ejb.persistence
 */
public abstract String getStreet();
/**
 * @ejb.interface-method
 * @ejb.persistence
 */
```

LISTING 9.4 Continued

```java
    public abstract void setStreet(String street);

    /**
     * @ejb.interface-method
     * @ejb.persistence
     */
    public abstract String getCity();
    /**
     * @ejb.interface-method
     * @ejb.persistence
     */
    public abstract void setCity(String city);

    /**
     * @ejb.interface-method
     * @ejb.persistence
     */
    public abstract String getState();
    /**
     * @ejb.interface-method
     * @ejb.persistence
     */
    public abstract void setState(String state);

    /**
     * @ejb.interface-method
     * @ejb.persistence
     */
    public abstract String getZipcode();
    /**
     * @ejb.interface-method
     * @ejb.persistence
     */
    public abstract void setZipcode(String zipcode);
```

You can now run XDoclet to generate the required files. Right-click CallCenterEJB in the Package Explorer view and select MyEclipse, Run XDoclet. A progress dialog will appear and close, and the Console view will display the output from Ant as it runs `xdoclet-build.xml` (see Listing 9.5). If all goes well, everything will be displayed in blue.

LISTING 9.5   MyEclipse XDoclet output

```
Buildfile: \\Brooklyn\Kickstart\09-J2EEAndMyEclipse\workspace\
➥CallCenterEJB\xdoclet-build.xml
N10004:
[ejbdoclet] (XDocletMain.start                 47 ) Running <remoteinterface/>
[ejbdoclet] Generating Remote interface for 'eclipse.kickstart.ejb.CustomerBean'.
[ejbdoclet] (XDocletMain.start                 47 ) Running <localinterface/>
[ejbdoclet] Generating Local interface for 'eclipse.kickstart.ejb.CustomerBean'.
[ejbdoclet] (XDocletMain.start                 47 ) Running <homeinterface/>
[ejbdoclet] Generating Home interface for 'eclipse.kickstart.ejb.CustomerBean'.
[ejbdoclet] (XDocletMain.start                 47 ) Running <localhomeinterface/>
[ejbdoclet] Generating Local Home interface for 'eclipse.kickstart.ejb.CustomerBean'.
[ejbdoclet] (XDocletMain.start                 47 ) Running <entitycmp/>
[ejbdoclet] Generating CMP class for 'eclipse.kickstart.ejb.CustomerBean'.
[ejbdoclet] (XDocletMain.start                 47 ) Running <utilobject/>
[ejbdoclet] Generating Util class for 'eclipse.kickstart.ejb.CustomerBean'.
[ejbdoclet] (XDocletMain.start                 47 ) Running <deploymentdescriptor/>
[ejbdoclet] Generating EJB deployment descriptor (ejb-jar.xml).
[ejbdoclet] (XDocletMain.start                 47 ) Running <jboss/>
[ejbdoclet] Generating jboss.xml.
[ejbdoclet] Generating jbosscmp-jdbc.xml.
_generation_:
BUILD SUCCESSFUL
Total time: 10 seconds
```

XDoclet adds the following files in your CallCenterEJB project:

- eclipse.kickstart.ejb.CustomerBeanEJB

- eclipse.kickstart.interfaces.CustomerBean

- eclipse.kickstart.interfaces.CustomerBeanHome

- eclipse.kickstart.interfaces.CustomerBeanLocal

- eclipse.kickstart.interfaces.CustomerBeanLocalHome

- eclipse.kickstart.interfaces.CustomerBeanUtil

- META-INF/ejb-jar.xml

- META-INF/jboss.xml

- META-INF/jbosscmp-jdbc.xml

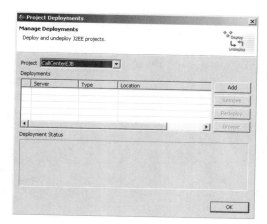

FIGURE 9.18 The Project Deployments dialog.

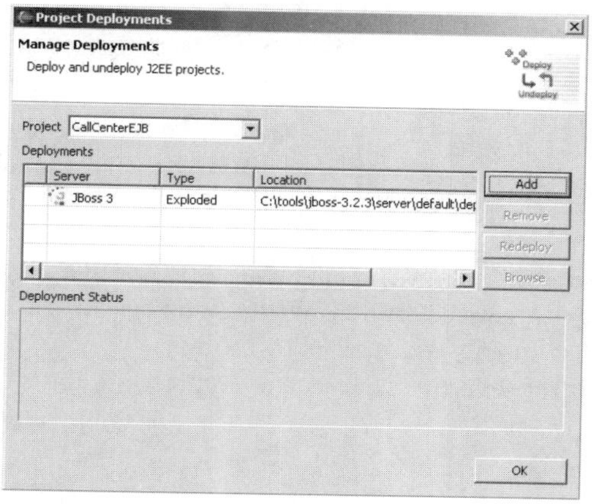

FIGURE 9.19 The Project Deployments dialog with the JBoss deployment entry.

It is very important for the deployment that the XML files be in the META-INF directory. If they are not, delete them, update the destDir property of the XDoclet <jboss> element in the project Properties, MyEclipse-XDoclet page, and then run XDoclet again.

The deployment of the EJB project is similar to the servlet deployment. Right-click CallCenterEJB in the Package Explorer and select MyEclipse, Add and Remove Project Deployments to open the Project Deployments dialog (see Figure 9.18). If CallCenterEJB is not the selected project, click the drop-down button and select CallCenterEJB. Because you have not deployed this project before, no deployment configurations will be available. Click Add to open the New Deployment dialog. In the Server field, select JBoss 3 and leave the Deploy Type field set to Exploded Archive. Click Finish to accept the server and to deploy the EJB for the first time. When the New Deployment dialog closes, the Deployments list in the Project Deployments dialog has an entry for JBoss that you will have to select whenever you want to redeploy the EJB (see Figure 9.19). For now, click OK to close the Project Deployments dialog.

Let's restart JBoss and take a look at its deployed components. The CustomerBean should show up as a deployed component. From the toolbar, click the triangle next to the MyEclipse app server button (the running guy with the smiling face behind him) and select JBoss 3, Start (or JBoss 3, Stop if you have JBoss running, and then JBoss 3, Start). In the middle of the JBoss output in the Console view, you can find entries specific to CustomerBean:

```
08:58:57,027 INFO  [MainDeployer] Starting deployment of package:
➥file:/C:/tools/jboss-3.2.3/server/default/deploy/CallCenterEJB.jar/
08:58:58,178 INFO  [EjbModule] Deploying CustomerBean
08:59:00,812 INFO  [CustomerBean] Table 'CUSTOMER' already exists
```

```
08:59:00,842 INFO  [EntityInstancePool] Started
jboss.j2ee:jndiName=ejb/CustomerBeanHome,plugin=pool,service=EJB
08:59:00,842 INFO  [EntityContainer]
➥Started jboss.j2ee:jndiName=ejb/CustomerBeanHome,service=EJB
08:59:00,842 INFO  [EjbModule]
➥Started jboss.j2ee:module=CallCenterEJB.jar,service=EjbModule
08:59:00,852 INFO  [EJBDeployer] Deployed: file:/C:/tools/jboss-3.2.3/
➥server/default/deploy/CallCenterEJB.jar/
08:59:00,932 INFO  [MainDeployer] Deployed package:
➥ file:/C:/tools/jboss-3.2.3/server/default/deploy/CallCenterEJB.jar/
```

There is the distinct possibility that the deploy may not work if you have conflicting JAR files in your JDK classpath. JBoss uses the Apache BCEL library to perform its EJB deploy, but unfortunately some of the XML/XSL parser support files also use the BCEL library. If you have any XML/XSL JAR files in your JDK endorsed directory, you should remove them; otherwise, the deploy to JBoss will fail. The endorsed directory under JAVA_HOME/lib is where JAR files can be placed that the JVM will use to override the standard JAR files that may need to be upgraded. Because of the special nature of the endorsed directory, any JAR files that are located there will be loaded first. Again, if you happen to have any XML/XSL JAR files, remove them so the EJB can deploy successfully to JBoss.

Open a browser to look at JBoss using its JMX admin console:

```
http://localhost:8080/jmx-console
```

Scroll down to jboss.j2ee. There are four entries for the EJB: three jndiName entries and one module entry (see Figure 9.20). The deployment has been successful. However, what good is a deployed EJB if a client cannot access it? The last step in this example is to modify CustomerSearchService to use CustomerBeanHome to retrieve the data in the Hypersonic database.

Updating the CustomerSearchService with JNDI

Before you change the code in CustomerSearchService, you must make the interfaces from CallCenterEJB visible to the CallCenterWeb project. Right-click CallCenterWeb and select Properties from the pop-up menu. In the Properties dialog, select Java Build Path on the left and the Projects tab on the right. Check the box next to CallCenterEJB and click OK.

You are now going to change the code in CustomerSearchService to use JNDI to look up the EJB factory (CustomerBeanHome), cast the reference from JNDI to the proper type, and then make a call to the default finder method to retrieve the customer using a phone number entered through the search.html page. In fact, there is more exception handling code involved than actual retrieval code (see Listing 9.6).

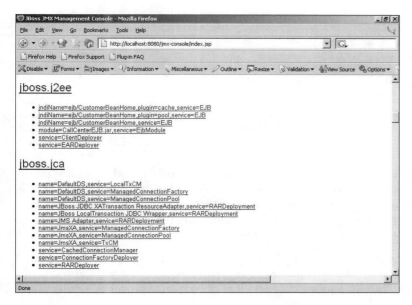

FIGURE 9.20 The JBoss JMX Agent View page displaying the `CustomerBean` entries.

LISTING 9.6 `CustomerSearchService.java`

```java
    public Hashtable searchUsing(String phoneNumber) {
        Hashtable result = new Hashtable(2);

//          result.put("name", "Thomas Anderson");
//          result.put("city", "Chicago");

        try {
            CustomerBean customer =
                CustomerBeanUtil.getHome().findByPhoneNumber(phoneNumber);
            result.put("name", customer.getName());
            result.put("street", customer.getStreet());
            result.put("city", customer.getCity());
            result.put("state", customer.getState());
            result.put("zipcode", customer.getZipcode());
        } catch (RemoteException e) {
            e.printStackTrace();
```

LISTING 9.6   Continued

```
      } catch (FinderException e) {
         e.printStackTrace();
      } catch (NamingException e) {
         e.printStackTrace();
      }
      return result;
   }
```

When you save `CustomerSearchService`, the compiler will notice that it cannot resolve many of the new symbols. Press Ctrl+Shift+O to resolve most of the symbols, and when Eclipse asks which CustomerBean symbol to use, make sure you select the `CustomerBean` interface located at `eclipse.kickstart.interfaces.CustomerBean`. Any remaining compile errors should be fixed by hand. Save the file to remove the fixed compile problems.

One of the Java classes generated by XDoclet is the `CustomerBeanUtil` class. This utility class wraps the call to JNDI and caches the reference to `CustomerBeanHome`. The exception-handling code notwithstanding, you added only one line of code to `CustomerSearchService`. With that, let's deploy the servlet to JBoss and run the Web application.

Deploying the servlet to JBoss means creating a new deployment configuration specific to JBoss. You could use the available deployment configuration for CallCenterWeb and deploy to Tomcat. However, if you decide to do this, remember that both Tomcat and JBoss use 8080 as their HTTP listener port, so one will have to be changed. For this example, deploying the servlet, JSP, and EJB to JBoss is convenient.

Right-click CallCenterWeb and select MyEclipse, Add and Remove Project Deployments to open the Project Deployments dialog once again. Ensure that CallCenterWeb is the selected project. Click Add to open the New Deployments dialog and select JBoss 3 as the server, leaving Deploy Type set to Exploded Archive. Click Finish. Once again, the creation of the deployment entry causes MyEclipse to deploy the project to the server without the use of the Redeploy button. Click OK to close the Project Deployments dialog.

Open a browser and go to `http://localhost:8080/CallCenter/search.html`. If you enter a random collection of letters into the Phone Number field, no results will be found, but if you enter the phone number 1-222-333-4444, you will see that the data was successfully retrieved from the database using the EJB (see Figure 9.21).

EJBs are complex. If you run into a problem, make sure you followed all the steps and that you typed in all the information correctly. Also, if you decide to change any of this code, you will have to restart JBoss.

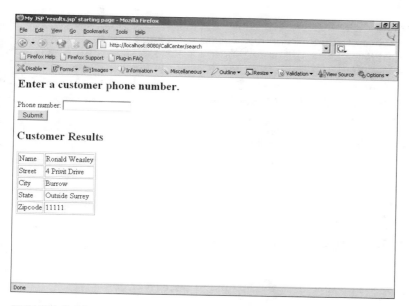

FIGURE 9.21   The results of the search on phone number 1-222-333-4444.

Debugging Servlets, JSPs, and EJBs

Debugging under MyEclipse is not much different from debugging a standard Java application, except that you must reset the MyEclipse Application Server Launcher information before starting the desired app server. Once the launch configuration is set, the Debug Perspective opens whenever you start the app server, and any code with breakpoints will stop when a breakpoint is reached.

To reset the MyEclipse app server launch configuration, open the Preferences dialog by selecting from the main menu Window, Preference. Select MyEclipse, JBoss 3, Launch from the tree view to the left and choose Debug mode in the Launch page to the right. Click OK to close Preferences.

Debugging a J2EE component within JBoss entails starting the app server, setting one or more breakpoints, and running the application from the browser. Restart JBoss by clicking the downward-pointing triangle next to the running guy with the smiling face behind him and selecting JBoss 3, Stop and then JBoss 3, Start. There are no breakpoints set, but you will set those next.

Open the following files: from the CallCenterWeb project open SearchServlet and CustomerSearchService and from CallCenterEJB open CustomerBean and CustomerBeanCMP. You are going to set one breakpoint in each file to demonstrate that each level can be examined in detail, regardless of the J2EE component type. You set breakpoints in Eclipse by double-clicking in the dark gray margin in the left of the editor or by right-clicking in the dark gray margin and selecting Toggle Breakpoint from the pop-up menu. In either case, a blue dot should appear next to the desired line of code.

In SearchServlet, set a breakpoint at the if in doPost():

```
if (isValid) {
    Hashtable info = _searchService.searchUsing(phoneNumber);

    request.setAttribute("results", info);
} else {
    request.setAttribute("errormsg", "Please enter a phone number.");
}
```

In CustomerSearchService, set a breakpoint at the first use of the result object:

```
result.put("name", customer.getName());
```

In CustomerBean, place a breakpoint at the end of ejbLoad():

```
public void ejbLoad() throws EJBException {
}
```

Set the last breakpoint in CustomerBeanCMP in setEntityContext() on the only line of code in the method. Objects of this type are used by the EJB container for life-cycle management:

```
public void setEntityContext(javax.ejb.EntityContext ctx)
    throws javax.ejb.EJBException
{
    super.setEntityContext(ctx);
}
```

The one piece of the Web application where you will not set a breakpoint is in the JSP. Native JSP debugging support is left up to the servlet engine vendor, and in this case JBoss uses Tomcat 4.1, which does not support native JSP debugging. If you were running this Web application using both Tomcat and JBoss individually, you would have been able to set a JSP breakpoint because Tomcat 5, the servlet engine you configured for the pure servlet example, supports native JSP debugging.

Let's look at the breakpoints one at a time. Open a browser and go to http://localhost:8080/CallCenter. Enter a phone number (1-222-333-4444) and click Submit. The Eclipse window jumps to the front of your screen, and the Confirm Perspective Switch dialog opens, asking for permission to switch to the Debug perspective. Click Yes. The Debug perspective opens with the debugger stopped at the conditional statement in the servlet. In the Variables view, you can see that isValid is true, so the next breakpoint will be called inside of CustomerBeanCMP. Press F8 to continue program execution.

From the servlet level you now enter the EJB level.

The next breakpoint is in setEntityContext() in CustomerBeanCMP. When an entity bean is created, part of its life cycle includes receiving the context under which it is running. The EJB object that intercepts all the calls to the entity bean represents the bean's context. At this point, you are now in the EJB environment debugging your CustomerBean because CustomerBeanCMP extends CustomerBean. The Debug view lists CustomerBeanCMP as the location of the breakpoint, and the Variables view displays the this reference and the incoming ctx object. Press F8 again to continue program execution.

The next breakpoint is in CustomerSearchService. Once the EJB has been found, it is ready to have its fields accessed. You can see in the Variables view the phoneNumber value, the Hashtable result that will carry the data back to the JSP, and a reference to a CustomerBean. Everything is well-positioned to access the needed data. Press F8.

The breakpoint in CustomerBean is finally hit. The ejbLoad() method is called to give the entity bean the opportunity to refresh its data in case it might have fallen out of sync. Because of this behavior, this breakpoint will be hit when the code accesses each of its fields. Press F8, and the breakpoint at ejbLoad() is hit again. Press F8 a few more times until the code runs to completion. Bring your browser to the front to display Ronald Weasley's information.

Open the Preferences dialog and go to MyEclipse, Applications Servers, JBoss 3, Launch to change the Launch Mode to Run.

Exporting the Finished Product

Now that you have a fully functional Web application, how do you deploy it outside of Eclipse? There are a number of ways to export the various projects. If you are deploying to one app server, a single EAR file would be most appropriate. If you are deploying the Web app to one server and the EJBs to another, you can create a separate EAR file for the Web application and another for the EJB component. However, the Web application does make use of the EJB utility class and two of the EJB interfaces, so those would also need to be exported as part of the Web application.

Let's export the single EAR file that will contain the Web application and the EJB. Return to the MyEclipse perspective. Up to this point, you have not used the Enterprise Application Project you created at the start of this chapter. It is useable in its current form because the CallCenterWeb project is associated with it, as can be seen from the contents of application.xml located in CallCenterEAR/META-INF:

```
<?xml version="1.0" encoding="UTF-8"?>
<!DOCTYPE application PUBLIC
➥"-//Sun Microsystems, Inc.//DTD J2EE Application 1.3//EN"
➥"http://java.sun.com/dtd/application_1_3.dtd">
<application>
    <display-name>CallCenter</display-name>
    <module id="myeclipse.1076791914090">
        <web>
            <web-uri>CallCenterWeb.war</web-uri>
            <context-root>/CallCenter</context-root>
        </web>
    </module>
</application>
```

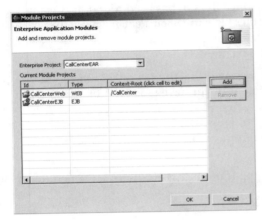

FIGURE 9.22   The CallCenterWeb and CallCenterEJB projects are associated with the CallCenterEAR enterprise module.

You must also associate the EJB project with the Enterprise Application Module. Right-click the CallCenterEAR project and from the pop-up menu select MyEclipse, Add and Remove Modules. When the Module Projects dialog opens, select CallCenterEAR as the Enterprise Project, if it is not already selected. Click Add to open the New Application Module dialog, which lists potential project candidates. Select CallCenterEJB and click Finish. Both projects are now associated with the CallCenterEAR enterprise project (see Figure 9.22). Click OK to close the Module Projects dialog.

Open application.xml again. The module entry for CallCenterEJB is the last element in the file:

```
<?xml version="1.0" encoding="UTF-8"?>
<!DOCTYPE application PUBLIC
➥"-//Sun Microsystems, Inc.//DTD J2EE Application
➥1.3//EN" "http://java.sun.com/dtd/application_1_3.dtd">
<application>
    <display-name>CallCenter</display-name>
    <module id="myeclipse.1076791914090">
        <web>
            <web-uri>CallCenterWeb.war</web-uri>
            <context-root>/CallCenter</context-root>
        </web>
    </module>
```

```
<module id="myeclipse.1079411233736">
    <ejb>CallCenterEJB.jar</ejb>
</module>
</application>
```

Before you export the EAR file, you must delete the existing deployment directories from within JBoss. Stop JBoss by selecting the downward-facing triangle next to the MyEclipse app server button on the toolbar and then selecting JBoss 3, Stop. If the Confirm Perspective Switch dialog opens, click No. When the Console view says, "Halting VM," it is now safe to delete the deployment directories. Using Window Explorer, navigate to the JBoss installation directory and delete the CallCenter.war and CallCenterEJB.jar directories from the jboss-3.2.3\server\default\deploy directory (see Figure 9.23).

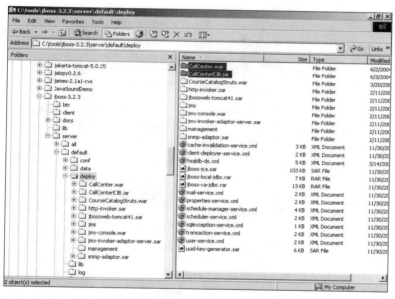

FIGURE 9.23 The two directories to delete from the JBoss deploy directory.

With the old files gone, you can safely deploy the EAR file to JBoss. Here are the steps to follow:

1. Bring the Eclipse window forward and restart JBoss.

2. When you are sure that JBoss has successfully started, right-click CallCenterEAR in the Package Explorer view and select MyEclipse, Add and Remove Project Deployments from the pop-up menu to open the Projects Deployment dialog.

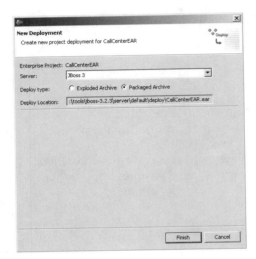

FIGURE 9.24   The New Deployment dialog with the `CallCenterEAR.ear` file to be deployed as a packaged archive.

3. Click Add to open the New Deployment dialog, select JBoss 3 as the server, and change Deploy Type from Exploded Archive to Packaged Archive (see Figure 9.24). Click Finish.

4. When the New Deployment dialog closes, the `CallCenterEAR.ear` file is now in the JBoss deploy directory. Click OK to close the Projects Deployment dialog.

Bring Windows Explorer forward and look in the JBoss server\default\deploy directory. `CallCenterEAR.ear` is sitting in the `deploy` directory, waiting for JBoss to start. If you open the file using an extraction program such as WinZip, you will see that `CallCenterWeb.war` and `CallCenterEJB.jar` are both contained within the EAR file.

Let's check on the quality of the `CallCenterEAR.ear` file by running the application again and confirming our results. Start JBoss from within Eclipse using the MyEclipse app server button on the toolbar. The JBoss output in the Console view mentions the `CallCenterEAR.ear` file:

```
13:01:48,309 INFO  [MainDeployer] Starting deployment of
➥package: file:/C:/tools/jboss-3.2.3/server/default/deploy/CallCenterEAR.ear
13:01:48,309 INFO  [EARDeployer] Init J2EE application:
➥file:/C:/tools/jboss-3.2.3/server/default/deploy/CallCenterEAR.ear
13:01:49,391 INFO  [EjbModule] Deploying CustomerBean
13:01:51,924 INFO  [CustomerBean] Table 'CUSTOMER' already exists
13:01:51,955 INFO  [EntityInstancePool] Started
jboss.j2ee:jndiName=ejb/CustomerBeanHome,plugin=pool,service=EJB
13:01:51,955 INFO  [EntityContainer]
➥Started jboss.j2ee:jndiName=ejb/CustomerBeanHome,service=EJB
13:01:51,955 INFO  [EjbModule] Started
➥jboss.j2ee:module=CallCenterEJB.jar,service=EjbModule
13:01:51,955 INFO  [EJBDeployer] Deployed:
➥file:/C:/tools/jboss-3.2.3/server/default/tmp/deploy/
➥tmp27025CallCenterEAR.ear-contents/CallCenterEJB.jar
13:01:52,065 INFO  [EmbeddedTomcatService] deploy,
➥ctxPath=/CallCenter, warUrl=file:/C:/tools/jboss-3.2.3/
➥server/default/tmp/deploy/
```

```
➥tmp27025CallCenterEAR.ear-contents/CallCenterWeb.war/
13:01:52,155 INFO  [Engine] SingleSignOnContextConfig[/CallCenter]:
➥Added certificates -> request attribute Valve
13:01:52,215 WARN  [EmbeddedTomcatService] Unable to invoke setDelegate on
➥class loader:org.jboss.web.tomcat.tc4.WebCtxLoader$ENCLoader@1a18ee2
13:01:52,215 INFO  [Engine] StandardManager[/CallCenter]: Seeding
➥random number generator class java.security.SecureRandom
13:01:52,215 INFO  [Engine] StandardManager[/CallCenter]:
➥Seeding of random number generator has been completed
13:01:52,215 INFO  [Engine] StandardWrapper[/CallCenter:default]:
➥Loading container servlet default
13:01:52,225 INFO  [Engine] StandardWrapper[/CallCenter:invoker]:
➥Loading container servlet invoker
13:01:52,335 INFO  [EARDeployer] Started J2EE application:
➥file:/C:/tools/jboss-3.2.3/server/default/deploy/CallCenterEAR.ear
13:01:52,335 INFO  [MainDeployer] Deployed package:
➥file:/C:/tools/jboss-3.2.3/server/default/deploy/CallCenterEAR.ear
```

Once JBoss is up and running, open your browser again and navigate to `http://localhost:8080/CallCenter`. Enter the phone number again (1-222-333-4444) and you will see the "Ronald Weasley" output as before.

In Brief

This chapter covered quite a bit of J2EE development ground in addition to test-driving much of the MyEclipse functionality. The integration of various plug-ins into a cohesive whole is not a trivial undertaking, but the MyEclipse plug-in works well in bringing J2EE capability well within the reach of all developers.

- Tomcat and JBoss are simple to install and use as platforms to develop and debug servlets, JSPs, and EJBs. You do not need MyEclipse to use these Java components, but MyEclipse gives you control over them from within Eclipse.

- The MyEclipse plug-in installation is straightforward. The JSP/HTML editor sets itself up as the default editor for JSP files and can be configured from the Preferences dialog. The XML editor can be used to view and edit project-specific files as well as external files.

- Enterprise application and Web projects are created using MyEclipse wizards.

- Servlets, JavaServer Pages, and Enterprise JavaBeans are implemented via MyEclipse wizards, with servlets and JSPs being deployed to either Tomcat or JBoss, and EJBs deployed just to JBoss. The deployment process is handled by a deployment wizard. MyEclipse supports deployment to 20 different servers.

- MyEclipse eases EJB development by using XDoclet to generate the files needed to deploy to the various supported servers.

- Debugging a servlet and an EJB running within JBoss is equivalent to debugging stand-alone Java code. The standard debug views are available, as are views to display break-points and values, among others. JSP native debugging is only available in app servers that support JSR045, which Tomcat 4.x does not.

- Exporting a complete EAR file to JBoss involves the modification of the `application.xml` file of the enterprise project. The MyEclipse Add Module Wizard controls what modules are added and updates the `application.xml` file on its own.

Developing Web Services Using the IBM Web Services Software Developer Toolkit

Web Services Software Development Kit

Although this book has been focusing on Eclipse 3.0, Web Services are too important to ignore. As mentioned in previous chapters, out-of-the-box Eclipse supports basic Java development, but no enterprise-level Java technologies. Sun has produced a Web services developer package for Java developers who want to work with Web services, but it does not have native support for Eclipse. The IBM Web Services Development Kit, which had been released earlier as a non-IDE–specific package, has been updated to work under Eclipse. The expectation is that soon after the release of Eclipse 3.0, the IBM WSDK will be updated to support it properly, but there are no guarantees. As of the writing of this chapter, IBM WebSphere Web Services Software Development Kit (WSDK) v5.1 will only work with Eclipse 2.1.1+, so the various examples in this chapter have been developed using Eclipse 2.1.3.

The IBM WSDK is based on Web Services Interoperability Organization (WS-I) Final Approved Basic Profile (BP) v1.0.

A WS-I Basic Profile consists of a grouping of Web service specifications. Web services are made up of a number of disparate technologies that are evolving independently of each other. WS-I Profiles help group together releases of Web service specifications in a manageable way. This is necessary because many technologies can be used (somewhat) interchangeably within a Web service. Because of the ever-changing release levels, it would be difficult to ensure that your Web service can coexist with all combinations of present, future, and past releases.

A profile defines what specifications are supported in a given release and how those technologies interact with one another. For Basic Profile v1, the following specifications/release levels are supported:

- SOAP 1.1

- UDDI 2.0

- WSDL 1.1

- XML Schema 1.0

Reviewing Web Services

In general, a *Web service* is a Web-based application that provides a service via XML-based messages that are transmitted via a network connection. A software system using resources such as Web services is called *service oriented*. By extension, a software architecture using this approach is known as a *service-oriented architecture*, or *SOA*. Typically, in a SOA approach, XML defines the message format, and the network addresses the message protocol.

The goal of SOAs (and Web services in particular) is to reduce the level of effort to interface disparate systems together. Over time, legacy systems accumulate, creating both opportunities and challenges. Service-oriented architectures address the need to bring together the various applications located in a company that are not easily integrated. The joining of these different systems in a way that allows them to be used in new and productive ways defines the Enterprise Application Integration (EAI) space.

The challenge of EAI is not a trivial one. Historically, the problems of systems integration were addressed by technologies such as CORBA, DCOM, and RMI, all of which are programmatic solutions. In practice, CORBA was too complex for many institutions, and DCOM and RMI were platform/language specific. The creation of a service-oriented architecture using programmatic solutions means that the systems being integrated have their data sources/services glued together by hand. The hand-coding of these legacy systems is well understood, but can lead to different kind of integration issues down the line. To avoid this problem, a number of EAI vendors adopted messaging as an alternative to a 100%-programmatic approach.

Systems integrated using messaging have a major advantage over systems programmatically integrated: They are very loosely coupled. When developers have to write glue code using a system-integration API such as CORBA, or even RMI, they are creating APIs that will change on rare occasion if at all. With messaging, the only thing with which a client should concern itself is the content of the message to be sent.

Enter Web services. This repacking of existing technology uses the advantages of both the programmatic and the loosely coupled solutions. Web services expose their API using the Web Services Description Language, an XML-formatted description file, yet they accept requests and return responses using the industry-standard XML message format SOAP (Simple Object Access Protocol). SOAP is many things, but it is first and foremost an agreed-upon format to exchange messages. A client to the Web service thinks it is making a language-specific API call when the reality is that a SOAP message is created and sent to the Web service. It translates the message into a method call that the Web service understands. The client knows what message the Web service accepts, and the Web service understands how to map the message to one of its methods. In addition, HTTP has turned out to be the de facto Web service wire protocol standard.

Web services have created a new migration path for legacy systems as well as a language-neutral/platform-neutral technology platform for use in enterprise applications.

Installing the WSDK Plug-In

If you only have Eclipse 3.0 installed on your machine, you will need to download 2.1.3 from http://www.eclipse.org. Multiple versions of Eclipse can coexist on the same machine if you install them into directories with different names. For example, you can extract the Eclipse files from the 2.1.3 zip file into a directory named c:\eclipse2.1.3.

Once you have the IBM WSDK-supported version of Eclipse installed, you must then obtain a copy of the IBM WebSphere/Eclipse Web Services Development Kit. You may do this by pointing your browser to the following page:

https://www6.software.ibm.com/dl/devworks/dw-wsdk-p

Once there, follow the prompts to begin the download. The first prompt will ask you to choose Windows or Linux download media. Select the Windows 2000/XP platform and then click Continue. We will not be focusing on any non-Windows installation directly in this book. After you go through the process of registering/logging in and downloading the file appropriate to your platform, you should have a file named wsdksetup.zip saved somewhere on your hard drive.

After the download is complete, open the zip file and extract the contents to a temporary directory. This zip file contains two files: setup.jar and wsdksetup.exe. Double-click wsdksetup.exe to start the install process (this file starts the InstallShield application).

Choose your desired language for the installer application and click Next. At this point, you will be presented with the WSDK Install Main Splash. Click Next.

Before You Begin

Before you invoke the WSDK installation process, you must uninstall any previous versions of the WSDK—even if you plan on reapplying the same install version.

To uninstall the WSDK, follow these steps:

1. Ensure that the Web Services Application Server is stopped by running the following command from a command prompt window:

   ```
   <WSDK-install-root>\bin\appserver stop
   ```

2. Open the Control Panel.

3. Select Add/Remove Programs.

4. Select IBM WebSphere SDK for Web Services, v5.1 from the list.

5. Click Change/Remove.

After the main splash page, the Product Installation screen will be displayed. Select the options for the Base WSDK command-line tools and the WSDK plug-ins for Eclipse 2.1.1 and then click Next (see Figure 10.1).

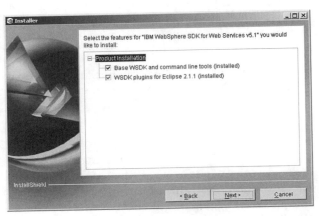

FIGURE 10.1   The WSDK product installation screen displaying the two items needed for the install.

Command-Line Tool Installation

If you have previously installed the WSDK command-line tools by themselves, you do not have to repeat the installation from scratch. In this case, you can enable the plug-in without having to reinstall the WSDK package. Consult the IBM WSDK Web site for details.

If you do decide to repeat the installation from scratch, be sure to uninstall any previous WSDK installations. Remember, this last point also applies to upgrading versions of the WSDK too.

The next install screen prompts you for the WSDK installation directory (see Figure 10.2). This directory can be a newly created subdirectory under your base Eclipse install, but it must not be the Eclipse directory itself.

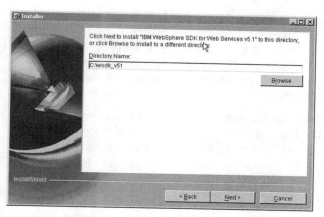

FIGURE 10.2   The WSDK installation directory setting.

Finally, you will be prompted for the Eclipse installation directory (see Figure 10.3). This is the directory of your current Eclipse (2.1.x) installation, not the desired installation directory of the plug-in.

It is important to note that the installation utility contains a bug. On Windows installs, if you are installing on a drive other than your local C: drive, you must make sure the target directory exists before proceeding to the next step. Consequently, on Windows, if you wish to install to a drive other than C: and that directory does not already exist, you must use Windows Explorer to create the parent directory outside of the install utility.

The next page asks for the root of the Eclipse installation directory. For many people, it will simply be C:\eclipse. If you are running multiple versions of Eclipse, enter the path to the specific version you wish to apply the plug-in (for example, c:\tools\eclipse2.1.3\eclipse).

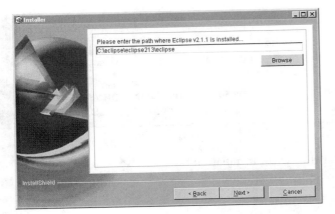

FIGURE 10.3   The core Eclipse installation directory setting.

When you click Next, the WSDK installation process will begin. Once the process is complete, you will have the option of viewing the Readme file or clicking Next a few more times until the Finish button is available. The WSDK can be accessed by selecting Start, Programs, IBM WebSphere SDK for Web Services v5.1 from the Windows toolbar.

Your WSDK installation is now complete. From this point on, when you desire to develop Web services using the IBM WSDK and Eclipse, you should use the Java Software Development Kit provided with the WSDK as the Java SDK used by Eclipse. This is important because APIs required by the plug-in might not be present in your current JDK installation. You have two ways to accomplish this. First, you can run Eclipse from the command line with the following option to force Eclipse to use a different JDK:

```
<Eclipse-root>\eclipse.exe -vm <WSDK-install-root>\appserver\java\jre\bin\javaw.exe
```

Second, as described in the final install page, you can select Launch Eclipse from the IBM WebSphere SDK for Web Services v5.1 menu.

When you start Eclipse for the first time, you will notice a message that states, "Please wait.... Completing the install." Once the install finalizes, the normal Eclipse window will appear. You will not see this finalization window again.

Several examples are provided by IBM with the WSDK plug-in. They include the following:

- Java Bean Web Service

- EJB Web Service

- EJB Client

- UDDI Publish and Unpublish

- UDDI Lookup and Invoke

- Complex Type Web Service

- One-way Messaging Web Service

- WSDL-based Web Service

- WS-Security Web Service

You can import these examples by right-clicking in the navigation window and then selecting New, Example.

In addition, IBM provides a WSDK Help application. You can start it by selecting Start, Programs, IBM WebSphere SDK for Web Services v5.1, WSDK Help.

Creating a Simple Java Bean Web Service

Now that we have installed the WSDK and reviewed the included examples, let's go through the steps involved in generating a Web service out of a JavaBean. The goal will be to create a simple JavaBean and then expose the bean's API as a Web service. Finally, the newly exposed Web service will be invoked both via the bean's API and via the newly created Web service. JavaBeans are a fixture in the Java landscape. They can contain business methods as well as accessors and mutators. A JavaBean acting as a facade to a larger system would be the perfect candidate for a Web service. The JavaBean would be well-defined, but decoupled from any clients making requests to the system the JavaBean represents.

Creating this Web service requires three steps:

1. Create a dynamic Web project.

2. Create a JavaBean class.

3. Create the Web service.

Remember, start Eclipse either from the command line, referring to the IBM WSDK Java SDK, or go to Start, Programs, IBM WebSphere SDK for Web Services v5.1, Launch Eclipse. Your normal Eclipse startup procedure will not work properly with the WSDK otherwise.

Create a New Dynamic Web Project

A Web service is, by nature of its name, defined as a Web application within Eclipse. Therefore, you need to define a dynamic Web project in which to develop your Web service application:

1. Select File, New, Project. (It does not matter what perspective you are in when you create the project.)

2. In the left pane of the New Project panel, select Web and in the right pane select Dynamic Web Project. Click Next.

FIGURE 10.4   The Dynamic Web Project page with the name of your project.

3. In the New Web Project panel, enter the name of your project (for example, BeanWebServiceExample), as shown in Figure 10.4.

4. Click Finish.

Open the BeanWebServicesExample project in the Package Explorer view. Note the folders that are created for you—in particular the JavaSource and WebContent folders. We will be using them in the coming steps.

Create a JavaBean Class

For the purposes of this example, you will create a simple JavaBean and then expose the bean's API as a Web service. Although you could use any JavaBean you like, you will define one in-place to ensure the lab will work the same for everyone.

As a refresher, a JavaBean is any Java class that adheres to a predefined set of naming conventions. Specifically, all internal instance variables that are to be exposed via the bean's interface are defined with method names such as get, set, has, is, and so on. For example, let's assume you have a private double instance variable called salary:

```
public double salary;
```

Its JavaBean APIs would consist of the following:

```
public double getSalary() ;
public void setSalary(double salary);
```

In a similar vein, suppose you have a boolean property named retired defined as this:

```
public double retired;
```

Its bean API would be defined as follows:

```
public boolean isRetired();
public boolean setRetired(boolean status);
```

In both cases, the first character of the field name has been changed to uppercase and the method name has been preceded with either a get/set or an is/set descriptor.

There are a host of other JavaBean requirements, but the aforementioned ones will be sufficient to get you through this example.

Follow these steps to create a JavaBean in your BeanWebServiceExample project. First, create a Java package to hold the code:

1. If you are not already there, switch to the Java perspective.

2. Right-click the BeanWebServiceExample, JavaSource folder.

3. Select New, Package. In the Name field, enter `com.kickstart.beanwebservice`.

4. Click Finish.

When you complete this task, note that Eclipse will have created a new package under the JavaSource folder. This package will contain all the generated code for your BeanWebServiceExample application.

To create the JavaBean, perform the following steps:

1. Right-click the newly created package and select New, Class.

2. In the New Java Class pane, enter `EmployeeBean` for the class name and deselect the public static void main(String[] args) and Constructors from Superclass options.

3. Click Finish. Eclipse will generate the Java stubs for your new class. Note the creation of the new class with the empty class definition within your JavaSource folder.

4. Define the two private field variables `salary` and `retired`:

```
private double salary = 0.;
private boolean retired = false;
```

5. You can generate the bean's getter and setter methods automatically:

   a. Right-click in the editor window.

   b. Select Source, Generate Getter and Setter.

   c. Select all the getter/setter combinations. You should have the two fields and four methods selected. Click OK and save the file.

At this point, the Getter/Setter Wizard will generate the applicable getter/setter methods. Your `EmployeeBean` class will take the form shown in Figure 10.5.

At this point, you have successfully created the `EmployeeBean` class within your dynamic Web project. Although we have been focusing our attention on the JavaSource folder, Eclipse has generated output in your WebContent folder. Specifically, when `EmployeeBean` was compiled, its output class was placed in the WebContent, WEB-INF, classes folder under the `com.kickstart.beanwebservice` package (see Figure 10.6).

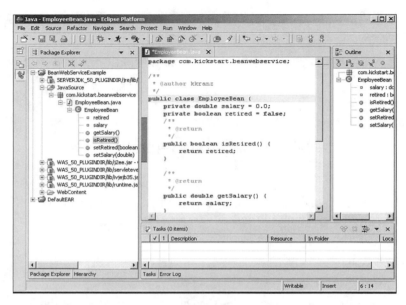

FIGURE 10.5 The EmployeeBean class with its getter/setter methods.

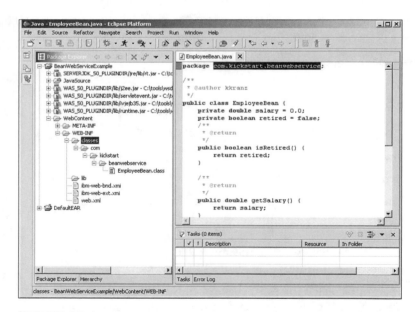

FIGURE 10.6 The Package Explorer view displaying the WebContent, WEB-INF, classes folder.

Create the Web Service

Now that the first two steps (creating the dynamic Web project and JavaBean class) have been completed, we can now turn our attention to generating the Web service itself.

Follow these steps to expose your EmployeeBean class as a Web service:

1. Switch to the Resource perspective.

2. In the Navigator view, right-click the newly created EmployeeBean.class file (located in the WebContent, WEB-INF, classes folder) and then select New, Other.

3. At this point, you are presented with the New dialog. The options selected will match those of the last time the New dialog was run (in this case, Web/Dynamic Web Project).

   To generate a Web service, select Web Services in the left pane and Web Service in the right pane. Click Next.

4. In the Web Services page, set the Web Service Type field to Java Bean Web Service. You may optionally select Test the Web Service and/or Launch the Web Services Explorer to test/inspect your results (see Figure 10.7). Click Next. If clicking Next does not move you to the next page, go to the Resources Perspective, open the .project file for BeanWebServiceExample, and remove the following lines:

```
<buildCommand>
    <name>com.ibm.etools.webtools.additions.linksbuilder</name>
    <arguments>
    </arguments>
</buildCommand>
```

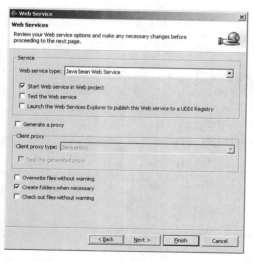

FIGURE 10.7 The Web Services page with its default information selected.

Once you remove the lines of code, restart Eclipse and try the preceding steps again. They should work with no problem. The builder referred to in the .project file does not exist, so the system runs into problems later.

5. If it is not already selected, select the current project (BeanWebServiceExample) as your Web service project and then click Next.

   We will not be concerning ourselves with the other options presented in this dialog, but you are free to experiment with them yourself. Specifically, the Test the Web Service and Launch the Web Service Explorer... options are useful when generating a Web service without the corresponding Web service client code, as we are doing here.

6. In the next page, if it's not already defined, set Web Services Java Bean Selection to `EmployeeBean.class` (the class created in the previous section) and then select Next.

7. The final page you will concern yourself with is the Web Service Java Bean Identity page. Here, you can choose which JavaBean methods you wish to expose as Web services—in this case, we will expose all four getter/setter methods (see Figure 10.8).

We will not be concerning ourselves with the encoding style, security, or custom mappings. You may click Finish at this point. If you chose any additional options in step 5, you would click Next to set these options.

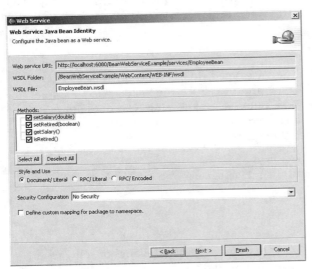

FIGURE 10.8   The Web Service Java Bean Identity page with all the accessor/mutator methods selected.

Once you have clicked Finish, the Web Services Wizard will begin to generate the Web services code for `EmployeeBean`. Specifically, under the WebContent, WEB-INF, classes folder, new Web services helper classes will be generated (see Figure 10.9). Additionally, under the WebContent, WEB-INF, wsdl and WebContent, wsdl folders, several XML, XMI, and WSDL files are generated. See the WEB-INF folder in the Navigator window in Figure 10.10.

You have now generated the necessary pieces to expose your JavaBean as a Web service. Let's run another test application to check on the state of your JavaBean-based Web service.

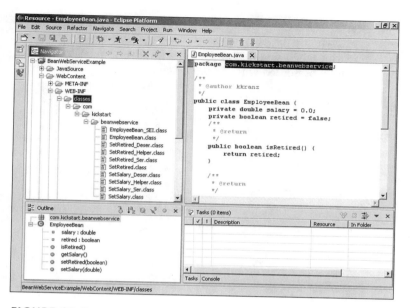

FIGURE 10.9 Web services helper classes found under WEB-INF, classes.

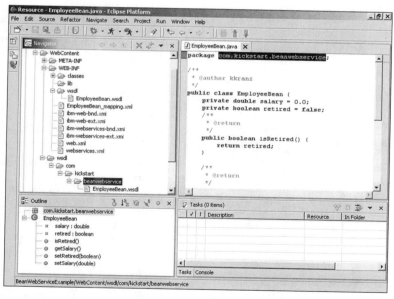

FIGURE 10.10 The list of generated XML, XMI, and WSDL files.

Right-click `EmployeeBean.wsdl` in either WebContent, WEB-INF, wsdl or WebContent, wsdl, com, kickstart, beanwebservice and then select Web Services, Test with WebServices Explorer. If you had selected Test the Web Service when you first created the JavaBean Web service (refer to Figure 10.7), you would also be presented with the Web Services Explorer (see Figure 10.11). In the Explorer, you will see your newly created Web services API. Furthermore, you will be able to invoke the APIs and observe their actions.

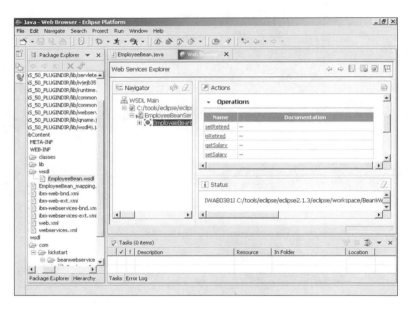

FIGURE 10.11   Web Services Explorer.

IBM-Provided WSDK Examples

Several examples are provided by IBM with the WSDK. They range from the simple (a JavaBean Web service like we created, but with the client code included) to more complicated scenarios. It is highly recommended that you review these examples and the associated sample tutorial available online. The sample tutorial can be found at

`https://www6.software.ibm.com/developerworks/education/ws-intwsdk51/`

These tutorials are beneficial because they not only discuss how to use the WSDK but also provide a more in-depth description on what Web services are and how to implement them.

In addition to describing the broad implementations of Web services, the IBM tutorial covers the use of the TCP/IP Monitor server. This server can be used by any application, not just Web services, to monitor messages sent via a TCP/IP port.

In Brief

Web services have turned out to be a strong addition to distribution systems, especially in the service-oriented architecture arena. The IBM Web Service Development Kit, as a plug-in to Eclipse, gives developers a chance to work with Web services in a controlled environment using a well-defined combination of technologies.

The WSDK, as a preview to Web services development, allowed you discover a number of things about Web services in general and the WSDK in particular:

- The WSDK is found on the IBM DeveloperWorks site and installing it is almost as simple to accomplish as installing Eclipse. However, as a plug-in that combines various technologies the WSDK must be installed properly to avoid potential conflicts with existing JDKs.

- A Web service is fundamentally a Web application. As such, you need to create a Dynamic Web Project from the New dialog.

- The WSDK lets you create Web services from either a JavaBean or an Enterprise JavaBean. The creation of the Web Services Description Language (WSDL) file is taken care of by the WSDK wizards.

- The WSDK TCP/IP Monitor can be used to intercept messages sent between clients and the Web service to examine the integrity of SOAP messages sent as requests and responses.

Struts Development Using MyEclipse

11

"A framework is the final reinvention of a wheel."

—Anonymous

J2EE, Struts, and Eclipse

Chapter 9, "J2EE and the MyEclipse Plug-In," discussed many of the wizards and editors available within the MyEclipse plug-in, which is itself an aggregation of plug-ins to make J2EE development more convenient.

J2EE is a collection of distinct technologies. Some of the technologies have a direct application with system integration (CORBA, RMI), data connectivity (JCA), security (JAAS), XML (JAXP), and email (JavaMail), just to name a few. However, of all the technologies associated with J2EE servlets, JavaServer Pages and Enterprise JavaBeans appear to be the most popular. Due to the popularity of Web applications, servlets and JSPs have been used in many applications. This accumulation of experience has led to a recognition of the commonality of designs used for the presentation layer—which leads us to Struts.

Struts

Struts is not an official part of the J2EE architecture, but it rests on J2EE technologies—in particular, servlets and JSPs—to accomplish its goals. It codifies standard Web development practices and, once you understand how the pieces fit and why they fit the way they do, makes development of the presentation side of a Web application simple. Struts is an open-source framework that defines a presentation architecture based on the Model-View-Controller design. The View component of the framework can be JSPs, Velocity, and/or XSLT, to name a few. The Controller component is a Struts-provided servlet that keeps a list of the objects you define, which drives the custom logic of your Web application. The Model component is your back-end system. It could be a custom datasource or a standard Java technology such as JDBC. Struts doesn't worry much about the model because that is the part of any system that is the most difficult to standardize.

Struts, as one of the more popular Web application frameworks, has the following moving parts:

- The Action class is the parent of a custom class that is responsible for handling incoming requests from the Web. This class is fine-grained in that it should handle one request. You are responsible for defining this class.

- An ActionForm is the parent of a custom class that maps directly to a form on some HTML page. The ActionForm could also be a superset of the fields, in case you have a form that spans multiple pages. You are responsible for defining this class.

- Zero or more HTML pages that send requests and zero or more JSPs (or other Action objects) that send responses back to the client. You are responsible for defining these pages and/or Action objects.

- The ActionServlet is the main switching point for the Struts framework. This is the only servlet needed for a Web application. The ActionServlet is responsible for receiving requests from the Web, determining which Action is responsible for a particular request, and routing the request to it. The configuration of the ActionServlet is defined in the Web application's web.xml file.

- The struts-config.xml file defines the configuration of a Struts-based application. It ties together the various pieces implemented by a developer. The ActionServlet uses this file to determine to which Action it should route incoming requests and with which ActionForm objects.

Also, support for dynamic forms (DynaActionForm), reusable presentation components (Tiles), and an external validator framework (the Validator framework) extends the capabilities of Struts even further.

For those of you already using frameworks such as Struts or WebWorks, you know using a proven design to implement your applications provides tremendous time savings. Many IDEs support Struts, and MyEclipse brings Struts support to Eclipse through the integration and extension of the Easy Struts plug-in, which was one of the early Eclipse plug-ins to support Struts.

Before installing MyEclipse, make sure you uninstall any existing Struts plug-ins. There may be conflicting configuration issues that are best avoided by using one plug-in task type at a time.

Finding and Installing MyEclipse and Tomcat

The "Downloading and Installing MyEclipse" section of Chapter 9 discusses the whys and wherefores of MyEclipse and walks you through the process of downloading and installing the plug-in, as well as downloading and installing Tomcat. If you have not installed either MyEclipse or Tomcat and need some help, refer to that section.

To use Tomcat within MyEclipse, you need to make sure MyEclipse is configured to support your version of Tomcat. If you have not yet configured MyEclipse to support Tomcat, again, refer to "Downloading and Installing MyEclipse" in Chapter 9 for the MyEclipse configuration information Tomcat needs to supply.

You are now ready to begin using MyEclipse to develop Struts applications.

Implementing a Web Application Using a Struts Module

Let's create a Web application to allow for the lookup of course information from a training company. An input page will ask for a course number, a course name, and an instructor name. If bad information is entered, the input page will let the user know which fields have a problem. If a course is found, the application will display information about it; otherwise, a "No course found" message will be displayed. You will put the main pieces together using the MyEclipse Struts wizards as well as the MyEclipse JSP editor.

The steps for creating a Struts application within MyEclipse are as follows:

1. Create a J2EE Web Module project.

2. Flag the Web Module project as Struts enabled.

3. Create the following three items in no particular order based on appropriateness:

   - Create an `ActionForm` that maps to the form in your starting HTML page. This step may be optional if the page you are coming from does not have a form.

   - Create an `Action`. If the `Action` processes an incoming form, use the `ActionForm` passed in as a method parameter.

   - Create a JSP that the `Action` can forward to, if necessary. An `Action` can execute and output HTML just like any other servlet, only it is not a servlet.

4. Update the `struts-config.xml` file to tie together the `ActionForm`, the `Action`, and the JSP (or any other target to which the `Action` might forward the request).

5. Deploy the Struts-based application to a Web server.

It is possible to create a Struts-based application with a JSP that gets routed back to itself, but it is not the intention of this chapter to go over Struts tips and tricks. Plenty of great Struts books are available that cover that kind of information. A few are listed in Appendix E, "Recommended Resources."

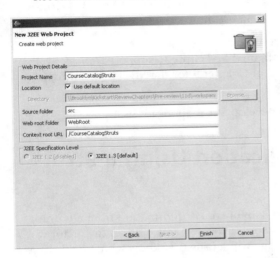

FIGURE 11.1   The New J2EE Web Project page, where you define the project name and the URL target for the project.

You start the process by creating a Web Module project and add Struts capabilities to it. Press Ctrl+N to open the New dialog; select Web Module Project beneath J2EE and click Next. Enter the project name CourseCatalogStruts (see Figure 11.1) and click Finish. If the Confirm Perspective Switch dialog opens asking for permission to switch to the MyEclipse perspective, click Yes. The project is once again set up the way a Web application should be: Under WebRoot you have a WEB-INF directory, a lib subdirectory, and a web.xml file to hold the configuration information needed by the Web server to properly deploy the application. There is also a META-INF directory, but it is really there for the use of the archiver, when you create and extract a WAR file.

The creation of a Web project is not sufficient to flag this project as a Struts-based project. Right-click the project and go to MyEclipse, Add Struts Capabilities. The New dialog opens on the Struts Support for MyEclipse Web Project page (see Figure 11.2). This page defines the information that will be inserted into web.xml. Struts Config Path is set to /WEB-INF/struts-config.xml. This path defines where the ActionServlet can find the Struts application configuration file. You can set this path to almost anywhere as long as a file exists at that location. In most circumstances, you will leave this value set to its default.

Leave the ActionServlet Name field set to action. Change the Base Package for New Classes field to eclipse.kickstart.struts and click Finish.

The Struts Wizard took care of the following tasks:

- The required Struts JAR files have been copied to WEB-INF/lib.

- The optional Tag Library Descriptor (TLD) files have been copied to WEB-INF. These files support the use of Struts custom JSP tags. In the development of a real application, you should create another directory under WEB-INF (for example, tld) where the TLD files should be moved. Web applications have a habit of aggregating support files, so the longer you can stay organized, the better. For this example, leave the files where the wizard placed them.

- The `struts-config.xml` file has been created with empty elements for the available tags that can contain information for use by the `ActionServlet`. The only missing tag is `plug-in`, but the MyEclipse Struts Editor will perform Code Assist if you type <p in the editor source page.

- The `web.xml` file, shown in Listing 11.1, has been updated with the `servlet` information needed by the Web server to load the `ActionServlet` when the Web server starts, and with default `init-params` for the `ActionServlet` to initialize itself. Also, a `servlet-mapping` is defined to route incoming resource requests that match the `*.do` pattern.

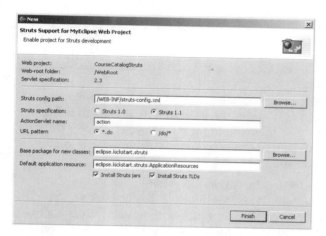

FIGURE 11.2   The New dialog's page for adding Struts support to an existing Web Module.

LISTING 11.1   `web.xml`

```
<?xml version="1.0" encoding="UTF-8"?>
<!DOCTYPE web-app PUBLIC "-//Sun Microsystems, Inc.//DTD Web Application 2.3//EN"
➥"http://java.sun.com/dtd/web-app_2_3.dtd">
<web-app>
    <servlet>
        <servlet-name>action</servlet-name>
        <servlet-class>org.apache.struts.action.ActionServlet</servlet-class>
        <init-param>
            <param-name>config</param-name>
            <param-value>/WEB-INF/struts-config.xml</param-value>
        </init-param>
        <init-param>
            <param-name>debug</param-name>
            <param-value>3</param-value>
```

LISTING 11.1   Continued

```
        </init-param>
        <init-param>
            <param-name>detail</param-name>
            <param-value>3</param-value>
        </init-param>
        <load-on-startup>0</load-on-startup>
    </servlet>
    <servlet-mapping>
        <servlet-name>action</servlet-name>
        <url-pattern>*.do</url-pattern>
    </servlet-mapping>
</web-app>
```

Now that the Struts project is created and properly initialized to support your development, you need to create an HTML page to accept input from the user, an `Action` class to manipulate the input and forward it to an output page, and an output HTML page to accept the data created by the `Action` class. Once again, MyEclipse comes to your aid with wizards to take care of creating stubbed versions of the files you need.

FIGURE 11.3
The struts-config.xml Outline view.

To open the Struts Wizard from the Package Explorer, open CourseCatalogStruts, WebRoot, WEB-INF and then double-click `struts-config.xml`. When the Struts editor opens, the Outline View displays a tree view of the contents of the file (see Figure 11.3). The Outline view is very important in the updating of the `struts-config.xml` file. Right-click `action-mappings` (the Struts element that ties together an input page, an action, and an output page) and select New Form, Action and JSP. This opens the New dialog at the Struts Form page (see Figure 11.4).

As a presentation-level piece, it is best to think of the functionality you are about to put together as satisfying a Use Case requirement for a larger application. For example, a user would navigate to the course search page to get information about a particular course, using a course number or description, or an instructor's name to discover which course he or she teaches. The input page, using a form, would take the user input and send it to a Struts `Action`, which would take care of retrieving course information. The Struts Form page collects the information needed by the code generator to create an initial input page and a `Form` class to contain the input data. The Struts Wizard uses the convention that every `Action` should have the granularity

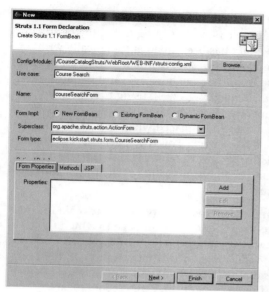

FIGURE 11.4 The Struts Form Wizard, complete with valid entries. (Due to resolution issues, the string Optional Details is covered by the Form Properties tab.)

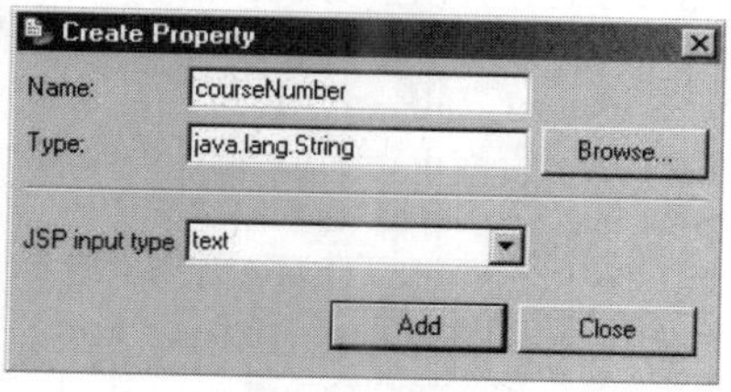

FIGURE 11.5 The Struts Create Property dialog with the courseNumber entry.

of a Use Case and therefore tries to name the Form and the Action after the Use Case. Because this is the Course Search Use Case, enter in the Use Case field Course Search. The Form Name field is automatically set to courseSearchForm, and the Form Type field is set to eclipse.kickstart.struts.form. CourseSearchForm. Using the drop-down button, change the Superclass setting from <default> to org.apache.struts.action.ActionForm.

At this point, the Form class is empty. To add form fields, click Add (found in the Form Properties section next to the empty text area). The dialog that appears allows you to set the name of the form field, the Java type to which it maps, an optional initial value, and the JSP input type (see Figure 11.5). One at a time, enter into the Name field courseNumber, courseName, and instructor, leaving Type set to java.lang.String, Initial Value set to blank, and the JSP Input Type set to text. Click Add until you have entered all three field names. When the dialog reopens for the fourth time, click Close. The Form Properties window lists courseNumber, courseName, and instructor as the defined form properties. Select the Methods tab and leave the top two selected methods, validate() and reset(), checked. Next, select the JSP tab and change the path from /form/courseSearch.jsp to /courseSearch.jsp. Click Next.

The next page of the wizard, Struts Action Declaration (see Figure 11.6), defines the action-mapping and action elements found in struts-config.xml. The entry in the Path field is the path alias used by the input HTML page to call the custom Action. In the HTML file, the path needs to end with .do if the Struts HTML tag library is *not* used. If the Struts HTML tag library is used, the Struts custom form tag will take care of adding .do to the form submission target. When you are done with the wizard (do not click Finish yet), you will find

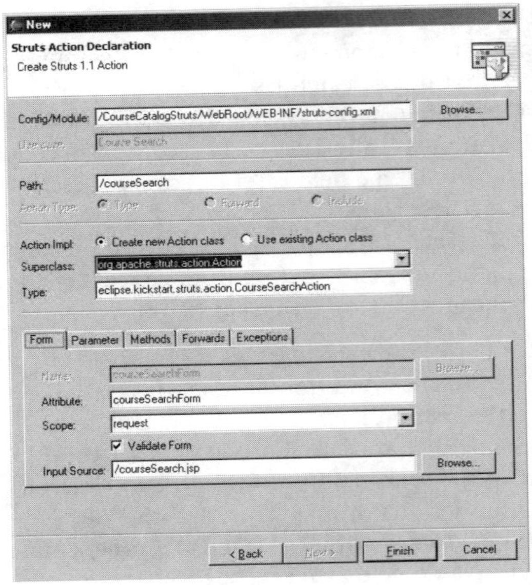

FIGURE 11.6 The Struts Action page displaying the ActionMapping information.

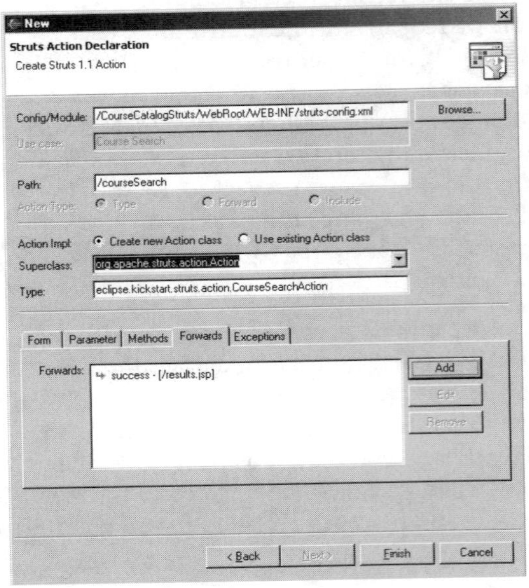

FIGURE 11.7 The Struts Action page with the "success" forward target set.

that the input JSP has a call to /courseSearch as the form action. Returning to the dialog, the Type field has been filled automatically with an acceptable Struts Action name based on the Use Case from the previous page, and the attribute name is filled in as well, using the form type name. The Scope dictates the scope object where the form will be placed when it is created by the Struts framework. The Scope defaults to request. This scope is acceptable because the search information is only valid for the initial search request.

Part of the responsibility of struts-config.xml is to map the input form page to which the ActionServlet should return if validation of the form fails. To match what was done in the previous dialog page, change the Input Source field on the Form tab from /form/courseSearch.jsp to just /courseSearch.jsp for user convenience. Leave the Parameter tab's Parameter field empty and make sure that the Methods tab has the execute() checked that takes in an HttpServletRequest/HttpServletResponse object (the first choice). The last tab you need to worry about, the Forwards tab, involves the JSP page to which the Action object should forward the response when it completes its task. The forward you define is specific to this Action; it is not a global forward. Click Add to open a dialog to enter a name for the forward target and the actual resource that should be called when the target name is used. In this case, enter the forward name success and the forward path /results.jsp (make sure it has a leading slash). Click Add to add the forward entry and then click Close to return to the New dialog (see Figure 11.7). Unfortunately, the wizard will not create a stubbed-out version of this file.

Close the New dialog by clicking Finish. The struts-config.xml file has two new entries: form-beans and action-mapping. The relevant code is shaded:

```xml
<?xml version="1.0" encoding="UTF-8"?>
<!DOCTYPE struts-config PUBLIC
➥"-//Apache Software Foundation//DTD Struts Configuration 1.1//EN"
➥"http://jakarta.apache.org/struts/dtds/struts-config_1_1.dtd">
<struts-config>
    <data-sources />
    <form-beans >
        <form-bean name="courseSearchForm"
➥type="eclipse.kickstart.struts.form.CourseSearchForm">
            <form-property name="instructor" type="java.lang.String" />
            <form-property name="courseName" type="java.lang.String" />
            <form-property name="courseNumber" type="java.lang.String" />
        </form-bean>

    </form-beans>

    <global-exceptions />
    <global-forwards />
    <action-mappings >
    <action
        attribute="courseSearchForm"
        input="/courseSearch.jsp"
        name="courseSearchForm"
        path="/courseSearch"
        type="eclipse.kickstart.struts.action.CourseSearchAction"
        unknown="false"
        validate="true">
    <forward
        name="success"
        path="/results.jsp"
        redirect="false"
        contextRelative="false" />
    </action>

    </action-mappings>

    <controller
        bufferSize="4096"
        debug="0"
        locale="false"
        nocache="false"
        inputForward="false" />
    <message-resources parameter="eclipse.kickstart.struts.ApplicationResources" />
</struts-config>
```

The struts-config.xml file has been modified, so save the file. Looking at the Outline view shows that the form-beans and action-mappings nodes have entries in them. For a more visual view of what you have just accomplished, click the Flow View tab located toward the bottom of the Struts editor window (see Figure 11.8). It displays the action as a flow from the starting input file (/courseSearch.jsp) to the Action object (/courseSearch.do) to the output target (/results.jsp).

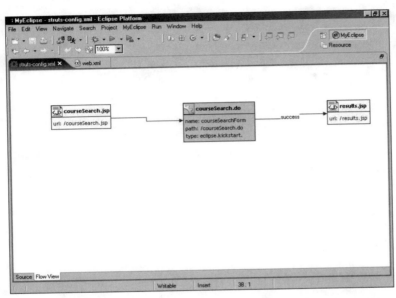

FIGURE 11.8 The Flow View displays the input, action, and output of the Struts components.

Implementing CourseSearchAction

From the Flow View, open CourseSearchAction by double-clicking /courseSearch.do. A cursory examination of the code shows that XDoclet has been hard at work generating the Struts files defined through the wizard. A look at the Javadoc for the class shows two XDoclet tags—@struts:action and @struts:action-forward (formatted to fit the page):

```
/**
 * MyEclipse Struts
 * Creation date: 06-07-2004
 *
 * XDoclet definition:
 * @struts:action path="/courseSearch" name="courseSearchForm"
 *                input="/courseSearch.jsp" validate="true"
 * @struts:action-forward name="/results.jsp" path="/results.jsp"
 */
```

The execute() method of CourseSearchAction has two lines of code: a line that assigns the generic Form object to a variable of type CourseSearchForm, and another line that throws an exception when the Action is called. Let's remove the exception and instead return the ActionForward that refers to your "success" target. The comments have been removed from the following code for brevity:

```
public class CourseSearchAction extends Action {

    public ActionForward execute(
        ActionMapping mapping,
        ActionForm form,
        HttpServletRequest request,
        HttpServletResponse response) {
        CourseSearchForm courseSearchForm = (CourseSearchForm) form;

        return mapping.findForward("success");
    }

}
```

By the time this code is executed, Struts has taken care of filling and validating the form object and, after the code calls the search object, forwarding the request to results.jsp through the use of the alias success. The use of a forward name as an indirection to the forward target makes your implementation much more flexible. If you need to change your forward target, you just need to change the configuration file, not the code.

You have two things left to do to complete the example and run it within Tomcat: update the CourseSearchForm and create a basic output page. Let's start by updating the CourseSearchForm to make the validate() and reset() methods relevant. The XDoclet-created code throws an UnsupportedOperationException when validate() is called, but the logic should be a little more reasonable:

```
public ActionErrors validate(
    ActionMapping mapping,
    HttpServletRequest request) {
    ActionErrors errors = new ActionErrors();

    if (instructor.trim().length() == 0) {
        errors.add("instructor", new ActionError("instructor.error"));
    }

    if (courseNumber.trim().length() == 0) {
        errors.add("courseNumber", new ActionError("courseNumber.error"));
    }
```

```
if (courseName.trim().length() == 0) {
    errors.add("courseName", new ActionMessage("name.error"));
}

return errors;
}
```

Make `reset()` assign an empty string to the various fields:

```
public void reset(ActionMapping mapping, HttpServletRequest request) {

    courseNumber = "";
    courseName = "";
    instructor = "";
}
```

Press Ctrl+Shift+O to remove compile problems related to missing imports.

The `validate()` method is now well-behaved. It creates an `ActionMessage` object each time there is a validation problem, and the `ActionServlet` is free to return the `ActionErrors` object to courseSearch.jsp. Of course, each of the `ActionMessage` objects is referencing a key in the `ApplicationResources.properties` file, which you have not updated. `ApplicationResources.properties` is found in the `eclipse.kickstart.struts` package. The strings referenced in each of the `ActionMessage` constructors constitute the keys:

```
# Resources for parameter 'eclipse.kickstart.struts.ApplicationResources'
# Project P/CourseCatalogStruts
instructor.error=Instructor name cannot be blank.
courseNumber.error=Course number cannot be blank.
name.error=Course name cannot be blank.
```

The input page, courseSearch.jsp, is already instrumented to handle an incoming `ActionErrors` object. Open courseSearch.jsp in the JSP editor. Each of the individual `<html:text>` lines has an associated `<html:error>`.

Let's create the output file results.jsp. In the Package Explorer view, select WebRoot in the CourseCatalogStruts project. Press Ctrl+N to open the New dialog and then select J2EE, Web, JSP. Click Next.

The JSP Wizard page only needs three pieces of information: the location to where the JSP should be written (File Path), the name of the JSP (File Name), and the template file to be used to create a starting file (Template to Use):

- **File Path**—/CourseCatalogStruts/WebRoot

- **File Name**—results.jsp

- **Template to Use**—Standard JSP Using Struts 1.1

After you've provided this information, click Finish.

The new JSP, `results.jsp`, is filled with setup information. Look for the line

```
This a struts page. <br>
```

In place of this line, substitute the following:

```
Course Number: <bean:write name="courseSearchForm" property="courseNumber"/><br>
Course Name:   <bean:write name="courseSearchForm" property="courseName"/><br>
Instructor:    <bean:write name="courseSearchForm" property="instructor"/><br>
```

Now you can save `results.jsp`.

Before you deploy, check the form target in `courseSearch.jsp`. The version of MyEclipse used in this chapter did not fill in the form action with the Struts action declared in the Struts Wizard. The form action in `courseSearch.jsp` should read `/courseSearch`. If it does not, update it to do so.

If you still have Tomcat running from the previous example, stop it by selecting the running guy with the smiling face behind him. Click the downward-pointing triangle and click Tomcat 5, Stop.

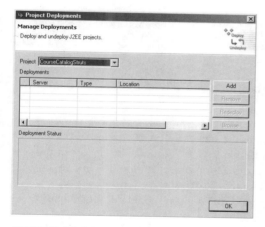

FIGURE 11.9 The Project Deployments dialog with no available deployment configurations.

From the Package Explorer, right-click the CourseCatalogStruts project and then click MyEclipse, Add and Remove Project Deployment to open the Project Deployments dialog. The Project Deployments dialog displays available projects and their deployment profiles. Select CourseCatalogStruts in the Project field if it is not the current project (see Figure 11.9). No deployment profiles are available for it, so you will have to create one the same way you created one for CallCenterWeb: by clicking Add and, when the New Deployment dialog opens, selecting Server Tomcat 5 and the deploy type Exploded Archive. The Deploy Location field will display the directory where the Web app will be installed (see Figure 11.10). Click Finish. Adding the Deployment profile for the first time takes care of doing the initial deployment. Click OK to complete the deployment and close the Project Deployments dialog.

Restart Tomcat by selecting Tomcat 5, Start from the toolbar. You are ready to go when Tomcat displays the following message:

```
INFO: Server startup in 18667 ms
```

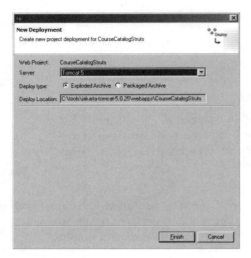

FIGURE 11.10   The completed deployment configuration for Tomcat 5.

Open a Web browser and point it to your Struts application:

```
http://localhost:8080/CourseCatalogStruts/
courseSearch.jsp
```

The HTML page displays a very plain look and feel, with just the three fields and two buttons. Without entering any information in the fields, click Submit. The `validate()` method will create `ActionMessage` objects for each of the fields, and the `ActionServlet` will call `courseSearch.jsp` to handle displaying the error messages contained in the `ActionErrors` object (see Figure 11.11). The `CourseSearchAction` has not been called as of yet.

Enter information in the various fields and click Submit. The `results.jsp` page displays the entered information (see Figure 11.12). Success! Your first Struts Web application using MyEclipse is done.

SHOP TALK

Struts and the Art of Layers and Indirection

The exercise you just ran through brings to mind a number of issues involved in the use of frameworks and indirection.

First of all, it is important to remember that a framework encapsulates many best practices, but it cannot encapsulate them all. Struts is no different and makes it a point to remind developers that they are responsible for the "M" part of the MVC design used in Struts. The model is the core of the application and needs the most work. The Struts example uses a form object to store the information from the input page, but it does not pass the form to any kind of search service, for the sake of brevity. However, even if there were a datasource of some kind, the `Action` should not pass the form in anyway. Passing the form would increase the coupling between the presentation and the data source layers. It would be up to the designer/implementer of the search service to create an object, or objects, to hold lookup criteria to increase the cohesion but decrease the coupling. Not knowing how a client is going to use the service would encourage the service to use this `SearchCriteria` object to do its job generically. It is the difference between having an `Action` do this:

```
// Cast the incoming form
SearchForm strutsSearchFromObject = (SearchForm)form;

// Get the search service to look up a course
searchService = … // Retrieve the SearchService from somewhere…
Course [] course = searchService.searchFor(strutsSearchFormObject);
```

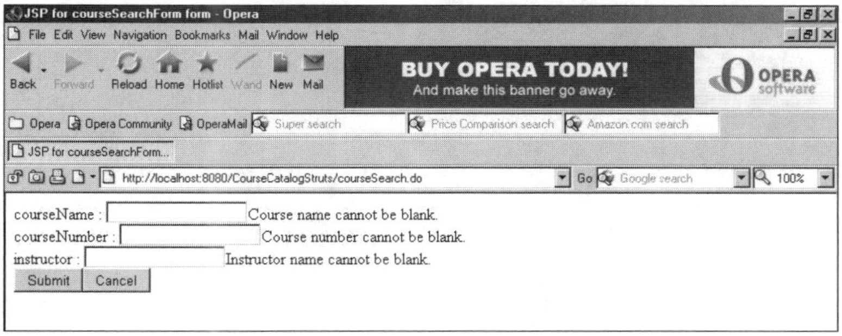

FIGURE 11.11   The course search page displaying error messages next to each field.

Struts is interesting enough that quite a bit of what you may have just discovered has less to do with Eclipse and more to do with Struts. The MyEclipse Wizards copied all the files you needed, created an input file, the `ActionForm`, the `Action`, and the `ApplicationResource` file. The MyEclipse JSP Wizard also has built-in templates to create JSP files that directly support the Struts tag libraries and Struts forms.

or this:

```
// Cast the incoming form
SearchForm strutsSearchFormObject = (SearchForm)form;

// Get the search service to look up a course
searchService = … // Retrieve the SearchService from somewhere…

// Copy the form information into a search service-specific object.
strutsSearchFormObject.copyTo(searchServiceCriteriaobject);
Course [] course = searchService.searchFor(searchServiceCriteriaobject);
```

By including the `CourseSearchForm` in the API of the `CourseSearchService` implies that the service is only being used by the `Action` and no one else, which is always a possibility, but not likely.

Does this mean that you would have to have code in various places in your `Action` to copy the data from the form to the criteria object? Not at all. Because the object controlling the data is the form, you would implement a `copyTo()` method in the form that would recognize the criteria object and take care of copying any data into it.

FIGURE 11.12   The output from `results.jsp`.

For the next few additions to the current example, you should stop Tomcat and close all your editor windows by pressing Ctrl+Shift+F4. The additions have to do with scenarios such as the following:

- All `Action` objects need to call a particular forward if certain information is entered.

- When an exception is thrown from any `Action`, the Web application should always display the same error page based on exception type.

- You will remove the code-based form altogether and use a configuration-driven form instead.

- You will configure a JDBC source for use by the Struts application.

MyEclipse gives you direct Struts support for these scenarios, in the creation of global forwards, global exceptions, `DynaActionForms`, and datasources. You will add one of each of these to the CourseCatalogStruts project, and you will modify the `CourseSearchAction` to use them all.

Adding Global Forwards

Let's create a global forward that the `CourseSearchAction` will use when an unknown course number is entered. A *global forward* is the mapping of a named resource that is available to all action-mapping elements. To create a global forward using MyEclipse, open `struts-config.xml`, go to the Outline view, right-click the `global-forward` node, and select New Forward to open the Struts 1.1 Forward Declaration dialog. You can declare global and local forwards using this dialog. By clicking a particular forward scope, you cause the wizard to assign the forward information either to a particular `Action` or to a global-forward element. For this example, ensure that Global Forward is the selected radio button in Forward Scope. Enter the forward name `unknown` and enter the forward path `/unknown.jsp` (see Figure 11.13). Click Finish. The `struts-config.xml` file is not saved by the wizard on completion, so save the file by pressing Ctrl+S. The `global-forward` element generated by the wizard displays the following information:

```
<global-forwards >
<forward
    name="unknown"
    path="/unknown.jsp"
    redirect="false"
    contextRelative="false" />

</global-forwards>
```

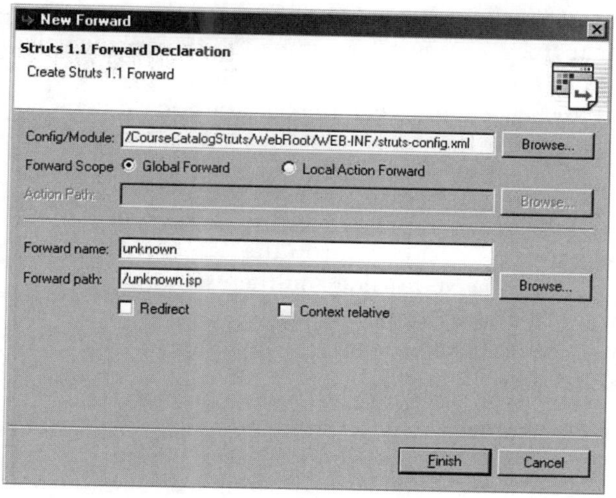

FIGURE 11.13   The New Forward dialog with a complete name and path.

Add a conditional to the Action so that all course numbers but one will cause the
unknown.jsp page to be displayed (you will create unknown.jsp next). Open
CourseSearchAction, located in the eclipse.kickstart.struts.action package, in the Java
editor. Update execute() to check for course number TT490. If the right course number
comes in, results.jsp is called and all other course numbers get unknown.jsp. Change
execute() to check for the incoming course number and return the proper ActionForward:

```
public ActionForward execute(
    ActionMapping mapping,
    ActionForm form,
    HttpServletRequest request,
    HttpServletResponse response) {
    CourseSearchForm customerSearchForm = (CourseSearchForm) form;

    ActionForward forward = null;
    if (customerSearchForm.getCourseNumber().equalsIgnoreCase("TT490")) {
```

```
        forward = mapping.findForward("success");
    } else {
        forward = mapping.findForward("unknown");
    }

    return forward;
}
```

With the following pieces in place, you can run the Struts application again. Start Tomcat, open you browser, navigate to http://localhost:8080/CourseCatalogStruts/courseSearch.jsp, enter "TT490" as the course number, and supply any information in the remaining two fields. Click Submit to see the usual results.jsp page. To see the call to unknown.jsp, click the Back button on your browser and change TT490 to TT491, or any other string that strikes your fancy. The result is an error from Struts to Tomcat stating that the request resource is unavailable. It is unavailable because you have not written unknown.jsp.

To create unknown.jsp in the Package Explorer, view select WebRoot in the CourseCatalogStruts project. Press Ctrl+N to open the New dialog and then select J2EE, Web, JSP. Click Next to go to the JSP Wizard page. Make sure File Path is set to /CourseCatalogStruts/WebRoot, File Name is set to unknown.jsp, and Template to Use is set to Standard JSP using Struts 1.1. Click Finish.

When the JSP editor opens, look for the following line:

```
This a struts page. <br>
```

In that line's place, put the following:

```
The following course was not found in the course catalog:<br>
<bean:write name="courseSearchForm" property="courseNumber" />
```

Redeploy the application either by clicking the button next to the MyEclipse Application Server button or by right-clicking the CourseCatalogStruts project and selecting Add and Remove Project Deployments. When the Project Deployments dialog opens, select CourseCatalogStruts as the project, select the Tomcat 5 server entry in the Deployments list, and click Redeploy.

Once again, open your browser and go to http://localhost:8080/CourseCatalogStruts/courseSearch.jsp. Enter a random course number and arbitrary information into the two remaining fields. When you click Submit, the ActionServlet will execute the CatalogSearchAction, which will ask the ActionServlet to forward the request to unknown.jsp, which in turn displays your page (see Figure 11.14).

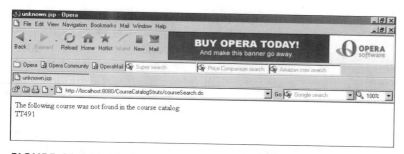

FIGURE 11.14 The browser displaying output from unknown.jsp.

Replacing Java-Based Forms with DynaActionForm

The next Struts technology supported in MyEclipse is the DynaActionForm. You can use DynaActionForm as a partial or complete replacement of your form, but when you use it as a complete replacement, you lose the ability to programmatically control the form's validation. An alternative to programmatic validation would be the Validator framework, which is part of the Jakarta Commons project. The Validator framework defines a reusable and extendible rule-based validation framework that lets you declare validation rules in an XML file as well as allows you to write your own rules that can be added to the framework. It is not directly related to Struts and therefore can be used to validate any kind of object. However, MyEclipse does not give you any direct support for the Validator framework. If you decide that the Validator framework is appropriate for your work, you would have to add the supporting pieces by hand. You will not be adding Validator support to any of the succeeding examples.

Let's look at both uses of the DynaActionForm and how MyEclipse supports them. The first one you will implement is the total replacement version. Rename the current form by right-clicking on CourseSearchForm and selecting from the pop-up menu Refactor, Rename. When the Rename Compilation Unit dialog opens, enter a new name of CourseSearchFormSave and make sure that no check boxes are selected. Click OK.

At this stage, you have a number of editors open. Close them all by using the keyboard short-cut Ctrl+Shift+F4. From the Package Explorer, double-click CourseCatalogStruts, WebRoot, WEB-INF, struts-config.xml. Delete the entry for CourseSearchForm by deleting the form-bean element between the form-beans tags. The new entry should be an open and close tag for form-beans. Save the struts-config.xml file:

```
<form-beans >
</form-beans>
```

In the Outline view, right-click form-beans and select New Form from the pop-up menu. When the New dialog opens, it opens on the same page you used when you first created the Struts application. Enter in the Use Case field Course Search. This will fill in the Form Name field with courseSearchForm, which is the name that will be entered in struts-config.xml as the form name. In Form Impl, click Dynamic FormBean, which changes the Dynamic Type field to use org.apache.struts.action.DynaActionForm. Click Add in the Form Properties section and enter the three field names courseNumber, courseName, and instructor, all with a type of java.lang.String. Remember to click Close when the Form Property dialog opens for the fourth time. Click Finish. The struts-config.xml file has been changed but not saved, so save the file.

The new form-beans entry now contains a type of org.apache.struts.action.DynaActionForm and three form-property elements, one for each of the form fields you entered. Take a look at your project: CourseSearchForm is not defined anywhere. In order for any code to access the form, it must now cast the form to be an object of type DynaActionForm and use the form's API to access the data:

```
<form-beans >
    <form-bean name="courseSearchForm" type="org.apache.struts.action.DynaActionForm">
        <form-property name="instructor" type="java.lang.String" />
        <form-property name="courseName" type="java.lang.String" />
        <form-property name="courseNumber" type="java.lang.String" />
    </form-bean>
</form-beans>
```

Open CourseSearchAction and change any references to CourseSearchForm to DynaActionForm. Remember to let the editor help you in typing out DynaActionForm (Ctrl+spacebar) and in correcting the import list (Ctrl+Shift+O). Also, change if() to look up the course number field using DynaActionForm.get():

```
public ActionForward execute(ActionMapping mapping, ActionForm form,
        HttpServletRequest request, HttpServletResponse response) {
    DynaActionForm customerSearchForm = (DynaActionForm) form;

    ActionForward forward = null;
    String courseNumber = (String) customerSearchForm.get("courseNumber");
    if (courseNumber.equalsIgnoreCase("TT490")) {
        forward = mapping.findForward("success");
    } else {
        forward = mapping.findForward("unknown");
    }

    return forward;
}
```

Save the file. Redeploy the Web application, restarting Tomcat if necessary. Your results should be the same as before: When you enter TT490 as the course number, the results.jsp page is displayed, and when you enter anything else as a course number, you get unknown.jsp. A different behavior will be when you leave any or all of the fields as blank, the ActionServlet does not send the form back to courseSearch.jsp; instead, it goes to either results.jsp or unknown.jsp.

Using a DynaActionForm, as convenient as the previous example portrays it to be, does lose validation that can be replaced using the Validator framework. Another option is to create a subclass of DynaActionForm, in conjunction with the definitions in struts-config.xml, and add validate() to the subclass. The use of this combination entails the following tasks:

- Subclassing DynaActionForm and adding validate().

- Changing the form-bean type entry to the subclass.

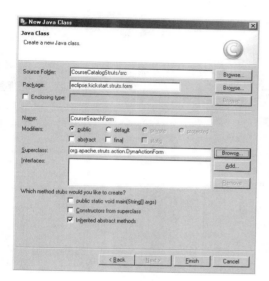

FIGURE 11.15 The New Java Class dialog with the information needed to generate the DynaActionForm subclass.

Let's create the hybrid DynaActionForm class. By rights, if you were doing this from scratch, you would use the MyEclipse Form Wizard to get you to where we are now, and the wizard would perform the following steps. Select the eclipse.kickstart.struts.form package in the CourseCatalogStruts project. Press Ctrl+N to open the New Java Class dialog; then select Java, Class and click Next. Enter in the Name field CourseSearchForm and click the Browse button next to the Superclass field. Entering the string dyn in the Superclass Selection dialog will bring DynaActionForm to the top of the list. Select it and click OK. The New dialog now has enough information to generate the stub class (see Figure 11.15). Click Finish.

When the CourseSearchForm opens in the Java editor, right-click anywhere in the editor and from the pop-up menu select Source, Override/ Implement Methods. The Override/Implement Methods dialog lists all the concrete and abstract methods available to your subclass. Scroll and open the ActionForm node, check validate(ActionMapping, HttpservletRequest), and click OK (see Figure 11.16).

Change validate() to perform a check on the form fields by getting the current field value from itself using the get() method and the desired field name:

```
public ActionErrors validate(
        ActionMapping mapping,
        HttpServletRequest request) {
        ActionErrors errors = new ActionErrors();

        String field = (String) get("instructor");
        if (field.trim().length() == 0) {
            errors.add("instructor", new ActionMessage("instructor.error"));
        }
```

```
        field = (String) get("courseNumber");
        if (field.trim().length() == 0) {
            errors.add("courseNumber", new ActionMessage("courseNumber.error"));
        }

        field = (String) get("courseName");
        if (field.trim().length() == 0) {
            errors.add("courseName", new ActionMessage("name.error"));
        }

        return errors;
    }
```

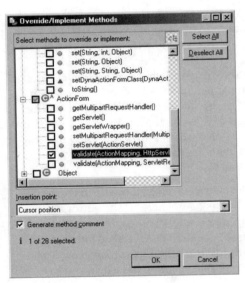

FIGURE 11.16 The list of available methods for CourseSearchForm to implement or override.

Now that you have a subclass of DynaActionForm, add it to struts-config.xml in the form-bean element type attribute (the shaded code):

```
<form-bean
    dynamic="true"
    name="courseSearchForm"
    type="eclipse.kickstart.struts.form.CourseSearchForm">
    <form-property name="instructor" type="java.lang.String" />
    <form-property name="courseNumber" type="java.lang.String" />
    <form-property name="courseName" type="java.lang.String" />
</form-bean>
```

Redeploy the application by selecting Add and Remove Project Deployments or by clicking the Redeployment button in the toolbar. Once you are redeployed, restart Tomcat, open your browser, and navigate to `http://localhost:8080/CourseCatalogStruts/courseSearch.jsp`. Click Submit without entering any information. The error messages will again be displayed.

Adding Global Exceptions

Action forwards define explicit targets that can be called by `Action` objects. Global exceptions define the flow for an exception that is not handled by your Web application. When an exception is caught by the `ActionServlet` and an exception element is defined within `struts-config.xml`, the framework retrieves the error message from the file where the messages are defined, wraps the string in an `ActionMessage` object, puts the `ActionMessage` object within an `ActionErrors` object, and passes the `ActionErrors` object to the forward target defined within the `exception` element. Let's create a global `exception` element that handles `IOExceptions` by sending an error message to an error page.

SHOP TALK

DynaActionForm Versus Subclassing ActionForm

If the `DynaActionForm` is so good, why is the `ActionForm` still supported in Struts? Why bother using one over the other? The answer is one of convenience: If you prefer to update configuration files instead of code, the `DynaActionForm` is a great way to go. Conventional wisdom goes like this: When a change needs to be made, you update `struts-config.xml` and continue on your way. Subclasses of `ActionForm` need to have code changed, which means that you have to take the file out of source control, you need to open an IDE to make the change, you need to run your tests to make sure that the change doesn't break anything or introduce new bugs, and so on.

I have to admit to feeling ambivalent about the `DynaActionForm`. As much as the `ActionForm` can appear to be more work, this is not as big a deal as it seems. If you are going to make a change to a form using `struts-config.xml`, you still need to take the file out of source control, you still need to update code somewhere to use the new field (or not use a deleted field), and you still need to run your tests to make sure that the change to the configuration file doesn't break anything else. (In my opinion, configuration file changes can create bugs that are much harder to track down than bugs created by code changes, unless you have good unit tests in place to prove otherwise.)

But what about the hassle of creating the Java class that maps to the form, defines the fields and their types, as well as the getter and setter methods? As you have seen in previous chapters, Eclipse lets you define a class using a wizard and takes care of generating the code to wrap access to instance fields from the editor. Also, defining the form using MyEclipse means the plug-in creates the `ActionForm` subclass for you with minimal effort.

There is one other advantage to creating the form as a subclass of `ActionForm`: The subclass's API to the instance fields is type-safe, whereas the `DynaActionForm` relies on you casting the various accesses to the data to the proper type.

Close all your editor windows except for `struts-config.xml` (double-click it to open it in the MyEclipse Struts editor if it is not already opened). In the Outline view, right-click `global-exceptions` and select from the pop-up menu New Exception to open the New Struts Exception dialog.

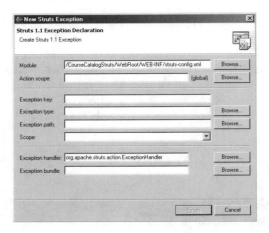

FIGURE 11.17 The New Struts Exception dialog.

The Struts 1.1 Exception Declaration page is divided up into three sections (see Figure 11.17):

- The location of the exception definition and its scope (global to all `Actions` or local to one)

- The type of exception this definition will handle, the error message to be displayed when it occurs, and the path to where the exception will be forwarded

- The type of the Java object that will handle the incoming exception and a resource file where it can look up the error message using the key from the previous section

All the fields in the wizard are required except for Action Scope and Exception Bundle. The exception will be assigned to the `global-exception` element if no action scope is declared; otherwise, the exception will be local to a particular action. The exception bundle defines a properties file that contains the error messages to be used when an exception is caught; if no file is declared, the file declared in `message-resources` is used.

Set the fields in the New Struts Exception dialog as follows:

- **Action Scope**—Leave this field blank.

- **Exception Key**—`ioe.error`.

- **Exception Type**—`java.io.IOException`. (Click the Browse button and use the dialog to find it.)

- **Exception Path**—`/error.jsp`.

- **Exception Handler**— `org.apache.struts.action.ExceptionHandler`.

- **Exception Bundle**—Leave this field blank.

Click Finish and save `struts-config.xml`. The `global-exceptions` element is ready for use. The `exception` element does not declare the use of `org.apache.struts.action.ExceptionHandler` because it is the default:

```
<global-exceptions >
   <exception
       key="ioe.error"
       path="/error.jsp"
       type="java.io.IOException" />

</global-exceptions>
```

For this first example of Struts-handled exceptions, you need to create an error page. Select CourseCatalogStruts, WebRoot and then press Ctrl+N to open the New dialog. Select J2EE, Web, JSP and click Next. In the JSP Wizard page, change the File Name field to error.jsp and leave the remaining two fields alone (Template to Use should be set to Standard JSP Using Struts 1.1). Click Finish.

In the error.jsp file, look for the line that reads

```
This a struts page. <br>
```

In place of this line, put in code to retrieve the ActionErrors object that is created when a java.io.IOException is caught:

```
<h1>Oh, no!  An error happened!</h1>
<html:errors />
```

Open the ApplicationResources.properties file found under CourseCatalogStruts, src, eclipse.kickstart.struts. Add a message with a key of ioe.error and save the file:

```
ioe.error=Major error trying to retrieve the data from the main server.<br>
```

The only thing left to do is have the CourseSearchAction throw an exception. Open CourseSearchAction in the Java editor and modify the condition to throw an java.io.IOException when a course number of "foobar" is entered. Make sure you add the throws Exception clause to execute():

```
public ActionForward execute(
    ActionMapping mapping,
    ActionForm form,
    HttpServletRequest request,
    HttpServletResponse response) throws Exception {
    DynaActionForm customerSearchForm = (DynaActionForm) form;

    String courseNumber = (String) customerSearchForm.get("courseNumber");
    ActionForward forward = null;
    if (courseNumber.equalsIgnoreCase("TT490")) {
        forward = mapping.findForward("success");
```

```
    } else if (courseNumber.equalsIgnoreCase("foobar")) {
        throw new IOException("Read/write error!");
    } else {
        forward = mapping.findForward("unknown");
    }

    return forward;
}
```

Stop Tomcat. The `struts-config.xml` file has been changed, and the only way for
`ActionServlet` to reread the file is to be reloaded. Redeploy the CourseCatalogStruts application using the Add and Remove Project Deployments dialog. Restart Tomcat within Eclipse,
and when Tomcat has completed its startup, open your browser and navigate to
`http://localhost:8080/CourseCatalogStruts/courseSearch.jsp`. Enter foobar into the
course number field, some arbitrary strings into the remaining two fields, and click Submit.
The `error.jsp` page will display with the message from the `ApplicationResources.proper-`
ties file (see Figure 11.18).

FIGURE 11.18   The `error.jsp` page displaying the error message from the thrown `IOException`.

If you subclassed `org.apache.struts.action.ExceptionHandler` to create your own exception handler, you could take the incoming exception and perform some intermediate operation before forwarding the request to the target forward.

Configuring a Struts Datasource

Another element defined within `struts-config.xml` is `data-source`. The definition of `data-`
`source` allows an `Action` to access a JDBC datasource from within your application. Because a
previous chapter defined a Hypersonic database, you will deploy your Struts-based application to JBoss and then you will modify `CatalogSearchAction` to access the `data-source`
defined in `struts-config.xml`.

If you have not installed and downloaded JBoss, refer to the "Downloading and Installing
JBoss" section of Chapter 9. It will walk you through the process of downloading and
installing JBoss, the configuration of the JBoss-supplied Hypersonic database, the execution
of the SQL to create a table, and the insertion of a few rows into the table.

On the assumption that you have JBoss downloaded, installed, and configured with its Hypersonic database set up with data, let's once again walk through creating a deployment configuration so that you can deploy to JBoss and test whether your Web application is still functioning.

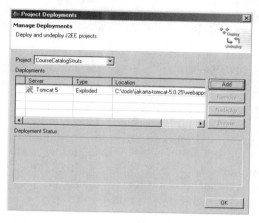

FIGURE 11.19 The Project Deployments dialog with the Tomcat deployment configuration.

Open the Project Deployments dialog by clicking the button next to the MyEclipse app server button on the toolbar, or you can right-click the CourseCatalogStruts project and select MyEclipse, Add and Remove Project Deployments from the pop-up menu. When the Project Deployments dialog opens, the Tomcat 5 deployment configuration appears as its only entry (see Figure 11.19). Select CourseCatalogStruts as the project and click Add. When the New Deployment dialog opens, select JBoss 3 as the server and select the deploy type Exploded Archive. Click Finish to return to the Project Deployments dialog, which now lists two deployment configurations: Tomcat 5 and JBoss 3. Click OK.

Once you selected JBoss as a deployment target, MyEclipse took care of deploying the application to it. If the configuration and deployment went well, you can call your Web application from a browser and see the input and output pages as you did before. To check the application, stop Tomcat (from the toolbar, select Tomcat 5, Stop) and then start JBoss (from the toolbar, select JBoss 3, Start). You cannot have Tomcat and JBoss running at the same time using their default configurations because they both use port 8080. JBoss is ready to go when you see the message telling you how long it took JBoss to start:

```
18:40:14,934 INFO  [Server] JBoss (MX MicroKernel) [3.2.3 (build:
↪CVSTag=JBoss_3_2_3 date=200311301445)] Started in 26s:137ms
```

Open your browser and navigate to the usual spot, http://localhost:8080/CourseCatalogStruts/courseSearch.jsp. To make sure your application is functioning, try the following scenarios:

1. Enter a course number of TT490 with any instructor and any course name. When you click Submit, you should get the results.jsp output. Click the Back button on your browser. Leave the instructor and name fields alone for the rest of the scenarios.

2. Change the course number to TT491 and click Submit. The output from unknown.jsp should appear. Click the Back button.

3. Change the course number to foobar and click Submit. The error.jsp page will display the "Oh, no! An error happened!" page.

If you were developing this as a real Web application, you would have had test fixtures in place to run these tests for you.

Before you can configure the Struts datasource, you have to put the JDBC driver you intend to use someplace where the Struts framework can find it and use it. If you had an external database running, this example could have been run from within Tomcat, as any JDBC driver will do as long as it is available to Struts. The use of JBoss is purely one of convenience.

Right-click CourseCatalogStruts, WebRoot, WEB-INF, lib and then select Import from the pop-up menu. When the Import dialog opens, select File System as the import source and click Next.

On the File System page, you need to navigate to the JBoss directory where the HSQL driver is located, which is <JBoss install directory>\server\default\lib. Click the top Browse button and navigate to the proper directory. When you have found the lib directory, click OK to enter the path into the From Directory field. The left window lists lib as a folder, and the right window lists the JAR files the directory contains. Put a check next to hsqldb.jar. The Into Folder field must read CourseCatalogStruts/WebRoot/WEB-INF/lib (see Figure 11.20). Click Finish. The hsqldb.jar file is now located in your project WEB-INF/lib directory.

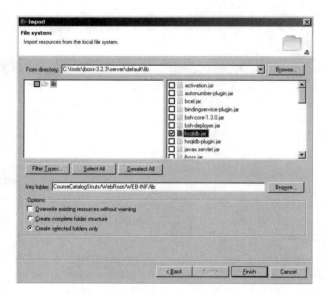

FIGURE 11.20   The File System import page with the required data.

One last thing before you can configure the struts-config.xml file: You need to put the HSQL driver JAR file in the build path of your project. The import should have taken care of that, but to be sure, from the Package Explorer open the Properties dialog by right-clicking the CourseCatalogStruts project name and selecting Properties from the pop-up menu. When the Properties dialog opens, select Java Build Path from the left and the Libraries tab from the right. The `hsqldb.jar` file should be one of the JAR files in the build path of your project. If it is not, click Add External JARs and navigate to your project workspace `WEB-INF/lib` directory and include it. If the `hsqldb.jar` file is there, click OK to close the Properties dialog.

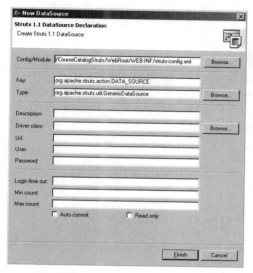

Open `struts-config.xml`. In the Outline view, right-click `data-sources` and select New DataSource from the pop-up menu to open the New DataSource dialog, where you define the Struts DataSource (see Figure 11.21). The first three fields are already filled and should be set as follows:

- **Config/Module Path**— `/CourseCatalogStruts/WebRoot/ WEB-INF/struts-config.xml`

- **Key**—`org.apache.struts.action. DATA_SOURCE`

- **Type**—`org.apache.struts.util. GenericDataSource`

FIGURE 11.21 The New DataSource dialog displaying the Struts 1.1 DataSource Declaration page.

The next section contains JDBC driver information:

- **Description**—This field can be left blank.

- **Driver Class**—`org.hsqldb.jdbcDriver`. (Use the Browse button to find it using the Superclass selection dialog.)

- **Url**—`jdbc:hsqldb:hsql://localhost:1701`. (This information is taken from the `hsqldb-ds.xml` file supplied with JBoss.)

- **User**—sa.

- **Password**—Leave this field blank.

The third section is datasource-configuration data:

- **Login Time Out**—Leave this field blank.

- **Min Count**—1. (This is the minimum number of connections to use.)

- **Max Count**—5. (This is the maximum number of connections to use.)

- **Auto Commit**—Check this option.

- **Read Only**—Leave this option unchecked.

Once all the preceding information is entered, click Finish. The data-sources element now contains the information needed to configure the default Struts datasource, GenericDataSource, at runtime:

```
<data-sources >
    <data-source>
        <set-property property="password" value="" />
        <set-property property="minCount" value="1" />
        <set-property property="maxCount" value="5" />
        <set-property property="user" value="sa" />
        <set-property property="driverClass" value="org.hsqldb.jdbcDriver" />
        <set-property property="description" value="" />
        <set-property property="url" value="jdbc:hsqldb:hsql://localhost:1701" />
        <set-property property="readOnly" value="false" />
        <set-property property="autoCommit" value="true" />
        <set-property property="loginTimeout" value="" />
    </data-source>

</data-sources>
```

Now that Struts has a JDBC datasource available for use by the Action, let's update the code for CourseSearchAction to use it. The first conditional is the only piece that has changed. No matter which instructor name is entered, the code will always use the name field from the customer table in the Hypersonic database:

```
if (courseNumber.equalsIgnoreCase("TT490")) {
    DataSource ds = getDataSource(request);
    Connection con = ds.getConnection();
    Statement stmt = null;
    ResultSet rs = null;
    try {
        stmt = con.createStatement();
        rs = stmt.executeQuery(
            "select * from customer where phone_number='1-222-333-4444'");
        rs.next();
        String name = rs.getString("name");
        customerSearchForm.set("instructor", name);
    } catch (SQLException e) {
        e.printStackTrace();
    } finally {
        con.close();
    }
    forward = mapping.findForward("success");
```

```
    } else if (courseNumber.equalsIgnoreCase("foobar")) {
        throw new IOException("Read/write error!");
    } else {
        forward = mapping.findForward("unknown");
    }
```

Stop JBoss, redeploy CourseCatalogStruts, and restart JBoss. Open your browser to `http://localhost:8080/CourseCatalogStruts/courseSearch.jsp` and enter TT490 for the course number, John Smith as the instructor, and Eclipse for the course name. Click Submit. The results.jsp output should have an instructor name of Ronald Weasley (see Figure 11.22).

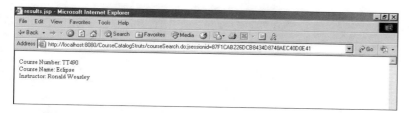

FIGURE 11.22 The final output of results.jsp showing the substitution of the name retrieved from the Hypersonic database.

Two Struts framework areas you are not going to try out using MyEclipse are the creation of controller components and the creation of message-resources because there is no direct support for either technology within MyEclipse.

In Brief

Struts developments using MyEclipse is easier than pulling the various pieces of the Struts framework together by hand. Not all aspects of Struts are supported within the plug-in, specifically the Validator framework and the controller configuration within struts-config.xml, but overall the support is solid and the various Struts pieces work with a minimum of effort.

- Struts projects are created from Web projects. Adding Struts capabilities to a Web project is accomplished by right-clicking the project and selecting MyEclipse, Add Struts Capabilities.

- Deployment of a Struts application to Tomcat is handled by a deployment wizard. The wizard works in conjunction with application server information entered in the Preferences dialog under MyEclipse, Application Servers.

- Global forwards are available to all `Actions` defined within `struts-config.xml`.

- `DynaActionForm` allows you to define a form without having to write an associated Java class, but you lose validation capability unless you create a subclass of `DynaActionForm` and include `validate()` or use the Validator framework.

- The `global-exceptions` element is supported by a MyEclipse wizard. Exceptions thrown by `Action` objects are caught by the `ActionServlet` and redirected to the forward target defined in the `global-exception` element.

- JDBC datasources are supported through a MyEclipse wizard that understands how to configure the default Struts JDBC datasource `GenericDataSource`.

UML Using Omondo

12

"Design like an analyst; analyze like a designer."

—Anonymous

UML and Eclipse

UML is a design technology that helps you communicate your design before, during, and after the actual process of system development. With nothing more than paper and pencil, you can describe your architecture in a way that is both simple and elegant. However, in the same way that the process of writing involves rewriting successive drafts, the process of design involves constant redesign due to the discovery of new facts. As fast as you can create your UML diagrams, they are out of date when the code starts to be written. Tools such as Rational Rose and Together/J tie the creation of certain development artifacts to their output (for example, class diagrams either create classes or reflect the current state of created classes), but depending on the capabilities of these tools, even they can run into problems keeping their diagrams in sync. Also, many UML diagramming tools are pure design tools when an analysis tool is just as important. UML tools, as numerous as they are, are not as common as they could be.

The short definition of UML, which stands for *Unified Modeling Language*, is that it is a graphical notation used to describe the various models of a software system. The long definition of UML is that UML aids in

- The process of requirements capture

- The formalized capture of systems concepts depicted as classes

- The understanding of how objects will interact with each other in specific scenarios

- The clarification of the life cycle of objects by identifying the various states to which an object can transition

- The organization of classes into packages and subsystems

- The depiction of the deployment of components in a final concrete system

UML 1.x defined nine diagrams, and the latest version of UML, version 2.0, defines 13 diagrams. UML has turned out to be so flexible that it is used in the modeling of nonsoftware processes as well.

It's most important function may be to communicate the current understanding of the software model to be implemented.

This chapter is not meant to be a tutorial on how to use UML. For those conversant in UML, EclipseUML has sufficient support for the base diagrams so that you can express not just the basics, such as Use Cases and class diagrams, but also state and activity diagrams as well as deployment. For a list of UML tutorials, refer to Appendix E, "Recommended Resources."

Understanding the Types of UML Diagrams

UML 2.0 has three categories of diagrams:

- **Structural**—The diagrams in this category describe the design, or *structure*, of the software system.

  The structural diagram types include Class, Object, Component, and Deployment.

- **Behavioral**—This category contains diagrams that depict the dynamic aspects of the software—how does it behave and under what conditions?

  The behavioral diagram types include Use Case, Sequence, Activity, Collaboration, and Statechart.

- **Management**—The various software and hardware components that represent the actual system are represented in the diagrams that fall under this category.

  The management diagram types include Packages, Subsystems, and Models.

The nine standard diagrams defined in the UML 1.x specification are detailed in the following list:

- **Use Case**—An analysis diagram that describes an actor's interaction with a system. Supporting documentation describes the course-grained goal an actor expects to achieve. An analyst would list the steps of the process an actor would perform to achieve the desired result if nothing goes wrong and the various alternate scenarios when things do go wrong. This is an important diagram because it defines what the system does as well as what it doesn't.

- **Class**—Class diagrams are used for both analysis and design. Many tools, including the EclipseUML plug-in, only support design-time class diagrams. The difference for a developer is that a design-time class diagram will not only define the relationships between class types, but will also use the naming conventions, package designations, field definitions, and so on of the implementation classes. A Class diagram is considered a static diagram because it only depicts *relationships* between the classes and not *interactions*.

- **Sequence**—A diagram that represents the dynamic interaction (messages sent) between classes. Actions flow left to right, with time progressing from top to bottom.

- **Collaboration**—A dynamic diagram similar to a sequence diagram. It displays objects and the flow of messages between them.

- **State**—A dynamic diagram that describes the various states in which an object can find itself as well as the events that cause an object to transition between those states.

- **Activity**—A dynamic diagram depicting object processes/data flow within a system among multiple objects.

- **Object**—A diagram of the objects in a system at a moment in time.

- **Component**—A static diagram that represents course-grained objects and their dependencies in a system. The component dependencies include implementation classes, binary files, scripts, and so on.

- **Deployment**—A static diagram of the hardware and software representation of a system.

The remaining four diagrams defined in UML 2.0—Composite Structure, Interaction Overview, Package, and Timing—will not be discussed in this chapter.

UML is not tied to any particular software development methodology. It is a graphical language and does not define any process for its use. A search of the Web for methodologies that use UML produces an overwhelming list of choices. You do not need a methodology to use UML, but knowing a methodology will make your work easier. If you are not sure where to begin, you can go to the Object Management Group's UML site at http://www.uml.org/ and begin digging into what UML really means. Don't let yourself get overwhelmed. The UML is a small number of diagrams with strong semantic meaning, but you should learn them one at a time and use them whenever possible to convey meaning.

The Omondo UML Plug-In

Omondo, a commercial software tool vendor, released a free version of its UML plug-in that has been available since Eclipse 2.0. EclipseUML supports the nine UML diagrams defined in the UML 1.x specification, with support expected for the remaining four diagrams defined in

UML 2.0. Some of the diagrams are purely for analysis, such as the Use Case diagram, whereas others are for both analysis and design, such as the Class diagram. The analysis diagrams tell you what you are implementing, whereas the design diagrams express how the system will be implemented. Within EclipseUML, an analysis diagram such as Use Case will not vary based on changes to the code in an Eclipse project. Design diagrams can reflect changes made to the class types as defined in the project at any given moment.

The EclipseUML plug-in can be found on the Omondo Web site. You will find both the free and the commercial version at `http://www.eclipseuml.com/`. Once you have successfully registered with Omondo, you can download the EclipseUML plug-in from `http://www.omondo.com/download/free/index.jsp`. The examples in this chapter use the EclipseUML Enterprise Edition, which you can download by clicking the Enterprise link on the left side of the Download page. This is not the free version but rather a 20-day time-boxed edition. This chapter will examine the feature set that overlaps the free version of EclipseUML.

The Download page for EclipseUML Enterprise Edition has an Auto-Installer you can download. The download used in this chapter is `eclipseUML_3M8_studioEdition-installer_1.0.0.20040524.jar`, though there may be a later version available by the time this book is published. Save the JAR file wherever you are used to saving downloaded files.

If you installed another version of EclipseUML for use with Eclipse 3.0, you must uninstall it before installing this new version.

Shut down Eclipse before performing the EclipseUML installation.

To install EclipseUML, you must execute the downloaded JAR file, `eclipseUML_enterpriseEdition-installer_0.9.520040319.jar`. If JAR files are already associated with `javaw`, double-click the installer JAR file to start the installer. If `javaw` has not been associated with JAR files, open a command-line window, change directories to where you have the EclipseUML file, and run `java` with the `-jar` option. Here is an example:

```
java -jar eclipseUML_enterpriseEdition-installer_1.0.0.20040524.jar
```

In either case, the installer will open a dialog to start the process by requesting that you select a language. Pick an appropriate language for your locale and click OK. You can accept most of the EclipseUML Wizard defaults except for the location of your Eclipse install. Make sure you enter the proper Eclipse directory because the EclipseUML plug-in is installed there. Once the wizard has completed the install, you can click Quit.

To check whether the installation was successful, open the Preferences dialog from the main menu by selecting Window, Preferences. If the install worked, you will see UML listed as a node in the list to the left. You are now ready to use EclipseUML in your next Java project.

Using UML to Facilitate Your Design

For the remainder of this chapter, you will create various diagrams to describe an online training system. The system will be described in terms of only two actors and a few of the tasks they want to accomplish when they use the system. The various diagrams will give you a starting point to implement the system, the completion of which will be left as an exercise for you, the reader.

To create the UML diagrams, you must have a project with which to associate them. Create a Java project named TrainingFirm by following these steps:

1. Start Eclipse if it is not already running.

2. Press Ctrl+N to open the New dialog.

3. Select Java Project and click Next.

4. In the Project Name field, enter TrainingFirm. If you want to save this project in another location, uncheck Create Project in Workspace and enter a new workspace location.

5. In the Project Layout section, the Create Separate Source and Output Folders option should be selected, but disabled. Click Next.

5a. If Project Layout is not disabled, cancel out of this dialog, open the Preferences dialog, and check the Java, New Project settings. New Project should be set to create src and classes directories for new projects. If New Project is not set to create src and classes, select Folders in the Source and Output Folder section and enter src as the source folder name and classes as the output folder name. Then return to step 2.

6. The Java Settings page should show TrainingFirm/src as the setting for Source Folder on Build Path and TrainingFirm/classes as the setting for Default Output Folder. Click Finish.

The UML model files you create can go anywhere in your project, but you should select somewhere. If you have project-wide diagrams, place them at the project level. Diagrams specific to certain areas of your system should be placed where they are most convenient. Create a folder called models under the TrainingFirm project by right-clicking TrainingFirm in the Package Explorer view. Then, from the pop-up menu, select New, Folder. When the New Folder dialog opens, enter the folder name models and click Finish.

Creating a Use Case Diagram

The training system has two primary users: a customer and a course coordinator. The customer needs to look up course information so he or she can register for a class, whereas the course coordinator is only concerned with making sure there are courses for which the customers can register. Their needs make up the requirements of this system. A Use Case diagram is not enough to communicate the information necessary to begin addressing the requirements of a system. The diagram is just the high-level view of the actors and their goals. As such, it is one of the only diagram types you can present to your users and expect them to understand it after a brief explanation. Let's delineate the Use Cases for this example:

Actor 1:

- **Course coordinator**—The course coordinator is responsible for entering new courses, scheduling classes to run on particular dates, and assigning instructors to the scheduled classes.

Use Cases:

- Schedule a class.

- Assign an instructor to a class.

- Enter a new course.

Actor 2:

- **Customer**—The customer uses the system to find scheduled classes and register one or more attendees for a course.

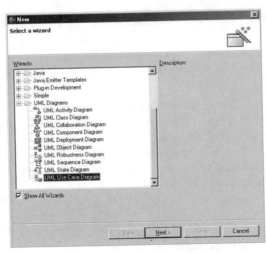

FIGURE 12.1   The New dialog displaying the available EclipseUML wizards.

Use Cases:

- Search for available courses.

- Register for a class.

Let's build the Use Case diagram for the two actors and their expectations:

1. From the Package Explorer view, select TrainingFirm and press Ctrl+N to open the New dialog.

2. Select UML Diagram, UML Use Case Diagram from the wizard list (see Figure 12.1). If the list of wizards is incomplete, check the box Show All Wizards and select the proper node. Click Next.

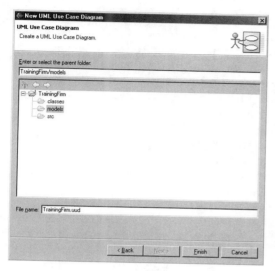

FIGURE 12.2 The New UML Use Case Diagram dialog.

3. In the tree view window, open the TrainingFirm node to reveal the classes, models, and src directories. Select models.

4. The File Name field should read TrainingFirm.uud. If not, enter the name in the field. The .uud extension stands for *UML Use Case diagram*. Because this diagram is generic to your project, leave it assigned to the models directory (see Figure 12.2). Click Finish.

Every EclipseUML diagram has a toolbar specific to the diagram on which you are working. Let's take a look at the Use Case toolbar in the creation of an initial diagram of the preceding actors and Use Cases (see Figure 12.3).

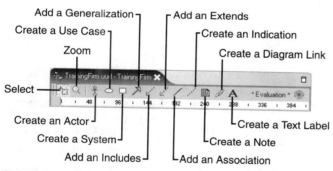

FIGURE 12.3 The Use Case diagram editor toolbar.

The Use Case diagram editor supports single/multiple selections, zoom, actors, Use Cases, systems, generalization/inheritance, includes/extends, associations, indications, notes, links, and labels. For this diagram, you will create the aforementioned actors and five Use Cases associated with them. Click the stick figure (third button from the left) and then click in the editor area. The New Actor dialog opens to receive the (optional) stereotype and name of the actor. You would enter a stereotype as a way of clarifying the role of the actor. For example, if the actor were a software system instead of a human, you might enter **HR System** as the stereotype. Leave Stereotype blank; in the Name field, enter **Course Coordinator** and click OK. The labeled UML icon for an actor is depicted in the Use Case editor (see Figure 12.4). At regular intervals, save the TrainingFirm.uud file.

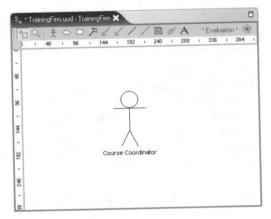

FIGURE 12.4   The Course Coordinator actor.

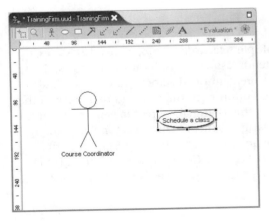

FIGURE 12.6   The Course Coordinator and its single "Schedule a class" Use Case.

Every actor that interacts with the system needs to have a Use Case associated with it. The Course Coordinator has three Use Cases: schedule a class, assign an instructor to a class, and enter a new course into the system. Add a Use Case by clicking the button with an oval (the button to the right of the actor button) and then clicking to the right of the Course Coordinator actor in the editor window. A New use case dialog opens. This dialog is divided into four documentation areas: Properties, Normal Flow, Alternative Flow, and Description. The Properties tab describes the name of the Use Case, whether it is *abstract* (meaning it is not a complete Use Case but rather dependent on other Use Cases), pre-conditions and post-conditions (how things must be prior to the Use Case being called and how they must be after the Use Case completes), and the Use Case's rank. Enter the information as shown in Figure 12.5.

The Normal Flow, Alternative Flow, and Description tabs are all freeform text areas. They are where you enter the scenario in which every-thing goes according to plan, the scenarios in which nothing goes according to plan and where they deviate from the good scenario, and general text about the Use Case that did not fit in the previous tabs. Click OK to close the New use case dialog and have the oval appear in the editor to the right of the actor (see Figure 12.6). Notice that the Outline view of the Use Case diagram is a thumbnail of the original diagram.

The actor and Use Case are missing one other thing: a line to associate them. Click the Add an Association button (the button on the toolbar with the slanted solid line) and click once on the actor and once on the Use Case. The actor and the Use Case are now connected (see Figure 12.7). Press Ctrl+S to save the TrainingFirm.uud file.

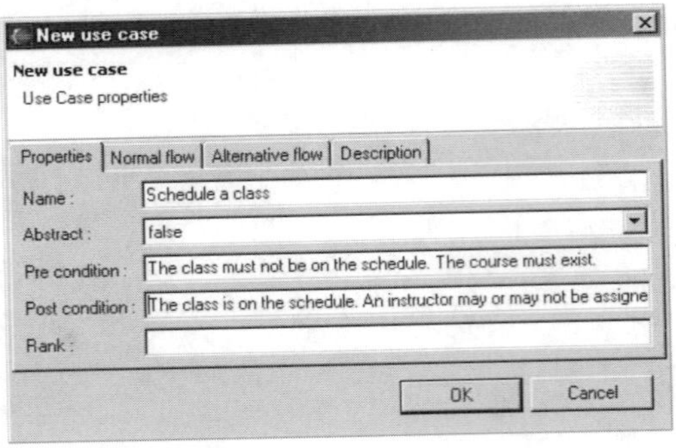

FIGURE 12.5   The New use case dialog with the properties of your first Use Case.

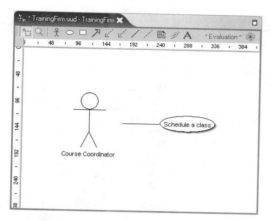

FIGURE 12.7 The actor, Use Case, and association line.

Let's add the remaining Use Cases for this actor:

1. Click the Use Case button and then click below the "Schedule a class" Use Case. When the New use case dialog opens, enter the following in the Properties tab:

   - **Name**—Assign an instructor to a class

   - **Abstract**—false

   - **Pre-condition**—The class may or may not have an instructor.

   - **Post-condition**—The class has an assigned instructor.

   - **Rank**—(leave blank)

2. Click OK to close the New use case dialog. You can drag and drop the icons to reposition them to your liking.

3. Click the Add an Association button, click the Course Coordinator actor, and then click the "Assign an instructor to a class" Use Case.

4. Perform the same steps for the Use Case "Enter a new course." Leave the Abstract, Pre-condition, Post-condition, and Rank fields blank.

The Customer actor needs to be added with its two Use Cases. Double-click the TrainingFirm.uud tab to give the Use Case editor more display room. Then follow these steps:

1. Click the Actor button and then click below the Course Coordinator actor. When the New Actor dialog opens, enter the name **Customer** and click OK.

2. Click the Use Case button and then click below the "Enter a new course" Use Case. When the New use case dialog opens, enter into the Properties tab **Search for available courses** in the Name field and click OK.

3. Click the Add an Association button, click the Customer actor, and then click the "Search for available courses" Use Case.

4. Perform the last two steps for the Use Case "Register for a class" (see Figure 12.8).

Finally, let's depict the various Use Cases as being part of one overall system. Click the Create a System button (fifth from the left) and draw a box around all the Use Cases. When the New System dialog opens, enter in the Name field **Training System** and then click OK.

The Use Cases will all be forced away from the Training System rectangle, so you will have to drag them back into the rectangle (see Figure 12.9).

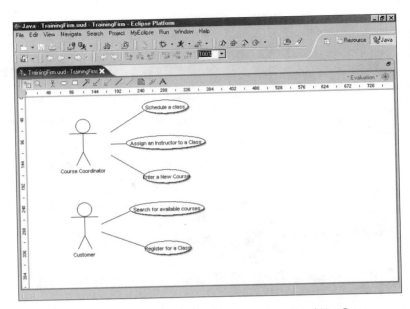

FIGURE 12.8   The Customer actor with its two associated Use Cases.

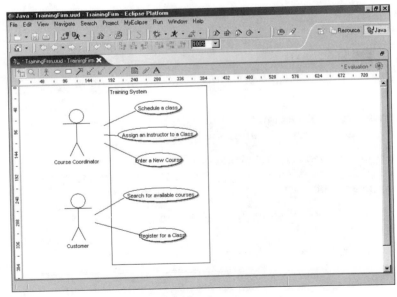

FIGURE 12.9   The completed Use Case diagram, including the system box.

As an analysis diagram, the Use Case diagram you just created still needs an associated document that discusses each individual Use Case from a process perspective: How does the process work when everything goes right? How does the process work when things go wrong? The various tabs, such as Normal Flow, provide the start of the documentation needed to get a deeper understanding of the task at hand. EclipseUML does support the printing of the information embedded in the diagrams as HTML pages, but that will not be covered in this chapter.

UML and Design by Chaos

Use Case diagrams are one of the few diagram types where there is minimal-to-no interaction with additional UML diagrams, with the exception of perhaps Sequence diagrams. As you grow your design, you will jump from Class diagram to Sequence diagram to State diagram to Component diagram to Deployment diagram, and so on, in the order in which your ideas take you. The diagrams are meant to support your thought process.

Using a Class Diagram

Using the brief information from the Use Case, you will now create a Class diagram displaying some of the classes that define the training domain and what the relationships are between the various classes. The intent in using EclipseUML is to let you define a domain model without getting bogged down in the details of creating classes, interfaces, and relationships. You give the wizard the package and class/interface name and grow the diagram until you have enough information to describe the problem domain.

Based on the prior Use Case descriptions, the following classes lend themselves to a first cut at a domain definition:

- **Class**—This is a particular course, at a particular location, on a particular date. It may have an assigned instructor.

- **Course**—This is one of many courses offered on particular subjects. It can be run onsite or offsite at a public training facility.

- **Instructor**—An instructor is a resource who knows the topic and is available to teach during a given time period. The instructor could be a contractor or a full-time employee.

- **Location**—A class can be held at a privately owned or rented facility. It has zero or more available rooms, and every available room can hold one or more students.

- **Address**—The basic information about where a training facility is located.

The Class diagram can be quite involved or trivial, depending on the amount of information you plan on conveying. For the training domain model, you have a combination of both, because this is not an exercise in designing a system but rather in how to create the diagrams using EclipseUML. There are many more classes you can add to this domain model, but you will work with the few listed here.

The steps to implement a class diagram are similar to the ones for the pervious diagram:

1. Create an empty diagram.

2. Use the icons on the editor toolbar to populate the diagram.

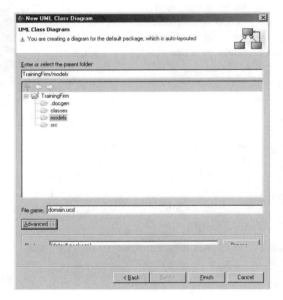

FIGURE 12.10 The UML Class Diagram page with the models directory as the target and the file name domain.ucd.

In addition, you will also define the relationships between the classes as either composition, aggregation, or none, add a note explaining the incomplete nature of the diagram, and add a title suitable for printing.

Let's create the diagram and add the classes, relationships, a note, and a title. Press Ctrl+N to open the New dialog and then select UML Diagrams, UML Class Diagram. Click Next.

In the UML Class Diagram page, select the TrainingFirm, models directory and change the File Name setting from (default diagram).ucd to domain.ucd (see Figure 12.10). The .ucd extension stands for *UML Class Diagram*. Click Finish. The domain.ucd file is created in the TrainingFirm, models directory, and the UML Class Diagram editor opens on an empty diagram.

The toolbars for all the diagrams have the Select and Zoom buttons as the first two available items. The next buttons are for the creation of packages, classes, interfaces, associations, inheritance, dependencies, indications, notes, links to other diagrams, and labels (see Figure 12.11). You will use most of these buttons by the time you are through with this diagram.

Double-click the tab domain.ucd to open the editor on the entire Eclipse workbench. Click Create a Class and then click in the center-top of the diagram. The New Java Class dialog

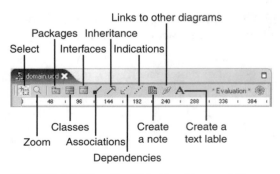

FIGURE 12.11 The UML Class Diagram Editor toolbar.

opens to collect the information needed by the wizard to create the class that corresponds to the diagram element. The wizard needs a minimum of information:

- **Source Folder**—TrainingFirm/src

- **Package**—training.domain

- **Name**—Class

- **Modifiers**—public

- **Superclass**—java.lang.Object

- **Which method stubs would you like to create?**—Only check Inherited Abstract Methods.

Click Finish. Somewhere on the diagram will be a rectangle with the name training::domain::Class. The double colon is the standard UML namespace notation, which corresponds to the Java package namespace when the double colons are changed to dots.

The procedure for adding classes to the diagram is mechanical: Click the Create a Class button (or right-click in the editor and select New, Class) and then click in an empty area of the diagram editor. When the New Java Class dialog opens, enter the package and name where the class should be generated and click Finish. Follow this procedure for Course, Location, Address, Outline, Contractor, and Employee, putting each of these classes in the training.domain package (see Figure 12.12). The classes that you add will not be placed exactly as shown in the figure, but you can drag and drop your icons to make your diagram look similar.

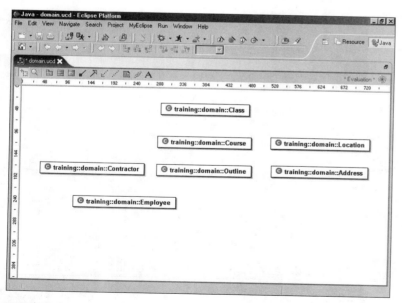

FIGURE 12.12   The Class diagram with seven classes, but no relationships.

This static UML diagram is a design diagram, not an analysis diagram. Every time you define a new class or interface for the diagram, a file is created with tagged Javadocs to keep the class and the diagram in sync. Double-click `Class` to open the file associated with the diagram object. The text file opens in the same text areas as the UML editor but in the lower half (see Figure 12.13). Because no associations are defined, the definition is thin:

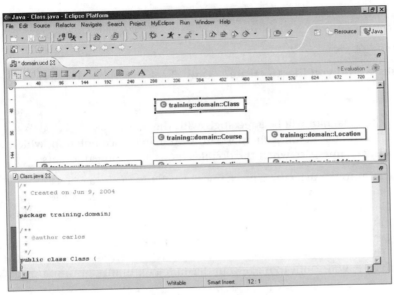

FIGURE 12.13   The full-screen editor area divided in half for the UML and text editors.

```
/*
 * File: Class.java
 * Created on Jun 9, 2004
 *
 */
package training.domain;

/**
 * @author carlos
 */
public class Class {

}
```

Close the text editor by clicking the X in the `Class.java` tab to restore the UML editor to full screen.

Now we'll add one more item—an interface. Right-click in the editor and from the pop-up menu select New, Interface. When the New Java Interface dialog opens, enter `training.domain` for Package and `Instructor` for Name and then click Finish. The diagram has all the needed definitions.

Adding associations to the diagram is more complex, but not by much. The relationships between the classes can be listed as follows:

- A Class has a Course, an Instructor, and a Location.

- A Location has an Address.

- A Course has an Outline.

- An Instructor is a Contractor or a full-time Employee.

There are many more class types and relationships that can be added to this model, but these will serve to depict aggregation, composition, and inheritance among the classes.

To associate `Class` with `Course`, click the Association button of the UML Class Editor toolbar. The cursor will turn into an arrow with an electric plug on one end. Moving the cursor over a class will cause the class to turn blue. Click once on `training::domain::Class` to select the first association point and then click once on `training::domain::Course` to define the second association point. A Properties dialog opens so you can enter the diagram information needed to define the association. The dialog has four tabs:

- **Connection**—This tab lists the two classes involved in the association and whether this is a named association.

- **1st Association End**—This tab describes the relationship from the perspective of what connects to it. For example, can an object on which it is dependent navigate back? What is the multiplicity of the relationship? What is the kind of association they share? What is the visibility of the relationship?

- **2nd Association End**—This tab contains the same information as the 1st Association End tab, but once again its information is from the perspective of the relationship class.

- **Router**—This tab defines how the association lines are drawn. Manual draws a straight line from one class to another, whereas Manhattan draws a line that will snake its way at 90 degree angles from one class to another. Anchor Type defines the start of the line—either in the middle of a side (Chopbox) or at the end of a side (Fixed at Edge). You should leave the Router properties set to their defaults (Manhattan and Chopbox).

In the Connection tab, give the association a name by entering **has a** for Label. The label is optional, but it will clarify the relationship of the two listed class types (see Figure 12.14).

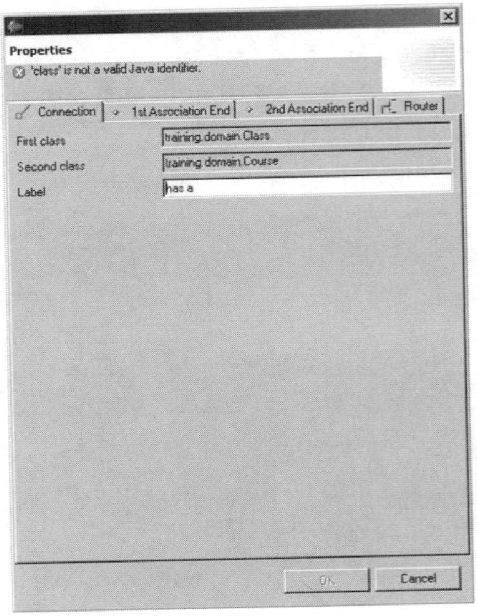

FIGURE 12.14 The Connection tab displaying the two ends of the relationship and the named association.

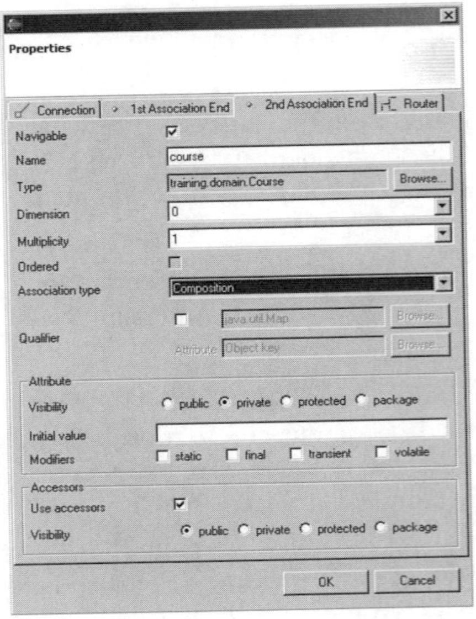

FIGURE 12.15 The association data for the Course class.

Click the 1st Association End tab and change Name from class to _class. The token class is a Java reserved word that cannot be used anyplace except to define a class. The error message at the top of the dialog disappears once the name is corrected. Course should not have the ability to navigate back to Class, so uncheck Navigable. All the fields except Navigable and Name become disabled. The properties of the Class association are its name and its lack of backward navigability (the class it is associated with cannot reference Class).

Click the 2nd Associated End tab. Course's association with Class is a one-to-one compositional relationship. The only fields that need to be changed are Multiplicity (set it to 1) and Association Type, which should be set to Composition (see Figure 12.15). Click OK.

When the diagram updates, the Class graphic may overlap the Course graphic. Class and Course have a clear compositional relationship named "has a," and Class is only allowed to have one Course (see Figure 12.16). Save domain.ucd by pressing Ctrl+S.

Perform the same steps for Class and Location using the same properties.

1. Click the Association button; then click Class, followed by Location.

2. When the Properties dialog opens, in the Connection tab enter **occurs at** for Label.

3. In the 1st Association End tab, uncheck Navigable and change Name from class to _class.

4. In the 2nd Association End tab, change Multiplicity to 1 and Association Type to Composition.

5. Click OK.

Perform the same steps for Class and Instructor, with a label of "is conducted by" in the Connection tab, no navigability in the 1st Association End tab, and Multiplicity set to 1 and Association Type set to Composition in the 2nd Association End tab.

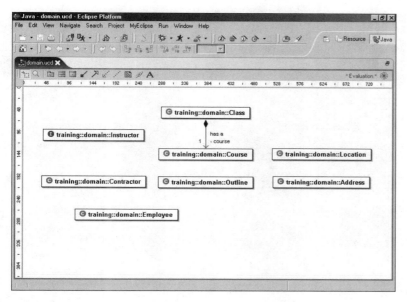

FIGURE 12.16   The incomplete Training Firm domain model.

Perform the same steps for Location and Address using the same properties. In the Connection tab, leave the Label field blank.

Perform the same steps for Course and Outline. Do not give their association a name and make their association type Aggregation. The diagram will show the line between Course and Outline with an empty diamond.

Depicting inheritance is simpler than associations. Both Contractor and Employee will inherit from Instructor. Click the Generalization button. Again, the cursor becomes an arrow with a plug attached to it, and when you move the cursor over one of the classes, it turns blue. Click Contractor and then click Instructor. The standard large, empty arrow-head appears, pointing from the subclass to the superclass. Perform the same steps with Employee and Instructor, only click in the arrowhead pointing from Contractor to Instructor. That completes the actual class diagram (see Figure 12.17).

As a final touch, create a note by clicking the toolbar's Note button. Click the empty area to the left and enter into the Note dialog **This is the domain model**. Click OK.

Next, click the Label button and enter the label **The Training System Domain Model** in the Label dialog. Click OK to close the dialog when you are done. The label that appears uses the default font settings. Right-click the label and from the pop-up menu select Change Font/Color.

When the Font dialog opens, change the size to 14 and click OK. The final diagram is now labeled and has a note (see Figure 12.18). Drag and drop sections of the diagram around until you are comfortable with the position of the various pieces.

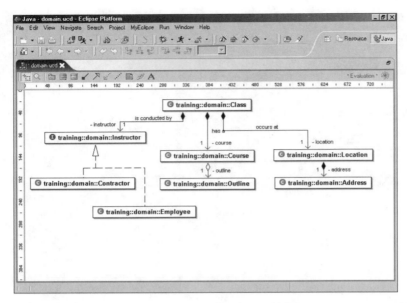

FIGURE 12.17   The Class diagram displaying aggregation, composition, and inheritance.

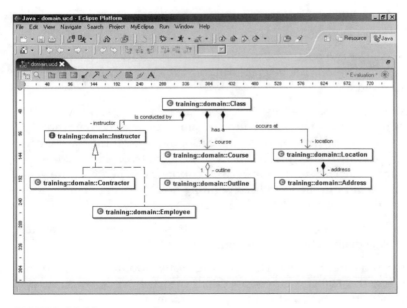

FIGURE 12.18   The final Class diagram.

Using a Sequence Diagram

A Sequence diagram is one of the dynamic UML diagrams. Whereas a Class diagram is time-less and context free, a Sequence diagram is grounded in time and context. Based on a particular scenario, objects are created and destroyed, messages are passed, and responses are returned. A Sequence diagram captures all this activity and in the order in which it happens. The classes of the domain model in their current incarnation are nothing more than wrappers around data structures. The objects also have responsibilities. For example, a Course object should be able to schedule itself and, in so doing, create a Class object; a Location object should be able to determine its availability based on capacity and resource data. The behavior among these objects is explored in dynamic diagrams such as the Sequence diagram.

For this example, in the act of scheduling a class, a Course Coordinator would search for a particular course and then schedule it based on an existing schedule, a date, and the number of days the class would run. The Course Coordinator interacts with the system through some kind of GUI, and the GUI would interact with various objects to complete the task. The Sequence diagram you create will show how the various objects will behave given the tasks they need to complete.

You need to create three classes that do not appear in the domain model: GUI, CourseCatalog, and CourseHome. Put all three in the package training.system.

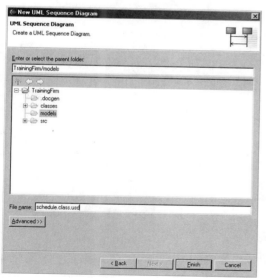

Let's walk through the process of creating a UML Sequence diagram, dragging and dropping classes onto the editor, and sending messages from one object to another. Begin by following these steps:

1. Select TrainingFirm, models in the Package Explorer view and press Ctrl+N to open the New dialog.

2. From the New dialog, select UML Diagrams, UML Sequence Diagram and then click Next.

3. From the New UML Sequence Diagram page, select models as the parent folder if it is not already selected and enter a filename of schedule.class.usd (see Figure 12.19). Click Finish.

FIGURE 12.19 The UML Sequence Diagram page with a parent folder of models and a filename of schedule.class.usd.

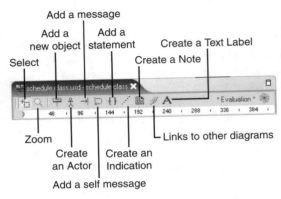

Add a message

Add a   Add a
new object | statement

Create a Text Label

Select

Create a Note

Zoom

Links to other diagrams

Create   Create an
an Actor   Indication

Add a self message

FIGURE 12.20   The UML Sequence Diagram toolbar.

An empty Sequence diagram opens with a new toolbar (see Figure 12.20). The Sequence Diagram Editor, in addition to the Select and Zoom capabilities, gives you the ability to do the following (from left to right, starting with the third button):

- Add new objects to the diagram.
- Create an actor.
- Send messages to objects.
- Have an object send a message to itself.
- Add a statement.
- Associate a note with any of the diagram elements.
- Create a link between this diagram and another diagram.
- Add a label to the diagram.

The three buttons you will use the most are the Add New Object, Create an Actor, and Add a Message buttons. The remaining six buttons will be used, but not as often as the others.

Now that you have a blank Sequence diagram available, let's add the actor (Course Coordinator) involved in the "Schedule a Class" Use Case. Click the Actor button. When the New Actor dialog opens, reenter **Course Coordinator** as the actor name and click OK. The actor is the primary object in this diagram and drives the interactions. The first thing the Course Coordinator does is interact with the GUI to search for a particular course. The GUI object retrieves the Course object from the CourseCatalog object, which goes to the CourseHome object to complete the lookup.

To add GUI, CourseCatalog, CourseHome, and Course to the diagram, you can either drag and drop the classes from the Package Explorer or click the Add New Object button. The following steps walk you through adding your first object to the diagram. None of the classes have methods defined, but the Sequence diagram allows you to sketch out what the flow should be before defining the API of the various objects. This version of EclipseUML does not add the methods to the class definitions.

1. Click the Add New Object button found on the toolbar.

2. Click directly to the right of the Course Coordinator actor to open the New dialog.

3. In the New dialog, click Browse to open the Object Class Selection dialog and type **gui**. Click OK.

4. The Type field will display `training.system.GUI`. Click OK. Save the file by pressing Ctrl+S.

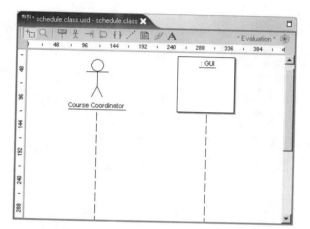

FIGURE 12.21 The Course Coordinator and the GUI object.

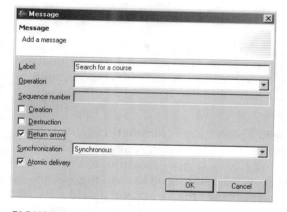

FIGURE 12.22 The Message dialog where you configure the name and type of message sent to an object.

The Sequence diagram displays only two items: the actor and an unnamed object of type GUI (see Figure 12.21). In standard UML, a data type name with a leading colon represents an object. The Course Coordinator needs to do two things: search for a course and then schedule the course. To have the Course Coordinator send these two messages, follow these steps:

1. Click the Add a Message button found on the toolbar.

2. Move the cursor just below the label of the actor (its head turns blue, so don't hold it there for too long) and click once.

3. Drag the cursor to the right until :GUI turns blue and then click once.

4. A Message dialog will open. Enter into the Label field **Search for a course**. At this point, you could name the operation (method) you need executed for this functionality, but for now leave the Operation field empty. Check the box next to Return Arrow and click OK (see Figure 12.22).

The diagram now has the Course Coordinator sending a search message to a GUI (see Figure 12.23). Following the previous steps, add a message going from the Course Coordinator to the GUI named **Submit scheduling information**.

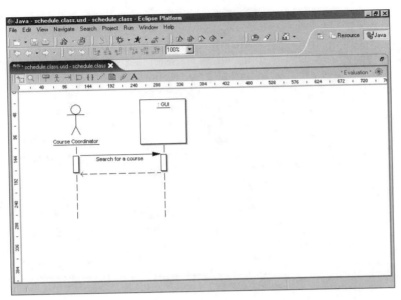

FIGURE 12.23   The Sequence diagram with one message being passed to the GUI.

The GUI needs an object to interact with to search for the desired course. Drag and drop the next object onto the diagram from the Package Explorer. If you expanded the editor, double-click the title bar of the diagram to restore it to its original size. From the Package Explorer, drag CourseCatalog to the left of :GUI in the diagram editor (see Figure 12.24). Double-click the title of the diagram to have it fill the window.

Click the Add a Message button to have :GUI send a message to :CourseCatalog asking it to search for the desired course. Move the cursor to the first white timebox directly below the :GUI object. When the :GUI object turns blue, click once and move the cursor to the :CourseCatalog object. When :CourseCatalog turns blue, click again to open the Message dialog. Enter into the Label field **Search for a course**. Check the Return Arrow field and click OK. The :GUI object is now asking the :CourseCatalog object to retrieve the course (see Figure 12.25).

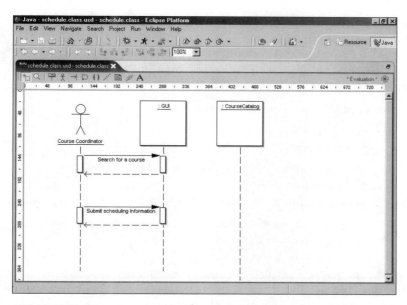

FIGURE 12.24   The Sequence diagram with an actor and two objects.

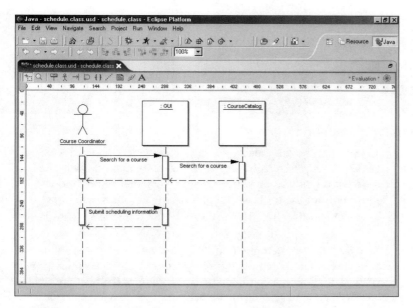

FIGURE 12.25   The Course Coordinator is sending a message to :GUI, which is sending a message to :CourseCatalog.

The :CourseCatalog object now needs to send a message to :CourseHome to find the proper course. Drag and drop CourseHome from the Package Explorer and then click Add a Message. Click once on the :CourseCatalog timebox and click under :CourseHome when it turns blue. When the Message dialog opens, enter as the label **Find course by number**, check Return Arrow, and then click OK.

The steps to create a sequence diagram can be broken down as follows:

1. Add an actor by clicking the Create an Actor button on the toolbar, clicking the diagram, and entering the actor's name.

2. Add an object by clicking the Add New Object button on the toolbar, clicking the diagram, and entering the object's class type. As an alternative, you can also drag and drop an object from the Package Explorer.

3. Add a message by clicking the Add a Message button on the toolbar, clicking the actor or object sending the message, and clicking the object receiving the message.

Using these steps, you can add another object, :Course, and have :CourseHome send it a "Load course data" message (see Figure 12.26). The second message being sent by the Course Coordinator should go to a Scheduler object, together with the Course, Location, and Date information.

SHOP TALK

UML, Design, and Extreme Programming

A myth of Extreme/Agile Programming is that there is little-to-no analysis or design involved. For some the term *emergent design*, or *emergent architecture*, has come to mean the blind growth of a system without any thought as to where it is going, even with the use of customer-driven and test-driven feedback. Nothing could be further from the truth. Although Extreme Programming does not advocate the use of UML, it certainly advocates design (albeit just-in-time test-driven design) every step of the way.

UML continues to play a strong role in lightweight methodologies. Past a certain point, communication about software direction and goals cannot be described through code. Objects abstract away issues and hide the detail behind APIs. Getting a complete understanding of the relationships between objects still demands a high-level, concise view of the objects and their relationships, and their interactions are still needed, whether a tool such as EclipseUML is used, or paper and pencil.

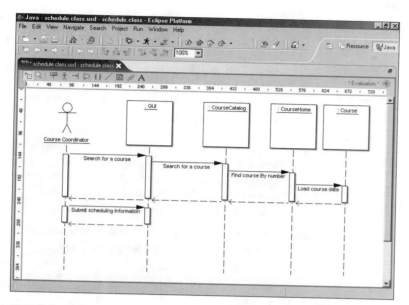

FIGURE 12.26 The final Sequence diagram displaying the flow of the search for a course to be scheduled.

Reverse Engineering

Another area where EclipseUML brings value to the table is in reverse engineering. The free version of EclipseUML only works with source code, but used in conjunction with a decompiler such as Jadclipse, it can produce diagrams that could prove useful in displaying dependencies and relationships that might otherwise be missed by looking over source code alone.

For example, if the classes created earlier in this chapter were handed over to you with the express intent that you understand their relationships, what better way to do that than to reverse engineer them and see how they relate?

Viewing Relationships

Close any editors you have open by pressing Ctrl+F4. In the Package Explorer, right-click the TrainingFirm, src, training.domain package and select Open UML to list the viewers you have available. Select Class Diagram Editor.

The Diagram options dialog gives you the option of displaying classes and interfaces within a package, along with their inheritance, association, and/or dependency relationships in any combination. Select Association and Inheritance and leave Scope set to package and Level at -1 (see Figure 12.27). Click OK.

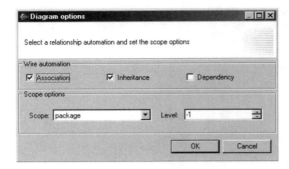

FIGURE 12.27 The Diagram options dialog, used to set the diagram defaults for reverse engineering.

The Package Content Select dialog opens to list all the available classes within the selected package. This is your opportunity to filter out classes you might not want to include in your reverse engineering. For this example, leave them all checked and click OK. The Class diagram that is produced is complete insofar as it displays the selected classes and their relationships. Any classes on which the displayed classes are dependent will not be displayed, unless they are part of the selected set. After some of the elements are moved around, the diagram looks similar to what you created earlier (see Figure 12.28).

You can reverse engineer code at the file, package, and project levels. A number of additional reverse-engineering tutorials are available at the Omondo site (`http://www.tutorial-omondo.com/reverse`).

SHOP TALK

UML and Test-driven Development

None of the examples in this chapter walk you through creating even a small app from front to back using EclipseUML. The reason for that is simple: You should not write your applications using a tool that does not encourage you to implement your system using tests. UML is a supporting technology, not the driving technology. Use EclipseUML, another vendor's UML tool, or paper and pencil, and the result is the same: A design that may or may not do what you intend it to do. During analysis, create Use Case diagrams and write up the scenarios using EclipseUML or index cards (though I would vote for EclipseUML because you can change and print out the diagrams).

When it comes time to begin turning the Use Cases into a domain model, create a separate project where your diagrams can be located and any of the generated classes/interfaces can be quarantined. Until you have written your system, you can only work with generalities, and those generalities can destroy the organization and stability of your Use Case–driven, test-driven implementation classes. Having Use Case, Class, and Sequence diagrams, at a minimum, gives you a solid direction to take your design, but you can only prove your design works through testing and continuous integration, not by drawing pictures.

UML is meant to help communicate software design and intent. This communication involves sharing your design vision with others both during and after the actual implementation. UML helps at both points in the process.

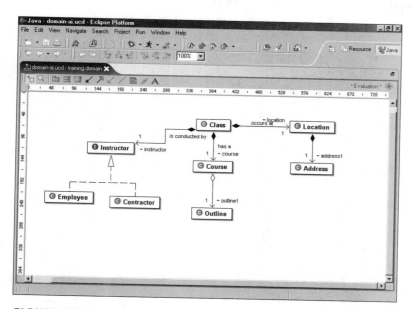

FIGURE 12.28 A class diagram generated from the existing code.

Configuring EclipseUML

The EclipseUML plug-in does come with a number of configurable properties. Because this version of EclipseUML is the Enterprise Edition and not the Free Version, and considering how many preferences there are, not all the listed preferences will be examined.

Open the Preferences dialog to look at EclipseUML's configurable properties. The high-level UML node, shown in Figure 12.29, gives you Startup, Toolbar, and Diagram Presentation Style choices. You can uncheck Show splash screen, select a flat or embossed button look for the toolbar, and select either images, text, or both, as well as select either a plain UML look (Omondo), the standard UML appearance, or a distinctly Eclipse look, which uses the Eclipse icons to denote classes, interfaces, and scope.

In the Class diagram node, setting Wire Automation to include Association is convenient if you perform reverse engineering (see Figure 12.30). The UML, Class Diagram, Colors page let's you add color to your diagrams by using it to highlight visibility, packages, classes and interfaces, and archetypes. Color can add additional semantic value to a diagram, so consider adding it to your diagram preferences.

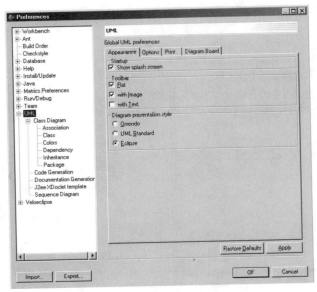

FIGURE 12.29   The UML node, with Appearance, Options, Print, and Diagram Board tabs.

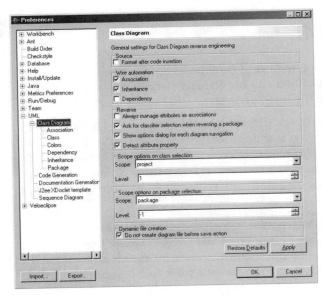

FIGURE 12.30   The UML, Class Diagram node with its defaults and Association set.

The UML, Code Generation node defines template classes that are used as the default implementation of wrappers methods that you would write to allow access to a property. For example, if you have a class that contains a `Collection`, the code-generation engine will add to the class the additional methods defined in the UML, Code Generation node for `Collections`. You can add additional types and methods that should be added to the class containing a listed type (see Figure 12.31). This is a very powerful feature.

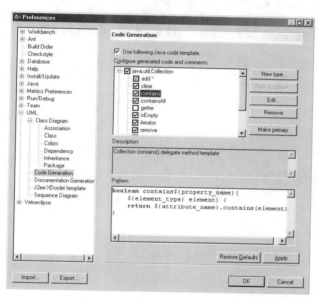

FIGURE 12.31 The UML, Code Generation node and one of the wrapper methods that would appear in the API of a class that contains a `Collection`.

In Brief

The Omondo plug-in is a great Eclipse UML tool that supports nine of the core UML diagrams defined by the UML 2.0 specification from the OMG. The flexibility of modifying, saving, and printing diagrams makes EclipseUML a valuable communication tool for any development team.

- The creation of an EclipseUML diagram is no different from the creation of many other resources. Once you choose a wizard, the system walks you through what it needs to create a drawing area where you can draw your diagram.

- Class diagrams have full support for the depiction of classes, interfaces, relationships, inheritance, composition, aggregation, and multiplicity. The sample class diagram used most of these features.

- Sequence diagrams in EclipseUML are more for communicating design than implementing design. When you enter messages, they are not checked against existing methods in the class types, though you can use existing methods if desired.

- Reverse engineering is as simple as right-clicking a file, package, or project and selecting an editor. EclipseUML takes care of the rest.

- The configuration of EclipseUML through the Preferences dialog affords you the opportunity to add color to your diagrams, set the defaults for many of the dialogs, and set code templates used by the code-generation engine to wrap object properties of certain types.

PART III

Extending Eclipse

The Eclipse Plug-In Architecture

13

If the Plug-in Developer Environment did not exist, it would be necessary to create it.

—Anonymous

Everything Is a Plug-In

The next three chapters will give you a great head start implementing the features you think are missing in Eclipse. It is Eclipse's plug-in architecture that has made it a tool developer's playground.

The Plug-In Architecture

Anyone who has done any kind of development in Eclipse has heard of its plug-in architecture. What exactly does plug-in development entail and what support does Eclipse give you to more easily develop custom plug-ins?

Plug-in development entails using the core Eclipse APIs to define new classes that will run as part of the base platform. In order to run as part of Eclipse, a plug-in must use one of a number of plug-in extension points. Inclusion into Eclipse also means that a plug-in has access to other plug-ins in the system, such as resources (projects, folders, and files), the workbench user interface components, the team plug-in, debugging, Java Development Tooling (JDT), and the Plug-in Development Environment (PDE). If the JDT and PDE were not present, you would still have access to all the other plug-ins, but development of a plug-in would not be a trivial undertaking.

The PDE allows developers to implement Eclipse plug-ins within Eclipse rather than through an external tool. The PDE is itself a plug-in and relies on the same core support to accomplish its tasks as every other Eclipse plug-in.

There are three types of Eclipse extensions:

- Plug-in
- Fragment
- Feature

A *plug-in* is a tool that adds functionality to Eclipse using Eclipse's extension points. In the same fashion that a servlet implements life-cycle methods such as init() and destroy(), a plug-in implements the methods from one of a number of interfaces, such as startup() and shutdown(). By submitting a plug-in to Eclipse, the core system takes care of lazy-loading the plug-in at runtime, calling startup() when the plug-in is first loaded and shutdown() when Eclipse wants the plug-in to clean up.

A *fragment* is a subset of the code set that makes up a plug-in. Because it can be incomplete, it does not have the same concept of life cycle that a plug-in does, but it's treated by Eclipse in the same way that the original plug-in was treated. When a fragment is deployed, Eclipse merges the fragment code with the original plug-in, making the update of behavior/functionality transparent to the plug-in user.

A *feature* is a collection of plug-ins that represents a set of functionality. It can be installed manually or delivered using the Update Manager. The plug-ins and their supporting files are packaged into a feature archive file that includes a feature manifest file, feature.xml, that describes the contents of the archive and the associated plug-ins. Whereas a plug-in is a complete tool and a fragment comprises the updated code for a plug-in, a feature is just the packaging of a collection of plug-ins for easy installation into Eclipse.

The Plug-In Extension Points

A large number of Eclipse-defined extension points are available. The extension points are divided up into the following areas:

- **Platform runtime**—Using one of the two extension points, you can define the global behavior of Eclipse itself. If you wanted to write an application that used the Eclipse core to the exclusion of everything else, this is the entry point to extend.

- **Workspace**—Entry points for resource builders, markers, project life-cycle behavior, and team behavior are found here. For example, resource builders are run when the project they are associated with changes. Project life-cycle behavior, on the other hand, is the purview of Eclipse natures. A *nature* is a fundamental aspect of a project, and a project can have one or more natures. An example of a nature would be a project that understands how to handle Java files or certain Java technologies such as EJBs or servlets.

- **Workbench**—This group has the largest number of extension points, and they all involve the user interface. A sampling of the extension points include support for new views and editors, the ability to reassign key bindings, support for drag-and-drop operations between unrelated views, and adding additional panels to the Preferences dialog.

- **Team**—The extension point that defines the sharing of projects, folders, and files.

- **Debug**—The extension points for debugging are divided among behavior and user interface points. The launching of applications are controlled from here as is the debugging of these applications.

- **Help**—Extending the Eclipse help table of contents or adding help for specific plug-in issues is handled through the help extension points. There is also an extension point into the Eclipse help search engine (which is Lucene, another open-source project).

- **Other**—Entry into the underlying Ant infrastructure, read-only content viewers, specialized search pages, and feature installers are all defined in this final grab bag of extension points.

Bear in mind that as you write additional plug-ins, you can also contribute extension points.

SHOP TALK

Perception and the Problem with Plug-ins

Plug-ins are not hard to implement.

The Eclipse Plug-in framework encompasses the main areas of tool development and standardizes how they are implemented. Some of the concepts appear to be on the edge, not because they truly are, but because they are object oriented, and, for developers who grew up with procedural languages, it is easy to forget that object-oriented frameworks are always going to stretch our synapses that much further until we wonder how we ever got along with these rather novel concepts. You might say that the SWT is not as full-featured as Swing (for now) and that as a tool-for-tool development environment, Eclipse has a large selection of hooks on which to hang your hat, which can make choosing a hook a challenging experience.

So what's the point?

All of the source code for all of Eclipse's plug-ins is available for your perusal as soon as you install Eclipse on your box. Implement by example and learn from the example of those who came before you.

Read. Test. Code. Have fun.

And remember: Plug-ins are not hard.

The Plug-In Developer Environment

The depth and breadth of extension points can make the selection of a proper entry point a daunting task. You should take advantage of the hundreds of plug-ins available to make the selection of one or more extension points more manageable. The purpose of a plug-in should be considered first rather than which is the appropriate entry point. Does you plug-in supply wizards? Is the plug-in configurable by the user? Are the resources under its control, if any, handled differently than other resources? The source code for all the plug-ins included with Eclipse is shipped with Eclipse for your convenience.

In addition, the Eclipse Plug-in Developer Environment does its best to make the task of implementing plug-ins as organized as possible through a combination of views, editors, wizards, and sample templates.

The Perspective and Its Views

The PDE perspective aggregates seven views to help in the development of plug-ins. Only two of the seven views are specific to plug-in development: the Plug-ins view and the Error Log. In order to describe the views in a worthwhile context, I implemented the HelloWorld plug-in example from the Eclipse help documentation. I will not describe the steps involved in creating the HelloWorld example because you will get the opportunity to implement a simple as well as a nontrivial plug-in in the next chapter. If you would like to follow along at a high-level, select from the main menu Window, Configure Activities. When the Configure Activities dialog opens, check the top Plug-in Development node.

The Package Explorer is the standard logical view of our projects and how they are organized. The only projects to be displayed in the Package Explorer are the projects you create for your development efforts. Click the Plug-ins view tab to see all the plug-ins available in Eclipse (displayed in Figure 13.1). Notice the plethora of additional plug-ins listed along with the project eclipse.kickstart.helloworld. On the other hand, the Package Explorer view only displays, in this case, the one project, regardless of its dependencies.

> **Modifying XML Files Considered Harmful**
>
> As convenient as XML can be, be wary of changing an XML file outside of a form editor. Editing XML is chancy at best and can lead to hard-to-correct configuration errors.

The Outline view is dependent on the selected resource. If a Java file is selected, it will display a tree view of the class, its package designation, its imports, its instance variables, and its methods. A .properties file will be displayed as a list of keys, whereas plain-vanilla XML and HTML files will not be displayed at all. On the other hand, a plugin.xml file will be shown as a collection of nodes that match the tab labels of the Plug-in Manifest Editor. Any resources contained in the tabs appear as outline subnodes. The Outline view is also there as a convenient way of causing the editor to skip to a particular location when you select an outline node.

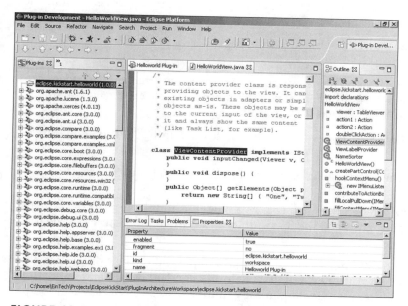

FIGURE 13.1 The HelloWorld plug-in example and the four out of seven visible views from the plug-in perspective.

The Properties view was originally discussed in Chapter 1, "Using the Eclipse Workbench." The list of available properties for a selected resource are listed in this view, but for more in-depth information you can right-click the resource and select Properties from the pop-up menu.

The Tasks view was also discussed in Chapter 1 as one of the fundamental workbench views. Tasks added directly to the view or through the use of Task Tags are listed here.

The Plug-ins view is displayed by selecting the Plug-ins tab located at the top of the Package Explorer view. Plug-in version numbers are displayed in parentheses to the right of the plug-in name. If you right-click one of the plug-ins, the pop-up menu gives you the following choices:

- **Open Dependencies**—Opens the Plug-in Dependencies view to list the dependencies needed by the selected plug-in.

- **References**—Opens the Search view to list any plug-ins that reference the selected plug-in.

- **Import as a Binary or Source Project**—Imports the selected plug-in into the Eclipse workbench as a plug-in project that includes all of the plug-in's required resources. Opening the project and, in turn, a JAR file and a package lists the various class files contained in the package. Importing the selected plug-in as a source project will include the source code if it's available.

- **Add to Java Search**—Adds the selected plug-in to the list of plug-ins to use for a search of plug-in references.

- **Select Dependent Plug-ins**—This selects zero or more plug-ins that are dependent on the plug-in you selected. For example, if you select org.eclipse.core.runtime, three OSGI plug-ins also will be selected.

- **Select Plug-ins in Java Search**—Every plug-in you selected using **Add to Java Search** will be selected.

- **Go Into**—Displays the selected plug-in in the Plug-ins view in isolation.

Any internal errors will be listed in the Error Log. As a plug-in is running as part of the main Eclipse process, the Error Log gives you the opportunity to see when problems arise due to your running code.

As mentioned in Chapter 2, "Writing and Running a Java Application," the Console provides a means for running processes within Eclipse to write to the standard output and standard error streams as well as read from standard input. Any runtime errors will display their output in the Console view of the development workbench, not the Runtime Workbench.

The Plug-in Manifest Editor

Double-clicking plugin.xml opens the Plug-in Manifest Editor (see Figure 13.2). Seven pages in total are available, with the seventh being the actual XML source to be saved in plugin.xml. If you start your plug-in project using the PDE Wizard, the plugin.xml file will contain enough defaults to start you off properly.

The Welcome page lists basic information about the plug-in and tips on how to work with it. The Welcome page can be hidden by scrolling to the bottom of the page and checking "Do not show this page next time." The Welcome page is of limited utility.

The Overview panel displays information about the name of your plug-in, any runtime libraries needed by Eclipse to run the plug-in, any required plug-ins, any extensions defined by this plug-in, and any extension points useable by other plug-ins.

The Dependency tab of the Plug-in Manifest Editor lists any additional plug-ins needed for a plug-in to function properly. At runtime, Eclipse loads plug-ins only as they are needed. If a plug-in will not work without the aid of another plug-in, you'll find quite a few plug-ins being loaded into the system.

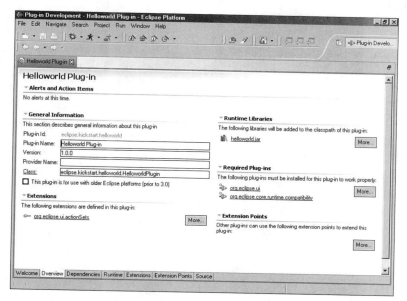

FIGURE 13.2 The Plug-in Manifest Editor displaying the Overview page containing general information about the plug-in.

The Runtime tab starts out just listing the plug-in JAR file, but as many JAR files can be added as are needed by the plug-in. Selecting any given runtime library enables the Library Type radio buttons. The default library type is one that contains both code and resource files. You can control the library file's visibility by setting the Library Exporting radio button to something other than Do Not Export. Exporting the entire library means that all of the plug-in API is visible to other plug-ins. When you select Export Using Content Filters, a list box appears, allowing you to enter either * (all code), [package name].* (only the classes of a particular package are visible), or a fully qualified class name. Only the classes listed in the specified packages will be made visible to other plug-ins. Directories found in Library Content contain source code that is included in the plug-in, whereas Package Prefixes lists package names for use by the ClassLoader to optimize the loading of classes at runtime. Clicking the triangle next to the Package Prefix label opens its list box.

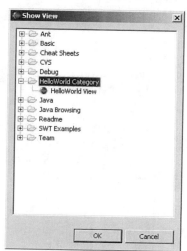

FIGURE 13.3 The Show View dialog displaying the HelloWorld Category and its associated HelloWorld View.

Extensions associate a view with a category. When you select Window, Show View, Other from the main menu, a dialog appears displaying various categories and their views. Figure 13.3 shows the Hello category and the Hello Greetings view. The Body Text is arbitrary text that will be associated with either the extension, the category, or the view.

All Extension Points lists any extension points being contributed by the plug-in. You decide on a unique ID within the plug-in, a name, and an extension point schema filename where the system will write the plug-in schema information. For example, the Eclipse core runtime has a file called `application.mxsd`, in addition to others, that is located in the Eclipse platform source directory (`%ECLIPSE_HOME%\plugins\org.eclipse.platform.source_3.0.0\src\ org.eclipse.core.runtime_3.0.0\schema`). This file describes the extension point in some depth and is used by the help system as well.

Resource Management

Resource management is accomplished through the use of a resource plug-in to access projects, folders, and files in a workspace. The current valid workspace, `IWorkspaceRoot`, is returned by the `ResourcesPlugin` class. The methods `IWorkspaceRoot.getProject()`, `IProject.getFolder()`, and `IFolder.getFile()` return the associated resources. Using the various resource APIs, you can move a resource, copy a resource, delete a resource, touch a resource, or set a resource to be a read-only resource. Resources, and their handling, are crucial to many plug-ins.

Workbench UI

Plug-ins do not need to have a GUI front end to be useful in Eclipse. However, because many of them have GUIs, Eclipse has two GUI toolkits, one built on top of the other, to assist you in integrating your functionality into the base IDE. The lowest-level toolkit is the Standard Widget Toolkit, or SWT. Like the original AWT layer in Java, it is one of the only platform-dependent parts of Eclipse. SWT is a Java-defined layer sitting on top of platform-dependent GUI components. Every platform that Eclipse runs on has its own native layer defined, but the Java layer remains unchanged. Although this could be seen as a step backward for Java GUI development, in fact a comparison of an AWT front end and an SWT front end clearly demonstrates how much better the implementation of SWT is over AWT. If you are wondering how Swing fares, bear in mind that Swing is a pure-Java GUI implementation and has never felt as responsive as GUIs written in compiled languages. That may change with the new Java 1.5 release, which promises to improve Swing performance.

The JFace toolkit is built on top of SWT. JFace is really a high-level GUI layer that caters to the needs of Eclipse. JFace supplies base components to create views and support events, control tasks through the use of progress components, and control UI resources such as fonts. Of course, the GUI needs of Eclipse are shared by many applications, and that makes JFace just as useful outside of the Eclipse environment.

Viewers are adapters to SWT widgets, allowing you to program against them using the more standard MVC pattern. A JFace component knows how to convert the data from your model into strings or images. Using the raw SWT component would force you to handle data conversion to and from the component by hand.

JFace actions are similar to listeners in the Java GUI world. You define an action and register it with the target component, thus separating the UI behavior from the UI. In addition, you can register various GUI components associated with an action, called *contributions*, with Eclipse to let the IDE worry about placing them in locations such as menus and toolbars.

UI resources are images such as fonts and icons. JFace takes care of most of the details of handling these images either directly, in your code, or indirectly, through configuration files such as plugin.xml.

When a task is started that may need to be paused or interrupted by the user, generally some kind of progress bar is used with a Cancel button that allows the user to halt execution. JFace supports this functionality at various levels. Any JFace class that implements IRunnableContext is a candidate for your code to register to monitor the progress of a task.

With all that, the workbench extension points also allow you to add your own panels to the Properties dialog as well as to other dialogs that display wizards and views.

Debug Support

You have two ways to use the debug support inherent in Eclipse:

- By debugging your plug-in using the JDT
- By allowing your plug-in to debug processes under its control

Eclipse supplies you with the ability to debug your plug-ins from within the environment. As of this writing, all plug-ins must implement their Eclipse layer in Java, which allows for the use of the JDT debugger.

However, Eclipse does support the ability for a plug-in to use the internal debug core to create custom launch capabilities or to create new debuggers. This capability does not mean that a plug-in has to supply a debugging feature, but rather that a plug-in that needs the ability to track a resource can do so either with the existing debugger, if appropriate, or by implementing a new kind of debugger build on top of the Eclipse debug API.

Of course, as useful as debugging can be, another starting point would be to write JUnit tests that exercise your plug-in instead. Writing a JUnit test to test your plug-in is not much more difficult than writing a regular JUnit test, only the test will now run within the Runtime Workbench instead of the standard workbench.

Help System

The help framework allows you to deploy help documentation as part of a plug-in or as its own plug-in. You are not forced into setting up your help files in any particular way. The only system expectations are that a table of contents (TOC) file exists and that the help files are in HTML. You supply the help plug-in with a table of contents file and a zip file, or directory, containing the HTML files, and the help system does the rest. Adding help for your plug-in is an almost trivial task. Chapter 15, "Implementing a Help Plug-in," walks you through a number of implementations.

Running a Plug-In from Within Eclipse

Because a plug-in is just another Java program, it is run like any other Java program. The difference is the environment under which the plug-in runs. When you are developing servlets, you deploy them to a servlet container and debug them from within Eclipse, which understands how to start them and connect to them as a debugging target. A plug-in runs within Eclipse itself, so it is necessary to start the plug-in in a new copy of Eclipse. This running and fully functional copy of Eclipse is known as the *Runtime Workbench*.

The Runtime Workbench

The Runtime Workbench is a copy of Eclipse that you have full control over. The same way you can write custom launch configurations for your running programs, you can create custom launch configurations for the Runtime Workbench. In addition, you can display the Plug-in Registry view from within any perspective displayed in the Runtime Workbench. Why bother displaying the plug-in registry? The plug-in registry displays only the plug-ins loaded in the workbench. Use the registry to ensure that your plug-in has been loaded and is running (see Figure 13.4).

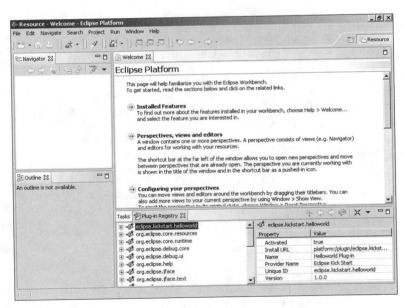

FIGURE 13.4 The Plug-in Registry displaying the plug-ins needed to run the Eclipse HelloWorld example, including the Hello World Example.

In Brief

With or without the Plug-in Development Environment, Eclipse is an extensible tool with many extension points and features that can be used to add new functionality to the IDE. The PDE makes the development of plug-ins—not a trivial undertaking, to be sure—a very doable task. The PDE encourages developers to create new facets in the Eclipse environment by giving them enough documentation, starting points, and building blocks to succeed.

You have been given a strong starting point for looking into plug-in development. Here are the main points we covered in this chapter:

- The Eclipse plug-in architecture allows almost everything in Eclipse to be extensible as well as removable. The base platform has the workspace, the workbench, the SWT and JFace toolkits, the help plug-in, and the team plug-in. In addition, Eclipse has the Java Development Tooling plug-in and the Plug-in Developer Environment.

- The functionality of all the plug-ins running in Eclipse are available to every other plug-in. These core plug-ins define the base extension points for all other plug-ins.

- The Plug-in perspective is made up of seven different views. Views such as the Outline view present different information about the current file in the editor based on the file type.

- The Plug-in Manifest Editor allows you to edit the `plugin.xml` file without worrying about XML syntax, unless you choose to edit the XML source directly.

- Resources in Eclipse are divided up between projects, folders, and files. The resource management API allows your plug-in to retrieve information about various resources and manipulate them as your plug-in sees fit.

- Because most plug-ins display some sort of information to their users, the workbench UI extension points give you the ability create wizards, views, and events as well as add your own custom panels to the system Properties dialog and add new categories to the View dialog.

- Not all plug-ins need the ability to debug a running process, but for the ones that do, Eclipse supplies the debug API to allow for the creation of unique launch configurations and to more easily create custom debuggers.

- Of all the plug-in areas in Eclipse, the help system is the simplest in which to add capability. In addition to the `plugin.xml` file, all the system needs is a table of contents and a directory filled with pages formatted in HTML.

- In order to run a plug-in so as to test it, Eclipse has the concept of the Runtime Workbench. The Runtime Workbench starts another copy of Eclipse, and only the copy loads up any new plug-ins. You can save custom launch configurations of the Runtime Workbench to simplify testing of the plug-in. You should always create JUnit tests of your plug-in as well.

Writing a Trivial (and Not So Trivial) Plug-In

14

Which came first: the plug-in or the IDE?

—Anonymous

The Hello World Console Plug-In

Writing a plug-in is not rocket science, nor is it as simple as printing "Hello, World" to a screen. There are many pieces to writing a plug-in, and this chapter covers how many of those pieces fit together. The examples in this chapter walk you through implementing the most simple of plug-ins, all the way through writing a medium complexity plug-in that displays a custom Preferences panel based on a new project type. After this chapter you should be able to add new natures and builders to existing project types as well as be able to create your own project types directly tied into the New Wizard and main Preferences dialog.

The Eclipse Cheat Sheets have a "Hello, World" example that walks you through the creation of a plug-in using the least number of steps because there is a plug-in wizard that has a "Hello, World" template already built in. If you like, you can start Eclipse right now and select Help, Cheat Sheets from the main menu. When the Cheat Sheet Selection dialog opens, select Create an Eclipse Plug-in Using PDE (see Figure 14.1).

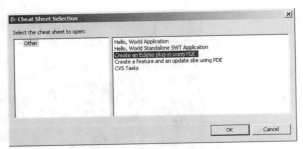

FIGURE 14.1 The Cheat Sheet Selection dialog with entries for a standalone Java application, an SWT application, a plug-in, a feature and update site, and CVS tasks.

FIGURE 14.2 Cheat Sheets view displaying the steps to follow to create the HelloWorld plug-in.

Follow the steps outlined in the Cheat Sheet view and you will have a fully functional "Hello, World" plug-in working in no time (see Figure 14.2). The built-in "Hello, World" plug-in adds a menu item in the main menu with a submenu that, when selected, opens up a dialog. You could perform the following steps and accomplish the exact same thing:

1. Press Ctrl+N to open the New dialog.

2. Select Plug-in Project and click Next.

3. Enter the project name **HelloWorld** and click Next.

4. In the Plug-in Content page, click Next.

5. Check the Create a Plug-in Using One of the Templates button and select the "Hello, World" template.

6. Click Finish. When the Confirm Perspective Switch dialog opens, click Yes to let it open the Plug-in Development perspective.

To check whether these steps accomplished their tasks, go to the main menu and select Run, Run As, Runtime Workbench. The Runtime Workbench, a complete Eclipse environment used for plug-in development, opens and displays the Sample Menu item in the main menu. Select the Sample Menu, Sample Action submenu to open the HelloWorld dialog (see Figure 14.3). The wizard has taken care of generating, in six steps, what you will create over the course of the next few pages, only the details will not be as hidden.

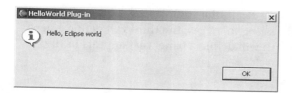

FIGURE 14.3 The dialog opened by the Hello, World plug-in when you select the Sample Menu, Sample Action menu item.

The plug-in architecture requires the following information from all plug-ins:

- General information about the plug-in, such as its ID, name, and version number

- The name of the JAR file that contains your plug-in code

- The name of any plug-ins your plug-in needs in order to function

- The names of one or more extension points to which your plug-in is contributing

In addition, you may also supply a list of extension point names your plug-in is making available for use by other plug-ins. This feature does assumes an implicit understanding of what other plug-ins may need from your plug-in and what valid extension points might be.

All plug-ins need to extend a parent class and zero-or-more interfaces. The class/interface they use depends on the extension point to which they are contributing, but the choice of class/interface will dictate the part of the Eclipse architecture with which they will function. The plug-in `HelloWorldConsolePlugin` will use `AbstractUIPlugin`, a super-class that supplies the plug-in with capabilities to directly interface with the underlying Eclipse Preferences store, dialog store, and images registry.

The next piece in the plug-in puzzle is the extension point to which your plug-in is contributing. You have many extension points to choose from. The Eclipse documentation has a list of all the extension points available as well as the classes and interfaces with which they are associated. As mentioned in the "Plug-in Extension Points" section of Chapter 13, "The Plug-In Architecture," there are seven different groupings of Eclipse extension points, and the only way to learn about them is to peruse the Eclipse documentation. In this chapter you will be exposed to a small number of extension points.

In general, plug-ins are loaded up when they're used for the first time. You will have to force Eclipse to load this first example because it has no interactive piece callable by a user of the Eclipse workbench. To accomplish this, your plug-in code will contribute to the `org.eclipse.ui.startup` extension point and implement the `IStartup` interface, which is required of any plug-in that is loaded at startup. This extension point will force your plug-in to be loaded when Eclipse is run.

The glue that binds your plug-in code to Eclipse is `plugin.xml`. This file contains the information that describes the plug-in, its dependencies, and any new extension points.

The first plug-in will print the string "Hello, world!" in the console view of the main workbench. The second example will print the same string in a view, the third will define a new project type with a custom wizard, and the fourth will define a panel that appears in the Preferences dialog.

Creating a Plug-In Project

Before you can create the plug-in project, you need to import any plug-ins on which your plug-in is dependent. Your first plug-in is dependent on the org.eclipse.ui plug-in. Select File, Import from the main menu. From the Import dialog, select External Plug-ins and Fragments as your import source and click Next. In the Import External Plug-ins panel, if you wish to see the source code, place a check next to Extract Source Archives and Create Source Folders in Projects; otherwise, leave everything set to the defaults. Click Next. The next panel, Selection, lists all the plug-ins available as dependencies. Scroll down until you find the org.eclipse.ui plug-in, select it, and click the Add Required Plug-ins button. The label directly below the list of plug-ins should read something like "21 out of 118 selected." Click Finish and give Eclipse a few seconds to load the various plug-ins into your workspace. Your Package Explorer should now contain the org.eclipse.ui plug-in and all its dependent plug-ins (all 20 of them).

Create a new plug-in project by pressing Ctrl+N and selecting Plug-in Project. Clicking Next will display the Plug-in Project page. Enter the project name as com.triveratech.helloworld.console. If you have a location where you prefer to save your projects, change the default location from <eclipse home>/workspace to your desired directory. The Project Settings section can be left with src and bin as the source and output folders, respectively. Leave the project as a Java project. Click Next.

The Plug-in Content page can be left alone. Note that the project name and the plug-in ID are identical. They do not have to be, but this fits in with the current Eclipse convention of giving the plug-in ID the same value as the project name. As naming conventions go, the thing to bear in mind is that the plug-in project should be named after the plug-in package. This convention makes it easier for you to track down any plugin.xml problems related to the plug-in's ID. The ID must be globally unique, so make sure your project name is also unique.

The Plug-in Class section has the class name for a plug-in life cycle class named ConsolePlugin. This class is used to create a singleton available to the system. It inherits from org.eclipse.ui.plugin.AbstractUIPlugin, which contains support for UI contributions to Eclipse. This entry can be left alone.

The plug-in runtime library, which can be named anything, defaults to using the last piece of the package name as the JAR filename, which in this case is console.jar. Click Next.

In the Templates page, you can leave the Create a Plug-in Using One of the Templates unchecked. The default plug-in structure will give you a `plugin.xml` file and the `ConsolePlugin` class mentioned earlier that extends `AbstractUIPlugin`. The project structure created is all you need for this example. Click Finish.

FIGURE 14.4 The Outline view of the `plugin.xml` file opened in the Manifest Editor.

If you did not create the initial plug-in described at the beginning of the chapter, you may get a Confirm Perspective Switch dialog. If the dialog appears, click Yes to have Eclipse open the Plug-in Development perspective.

From within the Plug-in Development perspective, `plugin.xml` will open in the Plug-in Manifest editor and the Outline view will display the various XML elements that define `plugin.xml` (see Figure 14.4). Select the Extensions tab of the Manifest Editor. No extensions are listed because you have not chosen any extension points yet. Click Add to display the New Extension dialog (see Figure 14.5). This is where you are given the choice of extension points with which to associate your code. As mentioned previously, you need to force Eclipse to load this sample plug-in at startup, so scroll down the list and select `org.eclipse.ui.startup`. Click Finish.

In the Eclipse plug-in help documentation (accessed by selecting Platform Plug-in Developer Guide, Reference, Extension Points Reference, Workbench, org.eclipse.ui.startup), the description states that any plug-in class that intends to use this extension point must implement interface `org.eclipse.ui.IStartup`. From the Package Explorer view, open the `com.triveratech.helloworld.console` project as well as `src` and the `com.triveratech.helloworld.console` package. Double-click `ConsolePlugin.java` to open it in the Java editor and add `implements IStartup` to the class declaration.

FIGURE 14.5 The New Extension dialog, where you select the plug-in extension point to associate with your code.

The editor flags the new symbol as needing to be fixed as soon as you finish typing. When the editor displays a light bulb in the left margin, move the cursor to the end of the word IStartup and press Ctrl+spacebar to have the editor automatically add the import to the file. Adding the import will now cause another light bulb to appear because the interface has one method that your plug-in must implement. Click the light bulb once to display a list of possible solutions to the problem. Double-click Add Unimplemented Methods, and the editor will create a stub method for earlyStartup(), the one method in IStartup. The light bulb disappears when you save the file.

Scroll to earlyStartup() and delete the TODO comment. Then add the following line:

```
System.out.println("Hello, world!");
```

Listing 14.1 shows the complete code listing.

LISTING 14.1   Creating a New Plug-In Project

```
package com.triveratech.helloworld.console;

import org.eclipse.ui.IStartup;
import org.eclipse.ui.plugin.*;
import org.osgi.framework.BundleContext;
import java.util.*;

/**
 * The main plugin class to be used in the desktop.
 */
public class ConsolePlugin extends AbstractUIPlugin implements IStartup {
    //The shared instance.
    private static ConsolePlugin plugin;

    //Resource bundle.
    private ResourceBundle resourceBundle;

    /**
     * The constructor.
     */
    public ConsolePlugin() {
        super();
        plugin = this;
        try {
            resourceBundle = ResourceBundle
                .getBundle("com.triveratech.helloworld.console.ConsolePluginResources");
        } catch (MissingResourceException x) {
```

LISTING 14.1   Continued

```
            resourceBundle = null;
        }
    }

    /**
     * This method is called upon plug-in activation
     */
    public void start(BundleContext context) throws Exception {
        super.start(context);
    }

    /**
     * This method is called when the plug-in is stopped
     */
    public void stop(BundleContext context) throws Exception {
        super.stop(context);
    }

    /**
     * Returns the shared instance.
     */
    public static ConsolePlugin getDefault() {
        return plugin;
    }

    /**
     * Returns the string from the plugin's resource bundle, or 'key' if not
     * found.
     */
    public static String getResourceString(String key) {
        ResourceBundle bundle = ConsolePlugin.getDefault().getResourceBundle();
        try {
            return (bundle != null) ? bundle.getString(key) : key;
        } catch (MissingResourceException e) {
            return key;
        }
    }

    /**
     * Returns the plugin's resource bundle,
     */
```

LISTING 14.1 Continued

```
    public ResourceBundle getResourceBundle() {
        return resourceBundle;
    }

    /*
     * (non-Javadoc)
     *
     * @see org.eclipse.ui.IStartup#earlyStartup()
     */
    public void earlyStartup() {
        System.out.println("Hello, world!");
    }
}
```

Running the Plug-In

For a plug-in to run as part of the Eclipse environment, you are required to export the JAR file with your code and the required `plugin.xml` file. This can be a very time- and labor-intensive operation because Eclipse needs to be stopped and restarted each time the plug-in is deployed in this manner. To circumvent this problem, Eclipse supports a runtime workbench environment that runs as a copy of Eclipse, allowing you to safely run and debug your plug-in.

To start the runtime workbench for this example, go to the main menu and select Run, Run As, Runtime Workbench. Another Eclipse workbench window will open, but the output from our plug-in does not appear in it. Bring the host workbench to the front, and you should see "Hello, world!" in the Console view (see Figure 14.6). The reason why the output appears in the host workbench and not the runtime workbench is that the host workbench, the one within which you implemented your plug-in, controls the input and output streams. Therefore, calling `System.out.println()` sends its output to the host workbench. This behavior is only true while you are using the runtime workbench. Once you write a plug-in and deploy it completely you will still see your output appear in the console window, but at that point there will only be the one copy of Eclipse running. You can now exit the runtime workbench.

And now the bad news: Performing an external deployment of this example will not work because the host workbench does not display fast enough for any output to be seen in the console. An external deployment of the HelloWorld View plug-in will be discussed in the next example.

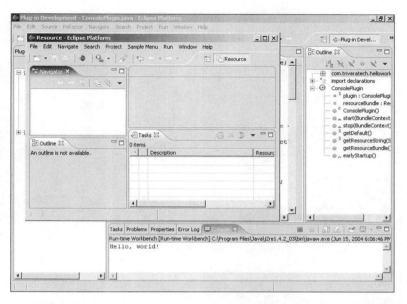

FIGURE 14.6   The runtime workbench in the foreground, and the host workbench in the background displaying "Hello, world!"

Debugging the Plug-In

Let's try to debug the plug-in. If `ConsolePlugin` is not open in the editor, double-click it from the Package Explorer. Change `earlyStartup()` to use a local variable containing the `"Hello, world!"` string and place a breakpoint in `earlyStartup()` at `System.out.println()`. The new version of `earlyStartup()` looks like this:

```java
public void earlyStartup() {
    String msg = "Hello, world!";
    System.out.println(msg);
}
```

Start the runtime workbench by selecting Run, Debug As, Runtime Workbench from the main menu. The Confirm Perspective Switch dialog will open alerting you to the fact that the Debug perspective should be opened if you are debugging the plug-in. Click Yes. The host workbench will display the Debug perspective after a few seconds, the runtime workbench will appear, and the host workbench will come forward with the debugger stopped at `System.out.println()`. If the host workbench does not come forward, you can force it forward by pressing Alt+Tab. The Variables view should be displayed in the upper-right window (if it's not, select Windows, Show View, Variables). One of the variables displayed should be `msg` with a value of `"Hello, world!"`. Double-click `msg` and when the Set Variable

Value dialog appears, enter the value **"Hello, from Eclipse!"**. Click OK and then press F8 to let the plug-in run without further interruption. The string "Hello, from Eclipse!" appears in the Console view at the bottom the screen (see Figure 14.7). Feel free to change msg by restarting the runtime workbench in debug mode multiple times and displaying different output.

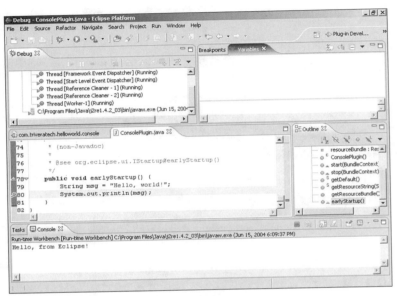

FIGURE 14.7 The host workbench displaying "Hello, from Eclipse!" in the console in the Debug perspective.

The Hello World View Plug-In

The previous example piggy-backed its behavior on the generic AbstractUIPlugin class and contributed to the org.eclipse.ui.startup extension point. You did not worry about filling in any but the most basic information in plugin.xml. This next example will create a view and use an SWT label to display the string "Hello, world!" It will contribute to the org.eclipse.ui.views extension point and create a new view category for itself.

A Plug-In with a View

Close all the editors from the previous example (press Ctrl+Shift+F4). Create a blank plug-in project by pressing Ctrl+N and selecting Plug-in Project. Click Next. Set the project name in the Plug-in Project page to com.triveratech.helloworld.view, uncheck Generate the Java Class That Controls the Project's Life Cycle and click Finish. Look in your Package Explorer and open the com.triveratech.helloworld.view project. Creating a blank plug-in project means that an empty src directory and a minimal plugin.xml file are created.

The Manifest Editor should already be opened, but if it is not, open the Manifest Editor by double-clicking the `plugin.xml` file for this new plug-in. You do not need to change or add anything to the Overview panel, but you should change the plug-in name to "HelloWorld View Plug-in" for legibility sake. Next select the Dependencies tab and click Add. In the Plug-in Selection dialog, check `org.eclipse.ui` and click Finish. Click Add again, and this time select `org.eclipse.core.runtime` from the list. As a view, your plug-in is dependent on both plug-ins being loaded into Eclipse before it can work. Listing `org.eclipse.ui` and `org.eclipse.core.runtime` in the Dependencies tab makes sure these external plug-ins will be available when you need it. Of course, while you develop the plug-in, you will also need these plug-ins in your project's build path. To add the two plug-ins, right-click in the Required Plug-ins window and select Compute Build Path from the pop-up menu. This action takes care of adding the two plug-ins to your project's build path. Press Ctrl+S to save your work so far.

The next tab to which you need to add information is Extensions. This tab is where you list the extension point to which your new class is going to contribute. Click the Add button, and the New Extension dialog is displayed. In the Extension Points tab scroll down and select `org.eclipse.ui.views`. Do not select the Sample View template that appears in the Available Templates window below the Available Extension Points. Click Finish, and `org.eclipse.ui.views` now appears in the list of extensions.

Your view needs to be available somewhere, so you need to create a category for it that appears in the Show View dialog. Right-click `org.eclipse.ui.views` and select New, Category. The category that appears is now associated with the extension point. Select the category entry, named `com.triveratech.example.helloworld.view.category1` (where the number 1 may be any digit), and change its Name in the input fields to the right of HelloWorld View Category. The name change will make it easier to find later. Save the file.

Once again, right-click the `org.eclipse.ui.views` extension and go to New, View. This view entry represents the HelloWorld view we have not yet implemented. Again, in the fields to the right, enter the following information:

- Change the Name property from `com.triveratech.example.helloworld.view.view1` to HelloWorld View.

- The Category value must be the ID from the previous category entry. It should be something like `com.triveratech.example.helloworld.view.category1`, but the number may be different. You should just cut and paste the string from the Category entry by selecting HelloWorld View Category in the Manifest Editor, going to its id field, selecting its contents, right-clicking, and selecting Copy from the pop-up menu. Return to the HelloWorld View entry and paste the value into the category field by right-clicking in the Category field and selecting Paste from the pop-up menu.

- Click the link/label of the Class field to open the Java Attribute Editor. Change the class name from `ViewPart1` to `HelloWorldView` and make the superclass `org.eclipse.ui.part.ViewPart`. Click Finish.

Within a few seconds the Java editor will open to your `HelloWorldView` class. There will be a light bulb in the left margin and errors listed in the Problems view. `ViewPart` is an abstract class with two abstract methods your HelloWorldView needs to implement. Click once on the light bulb and select Add Unimplemented Methods. Save the file to make the errors go away.

Now it is time to create the label that will appear in the view with the string "Hello, world!" Add the following two lines of code to `createPartControl()`:

```
Label label = new Label(parent, SWT.LEFT);
label.setText("Hello, world!");
```

This code will cause a light bulb to appear in the left margin of the editor. Click light bulb and select `Import 'Label' (org.eclipse.swt.widgets)` from the selection dialog. Save the file, and the gray X should disappear.

So what exactly is happening here? We are instantiating an SWT `Label` widget and telling it to add itself to a `Composite` object. An SWT `Composite` object is similar to an AWT/Swing `Panel` object in that it understands how to display the label on the screen.

You have two choices to run this plug-in: You can do a full deploy of this plug-in to the Eclipse `plugins` directory (or to an alternate plug-in directory of your choice), or you can use the runtime workbench. Let's do it both ways for this example, starting with the runtime workbench.

FIGURE 14.8   The Show View dialog displaying the HelloWorld View category.

Start the runtime workbench by choosing Run, Run As, Runtime Workbench. If you have not saved your `plugin.xml` file, the Save Resource dialog will appear asking you to choose which resources to save. The system will have all unsaved files listed and checked. If the dialog appears, click OK. Within a few seconds the Runtime Workbench will reappear, but the view will not be visible. Open the Show View dialog of the runtime workbench by selecting Window, Show View Other. If you properly set the category name of the view to match the ID of the category, you should see the Show View dialog with a folder named `HelloWorld View Category` (see Figure 14.8). Open the folder, and the HelloWorld View will be displayed. Double-click HelloWorld View or select HelloWorld View and click OK. The HelloWorld View appears as a new tab in the bottom view of the runtime workbench with the string "Hello, world!" as its only content (see Figure 14.9).

FIGURE 14.9   The runtime workbench displaying "Hello, world!" in a custom view.

Exit the runtime workbench. Now let's deploy this plug-in to the host workbench.

Deploying the Plug-In

Deploying the plug-in directly into Eclipse takes two steps:

1. Export the plug-in code as a JAR file.

2. Export the `plugin.xml` file.

Right-click the project name and select Export from the pop-up menu. The Export dialog's Select panel lists the various ways Eclipse can output your project, but for this exercise simply select JAR File. Click Next. When the JAR Package Specification panel appears, uncheck your project from the list on the left. Open your project folder to `src`, `com.triveratech.helloworld.view` and then select the check box next to the plug-in's package name (`com.triveratech.helloworld.view`). Make sure Export Generated Class Files and Resources is checked. The input field for the export destination of the JAR file should point to your Eclipse `plugins` directory, the project name of your plug-in (in this case, `com.triveratech.helloworld.view`), and the name of the JAR file. Your path should look something like this:

```
C:\eclipse\plugins\com.triveratech.helloworld.view\view.jar
```

The name of the JAR file must match the one listed in `plugin.xml`; otherwise, the system will not know which file to load. Click Finish. When the Confirm Create dialog opens, click Yes to allow it to create your plug-in directory.

Export the `plugin.xml` file by right-clicking it and selecting Export from the pop-up menu. When the Export dialog appears, select File System and click Next. The `plugin.xml` file should already be selected and checked. If it's not, check it. In the To Directory field, enter the full path where you just exported the JAR file, only without the JAR filename (for example, `C:\eclipse\plugins\com.triveratech.helloworld.view`). Use the Browse button to minimize spelling errors.

Click Finish and then exit and restart Eclipse. Go to Window, Show View, Other. Look for and open HelloWorld View Category. Double-click HelloWorld View. The Show View dialog will close, and the HelloWorld View should open in the lower-right corner of the workbench as another tab next to Console. If you do not close this view, every time you start Eclipse, the HelloWorld View will be visible from within the Plug-in perspective or whatever perspective you were using when you displayed the view from the Show View dialog.

Select Window, Show View, Plug-in Registry from the main menu. If the Plug-in Registry is not available as a choice, select Window, Show View, Other and open PDE Runtime, Plug-in Registry. The Plug-in Registry appears as an additional tab in the lower-right view next to HelloWorld View. It has the entire list of plug-ins available to Eclipse, including your just-exported `com.triveratech.helloworld.view`. Scroll down and you will find `com.triveratech.helloworld.view` in the Plug-in Registry (see Figure 14.10). You have now written two plug-ins: one that simply prints to a console, and another that creates its own custom view and label to display its message.

FIGURE 14.10 The Plug-in Registry displaying the `com.triveratech.helloworld.view` plug-in in the registry's list of available plug-ins.

The Hello World Project Wizard

At this point you should feel comfortable with plug-ins and their concepts. This next example will take you through the implementation of adding a new project type by hooking into Eclipse's internal resource system. This will not be a trivial exercise because you will add this new project type to the New Wizard, including adding a project builder, creating a custom wizard, adding pages to the main Preferences dialog to allow for the input of data specific to your new project type, and saving your preferences data.

You are going to implement this example in two parts:

- You are going to extend the wizard that creates new resources to display the new project type.

- You are going to complete the new project type by adding a nature and a builder to it.

The first task will be to extend the New wizard to display a new project type. Close any open editors before starting. Once again, you are going to create a new plug-in project. Click Ctrl+N, select Plug-in Project, and click Next. In the Plug-in Project Name page, make the project name `com.triveratech.helloworld.project` and click Next. The Plug-in Content page can be left alone, so click Finish.

The Importance of `org.eclipse.ui`

This is a good a time as any to discuss the `org.eclipse.ui` plug-in. Open the `org.eclipse.ui` project and go to `ui.jar`, `org.eclipse.ui.internal`. There is only one class in the JAR file, `UIPlugin`, but this class represents a major control point for the entire Eclipse plug-in system. `UIPlugin` is the wrapper to the workbench user interface and, as such, is one of the primordial plug-ins. You will rarely access it directly, but your plug-ins will interact with it on a regular basis.

The reason why you include `org.eclipse.ui` in your project's Java build path is for symbol recognition. When you are auto-generating Java code, the wizards expect the various classes and interfaces that appear in the generated code to be available; otherwise, they will not complete the code-generation phase.

The `plugin.xml` file is opened automatically using the Plug-in Manifest editor. Double-click the editor tab to see more of the lists and fields. In the Overview tab, change the plug-in name to HelloWorld Project Plug-in. Change to the Dependencies tab and add `org.eclipse.core.resources` and `org.eclipse.ui.ide` to the already listed `org.eclipse.ui` and `org.eclipse.core.runtime` (click Add, select `org.eclipse.core.resources` from the list of available plug-ins, click OK, and repeat for `org.eclipse.ui.ide`). Press Ctrl+S to save the work done on `plugin.xml` up to this point.

Your project is going to need these plug-ins added to its build path. Right-click in the Required Plug-Ins list and select Compute Build Path. That selection will take care of adding the listed plug-ins to your project's build path.

Select the Extensions tab. You are going to perform three steps:

1. Add the New Wizard extension point.

2. Create a category for the HelloWorld project type.

3. Define the class that will contain the various pages to be displayed in the New Wizard when a user selects the HelloWorld project type and then associate it with the category from step 2.

In order to add to the New dialog (the dialog that appears whenever you try to create a new resource), you will associate your plug-in with the `org.eclipse.ui.newWizards` extension point. Click Add, select the Extension Points tab, and select `org.eclipse.ui.newWizards` from the list of available extension points. Click Finish. Listing the extension has not accomplished anything yet. For that, you need to categorize and list the HelloWorld Wizard for use by the New Wizard.

Categories in Eclipse allow you to aggregate the various pieces of your plug-in under an arbitrary organization point. To create a new category, you must right-click org.eclipse.ui.newWizards and, from the pop-up menu, select New, Category. A category with the name com.triveratech.helloworld.project.category1 is added directly below the org.eclipse.ui.newWizards extension point. Select this new category and examine its values in the Extension Element Details to the right. Change the Name property of your new category to HelloWorld Project Category.

Let's add the HelloWorld Wizard to the extension point. Right-click org.eclipse.ui.newWizards and select New, Wizard. When the new entry appears, the Extension Element Details changes to display the entry's properties. For legibility, change the Name property from com.triveratech.helloworld.project.wizard1 to HelloWorld Project Wizard. Do not change the id field. The HelloWorld Project Wizard, which you have not yet implemented, is now registered with the org.eclipse.ui.newWizards extension point. Save the plugin.xml file.

Let's implement the com.triveratech.helloworld.project.NewWizard1 class. With the HelloWorld Project Wizard selected in the All Extensions list, click the class link in the Extension Element Details area to open the Java Attribute Editor dialog. Change the class name from NewWizard1 to HelloWorldWizard. The superclass, org.eclipse,jface.wizard.Wizard, is the base class for Eclipse wizards and org.eclipse.ui.INewWizard is the required interface that allows the Eclipse framework to interact with your new wizard. Click Finish. The class HelloWorldWizard will open in the Java editor.

Return to the Plug-in Manifest Editor and save plugin.xml. The class you have just generated is now the entry in the class field of the Extension Element Details for HelloWorld Project Wizard.

Finally, you need to associate the wizard with the category you defined earlier. Return to the HelloWorld Project Plug-in Manifest Editor and copy the ID from the HelloWorld Project Category's id property to the HelloWorld Project Wizard's Category property. Select each item one at a time to accomplish this. Click the HelloWorld Project Category item in the Extensions list box and copy the string in the id field. Next, click the HelloWorld Project Wizard item and paste the category ID string into the Category property. The wizard will now appear in its own category at runtime. Save the plugin.xml file.

In just a few steps, and a lot of explanation, you have extended the New dialog to include a custom wizard for a project type that does not exist. Let's see how well the pieces hold together.

Launch the runtime workbench (from the main menu select Run, Run As, Runtime Workbench). Press Ctrl+N, or select File, New, Other from the main menu, and the New dialog will open. The Wizards list contains the HelloWorld Project Category with the HelloWorld Project Wizard listed as a subnode (see Figure 14.11). The Finish button is disabled because we have not implemented anything that would tell the New dialog what to do next, and the Next button, though enabled, does nothing because our current implementation does not return any pages for the dialog to display.

FIGURE 14.11 The runtime workbench displaying the HelloWorld Project Category and the HelloWorld Project Wizard selection.

Cancel out of the New dialog and exit the runtime workbench. Let's fill in the `HelloWorldWizard` class created for us by the Java Class Selection Wizard and create a page for the New dialog to display.

In Eclipse, dialogs logically consist of one or more pages of information the user either accepts or changes. When the New dialog is displayed, it decides what to display next based on the item chosen in the list box. When a user selects the HelloWorld Wizard, the New dialog queries the `HelloWorldWizard` object for its first page so that the New dialog can display it for the plug-in. Your implementation of a wizard page controls what page is displayed at any given moment. When the user has arrived at the last page in a sequence, the pages are polled to check for completeness (`isPageComplete()` returns `true` for all the required pages) and the Finish button is enabled. Custom pages must implement the `IWizardPage` interface.

Eclipse supplies a set of default pages useable by anyone. As of Eclipse 2.1, they are as follows:

- `WizardDataTransferPage`

- `WizardExternalProjectImportPage`

- `WizardNewFileCreationPage`

- `WizardNewFolderMainPage`

- `WizardNewLinkPage`

- `WizardNewProjectCreationPage`

- `WizardNewProjectReferencePage`

- `WizardSelectionPage`

There are numerous existing wizard pages you can use without subclassing if you need to create new Java projects, classes, or interfaces, for example. You can extend the above classes and define your own behavior or you can use them as they are. For this example, you will use `WizardNewProjectCreationPage` as the opening page in the creation of a HelloWorld project.

Open `HelloWorldWizard.java` in the Java editor. Objects of this class type will contain the various pages to be displayed by the New dialog. Part of the life cycle of a wizard is the invoking of `addPages()`, which is defined in the `Wizard` class as an empty method. Overriding `addPages()` allows us to create all the pages we want, and calling the internal `addPage()` within the call to `addPages()` allows us to delegate the actual storage of our pages to the `Wizard` parent class. In the spirit of using Eclipse's features to make coding less tedious, right-click in the editor window of `HelloWorldWizard.java` and select Source, Override/Implement Methods. When the Override/Implement Methods dialog appears, put a check mark next to `addPages()` and click OK. The method `addPages()` will be inserted as the last method in `HelloWorldWizard`. Change the internals of the entire method to read as follows:

```
public void addPages() {
    WizardNewProjectCreationPage page = new WizardNewProjectCreationPage("page1");
    page.setDescription("Page 1 of HelloWorld New Wizard");
    page.setTitle("HelloWorld Wizard");
    addPage(page);
}
```

Remember to press Ctrl+Shift+O to resolve any missing imports. If the `WizardNewProjectCreationPage` is not found, return to `plugin.xml` and check that the required dependencies are all listed.

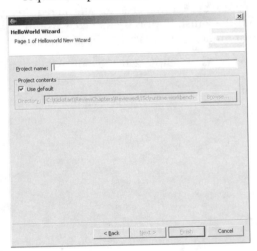

FIGURE 14.12 The runtime workbench displaying the first page of the HelloWorld Project Wizard.

If you run the runtime workbench after making these additions, you will be able to select the HelloWorld Wizard from the New dialog and the `WizardNewProjectCreationPage` will display without complaint (see Figure 14.12). However, because `performFinish()` returns `false`, entering a project name and clicking Finish does not close the dialog. You will fix that in the following code changes. Click Cancel to close the New dialog and exit the runtime workbench.

Double-click the `page` variable in `addPages()`. Right-click `page` while it is selected and, from the pop-up menu, select Refactor, Convert Local Variable to Field. The Convert Local Variable to Field dialog should display the variable as having an underscore in front of it, making it `_page`, the access modifier should be `private`, and Initialize In should be set to Current Method. (If `page` does not appear with a leading underscore, open the Eclipse Preferences dialog and go to Java, Code Style. Edit the Fields Variable type to use an underscore as a prefix.) Click OK. The Local field will now be an instance variable and the references to it will have been changed from `page` to `_page`.

This refactoring bought you the ability to add the following code to performFinish():

```java
public boolean performFinish()  {
    boolean result = false;

    System.out.println("project page.name = " + _page.getProjectName());
    System.out.println("project page.path = " + _page.getLocationPath());
    IProject project = _page.getProjectHandle();
    try {
        project.create(null);
        result = true;
    } catch (CoreException e) {
        e.printStackTrace();
    }

    return result;
}
```

This code will give you a number of red X's, all of which will be missing Java imports. Move your cursor to the end of each offending symbol and press Ctrl+spacebar to let the system add the imports for you or press Ctrl+Shift+O to do them all at once.

The first two lines of code make a call to System.out.println() so that you can see what kind of information the user has entered. You will not have this kind of code in a real plug-in because you should use either the JDK logging package or log4j.

The code in performFinish()accomplishes the following:

```java
IProject project = _page.getProjectHandle();
```

The WizardNewProjectCreationPage object, _page, takes care of creating an internal Eclipse implementation of a project object through the call to getProjectHandle(). The IProject object contains all the information entered by the user in the dialog page and also understands how to format the information into XML. Yes, in effect, Eclipse has created a default project type for you. The call to

```java
project.create(null);
```

takes care of writing the project information to an XML-formatted file named .project in the directory returned by _page.getLocationPath(). The _page object knows when the directory it is using is the default workspace path or an arbitrary path entered by the user. Of what value is the .project file? .project contains the list of natures and builders used by any particular project. It is not a file to be edited.

Let's start the runtime workbench again. When it appears, press Ctrl+N and select HelloWorld Project Category, HelloWorld Project Wizard and then click Next. The `WizardNewProjectCreationPage` is displayed with your title ("HelloWorld Wizard") and your description ("Page 1 of HelloWorld New Wizard"). Enter the project name `TestProject` and leave the `Project contents` directory set to the default runtime workbench directory. Click Finish. Something like the following should appear in the console view of the host (not the runtime) workbench:

```
project page.name = TestProject
project page.path = C:/tools/eclipse/runtime-workbench-workspace
```

Go to `%ECLIPSE_HOME%\runtime-workbench\TestProject` and look for the `.project` file. The contents of `.project` are pretty sparse:

```xml
<?xml version="1.0" encoding="UTF-8"?>
<projectDescription>
    <name>TestProject</name>
    <comment></comment>
    <projects>
    </projects>
    <buildSpec>
    </buildSpec>
    <natures>
    </natures>
</projectDescription>
```

The `<projects>`, `<buildSpec>`, and `<natures>` tags are empty. For a project type to be complete in Eclipse, the `<buildSpec>` and `<natures>` tags need to be filled in. What they need to be filled with is discussed in the next section.

Congratulations! You've created a brand new project. Now let's look at creating a brand new project type.

The Hello World Project Type

In Eclipse, a *project* is considered just another resource. What differentiates a project resource from a folder resource from a file resource? Logically, a project resource and a folder resource both represent directories on the filesystem. Projects can contain folders and/or files, and folders can contain folders and/or files, but projects cannot contain other projects. Programmatically, projects are plug-ins that contain one or more natures and one or more builders. Can projects exist without natures and/or builders? Yes, they can. However, without a nature, the project has no inherent behavior associated with any resources under its control.

A *builder* takes a resource and does something to it. A project can have multiple resources associated with it, and the builder associated with the project takes care of performing tasks such as creating, compiling, and deleting files, generating associated folders and/or files, and so on. The builder defines the life cycle of a project. A *nature* assigns that life cycle to a project.

In the previous example, you added a creation wizard to the New dialog that creates a project based on a user-defined name. This example will use tha7t project-creation capability and add a nature and a builder to the project, thereby creating a new project type. What is interesting about creating a new project type is that this is the first step toward extending an existing project by giving it an additional nature. For example, you can take the Java project type and add a J2EE nature to it.

Let's summarize the steps you will be taking:

1. Use the `com.triveratech.helloworld.project` project.

2. Add the following extension points to `plugin.xml`:

   ```
   org.eclipse.core.natures
   org.eclipse.core.resources.builders
   ```

3. Add a class that represents the implementation of the nature.

4. Add a class that represents the implementation of the builder.

5. Update the code in `HelloWorldWizard` to add the nature.

6. Update the code in `HelloWorldNature` to add the builder.

SHOP TALK

Adding Builders to Existing Project Types

The Java Development Tooling has one builder and one nature for Java project types. A J2EE project is also a type of Java project, but it has additional needs, such as validating the structure of the project and the deployment descriptors. If UML capability is added to a project, the UML capability will need its own set of builders and natures.

If you look at the `.project` files from a MyEclipse project, or a project that has UML diagrams, you will find builders and natures to enhance the build process. For example, MyEclipse adds an `IncrementalJSPBuilder` and a `webnature` (in addition to others) while the Omondo plug-in adds a `com.omondo.uml.std.Builder` and a `com.omondo.uml.std.Nature` to any project that uses its UML diagrams.

Just a word of caution: Adding builders to existing project types is not for the faint of heart. Builders are called when resources change within a project, so a slow builder can make developing within a particular project type a glacial event. If you must add one or more builders to an existing project type, make sure they are fast or will not scale. Before adding a nature/builder, consider using a resource change listener instead.

Start by selecting com.triveratech.helloworld.project and double-clicking the plugin.xml file if it is not already opened. When the plugin.xml file appears in the Plug-in Manifest Editor, select the Extensions tab. Remember, the Extensions tab is where you list the extension points to which you will be adding new functionality. Because you want to add a new nature and a new builder, you must click the Add button to display the New Extension dialog. From the Extension Points tab, scroll down and select org.eclipse.core.resources.natures and then click Finish. The All Extensions list should now have the org.eclipse.core.resources.natures extension point listed. If it is not selected, select it by clicking it once. Extension Details to the right displays three properties about this extension point: Id, Name, and Point.

Enter an Id, which is used by Eclipse to name the nature of helloworldnature. When Eclipse creates the .project file again, the name of your nature will appear as com.triveratech.helloworld.project.helloworldnature, which is a combination of the project name and the nature Id.

All this talk about creating natures is pretty useless unless you have a nature implementation class to take care of associating a builder with your project. In order to do that, you must add a runtime to the nature extension point and a run point to the runtime. Right-click org.eclipse.core.resources.natures and select New, Runtime. A new item called (runtime) will appear as a leaf to org.eclipse.core.resources.natures. Right-click (runtime) and select New, Run. The class name com.triveratech.helloworld.project.ProjectNature1 is created as your default nature implementation class. Let's make this name more legible. Select com.triveratech.helloworld.project.ProjectNature1 in All Extensions and, in the extension Element Details area, click the class link to open the Java Attribute Editor. Change the class name from ProjectNature1 to HelloWorldNature. The Interfaces window lists IProjectNature as the only interface to be implemented. The HelloWorldNature class, which will be generated by this wizard, is where you will insert code to associate your builder with your HelloWorld project type. Click Finish.

Return to the plugin.xml file to define the HelloWorld project builder. Because the steps are so similar to adding a nature extension point, just perform the following steps:

1. Select the HelloWorld Project Plug-in Manifest Editor tab.

2. Select the Extensions tab if it is not already displayed.

3. Click the Add button to get the New Extension dialog to appear.

4. From the Extension Points tab, select org.eclipse.core.resources.builders from the Available Extension Points list and click Finish.

5. Select org.eclipse.core.resources.builders from the All Extensions list. Go to the Extension Details area and change the Id to helloworldbuilder. This will be the name used internally to find your builder when the time comes.

6. From the All Extensions list in the Manifest Editor, right-click
   `org.eclipse.core.resources.builders` and select New, Builder. A leaf labeled
   `(builder)` appears.

7. Right-click `(builder)` and select New, Run. The class name
   `com.triveratech.helloworld.project.IncrementalProjectBuilder1` is generated.

8. Change the generated class name and force Eclipse to generate your stub builder class
   by clicking the `class` label of the Extension Element Details.

9. When the Java Attribute Editor dialog appears, change the class name from
   `IncrementalProjectBuilder1` to `HelloWorldBuilder`. Click Finish to generate the file.

10. Save the file `plugin.xml`.

These steps, which create a nature and a builder for your HelloWorld project type, beg the
question, Where do you associate the nature with the project type? The builder is associated
with a project by its nature. The nature is associated with the project through the class that
creates the project type. In this case, it occurs in `HelloWorldWizard`.

Go to the `HelloWorldWizard` file. In `performFinish()`, add the following code after the `try`
block containing `_project.create()`:

```
IProjectDescription projectDesc = null;
try {
    project.open(null);
    projectDesc = project.getDescription();
} catch (CoreException e1) {
    e1.printStackTrace();
}

String[] natureIds = projectDesc.getNatureIds();
String[] newNatureIds = new String[natureIds.length + 1];
System.arraycopy(natureIds, 0, newNatureIds, 0, natureIds.length);
newNatureIds[natureIds.length] = "com.triveratech.helloworld.project.helloworldnature";
projectDesc.setNatureIds(newNatureIds);
try {
    project.setDescription(projectDesc, null);
} catch (CoreException e2) {
    e2.printStackTrace();
}
```

Let's look at what this code does. Here's the call to `project.open(null)`:

```
project.open(null);
projectDesc = project.getDescription();
```

It gets the information generated by the prior call to project.create(). As Eclipse creates your default project information, you add your new nature to this already existing data. How do you add your nature? The remaining lines of code take care of that:

```
String[] natureIds = projectDesc.getNatureIds();
String[] newNatureIds = new String[natureIds.length + 1];
System.arraycopy(natureIds, 0, newNatureIds, 0, natureIds.length);
newNatureIds[natureIds.length] = "com.triveratech.helloworld.project.helloworldnature";
projectDesc.setNatureIds(newNatureIds);
try {
    project.setDescription(projectDesc, null);
} catch (CoreException e2) {
    e2.printStackTrace();
}
```

The first three lines take care of retrieving the existing natures from your project (which, in this case, is none) and allocates a new array large enough to hold the current natures and the new nature you want to add to this project type. The call to System.arraycopy() does a fast copy of the original array into your new larger array, and the next line assigns the name of your new nature, "com.triveratech.helloworld.project.helloworldnature", as the last entry in the new nature list. The next line of code assigns the new nature array list to the projectDesc object, where the original list came from, and the line of code after that assigns your modified projectDesc to the project.

The preceding code is fine as an example, but it is not safe. Before you add natures to a project type, you should always check to see whether the nature is already associated with the project so as to avoid adding duplicate natures.

To check whether your work will have an impact on your new project type, it is necessary to execute the runtime workbench and create a project of type HelloWorldProject. The name of the project does not matter. When you have finished creating your new project, go to the directory where the project was created. If you are not sure where that is, right-click the project and select Properties. The Info item lists the location in the panel to the right. The default is the Eclipse home directory followed by runtime-workbench\[project name]. If you called your project TestProject, it might be located under c:\eclipse\runtime-workbench\TestProject. Opening the .project file located in your project directory will display the following:

```
<?xml version="1.0" encoding="UTF-8"?>
<projectDescription>
    <name>TestProject</name>
    <comment></comment>
    <projects>
    </projects>
    <buildSpec>
    </buildSpec>
```

```
<natures>
    <nature>com.triveratech.helloworld.project.helloworldnature</nature>
</natures>
</projectDescription>
```

The name of the nature is indeed your project name plus the nature id property value you set in the Plug-in Manifest Editor.

Let's add the builder to the `HelloWorldProject` type, create another project of type `HelloWorldProject`, and examine the contents of the `.project` file again.

Open `HelloWorldNature.java` in the Java editor. When a nature is instantiated due to the creation of a project type, the nature's constructor is called, followed by a call to `setProject()` and a call to `configure()`. You should add any builders to the project type from within `configure()`. When a nature is being removed, you should delete any added builders when `deconfigure()` is called.

Update the `HelloWorldNature` class by adding an instance variable to hold the project reference when `setProject()` is called:

```java
private IProject _project;
```

Next, add the use of _project to `getProject()` and `setProject()`:

```java
public IProject getProject()  {
    return _project;
}

public void setProject(IProject project)  {
    project = project;
}
```

The `configure()` method would contain the code to associate the builder:

```java
public void configure() throws CoreException {
    IProjectDescription projectDesc = _project.getDescription();
    ICommand [] buildSpec = projectDesc.getBuildSpec();

    ICommand newCommand = projectDesc.newCommand();
    newCommand.setBuilderName("com.triveratech.helloworld.project.helloworldbuilder");
    ICommand [] buildSpecs = new ICommand[buildSpec.length + 1];

    System.arraycopy(buildSpec, 0, buildSpecs, 1, buildSpec.length);
    buildSpecs[0] = newCommand;
    projectDesc.setBuildSpec(buildSpecs);
    _project.setDescription(projectDesc, null);
}
```

The `ICommand` interface is located in `org.eclipse.core.resources`.

In similar fashion to your nature, the code uses _project to get the current crop of builders associated with the project, and the new builder is manually added to the list. In this case, you add the builder to the front of the list.

As mentioned earlier, you should always check for the existence of a builder prior to adding it because adding a builder more than once to a project can lead to severe performance issues and hard-to-track bugs. The following is the `configure()` method with the additional code (Listing 14.2):

LISTING 14.2   `HelloWorldNature.java`

```java
public void configure() throws CoreException {
    IProjectDescription projectDesc = _project.getDescription();
    ICommand[] buildSpec = projectDesc.getBuildSpec();
    boolean hasBuilder = false;

    for (int i = 0; i < buildSpec.length; ++i) {
        if (buildSpec[i]
            .getBuilderName()
            .equals("com.triveratech.helloworld.project.helloworldbuilder")) {
            hasBuilder = true;
            break;
        }
    }

    if (hasBuilder == false) {
        ICommand newCommand = projectDesc.newCommand();
        newCommand.setBuilderName("com.triveratech.helloworld.project.helloworldbuilder");
        ICommand[] buildSpecs = new ICommand[buildSpec.length + 1];

        System.arraycopy(buildSpec, 0, buildSpecs, 1, buildSpec.length);
        buildSpecs[0] = newCommand;
        projectDesc.setBuildSpec(buildSpecs);
        _project.setDescription(projectDesc, null);
    }
}
```

Now that you have a real-live builder associated with `HelloWorldProject` types, you need to be notified when any files in this project are modified. As usual, most of the work has been done for you.

The main entry point to your builder is through build(). What you will implement is a Visitor object that you pass in to an IResourceDelta object or an IProject object, either of which you get from Eclipse. For this example, you will implement the Visitor object as an inner class of your builder.

Design Patterns: Visitor

The Visitor pattern is one of the original 23 design patterns from the seminal book on the subject, *Design Patterns: Elements of Reusable Object-Oriented Software*, by Erich Gamma, Richard Helm, Ralph Johnson, and John Vlissides. A Visitor represents an operation to be performed on another object.[1] Of course, the visitor does not just perform an operation on another object; it is called from within the target object. This is why your Visitor, a subclass of IResourceVisitor, will be passed into either an IResourceDelta object or an IProject object. Either of these objects will decide when to call your IResourceVisitor object, but when they do, your object will be free to execute whatever logic you see fit.

Here are a couple things to bear in mind:

- The builder must inherit from IncrementalProjectBuilder (which HelloWorldBuilder does).

- It has one chance to initialize itself using startupOnIntialize().

The builder is instantiated when Eclipse is started and you have a project of your type available. Otherwise, the builder is not instantiated until you create a project of the proper type (in this case, a project of type HelloWorldProject). When you create a project of type HelloWorldProject, the builder is instantiated and build() is called to give the builder the opportunity to accomplish anything for which it was designed. Any time a change is made to the project (for example, adding a file or changing a file), the builder is called.

Just for fun, add a print statement to the builder's constructor:

```
System.out.println("HelloWorldBuilder.constructor()");
```

Also, add the following print statement to the builder's build() method:

```
System.out.println("HelloWorldBuilder.build()");
```

Run the runtime workbench and create a HelloWorldProject named TestBuilder. Look in the console window of the host workbench and you will see the following output:

---

1. *Design Patterns: Elements of Reusable Object-Oriented Software. Page 331.*

```
project page.name = TestBuilder
project page.path = C:/tools/eclipse/runtime-workbench-workspace
HelloWorldBuilder.constructor()
HelloWorldBuilder.build()
```

If you were to add a file to TestProject by pressing Ctrl+N and selecting Simple and File, you would see the line HelloWorldBuilder.build() again.

Although print statements are fine, let's implement an IResourceVisitor object and an IResourceDeltaVisitor object and see what happens when they are used in an IResourceDelta object and an IProject object. Add the code shown in Listing 14.3 to HelloWorldBuilder as private inner classes (remember to press Ctrl+Shift+O to create any missing imports).

LISTING 14.3   The Inner Classes of HelloWorldBuilder.java

```java
private class HelloWorldVisitor implements IResourceVisitor {
    public boolean visit(IResource resource) throws CoreException {
        System.out.println("HelloWorldVisitor.visit()");
        switch (resource.getType()) {
            case IResource.PROJECT :
                System.out.println("Project added: " + resource.getName());
                break;
            case IResource.FOLDER :
                System.out.println("Folder added: " + resource.getName());
                break;
            case IResource.FILE :
                System.out.println("File added: " + resource.getName());
                break;
        }

        return true; // visit child resources
    }
}

private class HelloWorldDeltaVisitor implements IResourceDeltaVisitor {
    public boolean visit(IResourceDelta delta) throws CoreException {
        System.out.println("HelloWorldDeltaVisitor.visit()");
        String type = null;
        switch (delta.getResource().getType()) {
            case IResource.ROOT :
                type = "ROOT";
                break;
            case IResource.PROJECT :
```

LISTING 14.3 Continued

```
                    type = "Project";
                    break;
                case IResource.FOLDER :
                    type = "Folder";
                    break;
                case IResource.FILE :
                    type = "File";
                    break;
            }

            switch (delta.getKind()) {
                case IResourceDelta.ADDED :
                    System.out.println(type + " added: " + delta.getResource().getName());
                    break;
                case IResourceDelta.CHANGED :
                    System.out.println(type + " changed: " + delta.getResource().getName());
                    break;
                case IResourceDelta.REMOVED :
                    System.out.println(type + " removed: " + delta.getResource().getName());
                    break;
            }

        return true; // visit child resources
    }
}
```

The first inner class, HelloWorldVisitor, is called when an
IncrementalProjectBuilder.AUTO_BUILD or IncrementalProjectBuilder.FULL_BUILD event
occurs. The creation of a project will cause this code to be executed, as will the manual
rebuild of the project. In the second inner class, HelloWorldDeltaVisitor, the code will
display information as folders and files are added, changed, or deleted from the project. Also,
notice that visit() for both inner classes returns true. This notifies the underlying system
that the code wants to be called for any child resources that may exist as well.

The last addition to make to your HelloWorldBuilder is to make build() look like this code:

```
    protected IProject[] build(int kind, Map args, IProgressMonitor monitor)
            throws CoreException {
        System.out.println("HelloWorldBuilder.build()");
        if (kind == IncrementalProjectBuilder.FULL_BUILD) {
            System.out.println("FULL_BUILD");
            getProject().accept(new HelloWorldVisitor());
```

```
            } else {
                IResourceDelta delta = getDelta(getProject());
                if (delta == null) {
                    System.out.println("AUTO_BUILD");
                    getProject().accept(new HelloWorldVisitor());
                } else {
                    System.out.println("INCREMENTAL_BUILD");
                    delta.accept(new HelloWorldDeltaVisitor());
                }
            }
            return null;
    }
```

The only three flags recognized by IncrementalProjectBuilder are FULL_BUILD, AUTO_BUILD, and INCREMENTAL_BUILD. For the purposes of this exercise, you will treat FULL_BUILD and AUTO_BUILD as the same. INCREMENTAL_BUILD is what happens when a resource is added or changed in some way, including being deleted from the project.

Be aware that the preceding code is a little wasteful. The code creates a new HelloWorldVisitor and HelloWorldDeltaVisitor every time build() is called, when the code could have created one object of each type and held the object references in instance variables.

Let's walk through some of the scenarios handled by the Visitors:

1. Run the runtime workbench.

2. Press Ctrl+N and create a project using the HelloWorld Project Wizard. Call it TestBuilderFull. Click Finish. Notice the output in the Console view of the host work-bench:

```
project page.name = TestBuilderFull
project page.path = C:/tools/eclipse/runtime-workbench-workspace
HelloWorldBuilder.constructor()
HelloWorldBuilder.constructor()
HelloWorldBuilder.build()
FULL_BUILD
**** HelloWorldVisitor.visit() ****
Project added: TestBuilerFull
**** HelloWorldVisitor.visit() ****
File added: .project
```

By creating a new project, which in turn created a .project file, a full build was triggered, which called HelloWorldVisitor.visit() to notify it that a new project was created. Because the method returned true, visit() was called again to process the .project file.

3. Press Ctrl+N again, only this time create a file by selecting Simple and File from the list boxes. Click Next to go to the next page and in the File Name field enter the name **TestFile.hw**. Click Finish. Check the output in the host workbench Console view:

```
INCREMENTAL_BUILD
**** HelloWorldDeltaVisitor.visit() ****
Project changed: TestBuilderFull
**** HelloWorldDeltaVisitor.visit() ****
File added: TestFile.hw
```

The project has changed, a file has been added to it, so visit() from HelloWorldDeltaVisitor is called. Because visit() also returns true, visit() is called again with another resource to be examined (in this case, the added file TestFile.hw).

4. The file TestFile.hw should already be opened in the default editor. Type anything in the editor and save the file. Examine the output in the host workbench Console view again. The output is exactly the same as before: The project changed because the file changed, and visit() is called once for each resource.

5. Delete TestFile.hw and look at the output in the host workbench. The project changed due to the file deletion, so visit() is called for the project and for the file:

```
INCREMENTAL_BUILD
**** HelloWorldDeltaVisitor.visit() ****
Project changed: TestBuilderFull
**** HelloWorldDeltaVisitor.visit() ****
File removed: TestFile.hw
```

You have built almost all the pieces to implement a custom project type plug-in in Eclipse. All that is left is the implementation of a wizard specific to your project type and the ability to add a preference page to the main Preferences dialog.

The HelloWorld Wizard

You need to implement a custom wizard when you have a specific task that cannot be added to an existing wizard extension point. For example, right-click a project and select Properties from the pop-up menu to display its custom wizard. The information available through the Properties Wizard would not be appropriate as an extension to any of the other existing wizards.

Although a project-specific wizard could offer any kind of functionality to the user, your wizard should not give the user the ability to accomplish a task best served by an already existing wizard; for example, if you need to create new resources, then contribute to the extension point of the New Wizard. A custom wizard *does not* contribute to an existing extension point. When an event occurs in the normal course of the plug-in's life, it displays the wizard in response.

Two steps are involved in implementing a wizard:

1. You must implement a class that inherits from either the IWizard interface, or Wizard, a convenience class, and has one or more pages to be displayed to accept user input. For the sake of convenience, you should inherit from Wizard because it takes care of many of the repetitive details of page handling.

2. You must wrap your wizard implementation inside of a WizardDialog, which will display a wizard with a standard look and feel and will take care of displaying the proper pages at the proper time.

Let's implement a custom wizard specific to HelloWorld projects. After selecting the com.triveratech.helloworld.project package from com.triveratech.helloworld.project project, press Ctrl+N and start the process of creating a new Java class. When the New Java Class page appears, the Source Folder and Package fields should be filled, and the only field you need to enter something into is the Name field. Therefore, enter HelloWorldCustomWizard as the name of your new class. Change the super-class from java.lang.Object to org.eclipse.jface.wizard.Wizard and click Finish.

The HelloWorldCustomWizard is ready to create pages. The Wizard class implements a method called addPage() that holds an object of type IWizardPage. You will implement addPages(), declared in the interface IWizard, create your pages, and save them for later use through a call to addPage() (implemented in Wizard). The class Wizard also implements addPages(), but the method is empty. Add the following code to your HelloWorldCustomWizard class:

```java
public boolean performFinish() {
    return true;
}


public void addPages() {
    String pageName = "HelloWorld Custom Wizard Page";
    String title = "HelloWorld Custom Wizard";
    String description = "This is the first and only page of this custom wizard.";

    WizardPage page1 = new HelloWorldWizardPage(pageName);
    page1.setTitle(title);
    page1.setDescription(description);

    addPage(page1);
}
```

Correct most of the red X's that appear by moving the cursor to the end of the underlined symbol and pressing Ctrl+spacebar (or just press Ctrl+Shift+O to handle all your missing imports). The one problem that is not so easily fixed is the declaration of HelloWorldWizardPage. Single-click the yellow light bulb/red X icon and select from the Quick Fix window Create Class HelloWorldWizardPage. The first page of the New dialog to define a new Java class will appear. Because the code inside of addPages() is assigning your custom page to a variable of type WizardPage, the New wizard has guessed that you want to inherit from that class, and it has guessed right. Click Finish.

When HelloWorldWizardPage opens in the Java editor, it will notify you of a missing default constructor. Click the light bulb in the left margin and select Add Constructor 'HelloWorldWizardPage(String)'. Save the file.

By defining a Wizard class and a WizardPage class, you have declared the minimum number of classes needed to implement the custom wizard (excluding the WizardDialog wrapper class, of course). In HelloWorldWizardPage change createControl() to the following:

```
public void createControl(Composite parent) {
    Label label = new Label(parent, SWT.WRAP | SWT.CENTER);
    label.setText("Hello World");

    setControl(parent);
}
```

Press Ctrl+Shift+O to satisfy the import requirements. If the Organize Imports dialog opens asking which Label symbol to import, select org.eclipse.swt.widgets.Label. Once again, you are using a basic SWT GUI Label component with the string "Hello, World" as its content. When the wizard appears, it will be an informational dialog (or at least as informational as a greeting can be).

Now that the wizard and the panel that constitutes the wizard's GUI have been implemented, you need to open the wizard based on an external event. For this example, the event will be tied to a pop-up menu.

To add your own menu item to the pop-up menu, you will need to contribute to the org.eclipse.ui.popupMenus extension point. That entails adding the extension point to the plugin.xml file, adding configuration criteria, and adding an action object that will be executed when the configuration criteria are met. Open the plugin.xml file for the com.triveratech.helloworld.project project and select the Extensions tab. Click the Add button, select org.eclipse.ui.popupMenus from the Extension Points tab, and click Finish. You have now declared that you are contributing to a pop-up menu.

There are two kinds of pop-up menu contributions: one that appears based on a particular object type, and one based on the pop-up menu within a particular view. For this example, you will extend the pop-up menu when you select a resource of a particular type. In this case, the resource will be a file with the extension .hw. Still within the plugin.xml file, right-click the `org.eclipse.ui.popupMenus` node and select New, objectContribution. Follow these steps to add or change the values for the new object contribution:

1. Change the id field from `com.triveratech.helloworld.project.objectContribution1` to `com.triveratech.helloworld.project.popupfor.files`. This give us a more legible ID for this contribution.

2. Change objectClass from `com.triveratech.helloworld.project.object1` to `org.eclipse.core.resources.IFile`. Because this pop-up menu appears based on the type of resource chosen, you are telling the pop-up menu to only display this new menu item when the resource chosen is a file. It may be necessary for you to type in the full class name of IFile because the Browse button will only display types contained within your projects.

3. Enter the string `*.hw` into the nameFilter property. This narrows the selection criteria even more. The new pop-up menu item will only appear when the pop-up is selected on a file and the file has an extension of `.hw` (for example, `TestFile.hw`).

This configuration has not yet defined the pop-up menu item. Let's do that next. Right-click the object contribution `com.triveratech.helloworld.project.popupfor.files` and select New, Action. Once again, change the following values found in the Extension Element Details, but this time for the new action:

- **id**—Leave this value set to `com.triveratech.helloworld.project.action1`.

- **label**—Change this from the obscure `com.triveratech.helloworld.project.action1` to HelloWorld Custom Dialog. This is the label that will appear in the pop-up menu when the user right-clicks files with the `.hw` extension.

- **class**—Change `com.triveratech.helloworld.project.action1` to `com.triveratech.helloworld.project.popupfor.HelloWorldActionDelegate`. Later you will implement this class as a subclass of interface `org.eclipse.ui.IObjectActionDelegate`. Remember, this action is looking for a particular object type, so the action delegate must reflect this data type.

- **menubarPath**—Enter additions into this field. This string is an internal constant, which means you want to create a new top-level menu. By using "additions," the menu item HelloWorld Custom Dialog will appear in its own cordoned-off area of the pop-up menu. For the full list of constants and their meanings, go to `org.eclipse.ui.IWorkbenchActionConstants`. A large number of constants are defined for use in the creation of standard and global actions and menus.

- **enablesFor**—Enter 1 into this field. This property allows you to control the visibility of the pop-up menu item HelloWorld Custom Dialog. The property enablesFor tells the menu item to appear if no items, zero or one item, one or more items, two or more items, an exact number of items, or any number of resource items are selected. The value 1 for enablesFor means the menu item will appear only if one file is selected. If enablesFor is set to 3, the pop-up menu item would only appear if three items are selected, no more and no less.

It is time to implement the `HelloWorldActionDelegate` class. Click the link class in the Extension Element Details section. When the Java Attribute Editor dialog appears, click the Add button and enter `IObjectActionDelegate` as a required interface. Ensure that the Inherited Abstract Methods check box is checked. Then click Finish.

Three methods appear in your `HelloWorldActionDelegate`, but the only one you are going to worry about for this example is `run()`. Change `run()` to the following:

```
public void run(IAction action) {
    System.out.println("In HelloWorldActionDelegate.run()");

    // Create the custom wizard.
    HelloWorldCustomWizard wizard = new HelloWorldCustomWizard();

    // Create the wizard dialog that will wrap your custom wizard.
    WizardDialog dialog = new WizardDialog(PlatformUI.getWorkbench().getActiveWorkbenchWindow().getShell(),wizard);

    // Open the wizard dialog
    dialog.open();
}
```

FIGURE 14.13 The HelloWorld Custom Dialog menu item displayed in the pop-up menu.

Press Ctrl+Shift+O to include any missing import statements. Save the file. The method `run()` instantiates an object of type `HelloWorldCustomWizard`, which is really just a container for the pages to be displayed in the real dialog, and instantiates a `WizardDialog`, passing in the workbench shell and your wizard. The workbench shell passed into the `WizardDialog` constructor is the highest (or top-level) shell available in Eclipse. This shell constitutes the windows that make up Eclipse. By passing in the shell, you afford the constructor the opportunity to find a parent window to which it can attach itself. The last thing `run()` does is open the dialog. You are done implementing and gluing your custom wizard to Eclipse.

Run the runtime workbench. You should still have the `TestBuilderFull` project displayed in the Package Explorer. `TestFile.hw` appears in the Package Explorer as a leaf to `TestBuilderFull`. Right-click `TestFile.hw` and you should see HelloWorld Custom Dialog as the menu item after Refresh in the pop-up menu (see Figure 14.13). Select HelloWorld Custom Dialog, and the HelloWorld Custom dialog appears with its snappy description and eye-catching label (see Figure 14.14). When you are done, you may exit the runtime workbench.

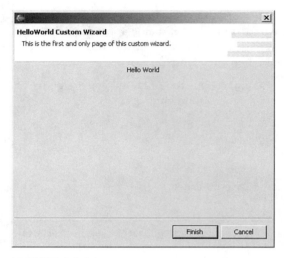

FIGURE 14.14   The HelloWorld Custom dialog.

Now that you have managed to create a new project type, add your new project type to the New dialog, and create a custom dialog for use by your project type, there is only one thing left to do: Add custom preferences.

The Hello World Preferences Panel

The Preferences dialog is the ultimate database of global configuration data in Eclipse. The information entered by a user becomes available as soon as the user clicks the OK button, and plug-ins are free to use the data as they see fit.

I expect that most, if not all, plug-ins would take advantage of the hook into the Preferences dialog as a simple way of allowing the user to customize the plug-ins' behavior. What is the hook into the Preferences dialog? As you might guess, the preferences extension point is the hook into the dialog.

The steps to adding one or more pages to the Preferences dialog are as follows:

1. Add `org.eclipse.ui.preferencesPages` to the Extensions tab of `plugin.xml`.

2. Add one or more new pages to the extension point.

3. Select one new page at a time and define/generate a new Java class that represents the page to be displayed.

4. Implement each of the new preferences pages using SWT to generate the form and override one or more of the methods defined to be called based on a user action such as clicking the OK button.

That is it. Of course, the default data for the form and the new data entered by the user needs to be available somewhere. The JDT defines a default preferences store mechanism so you don't have to worry about where to store the data. You access this default preference store by asking for it from the `AbstractUIPlugin` you normally extend when you first create a plug-in. The default preference store is a file located in the `plugin` directory. You have not had to use `AbstractUIPlugin` until now, so you will create one in the next exercise.

Adding to the Preference Dialog

In the `com.triveratech.helloworld.project` package (not *project*) is a class named `ProjectPlugin`. In the Package Explorer view, right-click the `ProjectPlugin` file and select

Refactor, Rename from the pop-up menu. Change the class name from `ProjectPlugin` to `HelloWorldPlugin`. Check Update References and Update Fully Qualified Name in non-Java Files. In the File Name Patterns field, enter `*.xml`. Click Preview. The Rename Compilation Unit dialog will list three items: the internal rename of the class, the external rename of the file, and the modification of `plugin.xml`, which contains the old class name. Click OK. Check the Overview tab of `plugin.xml` to ensure that the class name has been properly update to read `com.triveratech.helloworld.project.HelloWorldPlugin`.

At runtime, the system will instantiate an object of `HelloWorldPlugin` and leave it lying around during the life of the plug-in. If you want to use the capabilities available through this object, you need to be able to ask for it. One way to do that is to have a static method you can call on the `HelloWorldPlugin` class that will return the instantiated object. The code generator has already taken care of doing that for you by defining a static reference to `HelloWorldPlugin` and defining a static method to return that reference called `getDefault()`.

Open `HelloWorldPlugin.java`. Because the plug-in options should be in the plug-in class, let's define the following option constant there:

```
public static final String GREETING = "HelloWorldPlugin.GREETING";
```

SHOP TALK

The Importance of Being Constant

Constants such as GREETING, defined in HelloWorldPlugin, can be defined in numerous places. As a point of style, you should never use string or numeric literals in your code; rather you should define constants that are easy to use and understand. With that said, private and protected constants are easy to define because they go in the class that needs them—no one can see them anyway (and only the subclasses can see the protected ones). Public constants are an issue. If they are defined in the class that needs them, anyone else who needs them has to drag around the code from the class where the constants are defined. If you define the constants in an interface with an API, you run the risk of runtime issues if the API changes.

Public constants need a home that is theirs alone. For example, if you are writing Data Access Objects (DAOs), it is a good idea to create constants for the various tables and column names to which the objects map, independent of the persistence code. This allows you to update just the constants if they need to be updated or just the code if it needs to be updated. Must it be done like this? No, of course not. However, any other code you write that relies on those names can easily use them and not worry about API changes.

Unsolicited advice: Use constants liberally and put public constants in an interface with no additional API information.

Return to plugin.xml. You are going to add the preferences extension point by selecting the Extensions tab and clicking Add. When the New Extension dialog opens, scroll down to org.eclipse.ui.preferencesPages and click Finish. The preferencesPage extension point is the last item in the list. In order for the Preferences dialog to know which page should be displayed when a user selects the HelloWorld preference node, you need to right-click org.eclipse.ui.preferencesPages and select New, Page to add this information.

This addition to the preferencesPages extension is where you define the name of the node that will appear in the Preferences dialog as well as the object that represents the page of information the user will configure. Leave the Id field alone, change the Name field to HelloWorld, and change the Class name to com.triveratech.helloworld.project.WorkbenchPreferencePage (in other words, just remove the last character in the class name, which should be the number 1).

Create the WorkbenchPreferencePage by clicking the Class link in the Extension Element Details section. When the Java Attribute Editor dialog opens, all the fields should be filled in, including the superclass org.eclipse.jface.preference.PreferencePage and interface org.eclipse.ui.IWorkbenchPreferencePage. Click Finish to open WorkbenchPreferencePage in the Java editor.

The constant GREETING, defined in HelloWorldPlugin, will be used in WorkbenchPreferencePage in the performXXX() methods. First, modify the WorkbenchPreferencePage by adding an instance field and changing createControl() as follows:

```
private Text _greeting;

protected Control createContents(Composite parent) {
    Label label = new Label(parent, SWT.CENTER);
    label.setText("Greeting");
    _greeting = new Text(parent, SWT.SINGLE | SWT.BORDER);

    return parent;
}
```

In this code, the label has been changed to "Greeting" and an input field has been added. The plan is for a user to change the HelloWorld preference, which will change the label in the HelloWorldCustomDialog. If you execute the runtime workbench, you will see the GUI change in the HelloWorld page of the Preferences dialog, but the value has not yet been propagated to the HelloWorldCustomDialog (see Figure 14.15).

When a value has been entered into a Preferences page, that value can be persisted in the preferences store. Your WorkbenchPreferencePage will need to implement three methods: doGetPreferenceStore(), performOK(), and performDefault(). All three are defined in the parent class `PreferencePage`. The first, `doGetPreferenceStore()`, is nothing more than a call to your static `HelloWorldPlugin.getDefault()` method to get a handle on the `AbstractUIPlugin` method `getPreferenceStore()`. The next two methods, `performOK()` and `performDefault()`, are all event handlers. When the OK button is clicked, you save the new information into the preference store for later use. If the Default button is clicked, you update the preference store with your default greeting to "world." The code for the two methods is shown in Listing 14.4.

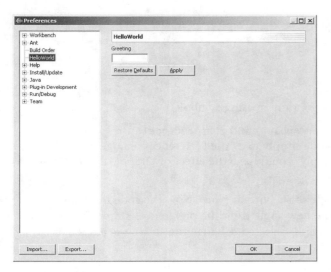

FIGURE 14.15   The HelloWorld Preferences page.

LISTING 14.4   WorkbenchPreferencePage.java

```
protected IPreferenceStore doGetPreferenceStore() {
    System.out.println("WorkbenchPreferencePage.doGetPreferenceStore()");
    return HelloWorldPlugin.getDefault().getPreferenceStore();
}

protected void performDefaults() {
    System.out.println("WorkbenchPreferencePage.performDefaults()");
    IPreferenceStore prefStore = getPreferenceStore();
    prefStore.setValue(HelloWorldPlugin.GREETING, "world");
    HelloWorldPlugin.getDefault().savePluginPreferences();

    _greeting.setText(prefStore.getString(HelloWorldPlugin.GREETING));
}
```

LISTING 14.4   Continued

```
public boolean performOk() {
    boolean result = false;
    System.out.println("WorkbenchPreferencePage.performOk()");
    IPreferenceStore prefStore = getPreferenceStore();
    prefStore.setValue(HelloWorldPlugin.GREETING, _greeting.getText());
        HelloWorldPlugin.getDefault().savePluginPreferences();

    result = true;

    return result;
}
```

Don't forget to press Ctrl+Shift+O to import any missing symbols.

The Apply and Cancel buttons call performApply() and performCancel(), respectively. For this example, if Cancel is clicked, the code simply exits the Preferences dialog, and the Apply button doesn't have any effect at all. Apply would have the effect of OK but does not exit the dialog.

The preceding code takes care of one side of the virtual fence. Now the code from the HelloWorldWizardPage needs to read the new value from the preferences store and display the new label when the pop-up menu item is selected. Change the code in createControl() to reflect the following code:

```
public void createControl(Composite parent) {
    Label label = new Label(parent, SWT.WRAP | SWT.CENTER);

    IPreferenceStore prefStore = HelloWorldPlugin.getDefault().getPreferenceStore();
    String greeting = prefStore.getString(HelloWorldPlugin.GREETING);

    label.setText("Hello, " + greeting + "!");

    setControl(parent);
}
```

This code is striking in its simplicity: It gets the preference store for this plug-in, gets the property value from the preference store based on the incoming key (HelloWorldPlugin.GREETING), and creates the new greeting. Can it get any better than that?

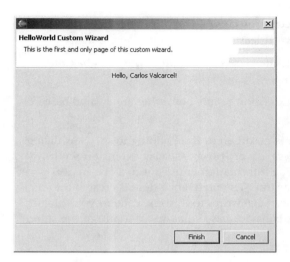

FIGURE 14.16 The HelloWorld Custom Dialog sending a greeting to an obscure author.

Time to check the work done so far for this piece. Start the runtime workbench, open the Preferences dialog (Window, Preferences) and select HelloWorld from the list to the left. Enter your name into the Greeting field and click OK. In the Package Explorer view, right-click TestFile.hw and from the pop-up menu select HelloWorld Custom Dialog. The hello message with the name you entered in the Preferences page appears (see Figure 14.16). Click Finish on the wizard, open the Preferences dialog again, change the name on the HelloWorld page, and click OK. Open the HelloWorld Custom Wizard and check out the new name. Finally, open the Preferences page again, go to the HelloWorld page, and click Restore Defaults. When you open the custom wizard, this time it should simply say "Hello, world!" We have come full circle.

In Brief

The creation of plug-ins in Eclipse is consistent and straightforward. The use of extension points make adding new functionality almost intuitive, but there are so many extension points that the real challenge is discovering the proper extension point with which to associate your class.

The chapter covered both basic and advanced topics related to plug-ins:

- Printing to the console from a plug-in is done with nothing fancier than the use of System.out or System.err.

- A view extends the ViewPart class and contributes to the org.eclipse.ui.views extension point. In order to see your view, it was necessary to add a category with which the view could associate. The Show View dialog allows you to select your custom view for display.

- The org.eclipse.ui.newWizards extension point is able to use HelloWorldWizard as an extension by displaying the pages it contains. In addition, Eclipse supplies a number of standard wizard pages such as WizardNewProjectCreationPage.

- Natures are the connecting points between projects and their life-cycle behavior, which is implemented by builders. Projects have at least one nature and one builder.

- Builders are called at various times in the life cycle of a resource. They can be called when files are created, updated, or deleted.

- Custom wizards are not contributed to extension points but rather are created based on some event that occurs in the system.

- Adding to the Eclipse Preferences dialog is no different from adding to the New dialog. The pages associated with the `org.eclipse.ui.preferencesPages` extension point will be displayed in the Preferences dialog. The information entered into a Preferences page can be stored in an Eclipse-supplied data store. The preference store is created for you by the underlying system. Your preference page writes to it, some code in your plug-in reads from it, and the plug-in adjusts its behavior based on what is found in the store.

Implementing a Help Plug-In

RTFM.

—Anonymous

Extension Points of the Eclipse Help Plug-In

You have finally reached the last chapter of this book (not counting the appendixes), and its topic is the topic most neglected by the developer community. The creation of documentation is by far the most forgotten part of the development process because it has zero impact on the executable that took so much time and effort to implement.

With that said, it is a truism of the development community that when a question is asked about some functionality of a delivered piece of software, the first response is "RTFM." The response is a valid one, but if no "M" was written, then reading it becomes quite a challenge. In the spirit of ease of use, Eclipse makes the addition of documentation to the workbench an almost mechanical function, but you will still have to write the content.

In most cases, implementing a help plug-in in Eclipse requires no code to be written. The help files should be written using HTML, so pick your favorite HTML editor and get writing. No matter that the plug-in help files go a long way toward explaining what a plug-in is, the rationale for writing it, how it should be used, and how it can be extended. Your users will be the better for it, and your first response to their questions can once again be that famous acronym. For an overview of how to use the Help system, refer to Appendix A, " Navigating Through Eclipse Help."

Three kinds of help are available in Eclipse:

- Normal documentation

- Infopops, also known as *context-sensitive help*

- Active help

The examples in this chapter will cover the implementation of all the various types of help.

To implement a help plug-in, you follow these steps:

1. Write your documentation as a collection of HTML files. The directory structure you create should reflect the topics being covered. There should be one high-level directory where the pages and subdirectories exist.

2. Define one or more XML-formatted table of contents files that reflect the various topics in your help files. The topics point to the entry point HTML files to be displayed in the help content window.

3. Define a `plugin.xml` file that points to your table of contents files.

4. Deploy your HTML files in a Zip file named `doc.zip` and package the table of contents and the `plugin.xml` files to be installed under the Eclipse `plugins` directory. Restart Eclipse and look for your files in the help system.

Eclipse has a sample online help called Online Help Sample. You can view it from the standard Help window. It is made up of a number of table of contents files and doesn't say any more than the pages you will create in this chapter. If you want to look at the files for this example, go to your Eclipse `plugins` directory and look in `org.eclipse.help.examples.ex1_3.0.0`.

Five Ways to Implement a Help Plug-In

Let's walk through a few help plug-in scenarios:

- Using one table of contents file that links the HTML files to topics.

- Using multiple table of contents files to tie together the directory tree that contains the help documentation to describe a more complex organization of help files.

- Extending existing help files using a nested documentation structure.

- Extending the help plug-in with a context-sensitive help item called an *infopop*.

- Creating a help plug-in that executes Java code from JavaScript embedded in the help pages, also known as *Active help*.

The plug-in piece of a help plug-in is the final glue that holds everything together. The plug-in is not the most important part of a help plug-in. It is the delivery mechanism of the help files, and the help files are the most important part. The `plugin.xml` file tells the help system which table of contents file (or files) to use, and the table of contents files tell the help system how the actual help files are laid out. There is nothing else to adding help files to Eclipse.

One caveat, though: There is no easy way to test help plug-ins. You develop them, deploy them, and see how well they show up in the host workbench Help window. Every example that follows will deploy to the Eclipse `plugins` directory.

One Table of Contents File

In this first exercise, you will display four HTML files with minimal content, but the files will be unique. After that, you will create separate table of contents files for two of the pages, which will then turn these pages into their own sub-books.

It is possible to use the various wizards and editors available in Eclipse to build this plug-in, but instead you will edit the `plugin.xml` file directly. Implementing a help plug-in is all about making sure the `plugin.xml` file contains the proper extension point (`org.eclipse.help.toc`) and the location of your table of contents files.

First, you'll start with the base plug-in project and create the documentation directory structure so that your HTML pages have a place to live. After that, you will create a few files so you have something to display when the plug-in is deployed.

Before you start this exercise, let's make two assumptions:

- You are organizing the help documentation for your group.
- Two other people are writing documentation for inclusion in this plug-in.

In this first exercise, you will create a new plug-in project and include your overview HTML files. Therefore, create a blank plug-in project by pressing Ctrl+N. When the New Wizard appears, select Plug-in Project from the default list of resources you can create and click Next. Eclipse convention dictates that a help plug-in must use `.doc` as part of the plug-in name, so in the Project Name field enter `com.eintech.help.doc` and click Next. In the Plug-in Project Structure page, in the Project Settings section, select Create a Simple Project and click Next. On the Templates page click Finish.

Before you add your HTML files to the project, let's add the file association for HTML pages to make Eclipse open your file within the IDE instead of sending the file to the browser for "editing." From the main menu select Window, Preferences, and from within the Preferences dialog select Workbench, File Associations. Click the top Add button. When the New File Type dialog opens, enter the string `*.html`. Click OK, and the new file type is added to the existing list of known file types. Now you need to add a default editor to go with this new file type. Click Add for the lower window. When the Editor Selection dialog opens, select JSP Editor and click OK. Now any files ending with .html will be opened using the JSP editor (which is just a text editor).

Now you'll add four HTML files to your new plug-in project. Right-click your project name and select New, Folder. When the New Folder dialog appears, enter into the Folder Field the name **help**. This will represent the highest directory in your help file system. Right-click the help directory and select New, File. Enter **titlepage.html** in the File Name field, click Finish, and then enter the following HTML into the file when it opens in the editor:

```html
<html>
  <head>
    <title>Eclipse Kick Start Title Page</title>
  </head>
  <body>
    <h2>Eclipse Kick Start Title Page</h2>
    Pretend this is a really cool title page.
  </body>
</html>
```

This HTML file will be displayed when a user selects your help document. In effect, it is your title page. Create another HTML file under the help directory called overview.html. Enter the following HTML into overview.html:

```html
<html>
  <head>
    <title>Example Help Overview Page</title>
  </head>
  <body>
    <h2>Overview</h2>
    This is the introduction page to the Eclipse Kick Start example help pages.
  </body>
</html>
```

Create another HTML file under the help directory called guide.html. This new file should contain the following:

```html
<html>
  <head>
    <title>Example Help Guide Intro Page</title>
  </head>
  <body>
    <h2>Guide</h2>
    This is the guide page to the Eclipse Kick Start example help pages.
  </body>
</html>
```

You have one more HTML file to create: `reference.html`. Give it the following content:

```
<html>
  <head>
    <title>Eclipse Kick Start Reference Page</title>
  </head>
  <body>
    <h2>Eclipse Kick Start Reference Page</h2>
    This is the reference page to the Eclipse Kick Start example help pages.
  </body>
</html>
```

Now that you have some help files to view, you must create an XML file that represents the table of contents for these files. Right-click the help project name and select New, File from the pop-up menu. Create a file named `toc.xml`. This file is your table of contents file and can be named anything you want. Only four XML tags are valid for a table of contents file: `toc`, `topic`, `anchor`, and `link`. For this example, `toc`, the root tag, will have three `topic` tags, one for each help area in this documentation.

Place the following information in `toc.xml`:

```
<?xml version="1.0" encoding="UTF-8"?>
<toc label="Eclipse Kick Start Table of Contents" topic="help/titlepage.html">
    <topic label="Overview" href="help/overview.html"/>
    <topic label="Guide" href="help/guide.html"/>
    <topic label="Reference" href="help/reference.html"/>
</toc>
```

The `toc` tag uses the `label` and `topic` attributes. The `label` value is the string to be used as the title of the book when the Help window first opens. The `label` tag is a required attribute, and `toc.xml` will cause errors to be generated if `label` is missing. The `topic` tag, on the other hand, is optional. If it is missing, no content will appear in the content window when the user selects your book title. For an example of a help book that does not have a topic page, go to the main menu and select Help, Help Contents. Then go to the Workbench User Guide and select the book title. No content appears in the content window. On the other hand, the Online Help Sample has an HTML file defined as its topic page. Based on the `toc` tag, your help book will have the title "Eclipse Kick Start Table of Contents" and a content page named `titlepage.html`.

In `toc.xml`, the `toc` tag has three nested topics. The `topic` tag has a required `label` attribute and an optional `href` attribute. The labels in this case are Overview, Guide, and Reference, and they are the names of the pages that will be displayed when a user selects the Eclipse Kick Start Table of Contents help link. The HTML files listed in the `href` attribute represent the help information that will be displayed in the content window.

To summarize the table of contents file, the `toc` tag has a label that will be displayed next to the book icon in the Help window. It also has a file that will display content in the content view of the Help window when the title is selected. When the title is selected, the nested topics will be listed next to page icons using the individual labels associated with each topic. The content to be displayed when the user selects a topic is the HTML file listed in the `href` attribute.

Now you need to tie the `toc.xml` file to the `plugin.xml` file to be used by the Eclipse help subsystem.

A `plugin.xml` file was created as part of the `com.eintech.help.doc` plug-in project. The `plugin.xml` file will not automatically open, so open it in the Plug-in Manifest Editor. Select the Overview tab and change the plug-in name to **Eclipse Kick Start Help Example**. Select the plugins.xml tab and then enter the rest of the XML information needed by `plugin.xml` by hand:

```xml
<?xml version="1.0" encoding="UTF-8"?>
<?eclipse version="3.0"?>
<plugin
   id="com.eintech.help.doc"
   name="Eclipse Kick Start Help Example"
   version="1.0.0"
   provider-name="EINTECH">

   <extension point="org.eclipse.help.toc">
      <toc file="toc.xml" primary="true"/>
   </extension>
</plugin>
```

The extension point for this plug-in is `org.eclipse.help.toc`. The nested `toc` tag defines your contribution to this extension. Your contribution is the table of contents file, `toc.xml`, and you also flag this file as the primary table of contents file. You will see later how `plugin.xml` expects to have a list of every table of contents file included in this plug-in, but only one of them is lucky enough to be the file that defines the book used by the user. By you setting `primary` to `true`, the extension point knows which file to use in the Navigation view. Save `plugin.xml`.

You are now ready to deploy your first help plug-in. You need to do three things:

1. Create a directory under `%ECLIPSE_HOME%/plugins` named `com.eintech.help.doc`.

2. Export the `help` directory as a Zip file. Right-click the `help` directory and select Export. When the Export dialog appears, select Zip file and click Next. Make sure the Options area has Compress the Contents of the File checked and Create Only Selected Directories selected. Click the Browse button and select the `%ECLIPSE_HOME%/plugins/com.eintech.help.doc` directory. Append to the path `doc.zip` so that the path looks something like `%ECLIPSE_HOME%/plugins/com.eintech.help.doc/doc.zip`. Click Finish.

3. Export the `plugin.xml` and `toc.xml` files to the help plug-in directory. Click once on `plugin.xml` and, holding down the Ctrl key, select `toc.xml` as well. With the two files selected, right-click one of them and select Export from the pop-up menu. When the Export dialog appears, select File System and click Next. Click the Browse button and select your help plug-in directory. Click Finish to close the Export dialog.

Now you need to restart Eclipse. When it has restarted, open the Help window by selecting Help, Help Contents. The results are displayed in Figure 15.1. Notice that four pages can be displayed: the three individual pages and the main title page.

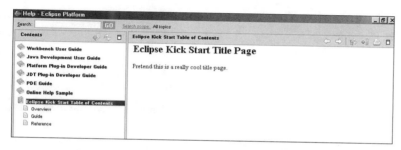

FIGURE 15.1 The Help window with the Eclipse Kick Start Table of Contents book selected and its three pages displayed (four HTML pages all together).

What if you wanted the Guide and Reference pages to be subsections of the help documentation rather than standalone pages? Let's add two more HTML files to the project and turn Guide and Reference into subsections. Create another HTML file under the `help` directory named `guide1.html` and enter the following content into it:

```
<html>
  <head>
    <title>Example Help Guide Page 1</title>
  </head>
  <body>
    <h2>Guide</h2>
    This is the first guide page to the Eclipse Kick Start example help pages.
  </body>
</html>
```

Create another HTML file named `reference1.html` and enter the following into it:

```
<html>
  <head>
    <title>Eclipse Kick Start Reference Page</title>
  </head>
  <body>
    <h2>Reference 1 Page</h2>
```

```
      This is the first reference page to the Eclipse Kick Start example help pages.
   </body>
</html>
```

Open `toc.xml` and change `topic` for Guide and Reference to look like this:

```
<?xml version="1.0" encoding="UTF-8"?>
<toc label="Eclipse Kick Start Table of Contents" topic="help/titlepage.html">
    <topic label="Overview" href="help/overview.html"/>
    <topic label="Guide sub-section" href="help/guide.html">
        <topic label="Guide" href="help/guide1.html"/>
    </topic>
    <topic label="Reference sub-section" href="help/reference.html">
        <topic label="Reference" href="help/reference1.html"/>
    </topic>
</toc>
```

Export the `help` directory again as `doc.zip` and export `toc.xml`. The `plugin.xml` file did not change at all, so you do not have to redeploy it. Stop and restart Eclipse. Open the Help window and select Eclipse Kick Start Table of Contents, which will look like Figure 15.2. If your help documentation does not demand a complex organization, consider declaring all of the HTML in one table of contents file.

FIGURE 15.2 The Help window with the Eclipse Kick Start Table of Contents book selected and its two subsections.

Multiple Table of Contents File

Let's look at how the `plugin.xml` file would be modified to support multiple table of contents files. You created two subsections in the last example. In this example, you will separate them out in their own table of contents files and integrate them into both `toc.xml` and `plugin.xml`.

Right-click the project and create two new XML files named `guide.xml` and `reference.xml`. Enter the following XML into `guide.xml`:

```xml
<?xml version="1.0" encoding="UTF-8"?>
<toc label="Guide sub-section" topic="help/guide.html">
    <topic label="Guide" href="help/guide1.html"/>
</toc>
```

Enter the following XML into reference.xml:

```xml
<?xml version="1.0" encoding="UTF-8"?>
<toc label="Reference sub-section" topic="help/reference.html">
    <topic label="Reference" href="help/reference1.html"/>
</toc>
```

Change toc.xml to the following:

```xml
<?xml version="1.0" encoding="UTF-8"?>
<toc label="Eclipse Kick Start Table of Contents" topic="help/titlepage.html">
    <topic label="Overview" href="help/overview.html"/>
    <topic label="Guide sub-section" >
        <link toc="guide.xml"/>
    </topic>
    <topic label="Reference sub-section">
        <link toc="reference.xml"/>
    </topic>
</toc>
```

Instead of nested topic tags, you nest a link tag. The link tag points to another table of contents file rather than an HTML file. However, listing the XML file in toc.xml is not enough. The plugin.xml file must have declared all the table of contents files being used by this plug-in. Your plugin.xml file should now look like this:

```xml
<?xml version="1.0" encoding="UTF-8"?>
<?eclipse version="3.0"?>
<plugin
    id="com.eintech.help.doc"
    name=" Eclipse Kick Start Help Example"
    version="1.0.0"
    provider-name="EINTECH">

    <extension point="org.eclipse.help.toc">
        <toc file="toc.xml" primary="true"/>
        <toc file="guide.xml"/>
        <toc file="reference.xml"/>
    </extension>

</plugin>
```

The significant change is the addition of two `toc` tags that declare `guide.xml` and `reference.xml` as two potential table of contents files. Only one of the `toc` tagged files is allowed to be the primary, so you'll leave `primary=true` for `toc.xml` alone. Listing these two file in `plugin.xml` only states your intentions to use them. Unless a table of contents file (in this case, `toc.xml`) uses them, these two new files will not appear in the help system at all.

You did not change the HTML files, so do not redeploy them. Select all four XML files you just created/edited and export them to the `plugins` directory. Stop and restart Eclipse and then open the Help window again. The content displayed should look exactly the same as before. What you have gained by breaking up the subsections into distinct table of contents files is the ability to have other people work on separate topics independent of each other. As long as the individual table of contents files are declared in `plugin.xml` and referenced within a higher-level table of contents file, their inclusion becomes transparent.

Nested Documentation Structures

Another kind of help extension is the nested documentation structure, which consists of synchronized `anchor/link_to` tags. One table of contents (TOC) file can list anchors, and another TOC file can list links that match up with the anchor points. This capability gives you the ability to add to existing documentation as well as to your own documentation just by deploying a new TOC file in a plug-in.

On the other hand, if you are only concerned with your own documentation and you want to make the structure extendable, you should consider what nested documentation structures can do for you. Once a version of a particular help structure is complete, it is just as complex to modify as it is to change the object model of an almost-complete system (if you've never had to update Web sites with a few hundred static pages, you don't know what you're missing).

The `<anchor>` tag designates the entry point into a particular slot in the TOC file. The `<toc link_to>` attribute designates the beginning of new help content to be inserted at the `<anchor>` point. You'll now add anchors to your existing `toc.xml` file and create a new TOC file that contributes to the anchor point.

Open `toc.xml` from your `com.eintech.help.doc` project. Add the following tag after the Overview topic:

```
<anchor id="afterOverview"/>
```

After the Guide link, add the following:

```
<anchor id="afterGuide"/>
```

After the Reference link, add this:

```
<anchor id="afterReference"/>
```

Your `toc.xml` file should look like Listing 15.1.

LISTING 15.1   `toc.xml`

```xml
<?xml version="1.0" encoding="UTF-8"?>
<toc label="Eclipse Kick Start Table of Contents" topic="help/titlepage.html">
    <topic label="Overview" href="help/overview.html"/>
    <anchor id="afterOverview"/>

    <topic label="Guide sub-section" >
        <link toc="guide.xml"/>
        <anchor id="afterGuide"/>
    </topic>

    <topic label="Reference sub-section">
        <link toc="reference.xml"/>
        <anchor id="afterReference"/>
    </topic>
</toc>
```

With that, you have added three anchor points into your help table of contents. Create three new HTML files in the `help` directory of your project (select the `help` directory in the Package Explorer view, press Ctrl+N, and select Simple, File from the New dialog) and call them `anchor1.html`, `anchor2.html`, and `anchor3.html`.

In `anchor1.html`, put the following content:

```html
<html>
  <head>
    <title>Anchor Page 1</title>
  </head>
  <body>
    <h2>Anchor Page 1</h2>
    This is Anchor page 1 of the Eclipse Kick Start example help pages.
  </body>
</html>
```

In `anchor2.html`, put the following content:

```html
<html>
  <head>
    <title>Anchor Page 2</title>
  </head>
  <body>
    <h2>Anchor Page 2</h2>
    This is Anchor page 2 of the Eclipse Kick Start example help pages.
  </body>
</html>
```

In anchor3.html, put the following content:

```
<html>
  <head>
    <title>Anchor Page 3</title>
  </head>
  <body>
    <h2>Anchor Page 3</h2>
    This is Anchor page 3 of the Eclipse Kick Start example help pages.
  </body>
</html>
```

These three additional files will be listed in a new TOC file. Select the com.eintech.help.doc project in the Package Explorer and press Ctrl+N. Create another TOC file by selecting Simple, File, clicking Next, and entering the filename **addoverview.xml**. Place the following tags in addoverview.xml:

```
<?xml version="1.0" encoding="UTF-8"?>
<toc label="Additional Overview" link_to="toc.xml#afterOverview" >
    <topic label="Additional Overview 1" href="help/anchor1.html"/>
</toc>
```

Notice the use of the link_to attribute in toc. The link_to attribute connects the additional content to the anchor points in toc.xml.

Add two more XML files to the same location. Call them addguide.xml and addreference.xml.

The file addguide.xml should contain the following content:

```
<?xml version="1.0" encoding="UTF-8"?>
<toc label="Additional Guide" link_to="toc.xml#afterGuide" >
    <topic label="Additional Guide 1" href="help/anchor2.html"/>
</toc>
```

The file addreference.xml should contain the following content:

```
<?xml version="1.0" encoding="UTF-8"?>
<toc label="Additional Reference" link_to="toc.xml#afterReference" >
    <topic label="Additional Reference 1" href="help/anchor3.html"/>
</toc>
```

The last modification you will have to make is to the plugin.xml file, which needs to know that it should pay attention to the contents of addoverview.xml, addguide.xml, and addreference.xml. Add three <toc> entries, one for each of the new TOC files, as follows:

```xml
<?xml version="1.0" encoding="UTF-8"?>
<?eclipse version="3.0"?>
<plugin
    id="com.eintech.help.doc"
    name=" Eclipse Kick Start Help Example"
    version="1.0.0"
    provider-name="EINTECH">

    <extension point="org.eclipse.help.toc">
        <toc file="toc.xml" primary="true"/>
        <toc file="guide.xml"/>
        <toc file="reference.xml"/>
        <toc file="addoverview.xml"/>
        <toc file="addguide.xml"/>
        <toc file="addreference.xml"/>
    </extension>

</plugin>
```

Again, Export the help files as a Zip file and the XML files as regular files to your `help` directory. Restart Eclipse and open up the Help window (Help, Help Contents). After selecting Eclipse Kick Start Table of Contents and opening up each of the sections, you should see three new subsections in your Help window (see Figure 15.3).

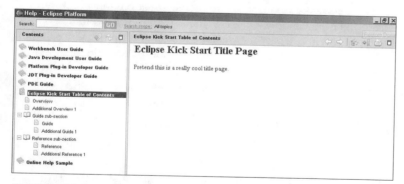

FIGURE 15.3   The Help window with the nested documentation additions.

Just for fun, let's update the `link_to` of `addoverview.xml` to point to the Workbench User Guide. This change will cause the Workbench User Guide to display the additional overview section after the Workbench User Guide, Concepts, Workbench section. Change `c:/tools/eclipse` to whatever the home directory is for your Eclipse installation. Then modify the `addoverview.xml` file to read as follows:

```xml
<?xml version="1.0" encoding="UTF-8"?>
<toc label="Additional Overview"
link_to="../org.eclipse.platform.doc.user/topics_Concepts.xml#c_afterworkbench" >
    <topic label="Additional Overview 1" href="help/anchor1.html"/>
</toc>
```

Export the file and restart Eclipse. Open the Help window and open Workbench User Guide, Concepts. Figure 15.4 displays the "Additional Overview 1" page embedded in the official Eclipse user documents.

SHOP TALK

Testing/Deploying Help Plug-ins

The two areas of concern in the creation of a help plug-in are the table of contents XML files and the content itself. In order to check the proper deployment of the plug-in, you must deploy the complete plug-in in a location where Eclipse can load it and make it available to the Help system.

The good news: Whenever you update the HTML files, all you need to do is re-zip the file and copy it into your deployment plug-in directory. You do not need to restart Eclipse, no matter when you update the page, because the Help window reads the file every time you click a navigation link. So, change the documentation, zip the files, copy the zip file into your deployment plug-in directory, and immediately check the change in the Help window. In fact, if you prefer to develop the content directly in the plug-ins directory and not deploy the documentation as a zip file, you can change the files in the target directory and skip the zip file step until you are ready to deliver. Just remember to set up a directory where your files will reside.

The bad news: Developing the table of contents files can be fraught with initial problems that may cause some frustration. Here are some examples:

- You cannot have an empty top-level book. All TOCs must have at least one topic.

- The TOC file is XML. Forget a closing tag (or worse, greater-than or less-than sign), and you could be looking for the cause of an error for a considerable length of time.

- The M9 release of Eclipse did have a caching issue that would force you to delete the current configuration of your Eclipse installation in order to see a change made to either the plugin.xml or the TOC file (or both) of a help plug-in. Any change made to those files would not be recognized until the contents of the eclipse/configuration directory was deleted.

This list is not a major concern; it's just something you need to bear in mind. Once the initial structure of your documentation is defined and the first set of pages appears, it will be smooth sailing. Your mileage may vary.

The most important thing to notice about this link is that the directory listed is not `org.eclipse.platform.doc.user_3.0.0` (or whatever version it happens to be when you use this book) but rather the plug-in name *without* the version number. If you include the version number, the help system will be unable to find the directory. Also, absolute paths will not work. Therefore, if you write help documentation that you need to link up with existing documents, you should put the new help plug-in directory in the same general vicinity as the docs you want to extend. In this case, `com.eintech.help.doc` is located in the `plugins` directory along with `org.eclipse.platform.doc.user_3.0.0`.

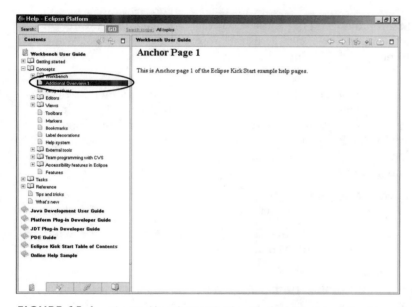

FIGURE 15.4   The Workbench User Guide with the help page defined in your help plug-in.

Context-Sensitive Help Using Infopops

An *infopop* is an undecorated help window that appear in one of three circumstances:

- A user presses F1 when a particular field has focus.
- A user presses F1 when a particular view has focus.
- A user presses F1 when a particular action is executed.

Let's look at all three circumstances.

Context-Sensitive Help When a Field Has Focus

In order to learn how to implement context-sensitive help on a field, you are going to create a pop-up menu item that displays a dialog with an input field. When you press F1 while the cursor is at the input field, an infopop window will appear with a few links that, when selected, cause the Help window to display and list the links displayed in the infopop. Because this is a chapter on help plug-ins, you will not get extensive background on the pop-up menu plug-in. Follow these steps and when you get to the section where the Eclipse help API impacts the code, I will point out what the code is doing and how to complete the implementation:

1. Create an empty plug-in project and name it `com.eintech.infopop`. That means when you get to the Plug-in Content page, click Finish. Eclipse may or may not ask you to switch to the Plug-in perspective. In any case, when the project is created, switch to the Plug-in perspective.

2. Right-click in the Package Explorer and select Import from the pop-up menu. Select External Plug-ins and Fragments as the import source. Click Next and click Next again on the Import External Plug-Ins page. In the Plug-ins and Fragments Found page, check `org.eclipse.ui` and `org.eclipse.help`. Click the Required Plug-Ins button, and 14 of the listed plug-ins should be selected. The complete count of plug-ins will vary based on how many plug-ins you may have already installed. Click Finish.

3. Double-click `plugin.xml` for this new project. Select the Dependencies tab and click Add. From the Plug-in Selection dialog, select `org.eclipse.help` and click Finish.

4. Select the Extensions tab. Click Add. In the New Extensions dialog, select the Extension Points tab, scroll down and select `org.eclipse.ui.popupMenus`. Click Finish.

5. Select `org.eclipse.ui.popupMenus` and in the Extension Details section set the Name property to **Confusing Input Dialog**. (If the dialog isn't confusing, why add help?) The Id field can stay blank.

6. Right-click `org.eclipse.ui.popupMenus` from within the All Extensions window and from the pop-up menu select New, objectContribution. Select `com.eintech.help.infopop.objectContribution1` in the All Extensions list and change the id property to `com.eintech.infopop.menuitem` and change objectClass to `org.eclipse.core.resources.IFile`. After clicking Finish, you may find that the Problems view displays an error due to the use of `IFile`. Return to the Dependencies tab and right-click in the Required Plug-Ins window. From the pop-up menu, select Compute Build Path. Any errors should disappear from the Problems view.

7. Right-click `com.eintech.infopop.menuitem` (objectContribution) and select New, Action from the pop-up menu. In the Extension Element Details section, set these fields as follows:

   - Set class to `com.eintech.infopop.MenuItemActionDelegate`.

   - Set enablesFor to 1.

- Set `label` to ConfusingDialogAction.

- Set `menubarPath` to additions.

8. Create the com.eintech.infopop.MenuItemActionDelegate class by clicking the class label. Click Finish to create the class file. Enter the following code into the class and save the file:

```java
package com.eintech.infopop;
import org.eclipse.jface.action.IAction;
import org.eclipse.jface.dialogs.InputDialog;
import org.eclipse.jface.viewers.ISelection;
import org.eclipse.swt.widgets.Composite;
import org.eclipse.swt.widgets.Control;
import org.eclipse.swt.widgets.Text;
import org.eclipse.ui.IObjectActionDelegate;
import org.eclipse.ui.IWorkbenchPart;
import org.eclipse.ui.PlatformUI;
import org.eclipse.ui.help.WorkbenchHelp;

public class MenuItemActionDelegate
    extends InputDialog
    implements IObjectActionDelegate {

    public MenuItemActionDelegate() {
        super(
            PlatformUI.getWorkbench().getActiveWorkbenchWindow().getShell(),
            "What is the answer to life, the universe and everything?",
            "Enter your answer here:",
            "0",
            null);

    }

    public void setActivePart(IAction action, IWorkbenchPart targetPart) {
    }

    public void run(IAction action) {
        this.open();
    }

    public void selectionChanged(IAction action, ISelection selection) {
    }
```

```
protected Control createDialogArea(Composite parent) {
    Composite dialogArea = (Composite)super.createDialogArea(parent);
    Text inputField = getText();
    WorkbenchHelp.setHelp(inputField, "com.eintech.infopop.infopops");
    return dialogArea;
}

}
```

Examine the code in `createDialogArea()`. One line of code is pertinent to this exercise:

```
WorkbenchHelp.setHelp(inputField, "com.eintech.infopop.infopops");
```

The first argument to the static `setHelp()` method is the component that will be associated with the infopop window. The second argument is the ID of the help information that will be used. Let's create the context-sensitive help information needed by our plug-in so that at runtime the Eclipse help system can associate the text component with the help content.

9. Now it's time to contribute to the help extension point. Return to the Plug-in Manifest Editor Extensions tab and click Add. On the Extension Points tab, select `org.eclipse.help.contexts`. Click Finish.

10. Right-click `org.eclipse.help.contexts` and select New, Contexts from the pop-up menu. Before you can continue, you must create a file that contains context-sensitive help information. Press Ctrl+N and from the New dialog select Simple, File. Click Next and enter the filename `contexts_Confusing.xml`. Context-sensitive help is described in this file using (what else?) XML. Because there can be more than one help context, the root tag is `<contexts>` with nested `<context>` tags. For this example, your context ID is going to be "infopops," and it should have a description of "Don't Panic!" along with references to HTML files that will be used when the infopop appears.

11. In the `com.eintech.infopop` project, create a directory called `help`. Create three files in it and name them `overview.html`, `guide.html`, and `references.html`. If you want to put HTML content in the files, you can, but for now you can leave them empty. If the infopop displays the labels assigned to it, the files will be accessed by default.

12. Place the following elements in `contexts_Confusing.xml`:

```
<contexts>
    <context id="infopops">
        <description>Don't Panic!</description>
        <topic href="help/overview.html" label="Who is Deep Thought?"/>
        <topic href="help/guide.html" label="Deep Thought Handbook"/>
        <topic href="help/references.html" label="Deep Thought API"/>
    </context>
</contexts>
```

13. Save the `contexts_Confusing.xml` file. The `<topic>` tags contain the reference to the HTML content using the `href` attribute, and the `label` attribute contains the text that will appear as the link in the infopop window.

14. Return to the `plugin.xml` Manifest Editor and select `com.eintech.infopop.contexts1`. In the Properties view, select the file value and click Browse. When the Resource Attribute Value dialog appears, select `contexts_Confusing.xml` and click OK. Save the `plugin.xml` file.

You are now ready to deploy the plug-in and run it. *Note that you must deploy the plug-in as a regular plug-in because the runtime workbench does not handle help plug-ins unless they are properly deployed.* There are three things you need to do:

1. Export the Java code for the pop-up menu action. Select the package (*not* the project) `com.eintech.infopop`. Right-click and select Export. The Export destination will be JAR file. Click Next and enter the path to the Eclipse `plugins` directory with the name of your plug-in as the directory and `infopop.jar` as the name of the JAR file. Use the following as an example of what you should enter (the directory where Eclipse is installed may be different):

   ```
   C:\tools\eclipse\plugins\com.eintech.infopop\infopop.jar
   ```

   When you click Finish, the wizard will ask if it can create the missing directory. Click Yes.

2. Right-click the `help` directory and select Export. The Export destination is Zip file. Click Next and enter the path to the Eclipse `plugins` directory with the name of your plug-in as the directory. Use the following as an example of what you should enter (again, the directory where Eclipse is installed may be different):

   ```
   C:\tools\eclipse\plugins\com.eintech.infopop\doc.zip
   ```

3. Select `contexts_Confusing.xml` and `plugin.xml` together from the Package Explorer and right-click the selection. When the pop-up menu appears, select Export. This time, make the Export destination the file system and click Next. Use the following as an example of what you should enter (again, the directory where Eclipse is installed may be different):

   ```
   C:\tools\eclipse\plugins\com.eintech.infopop
   ```

   Click Finish.

Restart Eclipse. Right-click any file as long as it is not a Java file. The pop-up menu will display ConfusingDialogAction as a menu item (see Figure 15.5). Select ConfusingDialogAction and an InputDialog should appear (if not, check whether the JAR file, the Zip file, and the two XML files have properly deployed). When the dialog appears, make sure that the cursor is in the input field and that the mouse arrow is visible and then press F1. An infopop window should appear (see Figure 15.6). Clicking any of the three links will force the Help window to appear with the three help links displayed in the left Navigator view.

FIGURE 15.5 The pop-up menu displaying the menu item ConfusingDialogAction.

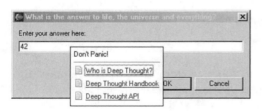

FIGURE 15.6 The Confusing dialog with the infopop window that should clarify everything.

Be aware: Calling an infopop of your own making may cause the help page to appear in a separate browser window and not in the standard Help dialog. This is acceptable because the help page will still appear.

Context-Sensitive Help When a View Has Focus
The code to add context-sensitive help to a view is exactly the same as what you just accomplished with the Confusing dialog. Rather than create a brand new view, let's reuse view project com.eintech.helloworld.view from Chapter 14, "Writing a Trivial (and Not So Trivial) Plug-In," and just copy over the pieces we need (the help files and the contexts_Confusing.xml file). If you have not done the view portion of Chapter 14, I recommend that you do that now and return here to add the remaining pieces to add context-sensitive help to a view.

Make a copy of the `com.eintech.helloworld.view` project and call it `com.eintech.helloworld.view.infopop`. Make sure the project directory name is also changed to `com.eintech.helloworld.view.infopop`. If an X appears next to the project after you make the copy, open the `plugins.xml` file for `com.eintech.helloworld.view.infopop`, go to the Dependencies tab, and right-click in the Required Plug-Ins window. From the pop-up menu, select Compute Build Path to clean up any build problems.

Right-click the `help` directory from `com.eintech.infopop` and select Copy from the pop-up menu. Right-click `com.eintech.helloworld.view.infopop` and select Paste from the pop-up menu. The `help` directory should now be in your `com.eintech.helloworld.view.infopop` project. Do the same with the `contexts_Confusing.xml` file.

You have two things left to do: You need to contribute to the help extension point and update the code to assign the infopop to the component. Because you have already gone through the steps of adding the information through the Plug-In Manifest Editor, this time you will edit the XML source directly. Editing the XML will give you a peak under the hood.

Let's update the plug-in information for this new project. Double-click `com.eintech.helloworld.view.infopop`'s `plugin.xml` file. When the Plug-in Manifest Editor appears, select the plugins.xml tab. Press Ctrl+F and enter `com.eintech.helloworld.view` in the Find field and `com.eintech.helloworld.view.infopop` in the Replace With field. Click Replace All to make all the various IDs consistent with the new package name. Save the file by pressing Ctrl+S. With that done, you need to add any additional extension points required by the plug-in. Recall from the previous exercise that the help extension point was `org.eclipse.help`. Add the following line into the `<requires>` tag:

```
<import plugin="org.eclipse.help"/>
```

Once you've done that, the `<requires>` tag should look more like the following code:

```
<requires>
    <import plugin="org.eclipse.ui"/>
    <import plugin="org.eclipse.help"/>
</requires>
```

To complete the updates to `plugin.xml`, add the following code at the bottom of the file but before the closing `<plugin>` tag:

```
<extension
      point="org.eclipse.help.contexts">
    <contexts
         file="contexts_Confusing.xml">
    </contexts>
</extension>
```

This constitutes all that you need to do to configure the plug-in to support the context-sensitive help.

With the configuring out of the way, let's update the view code to support the infopop. You are going to update the code so that it does the following:

- Supports an input field that will control the view's focus. You will force focus to that field.

- Adds the exact same call to setHelp() as before.

In the com.eintech.helloworld.view.infopop project, right-click the com.eintech.helloworld.view package and select Refactor, Rename. Change the name to com.eintech.helloworld.view.infopop and click OK. Double-click HelloWorldView.java to open the file in the Java editor and change the code in createPartControl() to the following code. All this code is doing is creating an input text field and making the call to setHelp():

```
private Text _field;

public void createPartControl(Composite parent) {
    parent.setLayout(new RowLayout());
    Label label = new Label(parent, SWT.LEFT);
    label.setText("Answer");
    _field = new Text(parent, SWT.BORDER | SWT.SINGLE);

    WorkbenchHelp.setHelp(_field, "com.eintech.helloworld.view.infopop.infopops");
}
```

Notice that the context ID is the new name you gave to the project and to the various IDs in plugin.xml. If this ID is incorrect, the infopop will not appear when F1 is pressed.

In order to give the input field focus when the view is opened, you need to update setFocus() as follows:

```
public void setFocus() {
    _field.setFocus();
}
```

You will have all kinds of red X's appearing due to missing/incorrect imports. Press Ctrl+Shift+O to have the editor insert and remove the appropriate imports for you. Save the file.

Because this is a help plug-in, Eclipse demands that you deploy it in order to see the final effect. Deploy this plug-in using the following steps:

1. Deploy the Java code in a JAR file. Right-click the
   `com.eintech.helloworld.view.infopop` package and select Export. When the Export
   dialog appears, select JAR file, click Next, and then enter the following into the JAR file
   field:

   `C:\tools\eclipse\plugins\com.eintech.helloworld.view.infopop\view.jar`

   Your path to Eclipse may vary. If the path is different, use your path. Make sure you call
   the JAR file `view.jar` because the `plugin.xml` file states that `view.jar` is the file the
   plug-in is supplying to the system. Click Finish. The wizard may ask if you want to
   create `com.eintech.helloworld.view.infopop` because it does not yet exist. Click Yes.

2. Deploy the help files as a Zip file. Right-click the `help` directory and select Export. This
   time, when the Export dialog appears, select the Zip file, click Next, and enter the
   following into the To Zip File field:

   `c:\tools\eclipse\plugins\com.eintech.helloworld.view.infopop\doc.zip`

   Make sure this path is valid for your Eclipse installation. Click Finish.

3. Deploy the `plugin.xml` and context-sensitive help files to the destination plug-in directory. Select both files by selecting one of them, pressing Ctrl or Shift, and pressing the
   down-arrow button (or hold Ctrl and click each file with the mouse). Right-click the
   selection and select Export. When the Export dialog appears, select File System, click
   Next, and enter the following into the To Directory field:

   `c:\tools\eclipse\plugins\com.eintech.helloworld.view.infopop`

   Once again, after making sure the path is valid on your system, click Finish.

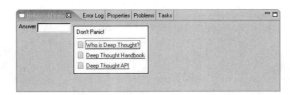

FIGURE 15.7 The Deep Thought context-sensitive help links associated with a view.

In order to see the effect of the plug-in, you
must restart Eclipse. When Eclipse reappears,
select Window, Show View, Other from the
main menu and select HelloWorld View
Category, HelloWorld View from the Show
View dialog. After you click OK, the
HelloWorld view should appear at the bottom
of the workbench. Press F1 and the infopop
should appear (see Figure 15.7).

Context-Sensitive Help When an Action Is Executed

There aren't many ways left to use the Eclipse help system. In fact, there are only two: You
can associate an action with an infopop through the `plugin.xml` file, and you can implement
a `HelpListener` and register it with any UI component or action that has an
`addHelpListener()` or `setHelpListener()`. I am a big fan of programming by configuration,
so let's do that one first.

Close all your open editors and then open `plugin.xml` for the `com.eintech.infopop` project. Select the Extensions tab and go to `org.eclipse.ui.popupMenus`, `com.eintech.infopop.` `menuitem (objectContribution)`, `ConfusingDialogAction (action)`. If you are having a hard time reading the contents of the list, double-click the editor title bar to give the editor more room. In the Extension Element Details section, note the property `helpContextId`. When you wrote `MenuItemActionDelegate`, which is the action that is executed when you right-click a file and select ConfusingDialogAction, you made a call to `WorkbenchHelp.` `setHelp()` with a context ID of `com.eintech.infopop.infopops`. This time, enter the context ID, `com.eintech.infopop.infopops`, in the field named `helpContextId`. That's it! You're finished configuring an infopop context-sensitive help item for action targets. To see it in action, you must export the `plugin.xml` file to `com.eintech.infopop`, restart Eclipse, right-click a file in the Package Explorer view, and move your arrow to the ConfusingDialogAction menu item (but don't select it). Then, while the arrow is on the pop-up menu item, press F1. The infopop will appear wherever the cursor happens to be (see Figure 15.8).

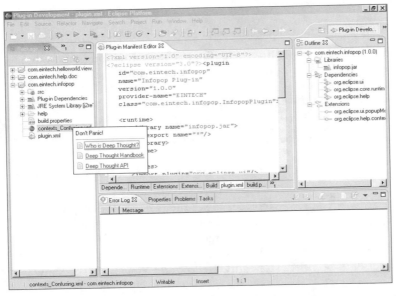

FIGURE 15.8 The Deep Thought context-sensitive infopop window where the pop-up menu used to be.

To achieve the same result through code, your plug-in needs to contribute a `HelpListener` to any object willing to register and talk to it. Your `HelpListener` can execute any logic it wants, but to cause an infopop window to appear, the code will have to make a call to `WorkbenchHelp.displayHelp()`. Object types that know about `HelpListener` objects are GUI components and actions. GUI components that extend `org.eclipse.swt.widgets.Control` inherit `addHelpListener()` by default, and when F1 is pressed the `HelpListener`'s `helpRequest()` method is called. Because the method is called `addHelpListener()`, you are allowed to add as many `HelpListener` objects as you like. On the other hand, `Action` objects, which extend `org.eclipse.jface.action.Action` or implement the `org.eclipse.jface.IAction` interface, have the `setHelpListener()` method in their API. Conventionally, you should extend `Action` rather than implement `IAction` because `Action` contains useful default behavior. However, because the method is called `setHelpListener()`, you only get to assign one listener object per action.

Actions are `Command` objects that allow you to define behavior independent of the look of the GUI component that calls it. You can think of them as the brains behind the good looks. Because of this, you cannot take any of the help examples we have been working with so far and just add the single line of code you need to make your GUI component/action react to an F1 event. Instead, you will add a button to the HelloWorld view example and through the `HelpListener` cause the infopop window to appear.

Using the `com.eintech.helloworld.view.infopop` project, you will update `plugin.xml`, modify the code that creates the view, implement a `HelpListener`, and export the code to the plugins directory.

Open `com.eintech.helloworld.view.infopop.HelloWorldView` by double-clicking the filename. Add the following code for `HWHelpHandler` as a private inner class:

```
private class HWHelpHandler implements HelpListener {
    public void helpRequested(HelpEvent e) {
        WorkbenchHelp.displayHelp("com.eintech.helloworld.view.infopop.infopops");
    }
}
```

If you have done any AWT or Swing programming, this class should look familiar. This class will be called based on a particular event (in this case, a `help` event) being fired off by the component the listener is registered with. This listener will be registered with an SWT GUI component in the code soon to be added to `createPartControl()`.

Remove the call to `WorkbenchHelp.setHelp()` and add the last three lines of code to `createPartControl()`:

```
public void createPartControl(Composite parent) {
    parent.setLayout(new RowLayout());
    Label label = new Label(parent, SWT.LEFT);
    label.setText("Answer");
    _field = new Text(parent, SWT.BORDER | SWT.SINGLE);

    Button button = new Button(parent, SWT.LEFT);
    button.setText("Submit");
    button.addHelpListener(new HWHelpHandler());
}
```

The SWT GUI component `Button` extends `Control` and therefore has `addHelpListener()` as part of its API. When the button, which will have "Submit" as its label, has focus, pressing F1 causes `HWHelpHandler` to be called, which displays the infopop window with the content defined in `contexts_Confusing.xml`. This is quite different from what you did in the first infopop example. In the first example, you associated the `Label` component with a particular context ID, and the underlying help system took care of the rest. In this case, the code is opening the infopop window on its own when the user presses F1.

With the code changes in place, export the `HelloWorldView` code again in a JAR file named `view.jar`. Restart Eclipse.

If the HelloWorld view does not appear automatically, go to the main menu and select Window, Show View, Other and select HelloWorld View Category, HelloWorld View. Click OK. When the view appears, the cursor will be in the Answer text field. Press the Tab key to move the focus over to the Submit button. Press F1 and the infopop context-sensitive help will appear wherever your arrow happens to be (see Figure 15.9).

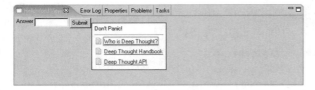

FIGURE 15.9   The Deep Thought context-sensitive infopop window opened by the `HelpListener` code.

Active Help

Active help is yet another facet of the Eclipse help system. Active help allows you to run Java code from within Eclipse using JavaScript. Because the JavaScript is so simple, let's go over that first.

Inside the HTML page there must be at least two tags: the `<script>` tag to activate JavaScript support in your HTML page and another tag to call the JavaScript method `liveAction()`. In `<script>`, the `language` attribute is set to `"JavaScript"` and the `src` attribute points to a JavaScript file named `livehelp.js` that defines a method called `liveAction()`:

```
<script language="JavaScript" src="../../org.eclipse.help/livehelp.js "></script>
```

The `<script>` tag must be located inside `<HEAD>`; otherwise, you will find that your call to `liveAction()` will not work. Also, it must have a closing tag. The JavaScript engine does not recognize the short form of the `<script>` tag.

The next part of the JavaScript/HTML puzzle is the call to `liveAction()`. Those of you familiar with JavaScript will not see anything new or novel. The call to `liveAction()` is embedded in the `href` attribute and is called when the user clicks the link. The signature to `liveAction()` is as follows:

```
function liveAction(pluginId, className, argument)
```

The `pluginId` argument refers to the name of the plug-in as defined in `plugin.xml`, whereas `classname` is the name of the class that should be called when the user clicks the link. The third argument is an arbitrary, optional string that will be passed to your class at runtime. As the string is passed at runtime, you dynamically generate the HTML and pass different information to the active help object. An example of the JavaScript call to your active help Java object would look like this:

```
<a href='javascript:liveAction(
    "com.eintech.help.activehelp.doc",
    "com.eintech.help.activehelp.doc.HelloWorldActiveHelp",
    "Kitty")'>An extremely obtuse piece of help text that needs active help
    in order to be clear.</a>
```

Every link on the HTML page where you want to have one or more active help links would need to be set up as illustrated in the preceding HTML.

The Java API of your object is also quite well defined. The class must implement the `ILiveHelpAction` interface and, because `ILiveHelpAction` inherits from `Runnable`, must implement two methods: `run()` and `setInitializationString()`. The `setInitializationString()` method is called prior to `run()`, so your object gets a chance to initialize itself before starting. There is one caveat to implementing the Java code for the active help: the active help code does not run within the GUI environment thread, so your main code needs to be surrounded by a call to `Display.syncExec()`.

The table of contents file (by convention called `toc.xml`) contains the usual information about the directory hierarchy of the HTML files. For the purposes of this exercise, you will create a very shallow `toc.xml` file with only one HTML file.

The `plugin.xml` file contains the standard help definitions: the table of contents files and the JAR file of any code that is part of this plug-in. A minimum active help `plugin.xml` file would contain the plug-in descriptive data (ID, name, and so on), the name of the runtime JAR file, which contains the Java code to be called by the JavaScript, and a list of one or more table of contents files.

Using the information just covered, let's create an active help project. You will write an active help–enabled HTML file, a Java class to open a dialog when the link is selected, and a `plugin.xml` file to glue the pieces together. Most of the steps assume you understand how to create items such as blank plug-in projects and do not go into fine detail about how to accomplish certain Eclipse tasks.

Create a plug-in project. Call the project `com.eintech.help.activehelp.doc`. Call the plug-in runtime library `activeHelloHelp.jar`, click Next, uncheck Generate the Java Class that Controls the Plug-in's Life Cycle, and then click Finish.

Create a new folder directly under your project folder called `help`. The `help` directory is where your active help HTML file will go. Right-click the `help` directory and select New, File. When the New File dialog appears, enter the name **HelloHelp.html** and click Finish. If the file does not open in the editor window, double-click it to force it to appear in the editor area. Enter the following HTML into `HelloHelp.html`:

```html
<html>
  <head>
    <title>Example Active Help Page</title>
    <script language="JavaScript" src="../../org.eclipse.help/livehelp.js">
    </script>
  </head>
  <body>
    <h2>Active Help</h2>
    This text is too confusing to understand.  Click
    <a href='javascript:liveAction(
      "com.eintech.help.activehelp.doc",
      "com.eintech.help.activehelp.doc.HelloWorldActiveHelp",
      "Kitty"
    )'>
    here</a> for more information.
  </body>
</html>
```

This HTML declares the use of JavaScript in `<HEAD>` and declares the call to `liveAction()` at the link point for the word *here*. You are now done with the HTML part of this example.

Create a table of contents file by right-clicking the project name, selecting New, File, and naming the file `toc.xml`. Open `toc.xml` and enter the following:

```xml
<?xml version="1.0" encoding="UTF-8"?>
<toc label="Eclipse Kick Start Active Help Example" topic="help/HelloHelp.html">
    <topic label="Confusion" topic="help/HelloHelp.html">
</toc>
```

The Help system does not like empty `<toc>` elements, so you are forced to create a `<topic>` element so that the new documentation will appear in the Help window.

Before you create the new class, open `plugins.xml` (if it is not already open) and click the Dependencies tab. In the Required Plug-Ins section, click Add, select `org.eclipse.help` and `org.eclipse.ui`, and add them to the list one at a time. When you are done, right-click in the Required Plug-Ins window and select from the pop-up menu Compute Build Path.

Create a new Java class, call it `HelloWorldActiveHelp`, give it a package name of `com.eintech.help.activehelp.doc`, and add `ILiveHelpAction` as one of the interfaces it is implementing. Click Finish to complete the creation of the class. Both `run()` and `setInitializationString()` should contain the following code:

```
private String _name;

public void setInitializationString(String data) {
    _name = data;
}
public void run() {
    Display.getDefault().syncExec(new HelloWorldInnerClass(_name));
}
```

Finally, add the following inner class to `HelloWorldActiveHelp`:

```
private class HelloWorldInnerClass implements Runnable {

    private String _name;

    public HelloWorldInnerClass(String name) {
        _name = name;
    }

    public void run() {
        IWorkbenchWindow window =
            PlatformUI.getWorkbench().getActiveWorkbenchWindow();
        if (window != null) {
            Shell shell = window.getShell();
            shell.setMinimized(false);
            shell.forceActive();
            // Open a message dialog
            MessageDialog.openInformation(window.getShell(), "Hello, " + _name,
            "Hello, " + _name);
        }
    }
}
```

The call to `syncExec()` in `run()` guarantees thread safety for the code that will execute when the user clicks the link. The only thing the inner class worries about is opening up a `MessageDialog` and displaying a string. The Java part is now complete.

Finally, once again open `plugin.xml`. Next, go to the Extensions tab, click Add, and select `org.eclipse.help.toc`. Click Finish. Right-click `org.eclipse.help.toc` and select New, toc.

With `com.eintech.help.activehelp.doc.toc1` selected, click the Browse button to the right of the file input field and `toc.xml` file. Click the check box labeled "primary" to set its value to `true`. Save `plugin.xml`. The `plugin.xml` piece is now complete.

You can deploy the plug-in with the usual steps:

1. Export the help file to
   `%ECLIPSE_HOME%/plugins/com.eintech.help.activehelp.doc/doc.zip`. Make sure the Create Only Selected Directories radio button is selected. Eclipse will notice that the directory does not exist. Select Yes when you are asked whether the system should create the directory for you.

2. Export the Java code to
   `%ECLIPSE_HOME%/plugins/com.eintech.help.activehelp.doc/activeHelloHelp.jar` (select the `com.eintech.help.activehelp.doc` directory, right-click, and select Export, JAR file).

3. Export `toc.xml` and `plugin.xml` to
   `%ECLIPSE_HOME%/plugins/com.eintech.help.activehelp.doc`.

When you complete these three steps, you should have `doc.zip`, `activeHelloHelp.jar`, and `plugin.xml` under the `plugins` directory `com.eintech.help.activehelp.doc`.

Restart Eclipse and open the Help window. Select the Eclipse Kick Start Active Help Example link, and a page will appear with a standard-looking HTML link (see Figure 15.10). Click the link, and the host workbench will pop to the top and open a dialog displaying the string "Hello, Kitty" (see Figure 15.11).

FIGURE 15.10 The Help window displaying the sample page with an active help link.

FIGURE 15.11 The dialog opened by the JavaScript from the Help window.

In Brief

Implementing a help plug-in is so simple that there are no specialized editors or support to be found within Eclipse. There is a Help template, which we did not discuss at any length, but it does nothing more than give you a sample `plugin.xml` and TOC file. We did cover a lot of ground in this chapter:

- A minimal help plug-in uses one table of contents file and is extendable to one main table of contents file and two nested table of contents files.

- Help plug-ins can also extend existing documentation, as you saw when you added to the existing Java Development Tooling documentation.

- Infopops, or *context-sensitive help*, rely on the registration of a help context ID with a UI component that calls the registered help when F1 is pressed. Context-sensitive help can be set up for an individual component, its container, a view, or an action.

- Active help is a combination of JavaScript and Java that executes some code within Eclipse when a user selects a link in the documentation.

PART IV

Appendices

Navigating Through Eclipse Help

"When all else fails read the instructions."

—Anonymous

Introduction to the Eclipse Help System

The help system in Eclipse contains as much help documentation as a plug-in author has decided to write and no more. In the case of Eclipse-delivered plug-ins, the documentation is quite extensive and really needs very little additional documentation to explain how to accomplish certain tasks (this book excluded, of course).

Three kinds of help are available in Eclipse:

- Normal
- Infopops, also known as context-sensitive help
- Active links

Normal documentation is displayed in a help window that gives you the ability to either select a topic directly, search for one or more terms in the documentation, or use bookmarks you set during a previous session with the help system. *Infopops* are floating windows that display help content and zero or more links to additional help based on where the cursor is when you press F1. *Active links* are executable links embedded in help files to execute some Java code within Eclipse to expand on the help information.

In addition to the previous functionality, you can also print the help files by selecting a topic and either clicking the printer button in the top-right toolbar or right-clicking the topic and selecting Print Target. The changing of fonts and colors will not be discussed in this appendix.

Let's discuss the various parts of help in a little more detail.

The Help Window

The Help window, where the standard documentation is found, is opened by selecting Help, Help Contents from the main menu. The Help window is divided into two areas: the navigation frame, on the left, and the viewer frame, on the right. As is customary in Eclipse, double-clicking the title of either frame causes the frame to fill the window, and double-clicking again restores the frame back to its original size and redisplays the hidden frame. The viewer frame will always display the chosen documentation, whereas the navigation frame can display one of four views.

Bookshelf Contents

The default Navigation frame view is the Bookshelf tab (the first tab to the far left), and it uses a book icon (see Figure A.1). The title of the view is Contents, and all the available documents are displayed unless you previously set up a working set, which would display a subset of the documentation. Working sets are discussed later in this appendix. When you single-click a book title, a tree view of the book's contents appears. If information is available at that link, its contents appear in the content window (see Figure A.2).

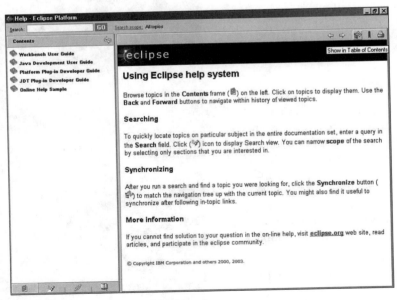

FIGURE A.1   The Navigation frame of the Help window displaying the Bookshelf's Contents view.

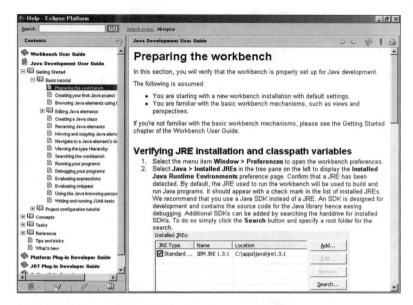

FIGURE A.2 A selected link with its contents on display.

Search

It is not until you have been using the help system for some period of time that you will become familiar with the location of various topics. Until then, you can use the Search Results view, which is the second tab of the Navigation frame and uses the flashlight icon. You do not need to select this tab because the search field is always available at the top of the Help window. When you enter search criteria, the results of the search will appear in the Search Results view, which displays itself when the search begins.

The rules of searching the documentation are as follows:

- The search is not case sensitive. In other words, ECLIPSE, eclipse, and EcLiPsE are all treated the same.

- AND, OR, and NOT are supported as search expression operators. AND is implied if no operator is explicitly defined. This translates into the following:

  - **J2EE email**—Returns pages where both words are used. The AND is implied.

  - **J2EE OR email**—Returns pages where one or the other word is used (possibly both, but not necessarily).

  - **J2EE NOT email**—Returns pages where J2EE appears and the word *email* does not appear.

- Double quotes delimit a list of words you expect to find together. The phrase "Hello world" would look for both words together in the order given.

- Single and multicharacter wildcards are supported (? and *, respectively). A search for "app?" returns two pages that match words such as *MyApp*, whereas a search for "app*" returns a huge number of pages that match words such as *AppletArgumentsTab* and *appropriate*.

- Use punctuation to delimit search words. Searching using "Hello world" or "hello.world" gives the exact same results. If you need the punctuation to be considered in the search (for example, to look for a particular filename with an extension), enclose the search item in double quotes. A search for Object.java without surrounding quotes returns three hits, whereas entering the filename with double quotes does not return any hits.

- Certain words are ignored by the search engine. Words such as *and, at, the, was,* and *with* are just a few of the words pruned out of a search expression. A full list of ignored words can be found in the Eclipse help documentation. Two things can be implied by this search capability:

  - Avoid using the listed words when possible because they will have no impact on the results.

  - Don't worry if you happen to use any of the listed words because the system ignores them anyway.

- The search engine uses a process called *word stemming* to take a term and search using variations of it. When the search engine finds a hit, the word is selected in the document for easy scanning. However, if you were to enter the word *write* in the search field, you would find that the "Active help" document listed as a result does not have the word *write* highlighted at all. That is because the search engine matched on *writing*, not on *write*.

Of course, the more plug-ins you have available, the more documentation you are liable to have to search to find specific help. A solution offered by the Eclipse help system is the ability to create a custom selection of help documents to be searched rather than the entire documentation set.

Let's create a document subset for the search engine to use when you give it a search term. Directly to the right of the Search field's Go button is the Search Scope link. Click the Search Scope link to bring up the first Help dialog. The Search All Topics radio button is selected by default. Select the Search Only the Following Topics radio button and then click New. The Help - Eclipse Platform dialog appears. In the List Name field, enter **Eclipse core search** and select the first five documents, as shown in Figure A.3.

FIGURE A.3   The Help dialog with a subset of selected documents.

Click OK to finish with the Help dialog and click OK again to close the Select Search Scope dialog.

The documentation you have in addition to the core set will determine what your searches look like. For example, because I have the EclipseUML plug-in documentation as part of my normal install, I can show how creating a search scope can limit the amount of information used by the search engine. Creating the preceding search scope, **Eclipse core search**, typing the acronym **UML** in the Search field, and then clicking Enter or Go will cause the Search Results view to state "Nothing found." If I then click the Search Scope link to open the Select Search Scope dialog again, reselect Search All Topics, click OK, and then run the search again. My Eclipse installation now displays 15 hits for the acronym UML.

Links

Directly related to context-sensitive help is the Links view. When you are using Eclipse and press F1, the help system takes a look at what has the current window focus and attempts a best guess at a help topic. When you press F1, an infopop window will appear, giving you a selection of links from which to choose. Clicking one will bring up the help window with a collection of related links in the Link view.

Close the Help window if you have it open. Open Eclipse up to the Java perspective and click once in the Outline view. Press F1 and an infopop appears, stating "View to show the outline (if applicable) of a resource being edited," along with the links Views and Outline View (see Figure A.4). Click either link, and the Help window reappears. The Link view displays two links—Views and Outline View—and the content window displays the help information for the link you selected. The Link view will always display as many links as are appropriate for the item that had the focus at the time you pressed F1.

Bookmarks

Bookmarks in the help system are the same as bookmarks in a browser. On the Eclipse Help window is a bookmark button, the second button from the right, that creates links leading to the bookmarked page.

To create a bookmark, open the Help window and select the Bookshelf tab. Select the Java Development User Guide and then Tips and Tricks. Click the Bookmark button and select the Bookmark tab at the bottom of the Navigator view. The Bookmark view displays a bookmark to the JDT Tips and Tricks page. If you wish to delete a bookmark, simply select the unwanted bookmark and press the Delete key. If you are more of a mouse person, right-click the link to be removed and select Delete from the pop-up menu.

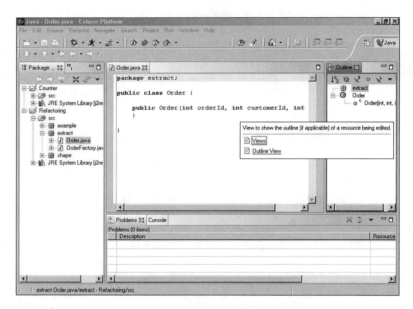

FIGURE A.4   The Java perspective displaying an infopop window for the Outline view.

Working Sets

Working sets are similar to the Search scope subset created earlier. You create a new Help working set by going to the Package Explorer view of the Java perspective, or the Plug-in perspective, of the main workbench. Clicking the last button of the view's toolbar, the button with the downward-pointing triangle, displays a drop-down menu with the menu item Select Working Set. Selecting that menu item causes the Select Working Set dialog to appear. If you created the "Eclipse core search" search scope in the previous example, you will see it listed here. In any case, if you click New, you will be asked to select a working set type. For our purposes, select Help and click Next. The New Working Set page is looking for the exact same information you entered when you created the Search scope entry. Create a name, select one or more working set content items, and click Finish.

Return to the Help window and click the Search Scope link. Your new working set appears in the list with any other sets you may have created.

Of what value are working sets? They afford you the opportunity to limit searches to whatever working set you have created and selected. Remember the Search dialog from the Java perspective? Open it up from the main menu by selecting Search, Search, or by pressing ctrl-H. Click the Help Search tab and then click Choose. Select the "Eclipse core search" subset, click OK, and then enter the string "plug-in" in the Search expression field. The search should return about 324 hits. A Search Scope item and a Help working set give you equivalent functionality.

Accessing the Eclipse Help Server Outside of Eclipse

As mentioned in Chapter 15, "Implementing a Help Plug-in," creating help plug-ins for Eclipse is almost trivial. Create your help pages as HTML, create a table of contents XML file describing the main directories of your HTML files, create a `plugin.xml` file telling Eclipse to use your table of contents XML file, and deploy. If you wanted to make your help pages available, you could run the Eclipse help server as a standalone process.

First of all, running Eclipse on your network with the Help window open makes the help system publicly available. The only problem is that the port the help server is listening on is determined arbitrarily by Eclipse at runtime. Let's change that by opening the Preferences dialog and telling Eclipse what port it should use when it runs the help server. Go to the Help, Help Server selection and add a hostname and port (for example, localhost and 8085). Click OK in the Preferences dialog and restart Eclipse.

Once you restart Eclipse, you will need to start the help server, which you do by running any kind of help functionality. Go to Help, Help Contents, and open the Help window. Leave it open.

Start a Web browser. Enter into the location field the hostname and port number you entered into the Preferences dialog. On my machine, I entered `http://localhost:8085`, and the main Eclipse help page was returned (see Figure A.5).

The preceding scenario, though convenient, is not secure. One way to make the Eclipse help server available in a more secure way is to configure your Web server to redirect requests from a public resource alias to the running help server. However, this is left as an exercise for the reader.

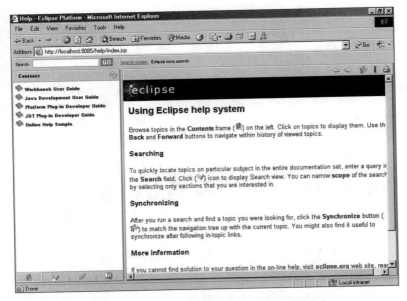

FIGURE A.5 The Eclipse help pages displayed using a Web browser.

Setting Up and Running a Local CVS Server

Getting a CVS Server for Windows

If you are setting up a CVS server for the first time, or just happen to need a CVS server to do your own personal local development, you can use a couple of different CVS servers to accomplish this. One CVS server I happened to run into in my search of the Web is CVSNT. You can download it from http://www.cvsnt.org/wiki. The CVSNT home page discusses various historical and documentation issues, but for this task you will concentrate on installing and configuring CVSNT on a Windows 2000 box and registering a repository. Chapter 7, "Painless Code Sharing Using Team Support," requires you to use a clean repository for the examples to better illustrate the interaction between the repository, Eclipse, and your code.

Installing CVSNT

At the time of this writing, the latest version of CVSNT was 2.0.3x, with the expectation of version 2.1 being released soon. Download the current release version because it should be more stable than the current development build.

Gotchas

Before you install CVSNT, make sure you follow these tips for the machine where you intend to install the server:

- The file system must be NTFS.

- Do not use a mapped drive. The file system must be local to the machine where CVSNT is running.

- Create directories \cvsrepo and \cvstemp at the root of the file system. This means either c:\cvsrepo and c:\cvstemp or, if you have local partitions available, d:\cvsrepo and d:\cvstemp (or whatever letter you have designated for the partition). Both \cvsrepo and \cvstemp must be at the root of the partition.

- As Administrator (or a user with administrator permissions), make sure that \cvstemp has Full Control permission set to Allow. You can check this by opening up Windows Explorer and right-clicking the cvstemp directory. When the Properties window opens, select the Security tab and look at the Permissions list. If Full Control is not set, then log off, log in as Administrator, and check the Allow box for Full Control permission on this directory.

All these gotchas are listed at http://www.cvsnt.org/wiki/InstallationTips. This page also displays pictures of the installation process.

When I installed CVSNT, I accepted all the defaults except for the installation directory. I have a separate directory where I install development tools, so when the moment came and the installer wanted confirmation as to the target directory, I entered my development tools directory. Feel free to leave the path set to c:\Program Files\cvsnt if c:\Program Files is where you install software like this server. Otherwise, enter your own custom path. Do *not* install the server in either c:\Winnt\Temp or anywhere in the c:\Documents and Settings area. Windows 2000 and Windows XP have user restrictions on those particular directories and would render your install useless. Bearing in mind the gotchas listed earlier, install CVSNT on the same box where the local disk containing the repository resides.

For paranoia's sake, reboot your box once you've set up the CVSNT server. Once you've done that, you should be ready to go. When you have successfully rebooted, check that the server is running by going to Start, Settings, Control Panel, Administrative Tools, Services. When the Services window appears, look in the table to the right. CVSNT and the CVSNT Locking Service should be both listed and their status should be set to Started. If CVSNT is not listed, the install did not complete for some reason. If CVSNT appears but it is not started, select CVSNT from the table and either click the Start button (the black triangle pointing to the right) or right-click the CVSNT service and select Start from the pop-up menu. If the CVSNT Locking Service is not started, then start it as well.

Configuring CVSNT

The CVSNT server should start on bootup, but if the word *Automatic* is not displayed in the Startup Type column, select Start, Control Panel, Administrative Tools, Service. When the Services window appears again, right-click CVSNT and select Properties. From within the Properties dialog, change the Startup Type setting to Automatic and click OK. Do the same for the CVSNT Locking Service if its Startup Type is not set to *Automatic*. The next time you reboot the CVS server, it will start automatically.

There are two parts to the installation of CVSNT. The first part installs the actual server on your machine, and the second installs an administrative client GUI to allow you to start, stop, install, and uninstall the CVSNT server. From the Windows desktop, select Start, Settings, Control Panel. Double-click CVS for NT, and a dialog will appear with four tabbed panels. The first panel, Service Status, lists the current status of the CVS Service and the CVS Lock Service. The first time you configure the server, the admin window should say Running. If you want to start or stop the server without going to the Windows Services window, you should use the CVS for NT client.

Registering a Repository

From the CVS for NT client window, click the Repositories tab. If you want to use this server with Eclipse, make sure the Repository Prefix box is unchecked. Eclipse complains when locating a CVS repository that has repository prefixes turned on.

The Valid Repository Roots list box should be empty. Click Add. The Enter Path to New Root dialog appears. Enter the drive name, /cvsrepo, and the name of a new repository (for example, kickstart). The new path should look something like c:/cvsrepo/kickstart. Click OK. Because the kickstart directory does not exist, a dialog appears asking for permission to create the directory. Click Yes. The various dialogs will disappear, and the new path will appear in the Valid Repository Roots list box. If the CVS server was running, return to the Service Status tab and click Stop. When the status displays Stopped, click Start. When the status changes to Running, you can click OK to exit the CVS to NT program.

You can run a quick test of your CVSNT setup by opening a command-line window (from the taskbar, click Start, Programs, Accessories, Command Prompt) and run CVS to list the contents of the repository you just created. In the previous paragraph, you create a repository. In the window, type the CVS command name, the -d option, the pserver protocol, your Windows login name, the machine name, and the repository location. For example, enter a command line similar to the following:

```
cvs -d :pserver:carlos@localhost:c:\cvsrepo\kickstart ls
```

You must use a colon (:) to separate the various components to be used by the CVS ls command:

```
C:\>cvs -d :pserver:carlos@localhost:c:\cvsrepo\kickstart ls
Listing modules on server
CVSROOT
```

If your output is similar to this, then your installation is working. If the cvs command instead complains with a message such as "Error reading from server," it is possible that you have a conflict with either your firewall or antivirus software. The only solution is to uninstall the firewall or antivirus software because even having it installed can cause CVSNT to fail. At one point I uninstalled four different programs to get CVSNT to work, found out which of the four was the problem, and then reinstalled my firewall and antivirus software. I have notified the vendor and hope they will work with the CVSNT folks to correct the problem.

Start Eclipse, if it is not already running, and go to the CVS perspective. Right-click in the CVS Repositories view and select New, Repository Location. Fill in the host field with the name of the machine the server is running on and enter the repository path as the absolute path of the repository, as listed in CVS for NT. Enter the username and password you created when you installed the CVS server and click Finish. Eclipse will display your new repository in the CVS Repositories view.

If you continue to have problems with the setup of CVSNT, read http://www.cvsnt.org/wiki/InstallationTips. When all else fails, send an email to carlos@valcarcel.com. I can't guarantee an answer, but you never know.

Running Ant Tasks from Within Eclipse

Eclipse supports Ant, a build tool written in Java, in much the same way Eclipse supports JUnit. The latest version of Eclipse adds a number of additional IDE conveniences, but let's concentrate on the basics and what you can accomplish with the current Ant functionality available within Eclipse. If you don't know Ant, then finish reading this book and go to http://ant.apache.org/ and download the latest version. A wealth of information about Ant is available online and in the bookstores.

Ant Editor

Create a Java project within Eclipse called AntTest. Create a simple file and call it build.xml. Ant defaults to reading a file named build.xml when it is run on the command line, but the list of build filenames that Eclipse will consider Ant files are defined in the Ant Preferences pages. The build.xml file should have opened when you created it, but if it did not, you can open it by double-clicking the file in the Package Explorer view. The Ant Editor should open the build.xml file, and the file should be empty.

Enter a less-than sign (<) and wait a second or two. The Content Assist window should open, displaying the only tag that makes any sense at this level—the <project> tag. Press Enter. The <project> tag appears complete with the "default" attribute set to an empty string. Because the cursor is already in the string, type "all". Move the closing <project> tag to a new line, like so:

```
<project default="all">
</project>
```

A red dot containing an X appears in the left margin of the editor. The Ant editor keeps track of the validity of the information in the file, and it cannot find the `"all"` target. Once you create the `"all"` target, in a few steps, the X will disappear. Insert a blank line between the `<project>` tags, press Tab, and enter another less-than sign. All the valid tags that can be nested at the project level are displayed for your convenience. Type the letters `pro`, and when `"property"` is displayed, press Ctrl+spacebar to expand the list of available templates. In addition to the standard `<property>` template, there is an additional entry with the label, "Ant property with name and value." Move the cursor down to this second `<property>` entry and press Enter. Now the editor has inserted a property tab with both the name and value attributes prepared to accept a name/value pair. The cursor is positioned within the quotes for the `"name"` attribute. Enter the string `"greeting"`. Press Tab to move to the `"value"` attribute. Type the string `"Hello"` as its value. Press Tab once again to move the cursor outside `<property>`. Repeat these steps to create two new `<property>` tags: one with a name of `"name"` and a value of `"world"`, and another with a name of `"punctuation"` and value of `"!"`.

Finally, create a target for the Ant file and call it `"all"`. Use the Content Assist window to find `<target>` and use its `name` attribute. Inside of `<target>`, enter `<echo>` with no attributes. In between the opening and closing `<echo>` tags, type the following string:

```
${greeting} ${name}${punctuation}
```

This basic Ant file now has three properties and one build target. Save `build.xml`, which should now look like this:

```xml
<project default="all">
    <property name="greeting" value="Hello,"/>
    <property name="name" value="world"/>
    <property name="punctuation" value="!"/>
    <target name="all">
        <echo>${greeting} ${name}${punctuation}</echo>
    </target>
</project>
```

The Outline view, to the right of the Ant editor, displays the Ant file in a tree view. The `<property>` tags are displayed as dollar signs surrounded by less-than and greater-than signs. Targets are displayed as empty green arrowheads, except for the default target, which has a filled-in blue arrowhead. If you select any of the nodes, the cursor will go to that tag (see Figure C.1).

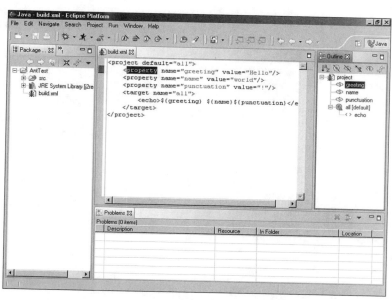

FIGURE C.1   The Outline view displaying the current Ant file as a tree.

Runtime Ant

In typical form, you have a number of ways to run the Ant file. Because this is the first time you are going to run this build file, select `build.xml` in the Package Explorer view and right-click to bring up the pop-up menu. From there, select Run Ant (see Figure C.2).

The Run Ant dialog will open, giving you the choice of which target to use (see Figure C.2). It will use the default target as its starting point, which in this case is "all." Click Run and watch the output of the selected target appear in the Console view (see Figure C.3).

The Ant plug-in remembers which target you have just run. This affords you the opportunity to run the Ant target in a number of different ways:

- By choosing Run, External Tools, External Tools from the main menu

- By clicking the running figure with the red toolbox behind it in the toolbar, which executes the last external tool command

- By clicking the down arrow next to the running figure with the red toolbox behind it in the toolbar, which allows you to select the external tool you want to run

- By right-clicking the Ant file and selecting Run Ant in the Package Explorer view

- By right-clicking the Ant file and selecting Run Ant in the Navigator view

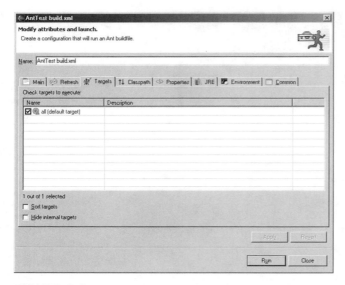

FIGURE C.2   The Run Ant dialog displaying the only available target.

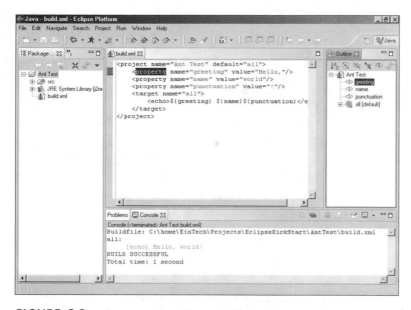

FIGURE C.3   The Output from the Ant build in the Console view.

You can change the target to run by right-clicking `build.xml` and selecting a new target from the Run Ant dialog or by selecting Run, External Tools, External Tools (you get the identical effect if you click the arrow next to the running figure with the red toolbox). In the latter case, you will need to create a new tool configuration for the Ant file or target you want to run.

Ant Preferences

Open the Preferences dialog (Window, Preferences) and select Ant in the tree view to the left. Three pages of configuration information are available, but only two will be discussed here.

The first page, shown in Figure C.4, contains the settings with which to run Ant. The Names field allows you to change the default file Ant will look at and lets you enter a comma-separated list of filenames Ant should use in its search for a valid build file. The first check box (which defaults to checked) displays a warning dialog about Ant's `tools.jar` file if this file is missing in a situation where you are running Ant and it tries to execute a task that it does not recognize. The `tools.jar` file contains the optional target extensions useable by Ant. If you don't use targets such as `<junit>`, it does not matter if `tools.jar` is in the classpath. However, if you use even one of the optional tasks, you must include `tools.jar` in Ant's classpath. The Ant, Runtime page is where you would add `tools.jar` to the classpath.

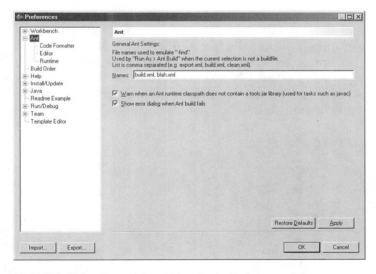

FIGURE C.4   General Ant settings in the Preferences dialog.

The Editor page's Appearance tab, shown in Figure C.5, is where you can set the substitution of spaces for tabs, enable/disable the overview ruler, set the display of line numbers, enable/disable the highlighting of the current line, and display the print margin. In the Code Assist tab, you control such things as when the Content Assist window appears and whether it should automatically insert selections when there is only one choice.

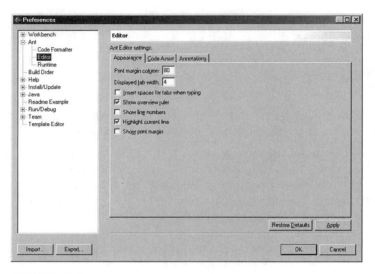

FIGURE C.5   The Ant Editor configuration tabs.

The Annotations tab, shown in Figure C.6, controls how the annotations appear in the editor. For example, when an error is encountered (for example, nonmatching XML tags), it is visually flagged using a red squiggly line on the line where the error appears as well as in the right border of the editor. To see annotations in action, remove the closing `</target>` tag and save the file. The error annotation appears immediately. The Annotations tab lets you control the color of the annotation and whether it will appear in the text, in the right editor border (known as the *overview ruler*), in both, or in neither.

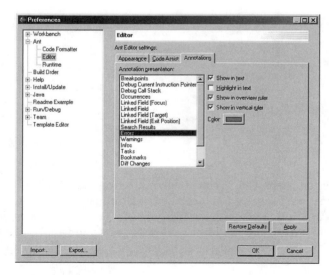

FIGURE C.6   The Annotations tab of the Ant Editor page.

The Ant View

The Ant view allows you to aggregate various Ant build files so that you can easily find them when you need them by simply adding them to the view (see Figure C.7). The Ant view is displayed by selecting Window, Show View, Ant. It is initially empty. Clicking the triple-plus-sign icon in the Ant view toolbar opens the Choose Location dialog, where you can select a project and add any Ant build files associated with the project (see Figure C.8).

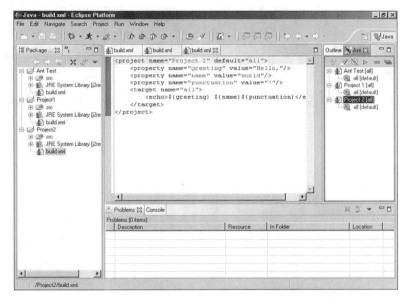

FIGURE C.7   The Ant view displaying multiple Ant files.

Once the build file is in the Ant view, right-click the target you want to execute and select Run (or Run Ant) from the pop-up menu. Again, any output from the build is displayed in the Console view.

Even with all this, a couple of pieces are missing in the Ant support. For example, there is no provision for converting tabs to spaces when you reformat the file. However, if you want to run the Ant task within a separate VM, open the External Tools dialog and go to the Ant launch configuration. Click the JRE tab, select Alternate JRE, and then either select a listed JRE or use the Installed JREs dialog to select a Java Runtime Environment within which to run Ant.

FIGURE C.8   The Choose Location dialog, where you select Ant files to aggregate in the Ant view.

Useful Editors

In Eclipse, the centerpiece of most perspectives continues to be the editor. Back in the days of vi, or worse, edlin, an editor was really nothing more than a way to edit a collection of up to 80 characters per line at a time. In today's environment, an editor must be capable of a minimal set of functionality, including colored-syntax support and auto-formatting. The Eclipse JDT editor is spoiling a new generation of developers by supplying suggested code fixes, arbitrary import statement ordering, and refactoring, just to mention a few. Of course, don't mention this to the Smalltalk guys; they've been using this stuff for years.

Given that this book has made a virtue of the use of open-source/free software, it would be incomplete if we did not cover the use of various editors to accomplish various editing tasks. The open-source community has been very generous in its contributions to Eclipse, so I apologize to those groups whose editors are not discussed here. The editors mentioned here are all free and/or open source, even though some have a version that can be purchased. If you have a favorite Eclipse plug-in editor that is not mentioned here, drop me a line (my email address is in the front of this book), and I will see about giving it a mention in a future edition.

So, what makes for a good Eclipse editor? The model promulgated by the Eclipse Java editor is a good place to start looking for features:

▶ Colored syntax

▶ Content Assist

▶ Resync on external changes

▶ Help

And here are some nice-to-haves:

▶ An outline view of the file contents

▶ Problems displayed in the Problems view

There are editors to support plain-vanilla text files, internal `build.properties` files, Ant `build.xml` files, EMF (Eclipse Modeling Framework) files, plug-in manifest files, JAR description files, Java scrapbook files, and, of course, Java files. There is no default editor in Eclipse, or the JDT, to support XML, JSPs, or WSDL. JDT does come with a default editor for properties files, but it is nothing more than a basic text editor.

If you decide to use one editor over another, it is in your best interests to set your editor as the default for that particular file type. To change the default, just go to Window, Preferences and select Workbench, File Associations. Select the file extension of your choice and either set one of the existing editors as the default or add the editor directly and then select it as the default.

XML

You should be able to open an XML file in an editor and be able to view its content in a tree view, similar to the Ant editor or the Plug-in Manifest Editor (which are, after all, just specific kinds of XML editors). Unfortunately, an XML tree view is a rather involved piece of functionality because the number of attributes is arbitrary and the file can contain arbitrary values that can be difficult to display. For example, the Ant editor displays a tree view of the tags in `build.xml`, but it only displays a subset of attributes, and no values, in its Outline view. (Try it. Create a `build.xml` file, add a target and a task, and then add an <echo> tag with a message either as an attribute or value. Neither appears in the Outline view.)

Available XML Editors

XMLBuddy   `http://www.xmlbuddy.com/`

XMen   `http://xmen.sourceforge.net/`

XMLBuddy

XMLBuddy is an XML editor with a number of features that make the creation of a plain-vanilla XML file easier. It has an XML perspective that is made up of the XML editor, a custom outline view, the standard Task view, and the Navigator view. You can either write the DTD first and then the XML file or write the XML file and have XMLBuddy best-guess the creation of a DTD. Eclipse already comes with a Template editor that is actually for use with Ant `build.xml` files, but it may open up on occasion when you try to open XML files. The Eclipse Template editor has an Eclipse logo in the Editor tab, whereas the XMLBuddy logo is a file with an X in it.

Let's create an XML file and see how well XMLBuddy behaves. We'll add a DTD file later because it does not have XSD support.

Download XMLBuddy from http://www.xmlbuddy.com/. Close all your editors and perspectives and then shut down Eclipse. Unzip the XMLBuddy file in your favorite Eclipse plug-in location. Then restart Eclipse.

Open the XML perspective (select Window, Open Perspective, Other from the main menu and then select XML when the Select Perspective dialog appears). Let's create an XML project

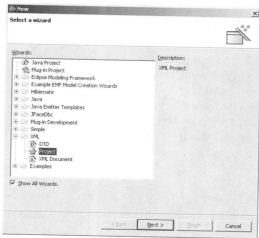

and then create an XML file to go with it. If you press Ctrl+N, the New dialog will have an XML entry in the tree view. Open the XML node and select Project (see Figure D.1). Click Next and enter a project name of XMLEditorTest. Click Finish.

Create an XML file. Using the New dialog, select XML, XML Document and then click Next. In the New Document Name field, enter the filename currency.xml. Click Finish. The XML editor should open automatically. The file starts out with three lines containing a default DOCTYPE and a fake XML root.

FIGURE D.1   The New dialog displaying the XML project type.

Change the word *root* in the DOCTYPE to *currency* and delete the <root></root> tags. Move the cursor to a blank line after the DOCTYPE and press Ctrl+spacebar. The Content Assist window opens and displays currency as the first entry.

Press Enter to print the opening and closing tags. The cursor is positioned at the end of the opening tag, giving you the opportunity to enter attributes. Move the cursor between the tags and press Enter. The closing tag is now on its own line and left-justified. The cursor is also indented and positioned on a new line.

Enter <name>. When you complete the opening tag with the greater-than sign, the closing tag appears automatically with the cursor positioned between the two tags. Move the cursor to the end of the line and press Enter to begin typing on a blank line. Now define description and exchange-rate tags inside of <currency> (not nested inside of <name>). The XML should look like the code shown here:

```
<!DOCTYPE currency>
<currency>
    <name></name>
    <description></description>
    <exchange-rate></exchange-rate>
</currency>
```

Back in the editor, enter USD as the value for <name>, US dollar as the value of <description>, and 1 as the value of <exchange-rate>. The contents of the file now looks like the following code:

```
<!DOCTYPE currency >
<currency>
    <name>USD</name>
    <description>US dollar</description>
    <exchange-rate>1</exchange-rate>
</currency>
```

In the meantime, the Outline view (in the lower-left corner) has been silently displaying the XML tags in a tree view every time you have made a change to the file. If you only want the Outline view to synchronize with the editor's contents on a file save, open Window, Preferences, XMLBuddy, Outline and uncheck Keep Outline Up-to-Date. The next time you change the tags, you will only see the Outline view change when you save the file. The Outline view does not display any string values surrounded by tags, but it will display the first attribute value. Add the attribute country to <name> and set it equal to "US". You will see the string US appear in the Outline view next to the name node (see Figure D.2). Remove the country attribute.

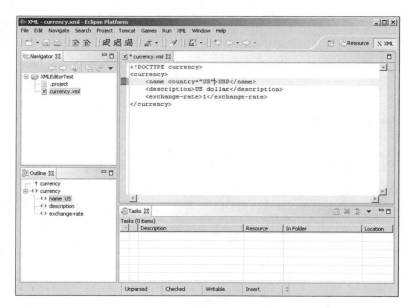

FIGURE D.2   The Outline view displaying the XML tags as nodes in a tree view.

Content Assist is available once you enter a DTD for the XML file to be validated against. Create a new file (press Ctrl+N, select XML, DTD) and name it currency.dtd. When the file opens, delete the line after <?xml> and add the following code after the <?xml> tag and save the file:

```
<!ELEMENT currency (name)>
<!ELEMENT name (#PCDATA)>
```

Return to currency.xml and change the first line:

```
<!DOCTYPE currency PUBLIC "" "currency.dtd">
```

Save currency.xml. From the main menu, select XML, Validate. Four errors will be found. The errors surfaced because you did not define the additional ELEMENTs in the DTD. However, the Problems view should be available for your use in tracking down errors of this type. It is not a default view in the XML perspective.

The Problems view exists to let you know which errors have occurred and where the errors can be located. Open the Problems view by selecting from the main menu Window, Open View, Other and from the Show View dialog by selecting Basic, Problems. Click OK, and the Problems view opens in the lower part of the XML perspective. However, the syntax errors still are not listed. This is because the Problems view uses an internal filtering mechanism to display only select errors. To add the XML syntax errors to the filter list, you need to go to the Problems view menu bar and click the downward-pointing triangle. Select Filters from the menu to open the Filters dialog. In the Show Items of Type list, scroll down to display XML Auto-Validate and XML Validate (see Figure D.3). Either check both items manually or click Select All and then click OK. This will cause the errors to be included rather than filtered out. The Problems view now displays the four errors.

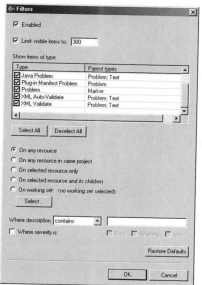

FIGURE D.3 The Filters dialog with the two XML validation error types selected.

To eliminate the errors, add the missing elements to currency.dtd using the following code as a guide:

```
<!ELEMENT currency (name,description,exchange-rate)>
<!ELEMENT name (#PCDATA)>
<!ELEMENT description (#PCDATA)>
<!ELEMENT exchange-rate (#PCDATA)>
```

Return to currency.xml again. Select XML, Validate again, and the errors should all disappear. Alternatively, you can just wait a few seconds and the auto-validate feature will check for you and remove the errors from the Problem view.

Just for the fun of it, let's add an attribute and try out the Content Assist feature. Add the following line to `currency.dtd`:

```
<!ATTLIST name country NMTOKEN #REQUIRED
              denomination NMTOKEN #REQUIRED>
>
```

Return to `currency.xml`, move the cursor to just after the word *name* in the <name> tag, and add a space. Press Ctrl+spacebar, and the Content Assist window will open, listing the two available attributes, `country` and `denomination` (see Figure D.4). If only one attribute was available, the editor would have inserted it automatically.

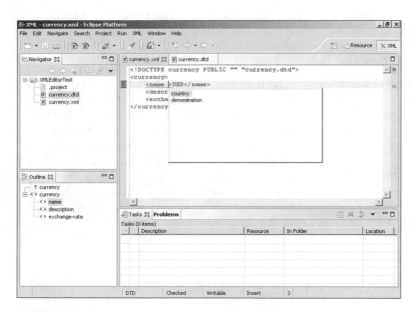

FIGURE D.4   The XMLBuddy editor displaying the Content Assist window.

Even though you created an XML project and you did all of the preceding in XMLBuddy's XML perspective, you can use XMLBuddy in any project. XMLBuddy sets itself as the default editor for XML files, and you can make it the default editor for other file types, such as HTML, by modifying the File Associations in the Preferences dialog under Workbench. As a matter of fact, it has rather good support for HTML, but there is no preview mode.

How well does XMLBuddy perform on the minimal list of features? It does have colored-syntax support (changeable from the Properties dialog), Content Assist if a DTD is available, auto-resync if the file is changed externally, and integrated Help. XMLBuddy also has a custom Outline view and sends validation errors to the Problems view.

JavaServer Pages

JavaServer Pages editors are in short supply for Eclipse. This is another area where WSAD is still ahead of the open-source pack. All have colored-syntax support, some have code assist, but only the MyEclipse package has a preview mode to allow you to see what you are building. None of them allow you to assemble the HTML in a visual fashion. The JSP editor I will use for this exercise is the one bundled with the MyEclipse package.

Available JavaServer Pages Editors

Lomboz—http://www.objectlearn.com

MyEclipse—http://www.myeclipseide.com/

Strecl—http://www.strecl.com/

The MyEclipse JSP Editor

The JSP editor bundled with the MyEclipse Enterprise Workbench happens to be a good JSP editor, primarily because it has a preview mode as well as colored-syntax support (Chapter 9, "J2EE and the MyEclipse Plug-In," has a much more in-depth look at the J2EE capabilities of MyEclipse). If you have not installed MyEclipse, but you would like to walk through this exercise, you must download and install the MyEclipse executable from the MyEclipse site and configure it the way it is described in Chapter 9 in the section "Installing and Configuring MyEclipse." The installation and configuration is straightforward.

Let's create a fresh page and see how the JSP editor works. The page will have an HTML form and table, a JSP expression, a JSP script, a JSP scriptlet, and finish off with a JSP tag. To keep this exercise as simple as possible, you should use Tomcat as the JSP container when you deploy the Web application, because this is a look at the editor's capabilities and not the app server's capabilities.

Open the MyEclipse perspective. Create a J2EE project by pressing Ctrl+N and selecting J2EE, Enterprise Application Project. Click Next and enter JSPEditorTest as the Project Name. In the Creation Tasks list, uncheck Define EJB Project Modules, leave Define Web Projects Modules checked, and click Next. Because a JSP is considered part of a Web application, you need to create a Web module for this enterprise application. Check the box Create Web Project Module and then click Finish. If a dialog appears asking to switch to the MyEclipse perspective, click Yes.

As mentioned in Chapter 9, two projects are created: JSPEditorTest and JSPEditorTestWeb. To create a new JSP, return to the Package Explorer, open JSPEditorTestWeb, select WebRoot, and press Ctrl+N. When the New dialog appears, select J2EE, Web, JSP. Click Next. Change the default filename from MyJsp.jsp to index.jsp. If you press the down arrow of the Template to Use field, you will see that MyEclipse supports the creation of JSPs, struts, and plain-vanilla HTML pages. Leave Template to Use set to "1) Default JSP template" and check that the file path is /JSPEditorTestWeb/WebRoot. Click Finish. The wizard creates an index.jsp file with reasonable content:

```
<%@ page language="java" import="java.lang.*,java.util.*" %>
<%
String path = request.getContextPath();
String basePath = "http://"+request.getServerName()+":"+request.getServerPort()+path+"/";
%>

<!DOCTYPE HTML PUBLIC "-//W3C//DTD HTML 4.01 Transitional//EN">
<html>
  <head>
    <base href="<%=basePath%>">

    <title>My JSP 'index.jsp' starting page</title>

    <meta http-equiv="pragma" content="no-cache">
    <meta http-equiv="cache-control" content="no-cache">
    <meta http-equiv="expires" content="0">

    <meta http-equiv="keywords" content="keyword1,keyword2,keyword3">
    <meta http-equiv="description" content="This is my page">

    <!--
    <link rel="stylesheet" type="text/css" href="styles.css">
    -->
  </head>

  <body>
    This is my JSP page. <br>
  </body>
</html>
```

Now delete everything in the file (Ctrl+A, Delete) and save it (Ctrl+S). You are going to build the page from scratch and see the effects of your work as you go along.

First, let's look at Content Assist. Type the opening less-than sign (<) and press Ctrl+spacebar. Type ht and then press Enter when the "html" tag appears in the Content Assist window. Enter a space after "HTML" but before the closing greater-than sign. Press Ctrl+spacebar again, and you should see the attributes dir, lang, and version in the Content Assist window. Select version and enter the string "1.0". Go to the next line, only this time just press

Ctrl+spacebar (do not type anything). The Content Assist window will open, and the second selection should be </HTML>. Press Enter, and the selection will be typed into index.jsp:

```
<html version="1.0" >
</html>
```

Put a blank line in between the two tags. Type the less-than sign (<) and press Ctrl+spacebar. The Content Assist window appears and displays the various HTML tags it understands. Type he and press Enter to complete <HEAD>. The closing tag for <HEAD> can be discovered by going to the end of the line and pressing Enter and Ctrl+spacebar. Do not type any of the tag characters. The Content Assist window will display </HEAD> as the second item in the list. Press the down arrow once or double-click </HEAD> with your mouse. All the tags behave this way: Create an opening tag by entering starting characters (or not) and close the tags by pressing Ctrl+spacebar without typing any starting characters. The closing tag will generally be the second item in the list.

Add the opening and closing <BODY> tags. Insert a line between the <BODY> tags, press Ctrl+spacebar, and you will see the Content Assist window with all the tags available in HTML (see Figure D.5). Type the characters <ce to bring up <CENTER> and then press Enter. Place the ending tag (</CENTER>) on a new line:

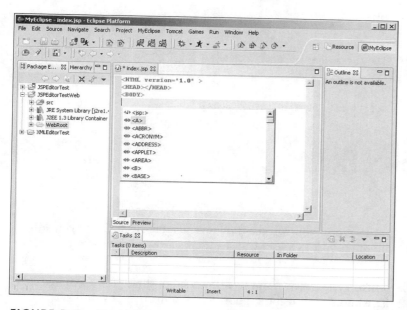

FIGURE D.5   The MyEclipse JSP editor displaying HTML Content Assist.

```
<HTML version="1.0" >
<HEAD></HEAD>
<BODY>
<CENTER>
</CENTER>
</BODY>
</HTML>
```

Insert a line between the <CENTER> tags and press Ctrl+spacebar again. Enter the opening and closing tags for <FORM>. Move the cursor to the end of the word *FORM* in the opening <FORM> tag and add a space. Press Ctrl+spacebar and add an empty action attribute. Add the following <TABLE> code:

```
<HTML version="1.0" >
<HEAD></HEAD>
<BODY>
<CENTER>
<FORM action="" >
    <table>
        <tr>
        Name:  <INPUT name="name" >
        </TR>
        <tr>
        Password:  <INPUT name="password" >
        </TR>
        <tr>
            <INPUT type="submit" name="submit" value="Submit" >
        </TR>
    </TABLE>
</FORM>
</CENTER>
</BODY>
</HTML>
```

If you look to the bottom of the editor, you will see the Preview tab. Select it, and you will see the page we have been building, just as a user will see it appear in a browser (see Figure D.6).

Return to the Source tab. Now that you have seen the editor's support for HTML colored syntax and HTML code assist, let's check out the support for JSP directives, expressions, scripts, and scriptlets. Here is a standard JSP expression:

```
<%= new Date()%>
```

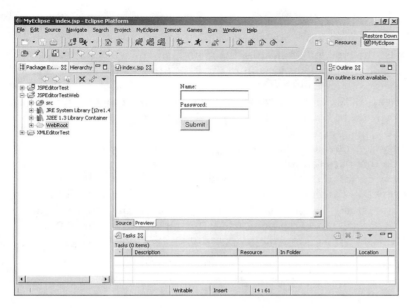

FIGURE D.6 The Preview page of the MyEclipse JSP editor.

Create another JSP, only this time call it `jsptest.jsp`. Delete everything from inside `jsptest.jsp`, just like you did for `index.jsp`. Create a table with one row and two columns to display this date in an organized fashion. The first column should have a label such as "Today's date:" and the second column should have the JSP expression:

```
<HTML>
<HEAD></HEAD>
<BODY>
  <CENTER>
    <FORM action="">
      <TABLE>
        <CAPTION><H2> MyEclipse JSP Example for Eclipse Kick Start</H2></CAPTION>
        <TR>
          <TD>Today's Date:</TD>
          <TD><%=new Date()%></TD>
        </TR>
      </TABLE>
      <INPUT type="submit" name="submit">
    </FORM>
  </CENTER>
</BODY>
</HTML>
```

Save the file. Depending on your compiler's pickiness level, one or more errors should appear in the Problems view (which you must open by hand because it is not a default view for the MyEclipse perspective). Open the Problems view from the main menu by selecting Window, Show View, Other and selecting the Problems view from the Basic category. Of course, opening the Problems view leads to the same problem you had with the last plug-in: New problem categories now exist, and the Problems view does not know about them. Once again, go to the Problems view menu bar, click the downward-pointing triangle, and select Filters. When the Filters dialog opens, click Select All to select all the current error types and then click OK. The Problems view now displays at least one error. The error you need to correct is the one telling you that Date cannot be resolved. You can fix this particular compiler error by moving the cursor to the end of the word *Date* and pressing Ctrl+spacebar. The Content Assist window will once again appear, only this time it is displaying a list of package names from which to choose. When you select java.util.Date, the editor will place the <%@ page %> directive at the top of the file, completing the import of java.util.Date. When you save jsptest.jsp, the syntax error will disappear from the Problems view.

Let's add an instance variable to the page and call it from an expression. Add a SimpleDateFormat object called _format to the area below the page directive:

```
<%@ page import="java.text.SimpleDateFormat" %>
<%@ page import="java.util.Date" %>
<%!private static DateFormat _format =
    new java.text.SimpleDateFormat("MM/dd/yyyy");
%>
```

Add another row (<tr>) to your table with a label and an expression that calls the SimpleDateFormat object with a new Date object:

```
    <TR>
        <TD>Today's Date (MM/dd/yyyy):</TD>
        <TD><%=%></TD>
    </TR>
```

In the JSP expression, press Ctrl+spacebar after the equal sign (=) to see what is available for use. Press the underscore key, and you should see _format come up as the second choice. Press Enter on _format, type a period (.), and then press Ctrl+spacebar to look for format(). After finding format() and pressing Enter, create a new Date object as the method's argument. You should now have two rows—one with the default date formatting and another that uses MM/dd/yyyy (month/day/year):

```
<TABLE>
    <CAPTION>
    <H2>MyEclipse JSP Example for Eclipse Kick Start</H2>
    </CAPTION>
    <TBODY>
```

```
        <TR>
            <TD>Today's Date:</TD>
            <TD><%=new Date()%></TD>
        </TR>
        <TR>
            <TD>Today's Date (MM/dd/yyyy):</TD>
            <TD><%=_format.format(new Date())%></TD>
        </TR>
    </TBODY>
</TABLE>
```

Let's add a Java method to return the time in hours, minutes, and seconds and have a JSP expression call it. Return to the script section where you defined _format. Add a method called getCurrentTime(). In getCurrentTime(), create another SimpleDateFormat object with the format "hh:mm:ss". Have it create a Date object and format the time using the local SimpleDateFormat object:

```
<%!private static java.text.SimpleDateFormat _format =
    new java.text.SimpleDateFormat("MM/dd/yyyy");

    private String getCurrentTime() {
        java.text.DateFormat formatter = new java.text.SimpleDateFormat("hh:mm:ss");

        return formatter.format(new Date());
    }
%>
```

Add another row to your table, only this time call getCurrentTime(). You now have a JSP that displays standard HTML and uses scriptlets, scripts, expressions, and directives:

```
<TR>
  <TD>Today's Time (hh:mm:ss):</TD>
  <TD><%=getCurrentTime()%></TD>
</TR>
```

Use Content Assist the way you would if this were the Java editor. You will find it behaves in quite a similar fashion. If you like, you can select the Preview tab to look at the page in its current incarnation (see Figure D.7).

Deploy the Web module, start Tomcat, and open a Web browser to http://localhost:8080/JSPEditorTestWeb/jsptest.jsp. You should see a centered bold title on the first line, the current date displayed using the default formatting, the date in MM/dd/yyyy format, followed by the time in hh:mm:ss format, and a Submit button on the last line (see Figure D.8).

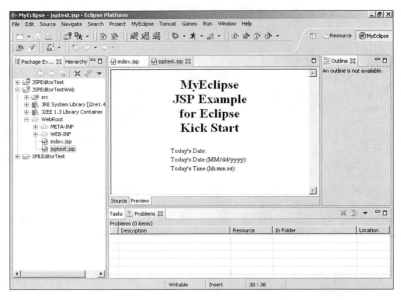

FIGURE D.7 The JSP without the Java-generated dynamic content.

FIGURE D.8 The final version of the JSP displayed within a browser.

If the editor seems to be missing functionality such as line numbers and a print margin, it is probably because you have not had a chance to configure it to your liking. Open the Preferences dialog and select MyEclipse, Editors, JSP/HTML Editor. You can configure the following functionality:

- ▶ Compile/don't compile on save.

- ▶ Set the print margins.

- ▶ Display an overview ruler.

- ▶ Show line numbers.

- ▶ Highlight the current line.

- ▶ Select colors for the various JSP/HTML tags.

- ▶ Set formatting options, such as tab size, the use of spaces instead of tabs, and so on.

Properties Files

The ubiquitous properties file in Java is one of the most neglected file types. Although it is indeed convenient to need nothing more than vi or Notepad to edit a standard `.properties` file, there are times when more sophistication comes in handy.

Eclipse comes with a default properties editor that is nothing more than a simple text editor with no colored-syntax support or fancy features. A properties file editor should allow you either to edit the file directly (for example, to add comments) or to use a GUI to manipulate the name/values pairs in a consistent fashion, perhaps to sort the names to make the list more manageable.

Available Properties Editors

Eclipse Property File GUI Editor—`http://eclpropfileedit.sourceforge.net/`

LaTeX Plugin For Eclipse—`http://sourceforge.net/projects/eclipse-latex/`

Eclipse Property File GUI Editor

The Eclipse Property File GUI Editor is a pure GUI-based editor. You add, edit, and delete properties from the GUI. It uses a table as its main interface, and it allows you to associate a comment with individual properties.

Download the installation from `http://eclpropfileedit.sourceforge.net/` and install it in your favorite plug-ins directory. Then start, or restart, Eclipse.

Create a simple file in a new or existing Java project and name it `test.properties`. The file should open with the Property File GUI Editor when you create the file (the Editor tab will have a red letter *P* within the document icon). Right-click `test.properties` and select Open With, Property File GUI Editor. The editor will open and display an empty table (see Figure D.9).

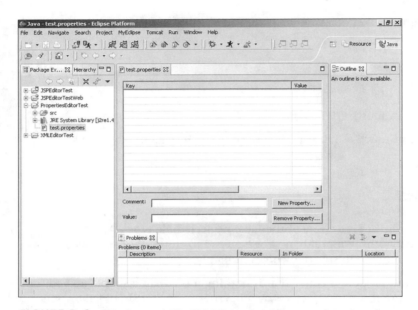

FIGURE D.9   The Property File GUI Editor when it is opened on an empty `.properties` file.

To add a property, click New Property. This will open the Create a New Property dialog, which allows you to enter a key (required), a value, and/or a comment. As shown in Figure D.10, enter the key "username," the value "Lindley," and the comment "This is a user name." Click New Property again and this time enter the key "password," the value "jedi," and the comment "This is a password." The table should display two properties, and if you select one of them, the value and comment associated with the property will be displayed in the two input fields below the table (see Figure D.11). Save the file.

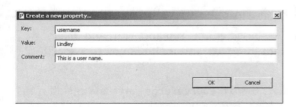

FIGURE D.10   The Create a new property dialog.

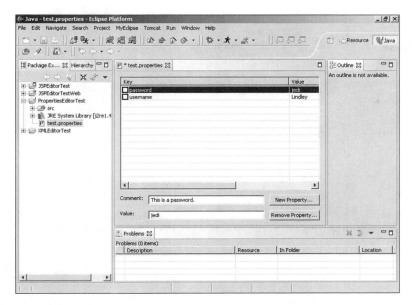

FIGURE D.11   The Property File GUI Editor displaying the two properties just entered.

Open the actual file in Notepad or some other basic editor outside of Eclipse. (If you are not sure where the file is located, right-click the file from within the Eclipse Package Explorer and select Properties. The absolute file path is displayed in the Properties For dialog.) The two properties will be listed with their individual comments. If you don't see them, make sure you have saved the file from within Eclipse:

```
#This is a password.
password=jedi

#This is a user name.
username=Lindley
```

To comment out one of the properties, select its check box. For example, select the check box for the password property and save it. Again, look at the file using an external editor:

```
#This is a password.
#password=jedi

#This is a user name.
username=Lindley
```

There are two ways to edit a property:

- ► Select the property in the table and update the existing information using the input fields below the table.

- ► Double-click one of the properties to open the Edit dialog. This is the only way to directly change the key.

Deleting a property is as simple as clicking Remove Property.

In Brief

Plenty of custom editor plug-ins are available for Eclipse. You had a chance to try out editors for XML, HTML, JSPs, WSDL, and Java properties files. By the time this book is published, there are bound to be many more.

Recommended Resources

This appendix presents a collection of resources directly or indirectly related to Java development and/or Eclipse use.

Eclipse Help Documentation

The Eclipse help documentation, shipped with the Eclipse install, is a great place to start to look for Eclipse reference tips. In writing this book, I found the following help docs to be a constant source of useful information:

▶ The Platform Plug-in Developers Guide: Simple Plug-in Example

▶ Eclipse Help Documentation, Workbench User Guide, Tasks, Using the Help System, Searching Online Help

▶ Eclipse Help Platform Plug-in Developer Guide, Reference, Extension Points Reference, Workbench, org.eclipse.ui.startup

▶ Eclipse Help Platform Plug-in Developer Guide, Programmer's Guide, Plugging into the Workbench, Basic Workbench Extension Points, org.eclipse.ui.popupMenus

▶ Eclipse Help Platform Plug-in Developer Guide, Programmer's Guide, Dialogs and Wizards, Wizard Dialogs

▶ Eclipse Help Platform Plug-in Developer Guide, Programmer's Guide, Preferences and Properties, Preferences

Projects and Tutorials

Eclipse—http://www.eclipse.org

You can find a number of interesting projects using Eclipse technology located at Eclipse.org that are worth your time and attention. Projects include support for Aspect-Oriented Programming (AOP), XML Schema (XSD), educational uses of Eclipse, Model-Driven Development (MDA), configuration management, and Web services.

JBoss—http://www.jboss.org

JBoss is a free open-source application server that supports the J2EE technology stack. It is a good server for learning about J2EE as well as running full-featured enterprise applications.

The Java Tutorial—http://java.sun.com/docs/books/tutorial

The Java J2EE Tutorial—http://java.sun.com/j2ee/1.4/docs/tutorial/doc/index.html

The Java Tutorial and the Java J2EE Tutorial are both excellent sources of information about Java and enterprise Java development. You can read them online or download them for offline use.

Introduction to Web services and the WSDK v5.1—http://www-106.ibm.com/developer-works/edu/ws-dw-ws-intwsdk51-i.html

This developerWorks tutorial is one of a collection of tutorials about implementing Web services using the IBM WebSphere SDK for Web services. It only works on Eclipse 2.1, but I expect it to be updated to support 3.0.

UML Tutorials

Practical UML: A Hands-On Introduction for Developers—http://bdn.borland.com/article/0,1410,31863,00.html

Embarcadero's UML Tutorial—http://www.embarcadero.com/support/uml_central.html#tutorials

Online Articles

Here are some other items you might find helpful:

▶ http://www.sdmagazine.com/columnists/martin/

This Web page contains a series of articles by Robert C. Martin on the continuing adventures of a developer slowly evolving into a test-driven development maven and the various missteps he makes along the way. This is an extremely fun read.

▶ `http://xprogramming.com/xpmag/virtualMockObjects.htm`

This article, titled "Virtual Mock Objects Using AspectJ with JUnit," presents a great perspective on the difficult task of testing parts of a system in a predictable fashion. Using AOP together with mock objects may turn out to be a useful extension to a test-driven system.

▶ `http://www.keyboardsamurais.de/mt/archives/000053.html`

In addition to the wealth of documentation about Tomcat at `http://jakarta.apache.org/tomcat/`, I found the "Tomcat Tutorial: HelloWorld for Complete Fools" to be both informative and fun.

▶ `http://www.omg.org/uml/`

Chapter 3, "UML Notation Guide," of the OMG-Unified Modeling Language v1.5 goes in depth into the notation of UML diagrams. It presents more information than you will ever need to know.

▶ `http://www-106.ibm.com/developerworks/opensource/library/os-ecfeat/`, October 14, 2003.

The Pat McCarthy article "Put Eclipse features to work for you: How to use Eclipse features to customize Eclipse behavior" is an informative look at implementing Eclipse plug-in features as well as how to install plug-ins using the Install/Update Manager.

Books

Beck, K. and E. Gamma. *Contributing to Eclipse*. Addison-Wesley. Reading, MA, 2004. ISBN 0-321-20575-8.

Beck, Kent. *Test-driven Development*. Addison-Wesley. Reading, MA, 2003. ISBN 0-321-14653-0.

Fowler, Martin. *Refactoring*. Addison-Wesley. Reading, MA, 2000. ISBN 0-201-48567-2.

Gamma, E. et al. *Design Patterns: Elements of Reusable Object-Oriented Software*. Addison-Wesley. Reading, MA, 1995. ISBN 0-201-63361-2.

Goodwill, J. and R. Hightower. *Professional Jakarta Struts*. Wiley Publishing, Inc. Indianapolis, IN, 2004. ISBN 0-764-54437-3.

Shavor, S. et al. *The Java Developer's Guide to Eclipse*. Addison-Wesley. Reading, MA, 2003. ISBN 0-321-15964-0.

Turner, J. and K. Bedell. *Struts Kick Start*. Sams Publishing. Indianapolis, IN, 2003. ISBN 0-67232-472-5.

Wells, Craig and Norman Richards. *XDoclet In Action*. Manning Publishing Co. Greenwich, CT, 2004. ISBN 1-932394-05-2.

Plug-Ins Used in This Book

Cactus—http://cvs.apache.org/builds/jakarta-cactus/nightly/

Eclipse-Games—http://eclipse-games.sourceforge.net/

Hibernate Synchronizer—http://www.binamics.com/hibernatesynch

JFaceDbc—http://jfacedbc.sourceforge.net/

Lucene—http://jakarta.apache.org/lucene/docs/index.html

MyEclipse—http://www.myeclipseide.com/

EclipseUML/Omondo—http://www.eclipseuml.com

PyDev—http://pydev.sourceforge.net/

Sysdeo Tomcat Plug-in—http://www.sysdeo.com/eclipse/tomcatPlugin.html

Index

A

removing, 59

setting, 63-64

Breakpoints view (Debug perspective), 20, 59-60, 64

build method, 345-347

builders, adding to projects, 338-349

C

Cactus, 127-139

deploying servlets, 130

downloading, 128

setUp method, 136

tearDown method, 136

tests

launch configuration, 137

running 138-139

writing, 132-137

website, 436

writing servlets, 128-129

Calculator project

creating, 30-31

classes, 33

interfaces, 32-33

JUnit tests, 34-35

scrapbook pages, 42

Java editor, 35-38

search capabilities, 42-48

Call Hierarchy view (Java perspective), 14

categories for views, creating, 329-330

Change Method Signature dialog box, 78

Change Method Signature refactor, 78-79

Cheat Sheets command, 319-320

Check Out As Project command, 148, 154

checking in CVS projects, 149-154

checking out CVS projects, 154-155

Class diagrams (UML), 277, 285-291

classes

creating, 33

interfaces, extracting, 79-81

JavaBean classes, 234-235

Javadoc comments, 16

relationships, viewing, 299-300

classes directory, 31

classpath, setting, 31

code (Java)

debugging, 57-58

Debug perspective, 58-60

remote debugging, 66-71

server-side, 66

standalone code, 61-66

refactoring, 73-74

Change Method Signature refactor, 78-79

Extract Method refactor, 83-87

Extracting Interface refactor, 79-81

Pull Up refactor, 81-83

Rename refactor, 75-78

and test-driven development, 73-74

J

M

N

O

Object diagrams (UML), 277

Omondo EclipseUML

configuring, 301-303

diagrams

Class, 285-291

creating, 279

overview, 276-277

Sequence, 293-298

Use Case, 279-285

downloading, 278

installing, 278

reverse engineering, 299-300

Online Help Sample, 362

Open Perspective button, 11

opening perspectives, 11

Debug, 58

Java, 30

Order class, 83-85

OrderFactory class, 83-87

org.eclipse.help extension point, 381

org.eclipse.help.contexts extension point, 378

org.eclipse.help.toc extension point, 363, 366, 389

org.eclipse.jface.action.Action extension point, 385

org.eclipse.jface.IAction interface, 385

org.eclipse.swt.widgets.Control extension point, 384

org.eclipse.ui plug-in, 322, 333

org.eclipse.ui.newWizards extension point, 333-334

org.eclipse.ui.popupMenus extension point, 351-352, 384

org.eclipse.ui.preferencesPages extension point, 356

org.eclipse.ui.startup extension point, 321-323

org.eclipse.ui.views extension point, 329

Outline view

Ant, 408

PDE perspective, 310

Resource perspective, 10-12

XMLBuddy, 418

Overview page (Plug-in Manifest Editor), 312

P

Package Explorer view, 16

PDE perspective, 310

Team

Branch, 155

Commit, 155

Merge, 156

Share Project, 150

Synchronize with Repository, 153

packages

adding to environment, 31

renaming, 75-78

X - Z

Your Guide to Computer Technology

www.informit.com